Ancient Legends of Ireland

Mystic Charms & Superstitions of Ireland
with Sketches of the Irish Past
By Lady Jane Francesca Agnes Wilde

©2020 Illustrated Books

Hardcover ISBN 13: 978-1-5154-4479-4
Trade Paperback ISBN 13: 978-1-5154-4480-0

Ancient Legends of Ireland

Mystic Charms & Superstitions of Ireland
with Sketches of the Irish Past
By Lady Jane Francesca Agnes Wilde

CONTENTS

PREFACE

The three great sources of knowledge respecting the shrouded part of humanity are the language, the mythology, and the ancient monuments of a country.

From the language one learns the mental and social height to which a nation had reached at any given period in arts, habits, and civilization, with the relation of man to man, and to the material and visible world.

The mythology of a people reveals their relation to a spiritual and invisible world; while the early monuments are solemn and eternal symbols of religious faith—rituals of stone in cromlech, pillar, shrine and tower, temples and tombs.

The written word, or literature, comes last, the fullest and highest expression of the intellect and culture, and scientific progress of a nation.

The Irish race were never much indebted to the written word. The learned class, the ollamhs, dwelt apart and kept their knowledge sacred. The people therefore lived entirely upon the traditions of their forefathers, blended with the new doctrines taught by Christianity; so that the popular belief became, in time, an amalgam of the pagan myths and the Christian legend, and these two elements remain indissolubly united to this day. The world, in fact, is a volume, a serial rather, going on for six thousand years, but of which the Irish peasant has scarcely yet turned the first page.

The present work deals only with the mythology, or the fantastic creed of the Irish respecting the invisible world—strange and mystical superstitions, brought thousands of years ago from their Aryan home, but which still, even in the present time, affect all the modes of thinking and acting in the daily life of the people.

Amongst the educated classes in all nations, the belief in the supernatural, acting directly on life and constantly interfering with the natural course of human action, is soon dissipated and gradually disappears, for the knowledge of natural laws solves many mysteries that were once inexplicable; yet much remains unsolved, even to the philosopher, of the mystic relation between the material and the spiritual world. Whilst to the masses—the uneducated—who know nothing of the fixed eternal laws of nature, every phenomenon seems to result from the direct action of some nonhuman power, invisible though ever present; able to confer all benefits, yet implacable if offended, and therefore to be propitiated.

The superstition, then, of the Irish peasant is the instinctive belief in the existence of certain unseen agencies that influence all human life; and with the highly sensitive organization of their race, it is not wonderful that the people live habitually under the shadow and dread of invisible powers which, whether working for good or evil, are awful and mysterious to the uncultured mind that sees only the strange results produced by certain forces, but knows nothing of approximate causes.

Many of the Irish legends, superstitions, and ancient charms now collected were obtained chiefly from oral communications made by the peasantry themselves, either in Irish or in the Irish-English which preserves so much of the expressive idiom of the antique tongue.

These narrations were taken down by competent persons skilled in both languages, and as far as possible in the very words of the narrator; so that much of the primitive simplicity of the style has been retained, while the legends have a peculiar and special value as coming direct from the national heart.

In a few years such a collection would be impossible, for the old race is rapidly passing away to other lands, and in the vast working-world of America, with all the new influences of light and progress, the young generation, though still loving the land of their fathers, will scarcely find leisure to dream over the fairy-haunted hills and lakes and raths of ancient Ireland.

I must disclaim, however, all desire to be considered a melancholy *Laudatrix temporis acti*. These studies of the Irish past are simply the expression of my love for the beautiful island that gave me my first inspiration, my quickest intellectual impulses, and the strongest and best sympathies with genius and country possible to a woman's nature.

Francesca Speranza Wilde

Introduction

The ancient legends of all nations of the world, on which from age to age the generations of man have been nurtured, bear so striking a resemblance to each other that we are led to believe there was once a period when the whole human family was of one creed and one language. But with increasing numbers came the necessity of dispersion; and that ceaseless migration was commenced of the tribes of the earth from the Eastern cradle of their race which has now continued for thousands of years with undiminished activity.

From the beautiful Eden-land at the head of the Persian Gulf, where creeds and culture rose to life, the first migrations emanated, and were naturally directed along the line of the great rivers, by the Euphrates and the Tigris and southward by the Nile; and there the first mighty cities of the world were built, and the first mighty kingdoms of the East began to send out colonies to take possession of the unknown silent world around them. From Persia, Assyria, and Egypt, to Greece and the Isles of the Sea, went forth the wandering tribes, carrying with them, as signs of their origin, broken fragments of the primal creed, and broken idioms of the primal tongue—those early pages in the history of the human race, eternal and indestructible, which hundreds of centuries have not been able to obliterate from the mind of man.

But as the early tribes diverged from the central parent stock, the creed and the language began to assume new forms, according as new habits of life and modes of thought were developed amongst the wandering people, by the influence of climate and the contemplation of new and striking natural phenomena in the lands where they found a resting-place or a home. Still, amongst all nations a basis remained of the primal creed and language, easily to be traced through all the mutations caused by circumstances in human thought, either by higher culture or by the debasement to which both language and symbols are subjected amongst rude and illiterate tribes.

To reconstruct the primal creed and language of humanity from these scattered and broken fragments, is the task which is now exciting so keenly the energies of the ardent and learned ethnographers of Europe; as yet, indeed, with but small success as regards language, for not more, perhaps, than twenty words which the philologists consider may have belonged to the

15

original tongue have been discovered; that is, certain objects or ideas are found represented in all languages by the same words, and therefore the philologist concludes that these words must have been associated with the ideas from the earliest dawn of language; and as the words express chiefly the relations of the human family to each other, they remained fixed in the minds of the wandering tribes, untouched and unchanged by all the diversities of their subsequent experience of life.

Meanwhile, in Europe there is diligent study of the ancient myths, legends, and traditions of the world, in order to extract from them that information respecting the early modes of thought prevalent amongst the primitive race, and also the lines of the first migrations, which no other monuments of antiquity are so well able to give. Traditions, like rays of light, take their colour from the medium through which they pass; but the scientific mythographic student knows how to eliminate the accidental addition from the true primal basis, which remains fixed and unchangeable; and from the numerous myths and legends of the nations of the earth, which bear so striking a conformity to each other that they point to a common origin, he will be able to reconstruct the first articles of belief in the creed of humanity, and to pronounce almost with certainty upon the primal source of the lines of human life that now traverse the globe in all directions. This source of all life, creed, and culture now on earth, there is no reason to doubt, will be found in *Iran*, or Persia as we call it, and in the ancient legends and language of the great Iranian people, the head and noblest type of the Aryan races. Endowed with splendid physical beauty, noble intellect, and a rich musical language, the Iranians had also a lofty sense of the relation between man and the spiritual world. They admitted no idols into their temples; their God was the One Supreme Creator and Upholder of all things, whose symbol was the sun and the pure, elemental fire. But as the world grew older and more wicked the pure primal doctrines were obscured by human fancies, the symbol came to be worshipped in place of the God, and the debased idolatries of Babylon, Assyria, and the Canaanite nations were the result. Egypt—grave, wise, learned, mournful Egypt—retained most of the primal truth; but truth was held by the priests as too precious for the crowd, and so they preserved it carefully for themselves and their own caste. They alone knew the ancient and cryptic meaning of the symbols; the people were allowed only to see the outward and visible sign.

From Egypt, philosophy, culture, art, and religion came to Greece, but the Greeks moulded these splendid elements after their own fashion, and poured the radiance of beauty over the grave and gloomy mysticism of Egypt. Everything hideous, terrible, and revolting was banished from the Greek Mythology. The Greeks constructed no theory of a devil, and believed in no hell, as a distinct and eternal abode for the lost souls of men. The Greek gods were divinely beautiful, and each divinity in turn was ready to help the mortal that invoked him. The dead in Hades mourned their fate because they could no longer enjoy the glorious beauty of life, but no hard and chilling dogmas doomed them there to the tortures of eternal punishment. Earth, air, the heavens and the sea, the storms and sunshine, the forests and flowers and the purple grapes with which they crowned a god, were all to the Greek poet-mind the manifestations of an all-pervading spiritual power and life. A sublime Pantheism was their creed, that sees gods in everything, yet with one Supreme God over all. Freedom, beauty, art, light, and joy, were the elements of the Greek religion, while the Eternal Wisdom, the Great Athené of the Parthenon, was the peculiar and selected divinity of their own half divine race.

Meanwhile other branches of the primal Iranian stock were spreading over the savage central forests of Europe, where they laid the foundation of the great Teuton and Gothic races, the destined world-rulers; but Nature to them was a gloomy and awful mother, and life seemed an endless warfare against the fierce and powerful elemental demons of frost and snow and darkness, by whom the beautiful Sun-god was slain, and who reigned triumphant in that fearful season when the earth was iron and the air was ice, and no beneficent God seemed near to help. Hideous idols imaged these unseen powers, who were propitiated by sanguinary rites; and the men and the god they fashioned were alike as fierce and cruel as the wild beasts of the forest, and the aspects of the savage nature around them.

Still the waves of human life kept rolling westward until they surged over all the lands and islands of the Great Sea, and the wandering mariners, seeking new homes, passed through the Pillars of Hercules out into the Western Ocean, and coasting along by the shores of Spain and France, founded nations that still bear the impress of their Eastern origin, and are known in history as the Celtic race; while the customs, usages, and traditions which their forefathers had learnt in Egypt or Greece were carefully preserved by them, and transmitted as heirlooms to the colonies they founded. From Spain the early mariners easily reached the verdant island of the West in which we Irish are more particularly interested. And here in our beautiful Ireland the last wave of the great Iranian migration finally settled. Further progress was impossible—the unknown ocean seemed to them the limits of the world. And thus the wanderers of the primal race, with their fragments of the ancient creed and mythic poet-lore, and their peculiar dialect of the ancient tongue, formed, as it were, a sediment here which still retains its peculiar affinity with the parent land—though the changes and chances of three thousand years have swept over the people, the legends, and the language. It is, therefore, in Ireland, above all, that the nature and origin of the primitive races of Europe should be studied. Even the form of the Celtic head shows a decided conformity to that of the Greek races, while it differs essentially from the Saxon and Gothic types. This is one of the many proofs in support of the theory that the Celtic people in their westward course to the Atlantic travelled by the coasts of the Mediterranean, as all along that line the same cranial formation is found. Philologists also affirm that the Irish language is nearer to Sanskrit than any other of the living and spoken languages of Europe; while the legends and myths of Ireland can be readily traced to the far East, but have nothing in common with the fierce and weird superstitions of Northern mythology.

This study of legendary lore, as a foundation for the history of humanity, is now recognized as such an important branch of ethnology that a journal entirely devoted to comparative mythology has been recently started in Paris, to which all nations are invited to contribute—Sclaves, Teutons, and Celts, Irish legends being considered specially important, as containing more of the primitive elements than those of other Western nations. All other countries have been repeatedly overwhelmed by alien tribes and peoples and races, but the Irish have remained unchanged, and in place of adopting readily the usages of invaders they have shown such remarkable powers of fascination that the invaders themselves became *Hibernicis ipsis Hiberniores*. The Danes held the east coast of Ireland for three hundred years, yet there is no trace of Thor or Odin or the Frost Giants, or of the Great World-serpent in Irish legend; but if we go back in the history of the world to the beginning of things, when the Iranian people were the only teachers of humanity, we come upon the true ancient source of Irish legend, and find that the original materials have been but very slightly altered, while amongst other nations the ground-work has been overlaid with a dense palimpsest of their own devising, suggested by their peculiar local surroundings.

Amongst the earliest religious symbols of the world are the Tree, the Woman, and the Serpent—memories, no doubt, of the legend of Paradise; and the reverence for certain sacred trees has prevailed in Persia from the most ancient times, and become diffused among all the Iranian nations. It was the custom in Iran to hang costly garments on the branches as votive offerings; and it is recorded that Xerxes before going to battle invoked victory by the Sacred Tree, and hung jewels and rich robes on the boughs. And the poet Saadi narrates an anecdote concerning trees which has the true Oriental touch of mournful suggestion:—He was once, he says, the guest of a very rich old man who had a son remarkable for his beauty. One night the old man said to him, "During my whole life I never had but this son. Near this place is a Sacred Tree to which men resort to offer up their petitions. Many nights at the foot of this tree I besought God until He bestowed on me this son." Not long after Saadi overheard this young man say in a low voice to his friend, "How happy should I be to know where that Sacred Tree grows, in order that I might implore God for the death of my father."

The poorer class in Persia, not being able to make offerings of costly garments, are in the habit of tying bits of coloured stuffs on the boughs, and these rags are considered to have a special virtue in curing diseases. The trees are often near a well or by a saint's grave, and are then looked upon as peculiarly sacred.

This account might have been written for Ireland, for the belief and the ceremonial are precisely similar, and are still found existing to this day both in *Iran* and in *Erin*. But all trees were not held sacred—only those that bore no eatable fruit that could nourish men; a lingering memory of the tree of evil fruit may have caused this prejudice, while the Tree of Life was eagerly sought for, with its promised gift of immortality. In Persia the plane-tree was specially reverenced; in Egypt, the palm; in Greece, the wild olive; and the oak amongst the Celtic nations. Sometimes small tapers were lit amongst the branches, to simulate by fire the presence of divinity. It is worthy of note, while on the subject of Irish and Iranian affinities, that the old Persian word for tree is *dar*, and the Irish call their sacred tree, the oak, *darragh*. [1]

The belief in a race of supernatural beings, midway between man and the Supreme God, beautiful and beneficent, a race that had never known the weight of human life, was also part of the creed of the Iranian people. They called them *Peris*, or *Feroüers* (fairies); and they have some pretty legends concerning the beautiful *Dukhtari Shah Periân*, the "Daughter of the King of the Fairies," for a sight of whose beauty men pine away in vain desire, but if it is granted to them once to behold her, they die. Every nation believes in the existence of these mysterious spirits, with mystic and powerful influence over human life and actions, but each nation represents them differently, according to national habits and national surroundings. Thus, the Russians believe in the phantom of the Ukraine, a beautiful young girl robed in white, who meets the wanderer on the lonely snow steppes, and lulls him by her kisses into that fatal sleep from which he never more awakens. The legends of the Scandinavians, also, are all set in the framework of their own experiences; the rending and crash of the ice is the stroke of the god Thor's hammer; the rime is the beard of the Frost Giant; and when Balder, their Sun-god, is beginning to die at Midsummer, they kindle pine-branches to light him on his downward path to hell; and when he is returning to the upper world, after the winter solstice, they burn the Yule-log, and hang lights on the fir-trees to illuminate his upward path. These traditions are a remnant of the ancient sun worship, but the peasants who kindle the Baal fires at Midsummer, and the upper classes who light up the brilliant Christmas-tree, have forgotten the origin of the custom, though the world-old symbol and usage is preserved.

The *Sidhe*, or Fairies, of Ireland, still preserve all the gentle attributes of their ancient Persian race, for in the soft and equable climate of Erin there were no terrible manifestations of nature to be symbolized by new images; and the genial, laughter-loving elves were in themselves the best and truest expression of Irish nature that could have been invented. The fairies loved music and dancing and frolic; and, above all things, to be let alone, and not to be interfered with as regarded their peculiar fairy habits, customs, and pastimes. They had also, like the Irish, a fine sense of the right and just, and a warm love for the liberal hand and kindly word. All the solitudes of the island were peopled by these bright, happy, beautiful beings, and to the Irish nature, with its need of the spiritual, its love of the vague, mystic, dreamy, and supernatural, there was something irresistibly fascinating in the belief that gentle spirits were around, filled with sympathy for the mortal who suffered wrong or needed help. But the fairies were sometimes wilful and capricious as children, and took dire revenge if any one built over their fairy circles, or looked at them when combing their long yellow hair in the sunshine, or dancing in the woods, or floating on the lakes. Death was the penalty to all who approached too near, or pried too curiously into the mysteries of nature.

To the Irish peasant earth and air were filled with these mysterious beings, half-loved, half-feared by them; and therefore they were propitiated by flattery, and called "the good people," as the Greeks call the dread goddesses "the Eumenides." Their voices were heard in the mountain echo, and their forms seen in the purple and golden mountain mist; they whispered amidst the perfumed hawthorn branches; the rush of the autumn leaves was the scamper of little elves—red, yellow, and brown—wind-delven, and dancing in their glee; and the bending of the waving barley was caused by the flight of the Elf King and his Court across the fields. They danced with soundless feet, and their step was so light that the drops of dew they danced on only trembled, but did not break. The fairy music was low and sweet, "blinding sweet," like that of the great god Pan by the river; they lived only on the nectar in the cups of the flowers, though in their fairy palaces sumptuous banquets were offered to the mortals they carried off—but woe to the mortal who tasted of fairy food; to eat was fatal. All the evil in the world has come by eating; if Eve had only resisted that apple our race might still be in Paradise. The Sidhe look with envy on the beautiful young human children, and steal them when they can; and the children of a Sidhe and a mortal mother are reputed to grow up strong and powerful, but with evil and dangerous natures. There is also a belief that every seven years the fairies are obliged to deliver up a victim to the Evil One, and to save their own people they try to abduct some beautiful young mortal girl, and her they hand over to the Prince of Darkness.

Dogmatic religion and science have long since killed the mythopoetic faculty in cultured Europe. It only exists now, naturally and instinctively, in children, poets, and the childlike races, like the Irish—simple, joyous, reverent, and unlettered, and who have remained unchanged for centuries, walled round by their language from the rest of Europe, through which separating veil science, culture, and the cold mockery of the sceptic have never yet penetrated.

Christianity was readily accepted by the Irish. The pathetic tale of the beautiful young Virgin-Mother and the Child-God, for central objects, touched all the deepest chords of feeling in the tender, loving, and sympathetic Irish heart. The legends of ancient times were not overthrown by it, however, but taken up and incorporated with the new Christian faith. The holy wells and the sacred trees remained, and were even made holier by association with a saint's name. And to this day the old mythology holds its ground with a force and vitality untouched by any symptoms of weakness or decay. The Greeks, who are of the same original race as our people, rose through the influence of the highest culture to the fulness and perfectness of eternal youth; but the Irish, without culture, are eternal children, with all the childlike instincts of superstition still strong in them, and capable of believing all things, because to doubt requires knowledge. They never, like the Greeks, attained to the conception of a race of beings nobler than themselves—men stronger and more gifted, with the immortal fire of a god in their veins; women divinely beautiful, or divinely inspired; but, also, the Irish never defaced the image of God in their hearts by infidelity or irreligion. One of the most beautiful and sublimely touching records in all human history is that of the unswerving devotion of the Irish people to their ancient faith, through persecutions and penal enactments more insulting and degrading than were ever inflicted in any other land by one Christian sect upon another.

With this peculiarly reverential nature it would be impossible to make the Irish a nation of sceptics, even if a whole legion of German Rationalists came amongst them to preach a crusade against all belief in the spiritual and the unseen. And the old traditions of their race have likewise taken firm hold in their hearts, because they are an artistic people, and require objects for their adoration and love, not mere abstractions to be accepted by their reason. And they are also a nation of poets; the presence of God is ever near them, and the saints and angels, and the shadowy beings of earth and air are perpetually drawing their minds, through mingled love and fear, to the infinite and invisible world. Probably not one tradition or custom that had its origin in a religious belief has been lost in Ireland during the long course of ages since the first people from Eastern lands arrived and settled on our shores. The Baal fires are still lit at Midsummer, though no longer in honour of the sun, but of St. John; and the peasants still make their cattle pass between two fires—not, indeed, as of old, in the name of Moloch, but of some patron saint. That all Irish legends point to the East for their origin, not to the North, is certain; to a warm land, not one of icebergs, and thunder crashes of the rending of ice-bound rivers, but to a region where the shadow of trees, and a cool draught from the sparkling well were life-giving blessings. Well-worship could not have originated in a humid country like Ireland, where wells can be found at every step, and sky and land are ever heavy and saturated with moisture. It must have come from an Eastern people, wanderers in a dry and thirsty land, where the discovery of a well seemed like the interposition of an angel in man's behalf.

We are told also by the ancient chroniclers that serpent-worship once prevailed in Ireland, and that St. Patrick hewed down the serpent idol *Crom-Cruadh* (the great worm) and cast it into the Boyne (from whence arose the legend that St. Patrick banished all venomous things from the island). Now as the Irish never could have seen a serpent, none existing in Ireland, this worship must have come from the far East, where this beautiful and deadly creature is looked upon as the symbol of the Evil One, and worshipped and propitiated by votive offerings, as all evil things were in the early world, in the hope of turning away their evil hatred from man, and to induce them to show mercy and pity; just as the Egyptians propitiated the sacred crocodile by subtle flatteries and hung costly jewels in its ears. The Irish, indeed, do not seem to have originated any peculiar or national cultus. Their funeral ceremonies recall those of Egypt and Greece and other ancient Eastern climes, from whence they brought their customs of the Wake, the death chant, the mourning women, and the funeral games. In Sparta, on the death of a king or great chief, they had a wake and "keen" not common to the rest of Greece, but which they said they learned from the Phœnicians; and this peculiar usage bears a striking resemblance to the Irish practice. All the virtues of the dead were recited, and the Greek "Eleleu," the same cry as the "Ul-lu-lu" of the Irish, was keened over the corpse by the chorus of hired mourning women. The custom of selecting women in place of men for the chorus of lamentation prevailed throughout all the ancient world, as if an open display of grief was thought beneath the dignity of man. It was Cassandra gave the keynote for the wail over Hector, and Helen took the lead in reciting praises to his honour. The death chants in Egypt, Arabia, and Abyssinia all bear a marked resemblance to the Irish; indeed the mourning cry is the same in all, and the Egyptian lamentation "Hi-loo-loo! Hi-loo-loo!" cried over the dead, was probably the original form of the Irish wail.

The Greeks always endeavoured to lessen the terrors of death, and for this reason they established funeral games, and the funeral ceremonies took the form of a festival, where they ate and drank and poured libations of wine in honour of the dead. The Irish had also their funeral games and peculiar dances, when they threw off their upper garments, and holding hands in a circle, moved in a slow measure round a woman crouched in the centre, with her hands covering her face. Another singular part of the ceremony was the entrance of a woman wearing a cow's head and horns, as Io appears upon the scene in the Prometheus of Æschylus. This woman was probably meant to represent the horned or crescented moon, the antique Diana, the Goddess of Death. The custom of throwing off the garments no doubt originally signified the casting off the garment of the flesh. We brought nothing into this world, and it is certain we carry nothing out. The soul must stand unveiled before God.

In the islands off the West Coast of Ireland, where the most ancient superstitions still exist, they have a strange custom. No funeral wail is allowed to be raised until three hours have elapsed from the moment of death, because, they say, the sound of the cries would hinder the soul from speaking to God when it stands before Him, and waken up the two great dogs that are watching for the souls of the dead in order that they may devour them—and the Lord of Heaven Himself cannot hinder them if once they waken. This tradition of watching by the dead in silence, while the soul stands before God, is a fine and solemn superstition, which must have had its origin amongst a people of intense faith in the invisible world, and is probably of great antiquity.

The sound of the Irish keen is wonderfully pathetic. No one could listen to the long-sustained minor wail of the "Ul-lu-lu" without strong emotion and even tears; and once heard it can never be forgotten. Nor is there anything derogatory to grief in the idea of hired mourners; on the contrary, it is a splendid tribute to the dead to order their praises to be recited publicly before the assembled friends; while there is something indescribably impressive in the aspect of the mourning women crouched around the bier with shrouded heads, as they rock themselves to and fro and intone the solemn, ancient death-song with a measured cadence, sometimes rising to a piercing wail. They seem like weird and shadowy outlines of an old-world vision, and at once the imagination is carried back to the far-distant East, and the time when all these funeral symbols had a mysterious and awful meaning. Sometimes a wail of genuine and bitter grief interrupts the chant of the hired mourners. An Irish keen which was taken down from the lips of a bereaved mother some years ago, runs thus in the literal English version—

"O women, look on me! Look on me, women! Have you ever seen any sorrow like mine? Have you ever seen the like of me in my sorrow? Arrah, then, my darling, my darling, 'tis your mother that calls you. How long you are sleeping. Do you see all the people round you, my darling, and I sorely weeping? Arrah, what is this paleness on your face? Sure there was no equal to it in Erin for beauty and fairness, and your hair was heavy as the wing of a raven, and your skin was whiter than the hand of a lady. Is it the stranger must carry me to my grave, and my son lying here?"

This touching lament is so thoroughly Greek in form and sentiment that it might be taken for part of a chorus from the Hecuba of Euripides. Even the "Arrah" reminds one of a Greek word used frequently by the Greeks when commencing a sentence or asking a question, although the resemblance may be only superficial.

The tales and legends told by the peasants in the Irish vernacular are much more weird and strange, and have much more of the old-world colouring than the ordinary fairy tales narrated in English by the people, as may be seen by the following mythical story, translated from the Irish, and which is said to be a thousand years old:—

The Horned Women

A rich woman sat up late one night carding and preparing wool, while all the family and servants were asleep. Suddenly a knock was given at the door, and a voice called—"Open! open!"

"Who is there?" said the woman of the house.

"I am the Witch of the One Horn," was answered.

The mistress, supposing that one of her neighbours had called and required assistance, opened the door, and a woman entered, having in her hand a pair of wool carders, and bearing a horn on her forehead, as if growing there. She sat down by the fire in silence, and began to card the wool with violent haste. Suddenly she paused and said aloud: "Where are the women? They delay too long."

Then a second knock came to the door, and a voice called as before—"Open! open!"

The mistress felt herself constrained to rise and open to the call, and immediately a second witch entered, having two horns on her forehead, and in her hand a wheel for spinning the wool.

"Give me place," she said; "I am the Witch of the Two Horns," and she began to spin as quick as lightning.

And so the knocks went on, and the call was heard, and the witches entered, until at last twelve women sat round the fire—the first with one horn, the last with twelve horns. And they carded the thread, and turned their spinning wheels, and wound and wove, all singing together an ancient rhyme, but no word did they speak to the mistress of the house. Strange to hear, and frightful to look upon were these twelve women, with their horns and their wheels; and the mistress felt near to death, and she tried to rise that she might call for help, but she could not move, nor could she utter a word or a cry, for the spell of the witches was upon her.

Then one of them called to her in Irish and said—

"Rise, woman, and make us a cake."

Then the mistress searched for a vessel to bring water from the well that she might mix the meal and make the cake, but she could find none. And they said to her—

"Take a sieve and bring water in it."

And she took the sieve and went to the well; but the water poured from it, and she could fetch none for the cake, and she sat down by the well and wept. Then a voice came by her and said—

"Take yellow clay and moss and bind them together and plaster the sieve so that it will hold."

This she did, and the sieve held the water for the cake. And the voice said again—

"Return, and when thou comest to the north angle of the house, cry aloud three times and say, 'The mountain of the Fenian women and the sky over it is all on fire.'"

And she did so.

When the witches inside heard the call, a great and terrible cry broke from their lips and they rushed forth with wild lamentations and shrieks, and fled away to Slieve-namon, where was their chief abode. But the Spirit of the Well bade the mistress of the house to enter and prepare her home against the enchantments of the witches if they returned again.

And first, to break their spells, she sprinkled the water in which she had washed her child's feet (the feet-water) outside the door on the threshold; secondly, she took the cake which the witches had made in her absence, of meal mixed with the blood drawn from the sleeping family. And she broke the cake in bits, and placed a bit in the mouth of each sleeper, and they were restored; and she took the cloth they had woven and placed it half in and half out of the chest with the padlock; and lastly, she secured the door with a great cross-beam fastened in the jambs, so that they could not enter. And having done these things she waited.

Not long were the witches in coming back, and they raged and called for vengeance.

"Open! Open!" they screamed. "Open, feet-water!"

"I cannot," said the feet-water, "I am scattered on the ground and my path is down to the Lough."

"Open, open, wood and tree and beam!" they cried to the door.

"I cannot," said the door; "for the beam is fixed in the jambs and I have no power to move."

"Open, open, cake that we have made and mingled with blood," they cried again.

"I cannot," said the cake, "for I am broken and bruised, and my blood is on the lips of the sleeping children."

Then the witches rushed through the air with great cries, and fled back to Slieve-namon, uttering strange curses on the Spirit of the Well, who had wished their ruin; but the woman and the house were left in peace, and a mantle dropped by one of the witches in her flight was kept hung up by the mistress as a sign of the night's awful contest; and this mantle was in possession of the same family from generation to generation for five hundred years after.

The Legend of Ballytowtas Castle

The next tale I shall select is composed in a lighter and more modern spirit. All the usual elements of a fairy tale are to be found in it, but the story is new to the nursery folk, and, if well illustrated, would make a pleasant and novel addition to the rather worn-out legends on which the children of many generations have been hitherto subsisting.

In old times there lived where Ballytowtas Castle now stands a poor man named Towtas. It was in the time when manna fell to the earth with the dew of evening, and Towtas lived by gathering the manna, and thus supported himself, for he was a poor man, and had nothing else.

One day a pedlar came by that way with a fair young daughter.

"Give us a night's lodging," he said to Towtas, "for we are weary."

And Towtas did so.

Next morning, when they were going away, his heart longed for the young girl, and he said to the pedlar, "Give me your daughter for my wife."

"How will you support her?" asked the pedlar.

"Better than you can," answered Towtas, "for she can never want."

Then he told him all about the manna; how he went out every morning when it was lying on the ground with the dew, and gathered it, as his father and forefathers had done before him, and lived on it all their lives, so that he had never known want nor any of his people.

Then the girl showed she would like to stay with the young man, and the pedlar consented, and they were married, Towtas and the fair young maiden; and the pedlar left them and went his way. So years went on, and they were very happy and never wanted; and they had one son, a bright, handsome youth, and as clever as he was comely.

But in due time old Towtas died, and after her husband was buried, the woman went out to gather the manna as she had seen him do, when the dew lay on the ground; but she soon grew tired and said to herself, "Why should I do this thing every day? I'll just gather now enough to do the week and then I can have rest."

So she gathered up great heaps of it greedily, and went her way into the house. But the sin of greediness lay on her evermore; and not a bit of manna fell with the dew that evening, nor ever again. And she was poor, and faint with hunger, and had to go out and work in the fields to earn the morsel that kept her and her son alive; and she begged pence from the people as they went into chapel, and this paid for her son's schooling; so he went on with his learning, and no one in the county was like him for beauty and knowledge.

One day he heard the people talking of a great lord that lived up in Dublin, who had a daughter so handsome that her like was never seen; and all the fine young gentlemen were dying about her, but she would take none of them. And he came home to his mother and said, "I shall go see this great lord's daughter. Maybe the luck will be mine above all the fine young gentlemen that love her."

"Go along, poor fool," said the mother, "how can the poor stand before the rich?"

But he persisted. "If I die on the road," he said, "I'll try it."

"Wait, then," she answered, "till Sunday, and whatever I get I'll give you half of it." So she gave him half of the pence she gathered at the chapel door, and bid him go in the name of God.

He hadn't gone far when he met a poor man who asked him for a trifle for God's sake. So he gave him something out of his mother's money and went on. Again, another met him, and begged for a trifle to buy food, for the sake of God, and he gave him something also, and then went on.

"Give me a trifle for God's sake," cried a voice, and he saw a third poor man before him.

"I have nothing left," said Towtas, "but a few pence; if I give them, I shall have nothing for food and must die of hunger. But come with me, and whatever I can buy for this I shall share with you." And as they were going on to the inn he told all his story to the beggar man, and how he wanted to go to Dublin, but had now no money. So they came to the inn, and he called for a loaf and a drink of milk. "Cut the loaf," he said to the beggar. "You are the oldest."

"I won't," said the other, for he was ashamed, but Towtas made him.

And so the beggar cut the loaf, but though they ate, it never grew smaller, and though they drank as they liked of the milk, it never grew less. Then Towtas rose up to pay, but when the landlady came and looked, "How is this?" she said. "You have eaten nothing. I'll not take your money, poor boy," but he made her take some; and they left the place, and went on their way together.

"Now," said the beggar man, "you have been three times good to me to-day, for thrice I have met you, and you gave me help for the sake of God each time. See, now, I can help also," and he reached a gold ring to the handsome youth. "Wherever you place that ring, and wish for it, gold will come—bright gold, so that you can never want while you have it."

Then Towtas put the ring first in one pocket and then in another, until all his pockets were so heavy with gold that he could scarcely walk; but when he turned to thank the friendly beggar man, he had disappeared.

So, wondering to himself at all his adventures, he went on, until he came at last in sight of the lord's palace, which was beautiful to see; but he would not enter in until he went and bought fine clothes, and made himself as grand as any prince; and then he went boldly up, and they invited him in, for they said, "Surely he is a king's son." And when dinner-hour came the lord's daughter linked her arm with Towtas, and smiled on him. And he drank of the rich wine, and was mad with love; but at last the wine overcame him, and the servants had to carry him to his bed; and in going into his room he dropped the ring from his finger, but knew it not.

Now, in the morning, the lord's daughter came by, and cast her eyes upon the door of his chamber, and there close by it was the ring she had seen him wear.

"Ah," she said, "I'll tease him now about his ring." And she put it in her box, and wished that she were as rich as a king's daughter, that so the king's son might marry her; and, behold, the box filled up with gold, so that she could not shut it; and she put it from her into another box, and that filled also; and then she was frightened at the ring, and put it at last in her pocket as the safest place.

But when Towtas awoke and missed the ring, his heart was grieved.

"Now, indeed," he said, "my luck is gone."

And he inquired of all the servants, and then of the lord's daughter, and she laughed, by which he knew she had it; but no coaxing would get it from her, so when all was useless he went away, and set out again to reach his old home.

And he was very mournful and threw himself down on the ferns near an old fort, waiting till night came on, for he feared to go home in the daylight lest the people should laugh at him for his folly. And about dusk three cats came out of the fort talking to each other.

"How long our cook is away," said one.

"What can have happened to him?" said another.

And as they were grumbling a fourth cat came up.

"What delayed you?" they all asked angrily.

Then he told his story—how he had met Towtas and given him the ring. "And I just went," he said, "to the lord's palace to see how the young man behaved; and I was leaping over the dinner-table when the lord's knife struck my tail and three drops of blood fell upon his plate, but he never saw it and swallowed them with his meat. So now he has three kittens inside him and is dying of agony, and can never be cured until he drinks three draughts of the water of the well of Ballytowtas."

So when young Towtas heard the cats talk he sprang up and went and told his mother to give him three bottles full of the water of the Towtas well, and he would go to the lord disguised as a doctor and cure him.

So off he went to Dublin. And all the doctors in Ireland were round the lord, but none of them could tell what ailed him, or how to cure him. Then Towtas came in and said, "I will cure him." So they gave him entertainment and lodging, and when he was refreshed he gave of the well water three draughts to his lordship, when out jumped the three kittens. And there was great rejoicing, and they treated Towtas like a prince. But all the same he could not get the ring from the lord's daughter, so he set off home again quite disheartened, and thought to himself, "If I could only meet the man again that gave me the ring who knows what luck I might have?" And he sat down to rest in a wood, and saw there not far off three boys fighting under an oak-tree.

"Shame on ye to fight so," he said to them. "What is the fight about?"

Then they told him. "Our father," they said, "before he died, buried under this oak-tree a ring by which you can be in any place in two minutes if you only wish it; a goblet that is always full when standing, and empty only when on its side; and a harp that plays any tune of itself that you name or wish for."

"I want to divide the things," said the youngest boy, "and let us all go and seek our fortunes as we can."

"But I have a right to the whole," said the eldest.

And they went on fighting, till at length Towtas said—

"I'll tell you how to settle the matter. All of you be here to-morrow, and I'll think over the matter to-night, and I engage you will have nothing more to quarrel about when you come in the morning."

So the boys promised to keep good friends till they met in the morning, and went away.

When Towtas saw them clear off, he dug up the ring, the goblet, and the harp, and now said he, "I'm all right, and they won't have anything to fight about in the morning."

Off he set back again to the lord's castle with the ring, the goblet, and the harp; but he soon bethought himself of the powers of the ring, and in two minutes he was in the great hall where all the lords and ladies were just sitting down to dinner; and the harp played the sweetest music, and they all listened in delight; and he drank out of the goblet which was never empty, and then, when his head began to grow a little light, "It is enough," he said; and putting his arm round the waist of the lord's daughter, he took his harp and goblet in the other hand, and murmuring—"I wish we were at the old fort by the side of the wood"—in two minutes they were both at the desired spot. But his head was heavy with the wine, and he laid down the harp beside him and fell asleep. And when she saw him asleep she took the ring off his finger, and the harp and the goblet from the ground and was back home in her father's castle before two minutes had passed by.

When Towtas awoke and found his prize gone, and all his treasures beside, he was like one mad; and roamed about the country till he came by an orchard, where he saw a tree covered with bright, rosy apples. Being hungry and thirsty, he plucked one and ate it, but no sooner had he done so than horns began to sprout from his forehead, and grew larger and longer till he knew he looked like a goat, and all he could do, they would not come off. Now, indeed, he was driven out of his mind, and thought how all the neighbours would laugh at him; and as he raged and roared with shame, he spied another tree with apples, still brighter, of ruddy gold.

"If I were to have fifty pairs of horns I must have one of those," he said; and seizing one, he had no sooner tasted it than the horns fell off, and he felt that he was looking stronger and handsomer than ever.

"Now, I have her at last," he exclaimed. "I'll put horns on them all, and will never take them off until they give her to me as my bride before the whole Court."

Without further delay he set off to the lord's palace, carrying with him as many of the apples as he could bring off the two trees. And when they saw the beauty of the fruit they longed for it; and he gave to them all, so that at last there was not a head to be seen without horns in the whole dining-hall. Then they cried out and prayed to have the horns taken off, but Towtas said—

"No; there they shall be till I have the lord's daughter given to me for my bride, and my two rings, my goblet, and my harp all restored to me."

And this was done before the face of all the lords and ladies; and his treasures were restored to him; and the lord placed his daughter's hand in the hand of Towtas, saying—

"Take her; she is your wife; only free me from the horns."

Then Towtas brought forth the golden apples; and they all ate, and the horns fell off; and he took his bride and his treasures, and carried them off home, where he built the Castle of Ballytowtas, in the place where stood his father's hut, and enclosed the well within the walls. And when he had filled his treasure-room with gold, so that no man could count his riches, he buried his fairy treasures deep in the ground, where no man knew, and no man has ever yet been able to find them until this day.

A Wolf Story

Transformation into wolves is a favourite subject of Irish legend, and many a wild tale is told by the peasants round the turf fire in the winter nights of strange adventures with wolves. Stories that had come down to them from their forefathers in the old times long ago; for there are no wolves existing now in Ireland.

A young farmer, named Connor, once missed two fine cows from his herd, and no tale or tidings could be heard of them anywhere. So he thought he would set out on a search throughout the country; and he took a stout blackthorn stick in his hand, and went his way. All day he travelled miles and miles, but never a sign of the cattle. And the evening began to grow very dark, and he was wearied and hungry, and no place near to rest in; for he was in the midst of a bleak, desolate heath, with never a habitation at all in sight, except a long, low, rude shieling, like the den of a robber or a wild beast. But a gleam of light came from a chink between the boards, and Connor took heart and went up and knocked at the door. It was opened at once by a tall, thin, grey-haired old man, with keen, dark eyes.

"Come in," he said, "you are welcome. We have been waiting for you. This is my wife," and he brought him over to the hearth, where was seated an old, thin, grey woman, with long, sharp teeth and terrible glittering eyes.

"You are welcome," she said. "We have been waiting for you—it is time for supper. Sit down and eat with us."

Now Connor was a brave fellow, but he was a little dazed at first at the sight of this strange creature. However, as he had his stout stick with him, he thought he could make a fight for his life any way, and, meantime, he would rest and eat, for he was both hungry and weary, and it was now black night, and he would never find his way home even if he tried. So he sat down by the hearth, while the old grey woman stirred the pot on the fire. But Connor felt that she was watching him all the time with her keen, sharp eyes.

Then a knock came to the door. And the old man rose up and opened it. When in walked a slender, young black wolf, who immediately went straight across the floor to an inner room, from which in a few moments came forth a dark, slender, handsome youth, who took his place at the table and looked hard at Connor with his glittering eyes.

"You are welcome," he said, "we have waited for you."

Before Connor could answer another knock was heard, and in came a second wolf, who passed on to the inner room like the first, and soon after, another dark, handsome youth came out and sat down to supper with them, glaring at Connor with his keen eyes, but said no word.

"These are our sons," said the old man, "tell them what you want, and what brought you here amongst us, for we live alone and don't care to have spies and strangers coming to our place."

Then Connor told his story, how he had lost his two fine cows, and had searched all day and found no trace of them; and he knew nothing of the place he was in, nor of the kindly gentleman who asked him to supper; but if they just told him where to find his cows he would thank them, and make the best of his way home at once.

Then they all laughed and looked at each other, and the old hag looked more frightful than ever when she showed her long, sharp teeth.

On this, Connor grew angry, for he was hot tempered; and he grasped his blackthorn stick firmly in his hand and stood up, and bade them open the door for him; for he would go his way, since they would give no heed and only mocked him.

Then the eldest of the young men stood up. "Wait," he said, "we are fierce and evil, but we never forget a kindness. Do you remember, one day down in the glen you found a poor little wolf in great agony and like to die, because a sharp thorn had pierced his side? And you gently extracted the thorn and gave him a drink, and went your way leaving him in peace and rest?"

"Aye, well do I remember it," said Connor, "and how the poor little beast licked my hand in gratitude."

"Well," said the young man, "I am that wolf, and I shall help you if I can, but stay with us to-night and have no fear."

So they sat down again to supper and feasted merrily, and then all fell fast asleep, and Connor knew nothing more till he awoke in the morning and found himself by a large hay-rick in his own field.

"Now surely," thought he, "the adventure of last night was not all a dream, and I shall certainly find my cows when I go home; for that excellent, good young wolf promised his help, and I feel certain he would not deceive me."

But when he arrived home and looked over the yard and the stable and the field, there was no sign nor sight of the cows. So he grew very sad and dispirited. But just then he espied in the field close by three of the most beautiful strange cows he had ever set eyes on. "These must have strayed in," he said, "from some neighbour's ground;" and he took his big stick to drive them out of the gate off the field. But when he reached the gate, there stood a young black wolf watching; and when the cows tried to pass out at the gate he bit at them, and drove them back. Then Connor knew that his friend the wolf had kept his word. So he let the cows go quietly back to the field; and there they remained, and grew to be the finest in the whole country, and their descendants are flourishing to this day, and Connor grew rich and prospered; for a kind deed is never lost, but brings good luck to the doer for evermore, as the old proverb says:

"Blessings are won,

By a good deed done."

But never again did Connor find that desolate heath or that lone shieling, though he sought far and wide, to return his thanks, as was due to the friendly wolves; nor did he ever again meet any of the family, though he mourned much whenever a slaughtered wolf was brought into the town for the sake of the reward, fearing his excellent friend might be the victim. At that time the wolves in Ireland had increased to such an extent, owing to the desolation of the country by constant wars, that a reward was offered and a high price paid for every wolf's skin brought into the court of the justiciary; and this was in the time of Queen Elizabeth, when the English troops made ceaseless war against the Irish people, and there were more wolves in Ireland than men; and the dead lay unburied in hundreds on the highways, for there were no hands left to dig them graves.

The Evil Eye

There is nothing more dreaded by the people, nor considered more deadly in its effects, than the Evil Eye.

It may strike at any moment unless the greatest precautions are taken, and even then there is no true help possible unless the fairy doctor is at once summoned to pronounce the mystic charm that can alone destroy the evil and fatal influence.

There are several modes in which the Evil Eye can act, some much more deadly than others. If certain persons are met the first thing in the morning, you will be unlucky for the whole of that day in all you do. If the evil-eyed comes in to rest, and looks fixedly on anything, on cattle or on a child, there is doom in the glance; a fatality which cannot be evaded except by a powerful counter-charm. But if the evil-eyed mutters a verse over a sleeping child, that child will assuredly die, for the incantation is of the devil, and no charm has power to resist it or turn away the evil. Sometimes the process of bewitching is effected by looking fixedly at the object, through nine fingers; especially is the magic fatal if the victim is seated by the fire in the evening when the moon is full. Therefore, to avoid being suspected of having the Evil Eye, it is necessary at once, when looking at a child, to say "God bless it." And when passing a farmyard where the cows are collected for milking, to say, "The blessing of God be on you and on all your labours." If this form is omitted, the worst results may be apprehended, and the people would be filled with terror and alarm, unless a counter-charm were not instantly employed.

The singular malific influence of a glance has been felt by most persons in life; an influence that seems to paralyze intellect and speech, simply by the mere presence in the room of some one who is mystically antipathetic to our nature. For the soul is like a fine-toned harp that vibrates to the slightest external force or movement, and the presence and glance of some persons can radiate around us a divine joy, while others may kill the soul with a sneer or a frown. We call these subtle influences mysteries, but the early races believed them to be produced by spirits, good or evil, as they acted on the nerves or the intellect.

Some years ago an old woman was living in Kerry, and it was thought so unlucky to meet her in the morning, that all the girls used to go out after sunset to bring in water for the following day, that so they might avoid her evil glance; for whatever she looked on came to loss and grief.

There was a man, also, equally dreaded on account of the strange, fatal power of his glance; and so many accidents and misfortunes were traced to his presence that finally the neighbours insisted that he should wear a black patch over the Evil Eye, not to be removed unless by request; for learned gentlemen, curious in such things, sometimes came to him to ask for a proof of his power, and he would try it for a wager while drinking with his friends.

One day, near an old ruin of a castle, he met a boy weeping in great grief for his pet pigeon, which had got up to the very top of the ruin, and could not be coaxed down.

"What will you give me," asked the man, "if I bring it down for you?"

"I have nothing to give," said the boy, "but I will pray to God for you. Only get me back my pigeon, and I shall be happy."

Then the man took off the black patch and looked up steadfastly at the bird; when all of a sudden it fell to the ground and lay motionless, as if stunned; but there was no harm done to it, and the boy took it up and went his way, rejoicing.

*

A woman in the County Galway had a beautiful child, so handsome, that all the neighbours were very careful to say "God bless it" when they saw him, for they knew the fairies would desire to steal the child, and carry it off to the hills.

But one day it chanced that an old woman, a stranger, came in. "Let me rest," she said, "for I am weary." And she sat down and looked at the child, but never said "God bless it." And when she had rested, she rose up, looked again at the child fixedly, in silence, and then went her way.

All that night the child cried and would not sleep. And all next day it moaned as if in pain. So the mother told the priest, but he would do nothing for fear of the fairies. And just as the poor mother was in despair, she saw a strange woman going by the door. "Who knows," she said to her husband, "but this woman would help us." So they asked her to come in and rest. And when she looked at the child she said "God bless it," instantly, and spat three times at it, and then sat down.

"Now, what will you give me," she said, "if I tell you what ails the child?"

"I will cross your hand with silver," said the mother, "as much as you want, only speak," and she laid the money on the woman's hand. "Now tell me the truth, for the sake and in the name of Mary, and the good Angels."

"Well," said the stranger, "the fairies have had your child these two days in the hills, and this is a changeling they have left in its place. But so many blessings were said on your child that the fairies can do it no harm. For there was only one blessing wanting, and only one person gave the Evil Eye. Now, you must watch for this woman, carry her into the house and secretly cut off a piece of her cloak. Then burn the piece close to the child, till the smoke as it rises makes him sneeze; and when this happens the spell is broken, and your own child will come back to you safe and sound, in place of the changeling."

Then the stranger rose up and went her way.

All that evening the mother watched for the old woman, and at last she spied her on the road.

"Come in," she cried, "come in, good woman, and rest, for the cakes are hot on the griddle, and supper is ready."

So the woman came in, but never said "God bless you kindly," to man or mortal, only scowled at the child, who cried worse than ever.

Now the mother had told her eldest girl to cut off a piece of the old woman's cloak, secretly, when she sat down to eat. And the girl did as she was desired, and handed the piece to her mother, unknown to any one. But, to their surprise, this was no sooner done than the woman rose up and went out without uttering a word; and they saw her no more.

Then the father carried the child outside, and burned the piece of cloth before the door, and held the boy over the smoke till he sneezed three times violently: after which he gave the child back to the mother, who laid him in his bed, where he slept peacefully, with a smile on his face, and cried no more with the cry of pain. And when he woke up the mother knew that she had got her own darling child back from the fairies, and no evil thing happened to him any more.

*

The influence of the mysterious and malign power of the Evil Eye has at all times been as much dreaded in Ireland as it is in Egypt, Greece, or Italy at the present day. Everything young, beautiful, or perfect after its kind, and which naturally attracts attention and admiration, is peculiarly liable to the fatal blight that follows the glance of the Evil Eye. It is therefore an invariable habit amongst the peasantry never to praise anything without instantly adding, "God bless it;" for were this formula omitted, the worst consequences would befall the object praised.

The superstition must be of great antiquity in Ireland, for Balor, the Fomorian giant and hero, is spoken of in an ancient manuscript as able to petrify his enemies by a glance; and how he became possessed of the power is thus narrated:—

One day as the Druids were busy at their incantations, while boiling a magical spell or charm, young Balor passed by, and curious to see their work, looked in at an open window. At that moment the Druids happened to raise the lid of the caldron, and the vapour, escaping, passed under one of Balor's eyes, carrying with it all the venom of the incantation. This caused his brow to grow to such a size that it required four men to raise it whenever he wanted to exert the power of his venomed glance over his enemies. He was slain at last in single combat, according to the ancient legend, at the great battle of Magh-Tura [2] (the plain of the towers), fought between the Firbolgs and the Tuatha-de-Dananns for the possession of Ireland several centuries before the Christian era; for before Balor's brow could be lifted so that he could transfix his enemy and strike him dead with the terrible power of his glance, his adversary flung a stone with such violence that it went right through the Evil Eye, and pierced the skull; and the mighty magician fell to rise no more.

An interesting account of this battle, with a remarkable confirmation of the legends respecting it still current in the district, is given by Sir William Wilde, in his work, "Lough Corrib; its Shores and Islands." In the ancient manuscript, it is recorded that a young hero having been slain while bravely defending his king, the Firbolg army erected a mound over him, each man carrying a stone, and the monument was henceforth known as the *Carn-in-en-*

Fhir (the cairn of the one man). Having examined the locality with a transcript of this manuscript in his hand, Sir William fixed on the particular mound, amongst the many stone tumuli scattered over the plain, which seemed to agree best with the description, and had it opened carefully under his own superintendence.

A large flag-stone was first discovered, laid horizontally; then another beneath it, covering a small square chamber formed of stones, within which was *a single urn* of baked clay, graceful and delicate in form and ornamentation, containing incinerated human bones, the remains, there can be no reason to doubt, of the Firbolg youth who was honoured for his loyalty by the erection over him of the *Carn-in-en-Fhir* on the historic plains of Mayo.

After Balor, the only other ancient instance of the fatal effects of the malific Eye is narrated of St. Silan, who had a poisonous hair in his eyebrow that killed whoever looked first on him in the morning. All persons, therefore, who from long sickness, or sorrow, or the weariness that comes with years, were tired of life, used to try and come in the saint's way, that so their sufferings might be ended by a quick and easy death. But another saint, the holy Molaise, hearing that St. Silan was coming to visit his church, resolved that no more deaths should happen by means of the poisoned hair. So he arose early in the morning, before any one was up, and went forth alone to meet St. Silan, and when he saw him coming along the path, he went boldly up and plucked out the fatal hair from his eyebrow, but in doing so he himself was struck by the venom, and immediately after fell down dead.

The power of the Evil Eye was recognized by the Brehon laws, and severe measures were ordained against the users of the malign influence. "If a person is in the habit of injuring things through neglect, or of will, whether he has blessed, or whether he has not blessed, full penalty be upon him, or restitution in kind." So ran the ancient law.

The gift comes by nature and is born with one, though it may not be called into exercise unless circumstances arise to excite the power. Then it seems to act like a spirit of bitter and malicious envy that radiates a poisonous atmosphere which chills and blights everything within its reach. Without being superstitious every one has felt that there is such a power and succumbed to its influence in a helpless, passive way, as if all self-trust and self-reliant energy were utterly paralyzed by its influence.

Suspected persons are held in great dread by the peasantry, and they recognize them at once by certain signs. Men and women with dark lowering eyebrows are especially feared, and the handsome children are kept out of their path lest they might be overlooked by them.

Red hair is supposed to have a most malign influence, and it has even passed into a proverb: "Let not the eye of a red-haired woman rest on you."

Many persons are quite unconscious that their glance or frown has this evil power until some calamity results, and then they strive not to look at any one full in the face, but to avert their eyes when speaking, lest misfortune might fall upon the person addressed. [3]

The saving invocation, "God bless it!" is universally used when praise is bestowed, to prevent danger, and should a child fall sick some one is immediately suspected of having omitted the usual phrase out of malice and ill-will. Nothing is more dreaded by the peasantry than the full, fixed, direct glance of one suspected of the Evil Eye, and should it fall upon them, or on any of their household, a terrible fear and trembling of heart takes possession of them, which often ends in sickness or sometimes even in death.

*

Some years ago a woman living in Kerry declared that she was "overlooked" by the Evil Eye. She had no pleasure in her life and no comfort, and she wasted away because of the fear that was on her, caused by the following singular circumstance:—

Every time that she happened to leave home alone, and that no one was within call, she was met by a woman totally unknown to her, who, fixing her eyes on her in silence, with a terrible expression, cast her to the ground and proceeded to beat and pinch her till she was nearly senseless; after which her tormentor disappeared.

Having experienced this treatment several times, the poor woman finally abstained altogether from leaving the house, unless protected by a servant or companion; and this precaution she observed for several years, during which time she never was molested. So at last she began to believe that the spell was broken, and that her strange enemy had departed for ever.

In consequence she grew less careful about the usual precaution, and one day stepped down alone to a little stream that ran by the house to wash some clothes.

Stooping down over her work, she never thought of any danger, and began to sing as she used to do in the light-hearted days before the spell was on her, when suddenly a dark shadow fell across the water, and looking up, she beheld to her horror the strange woman on the opposite side of the little stream, with her terrible eyes intently fixed on her, as hard and still as if she were of stone.

Springing up with a scream of terror, she flung down her work, and ran towards the house; but soon she heard footsteps behind her, and in an instant she was seized, thrown down to the ground, and her tormentor began to beat her even worse than before, till she lost all consciousness; and in this state she was found by her husband, lying on her face and speechless. She was at once carried to the house, and all the care that affection and rural skill could bestow were lavished on her, but in vain. She, however, regained sufficient consciousness to tell them of the terrible encounter she had gone through, but died before the night had passed away.

It was believed that the power of fascination by the glance, which is not necessarily an evil power like the Evil Eye, was possessed in a remarkable degree by learned and wise people, especially poets, so that they could make themselves loved and followed by any girl they liked, simply by the influence of the glance. About the year 1790, a young man resided in the County Limerick, who had this power in a singular and unusual degree. He was a clever, witty rhymer in the Irish language; and, probably, had the deep poet eyes that characterize warm and passionate poet-natures—eyes that even without necromancy have been known to exercise a powerful magnetic influence over female minds.

One day, while travelling far from home, he came upon a bright, pleasant-looking farmhouse, and feeling weary, he stopped and requested a drink of milk and leave to rest. The farmer's daughter, a young, handsome girl, not liking to admit a stranger, as all the maids were churning, and she was alone in the house, refused him admittance.

The young poet fixed his eyes earnestly on her face for some time in silence, then slowly turning round left the house, and walked towards a small grove of trees just opposite. There he stood for a few moments resting against a tree, and facing the house as if to take one last vengeful or admiring glance, then went his way without once turning round.

The young girl had been watching him from the windows, and the moment he moved she passed out of the door like one in a dream, and followed him slowly, step by step, down the avenue. The maids grew alarmed, and called to her father, who ran out and shouted loudly for her to stop, but she never turned or seemed to heed. The young man, however, looked round, and seeing the whole family in pursuit, quickened his pace, first glancing fixedly at the girl for a moment. Immediately she sprang towards him, and they were both almost out of sight, when one of the maids espied a piece of paper tied to a branch of the tree where the poet had rested. From curiosity she took it down, and the moment the knot was untied, the farmer's daughter suddenly stopped, became quite still, and when her father came up she allowed him to lead her back to the house without resistance.

When questioned, she said that she felt herself drawn by an invisible force to follow the young stranger wherever he might lead, and that she would have followed him through the world, for her life seemed to be bound up in his; she had no will to resist, and was conscious of nothing else but his presence. Suddenly, however, the spell was broken, and then she heard her father's voice, and knew how strangely she had acted. At the same time the power of the young man over her vanished, and the impulse to follow him was no longer in her heart.

The paper, on being opened, was found to contain five mysterious words written in blood, and in this order—

Lady Jane Francesca Agnes Wilde

Sator.

Arepo.

Tenet.

Opera.

Rotas.

These letters are so arranged that read in any way, right to left, left to right, up or down, the same words are produced; and when written in blood with a pen made of an eagle's feather, they form a charm which no woman (it is said) can resist; but the incredulous reader can easily test the truth of this assertion for himself.

*

These popular stories are provokingly incomplete, and one cannot help regretting that the romance of "The Poet and the Farmer's Daughter" was not brought to a happy termination; but the Irish tales are in general rather incoherent, more like remembered fragments of ancient stories than a complete, well-organized dramatic composition, with lights well placed, and a striking catastrophe. The opening is usually attractive, with the exciting formula, "Once upon a time," from which one always expects so much; and there is sure to be an old woman, weird and witch-like, capable of the most demoniacal actions, and a mysterious man who promises to be the unredeemed evil spirit of the tale; but in the end they both turn out childishly harmless, and their evil actions seldom go beyond stealing their neighbours' butter, or abducting a pretty girl, which sins mere mortals would be quite equal to, even without the aid of "the gods of the earth" and their renowned leader, Finvarra, the King of the Fairies. The following tale, however, of a case of abduction by fairy power, is well constructed. The hero of the narrative has our sympathy and interest, and it ends happily, which is considered a great merit by the Irish, as they dislike a tale to which they cannot append, as an epilogue, the hearty and outspoken "Thank God."

The Stolen Bride

About the year 1670 there was a fine young fellow living at a place called

Querin, in the County Clare. He was brave and strong and rich, for he had his own land and his own house, and not one to lord it over him. He was called the Kern of Querin. And many a time he would go out alone to shoot the wild fowl at night along the lonely strand and sometimes cross over northward to the broad east strand, about two miles away, to find the wild geese.

One cold frosty November Eve he was watching for them, crouched down behind the ruins of an old hut, when a loud splashing noise attracted his attention. "It is the wild geese," he thought, and raising his gun, waited in death-like silence the approach of his victim.

But presently he saw a dark mass moving along the edge of the strand. And he knew there were no wild geese near him. So he watched and waited till the black mass came closer, and then he distinctly perceived four stout men carrying a bier on their shoulders, on which lay a corpse covered with a white cloth. For a few moments they laid it down, apparently to rest themselves, and the Kern instantly fired; on which the four men ran away shrieking, and the corpse was left alone on the bier. Kern of Querin immediately sprang to the place, and lifting the cloth from the face of the corpse, beheld by the freezing starlight, the form of a beautiful young girl, apparently not dead but in a deep sleep.

Gently he passed his hand over her face and raised her up, when she opened her eyes and looked around with wild wonder, but spake never a word, though he tried to soothe and encourage her. Then, thinking it was dangerous for them to remain in that place, he raised her from the bier, and taking her hand led her away to his own house. They arrived safely, but in silence. And for twelve months did she remain with the Kern, never tasting food or speaking word for all that time.

When the next November Eve came round, he resolved to visit the east strand again, and watch from the same place, in the hope of meeting with some adventure that might throw light on the history of the beautiful girl. His way lay beside the old ruined fort called *Lios-na-fallainge* (the Fort of the Mantle), and as he passed, the sound of music and mirth fell on his ear. He stopped to catch the words of the voices, and had not waited long when he heard a man say in a low whisper—

"Where shall we go to-night to carry off a bride?"

And a second voice answered—

"Wherever we go I hope better luck will be ours than we had this day twelvemonths."

"Yes," said a third; "on that night we carried off a rich prize, the fair daughter of O'Connor; but that clown, the Kern of Querin, broke our spell and took her from us. Yet little pleasure has he had of his bride, for she has neither eaten nor drank nor uttered a word since she entered his house."

"And so she will remain," said a fourth, "until he makes her eat off her father's table-cloth, which covered her as she lay on the bier, and which is now thrown up over the top of her bed."

On hearing all this, the Kern rushed home, and without waiting even for the morning, entered the young girl's room, took down the table-cloth, spread it on the table, laid meat and drink thereon, and led her to it. "Drink," he said, "that speech may come to you." And she drank, and ate of the food, and then speech came. And she told the Kern her story—how she was to have been married to a young lord of her own country, and the wedding guests had all assembled, when she felt herself suddenly ill and swooned away, and never knew more of what had happened to her until the Kern had passed his hand over her face, by which she recovered consciousness, but could neither eat nor speak, for a spell was on her, and she was helpless.

Then the Kern prepared a chariot, and carried home the young girl to her father, who was like to die for joy when he beheld her. And the Kern grew mightily in O'Connor's favour, so that at last he gave him his fair young daughter to wife; and the wedded pair lived together happily for many long years after, and no evil befell them, but good followed all the work of their hands.

This story of Kern of Querin still lingers in the faithful, vivid Irish memory, and is often told by the peasants of Clare when they gather round the fire on the awful festival of *Samhain*, or November Eve, when the dead walk, and the spirits of earth and air have power over mortals, whether for good or evil.

Fairy Music

The evil influence of the fairy glance does not kill, but it throws the object into a death-like trance, in which the real body is carried off to some fairy mansion, while a log of wood, or some ugly, deformed creature is left in its place, clothed with the shadow of the stolen form. Young women, remarkable for beauty, young men, and handsome children, are the chief victims of the fairy stroke. The girls are wedded to fairy chiefs, and the young men to fairy queens; and if the mortal children do not turn out well, they are sent back, and others carried off in their place. It is sometimes possible, by the spells of a powerful fairy-man, to bring back a living being from Fairy-land. But they are never quite the same after. They have always a spirit-look, especially if they have listened to the fairy music. For the fairy music is soft and low and plaintive, with a fatal charm for mortal ears.

One day a gentleman entered a cabin in the County Clare, and saw a young girl about twenty seated by the fire, chanting a melancholy song, without settled words or music. On inquiry he was told she had once heard the fairy harp, and those who hear it lose all memory of love or hate, and forget all things, and never more have any other sound in their ears save the soft music of the fairy harp, and when the spell is broken, they die.

It is remarkable that the Irish national airs—plaintive, beautiful, and unutterably pathetic—should so perfectly express the spirit of the Céol-Sidhe (the fairy music), as it haunts the fancy of the people and mingles with all their traditions of the spirit world. Wild and capricious as the fairy nature, these delicate harmonies, with their mystic, mournful rhythm, seem to touch the deepest chords of feeling, or to fill the sunshine with laughter, according to the mood of the players; but, above all things, Irish music is the utterance of a Divine sorrow; not stormy or passionate, but like that of an exiled spirit, yearning and wistful, vague and unresting; ever seeking the unattainable, ever shadowed, as it were, with memories of some lost good, or some dim foreboding of a coming fate—emotions that seem to find their truest expression in the sweet, sad, lingering wail of the pathetic minor in a genuine Irish air. There is a beautiful phrase in one of the ancient manuscripts descriptive of the wonderful power of Irish music over the sensitive human organization: "Wounded men were soothed when they heard it, and slept; and women in travail forgot their pains." There are legends concerning the subtle charm of the fairy music and dance, when the mortal under their influence seems to move through the air with "the naked, fleshless feet of the spirit," and is lulled by the ecstasy of the cadence into forgetfulness of all things, and sometimes into the sleep of death.

The Fairy Dance

The following story is from the Irish, as told by a native of one of the Western Isles, where the primitive superstitions have still all the freshness of young life.

One evening late in November, which is the month when spirits have most power over all things, as the prettiest girl in all the island was going to the well for water, her foot slipped and she fell. It was an unlucky omen, and when she got up and looked round it seemed to her as if she were in a strange place, and all around her was changed as if by enchantment. But at some distance she saw a great crowd gathered round a blazing fire, and she was drawn slowly on towards them, till at last she stood in the very midst of the people; but they kept silence, looking fixedly at her; and she was afraid, and tried to turn and leave them, but she could not. Then a beautiful youth, like a prince, with a red sash, and a golden band on his long yellow hair, came up and asked her to dance.

"It is a foolish thing of you, sir, to ask me to dance," she said, "when there is no music."

Then he lifted his hand and made a sign to the people, and instantly the sweetest music sounded near her and around her, and the young man took her hand, and they danced and danced till the moon and the stars went down, but she seemed like one floating on the air, and she forgot everything in the world except the dancing, and the sweet low music, and her beautiful partner.

At last the dancing ceased, and her partner thanked her, and invited her to supper with the company. Then she saw an opening in the ground, and a flight of steps, and the young man, who seemed to be the king amongst them all, led her down, followed by the whole company. At the end of the stairs they came upon a large hall, all bright and beautiful with gold and silver and lights; and the table was covered with everything good to eat, and wine was poured out in golden cups for them to drink. When she sat down they all pressed her to eat the food and to drink the wine; and as she was weary after the dancing, she took the golden cup the prince handed to her, and raised it to her lips to drink. Just then, a man passed close to her, and whispered—

"Eat no food, and drink no wine, or you will never reach your home again."

So she laid down the cup, and refused to drink. On this they were angry, and a great noise arose, and a fierce, dark man stood up, and said—

"Whoever comes to us must drink with us."

And he seized her arm, and held the wine to her lips, so that she almost died of fright. But at that moment a red-haired man came up, and he took her by the hand and led her out.

"You are safe for this time," he said. "Take this herb, and hold it in your hand till you reach home, and no one can harm you." And he gave her a branch of a plant called the *Athair-Luss* (the ground ivy). [4]

This she took, and fled away along the sward in the dark night; but all the time she heard footsteps behind her in pursuit. At last she reached home and barred the door, and went to bed, when a great clamour arose outside, and voices were heard crying to her—

"The power we had over you is gone through the magic of the herb; but wait—when you dance again to the music on the hill, you will stay with us for evermore, and none shall hinder."

However, she kept the magic branch safely, and the fairies never troubled her more; but it was long and long before the sound of the fairy music left her ears which she had danced to that November night on the hillside with her fairy lover.

Fairy Justice: A Legend of Shark Island

The "Red-haired Man," although he is considered very unlucky in actual life, yet generally acts in the fairy world as the benevolent *Deus ex machina*, that saves and helps and rescues the unhappy mortal, who himself is quite helpless under the fairy spells.

There was a man in Shark Island who used to cross over to Boffin [5] to buy tobacco, but when the weather was too rough for the boat his ill-temper was as bad as the weather, and he used to beat his wife, and fling all the things about, so that no one could stand before him. One day a man came to him.

"What will you give me if I go over to Boffin," said he, "and bring you the tobacco?"

"I will give you nothing," said the other. "Whatever way you go I can go also."

"Then come with me to the shore," said the first man, "and I'll show you how to get across; but as only one can go, you must go alone."

And as they went down to the sea, they saw a great company of horsemen and ladies galloping along, with music and laughter.

"Spring up now on a horse and you will get across," said the first man.

So the other sprang up as he was told, and in an instant they all jumped right across the sea and landed at Boffin. Then he ran to buy the tobacco and was back again in a minute, and found all the same company by the seashore. He sprang again upon a horse and they all jumped right into the sea, but suddenly stopped midway between the two islands, where there was a great rock, and beyond this they could not force the horses to move. Then there was great disquietude amongst them, and they called a council.

"There is a mortal amongst us," they said. "Let us drown him."

And they carried the man up to the top of the rock and cast him down; and when he rose to the surface again they caught him by the hair, and cried—

"Drown him! Drown him! We have the power over life and death; he must be drowned."

And they were going to cast him down a second time, when a red-haired man pleaded for him, and carried him off with a strong hand safe to shore.

"Now," said he, "you are safe, but mind, the spirits are watching you, and if ever again you beat your poor good wife, and knock about the things at home just to torment her out of her life, you will die upon that rock as sure as fate." And he vanished.

So from that time forth the man was as meek as a mouse, for he was afraid; and whenever he went by the rock in his boat he always stopped a minute, and said a little prayer for his wife with a "God bless her." And this kept away the evil, and they both lived together happily ever after to a great old age.

This is but a rude tale. Yet the moral is good, and the threat of retributive justice shows a laudable spirit of indignation on the part of the fairy race against the tyranny of man over the weaker vessel.

The Priest's Soul

An ethical purpose is not often to be detected in the Irish legends; but the following tale combines an inner meaning with the incidents in a profound and remarkable manner. The idea that underlies the story is very subtle and tragic; Calderon or Goethe might have founded a drama on it; and Browning's genius would find a fitting subject in this contrast between the pride of the audacious, self-relying sceptic in the hour of his triumph and the moral agony that precedes his punishment and death.

In former days there were great schools in Ireland where every sort of learning was taught to the people, and even the poorest had more knowledge at that time than many a gentleman has now. But as to the priests, their learning was above all, so that the fame of Ireland went over the whole world, and many kings from foreign lands used to send their sons all the way to Ireland to be brought up in the Irish schools.

Now at this time there was a little boy learning at one of them who was a wonder to every one for his cleverness. His parents were only labouring people, and of course very poor; but young as he was, and poor as he was, no king's or lord's son could come up to him in learning. Even the masters were put to shame, for when they were trying to teach him he would tell them something they never heard of before, and show them their ignorance. One of his great triumphs was in argument; and he would go on till he proved to you that black was white, and then when you gave in, for no one could beat him in talk, he would turn round and show you that white was black, or may be that there was no colour at all in the world. When he grew up his poor father and mother were so proud of him that they resolved to make him a priest, which they did at last, though they nearly starved themselves to get the money. Well, such another learned man was not in Ireland, and he was as great in argument as ever, so that no one could stand before him. Even the Bishops tried to talk to him, but he showed them at once they knew nothing at all.

Now there were no schoolmasters in those times but it was the priests taught the people; and as this man was the cleverest in Ireland all the foreign kings sent their sons to him as long as he had house-room to give them. So he grew very proud, and began to forget how low he had been, and worst of all, even to forget God, who had made him what he was. And the pride of arguing got hold of him, so that from one thing to another he went on to prove that there was no Purgatory, and then no Hell, and then no Heaven, and then no God; and at last that men had no souls, but were no more than a dog or a cow, and when they died there was an end of them. "Who ever saw a soul?" he would say. "If you can show me one, I will believe." No one could make any answer to this; and at last they all came to believe that as there was no other world, every one might do what they liked in this; the priest setting the example, for he took a beautiful young girl to wife. But as no priest or bishop in the whole land could be got to marry them, he was obliged to read the service over for himself. It was a great scandal, yet no one dared to say a word, for all the kings' sons were on his side, and would have slaughtered any one who tried to prevent his wicked goings-on. Poor boys! they all believed in him, and thought every word he said was the truth. In this way his notions began to spread about, and the whole world was going to the bad, when one night an angel came down from Heaven, and told the priest he had but twenty-four hours to live. He began to tremble, and asked for a little more time.

But the angel was stiff, and told him that could not be.

"What do you want time for, you sinner?" he asked.

"Oh, sir, have pity on my poor soul!" urged the priest.

"Oh, ho! You have a soul, then," said the angel. "Pray, how did you find that out?"

"It has been fluttering in me ever since you appeared," answered the priest. "What a fool I was not to think of it before."

"A fool indeed," said the angel. "What good was all your learning, when it could not tell you that you had a soul?"

"Ah, my lord," said the priest, "if I am to die, tell me how soon I may be in Heaven?"

"Never," replied the angel. "You denied there was a Heaven."

"Then, my lord, may I go to Purgatory?"

"You denied Purgatory also; you must go straight to Hell," said the angel.

"But, my lord, I denied Hell also," answered the priest, "so you can't send me there either."

The angel was a little puzzled.

"Well," said he, "I'll tell you what I can do for you. You may either live now on earth for a hundred years enjoying every pleasure, and then be cast into Hell for ever; or you may die in twenty-four hours in the most horrible torments, and pass through Purgatory, there to remain till the Day of Judgment, if only you can find some one person that believes, and through his belief mercy will be vouchsafed to you and your soul will be saved."

The priest did not take five minutes to make up his mind.

"I will have death in the twenty-four hours," he said, "so that my soul may be saved at last."

On this the angel gave him directions as to what he was to do, and left him.

Then, immediately, the priest entered the large room where all his scholars and the kings' sons were seated, and called out to them—

"Now, tell me the truth, and let none fear to contradict me. Tell me what is your belief. Have men souls?"

"Master," they answered, "once we believed that men had souls; but, thanks to your teaching, we believe so no longer. There is no Hell, and no Heaven, and no God. This is our belief, for it is thus you taught us."

Then the priest grew pale with fear and cried out—"Listen! I taught you a lie. There is a God, and man has an immortal soul. I believe now all I denied before."

But the shouts of laughter that rose up drowned the priest's voice, for they thought he was only trying them for argument.

"Prove it, master," they cried, "prove it. Who has ever seen God? Who has ever seen the soul?"

And the room was stirred with their laughter.

The priest stood up to answer them, but no word could he utter; all his eloquence, all his powers of argument had gone from him, and he could do nothing but wring his hands and cry out—

"There is a God! there is a God! Lord have mercy on my soul!"

And they all began to mock him, and repeat his own words that he had taught them—

"Show him to us; show us your God."

And he fled from them groaning with agony, for he saw that none believed, and how then could his soul be saved?

But he thought next of his wife.

"She will believe," he said to himself. "Women never give up God."

And he went to her; but she told him that she believed only what he taught her, and that a good wife should believe in her husband first, and before and above all things in heaven or earth.

Then despair came on him, and he rushed from the house and began to ask every one he met if they believed. But the same answer came from one and all—"We believe only what you have taught us," for his doctrines had spread far and wide through the county.

Then he grew half mad with fear, for the hours were passing. And he flung himself down on the ground in a lonesome spot, and wept and groaned in terror, for the time was coming fast when he must die.

Just then a little child came by.

"God save you kindly," said the child to him.

The priest started up.

"Child, do you believe in God?" he asked.

"I have come from a far country to learn about Him," said the child. "Will your honour direct me to the best school that they have in these parts?"

"The best school and the best teacher is close by," said the priest, and he named himself.

"Oh, not to that man," answered the child, "for I am told he denies God, and Heaven, and Hell, and even that man has a soul, because we can't see it; but I would soon put him down."

The priest looked at him earnestly. "How?" he inquired.

"Why," said the child, "I would ask him if he believed he had life to show me his life."

"But he could not do that, my child," said the priest. "Life cannot be seen; we have it, but it is invisible."

"Then if we have life, though we cannot see it, we may also have a soul, though it is invisible," answered the child.

When the priest heard him speak these words he fell down on his knees before him, weeping for joy, for now he knew his soul was safe; he had met at last one that believed. And he told the child his whole story: all his wickedness, and pride, and blasphemy against the great God; and how the angel had come to him and told him of the only way in which he could be saved, through the faith and prayers of some one that believed.

"Now then," he said to the child, "take this penknife and strike it into my breast, and go on stabbing the flesh until you see the paleness of death on my face. Then watch—for a living thing will soar up from my body as I die, and you will then know that my soul has ascended to the presence of God. And when you see this thing, make haste and run to my school and call on all my scholars to come and see that the soul of their master has left the body, and that all he taught them was a lie, for that there is a God who punishes sin, and a Heaven and a Hell, and that man has an immortal soul, destined for eternal happiness or misery."

"I will pray," said the child, "to have courage to do this work."

And he kneeled down and prayed. Then when he rose up he took the penknife and struck it into the priest's heart, and struck and struck again till all the flesh was lacerated; but still the priest lived though the agony was horrible, for he could not die until the twenty-four hours had expired. At last the agony seemed to cease, and the stillness of death settled on his face. Then the child, who was watching, saw a beautiful living creature, with four snow white wings, mount from the dead man's body into the air and go fluttering round his head.

So he ran to bring the scholars; and when they saw it they all knew it was the soul of their master, and they watched with wonder and awe until it passed from sight into the clouds.

And this was the first butterfly that was ever seen in Ireland; and now all men know that the butterflies are the souls of the dead waiting for the moment when they may enter Purgatory, and so pass through torture to purification and peace.

But the schools of Ireland were quite deserted after that time, for people said, What is the use of going so far to learn when the wisest man in all

Ireland did not know if he had a soul till he was near losing it; and was only saved at last through the simple belief of a little child?

*

The allusion in this clever tale to the ancient Irish schools is based on historical fact. From the seventh to the tenth century Ireland was the centre of learning. The great Alfred of England was a student at one of the famous Irish seminaries, along with other royal and noble youths, and there formed a life-long friendship with the learned Adamnanl who often afterwards was a welcome guest at the Court of King Alfred. Other eminent Irishmen are known to history as the teachers and evangelizers of Europe. Alcuin, the Irish monk, became the friend and secretary of Charlemagne, and founded, at Aix-la-Chapelle, the first Grammar School in the imperial dominions. And the celebrated Clemens and Albinus, two Irishmen of distinguished ability and learning, aided the emperor not only in educating the people, but also to found a school for the nobles within his own palace.

The Fairy Race

The *Sidhe*, or spirit race, called also the *Feadh-Ree* or fairies, are supposed to have been once angels in heaven, who were cast out by Divine command as a punishment for their inordinate pride.

Some fell to earth, and dwelt there, long before man was created, as the first gods of the earth. Others fell into the sea, and they built themselves beautiful fairy palaces of crystal and pearl underneath the waves; but on moonlight nights they often come up on the land, riding their white horses, and they hold revels with their fairy kindred of the earth, who live in the clefts of the hills, and they dance together on the greensward under the ancient trees, and drink nectar from the cups of the flowers, which is the fairy wine.

Other fairies, however, are demoniacal, and given to evil and malicious deeds; for when cast out of heaven they fell into hell, and there the devil holds them under his rule, and sends them forth as he wills upon missions of evil to tempt the souls of men downward by the false glitter of sin and pleasure. These spirits dwell under the earth and impart their knowledge only to certain evil persons chosen of the devil, who gives them power to make incantations, and brew love potions, and to work wicked spells, and they can assume different forms by their knowledge and use of certain magical herbs.

The witch women who have been taught by them, and have thus become tools of the Evil One, are the terror of the neighbourhood; for they have all the power of the fairies and all the malice of the devil, who reveals to them secrets of times and days, and secrets of herbs, and secrets of evil spells; and by the power of magic they can effect all their purposes, whether for good or ill.

The fairies of the earth are small and beautiful. They passionately love music and dancing, and live luxuriously in their palaces under the hills and in the deep mountain caves; and they can obtain all things lovely for their fairy homes, merely by the strength of their magic power. They can also assume all forms, and will never know death until the last day comes, when their doom is to vanish away—to be annihilated for ever. But they are very jealous of the human race who are so tall and strong, and to whom has been promised immortality. And they are often tempted by the beauty of a mortal woman and greatly desire to have her as a wife.

The children of such marriages have a strange mystic nature, and generally become famous in music and song. But they are passionate, revengeful, and not easy to live with. Every one knows them to be of the Sidhe or spirit race, by their beautiful eyes and their bold, reckless temperament.

The fairy king and princes dress in green, with red caps bound on the head with a golden fillet. The fairy queen and the great court ladies are robed in glittering silver gauze, spangled with diamonds, and their long golden hair sweeps the ground as they dance on the greensward.

Their favourite camp and resting-place is under a hawthorn tree, and a peasant would die sooner than cut down one of the ancient hawthorns sacred to the fairies, and which generally stands in the centre of a fairy ring. But the people never offer worship to these fairy beings, for they look on the Sidhe as a race quite inferior to man. At the same time they have an immense dread and fear of the mystic fairy power, and never interfere with them nor offend them knowingly.

The Sidhe often strive to carry off the handsome children, who are then reared in the beautiful fairy palaces under the earth, and wedded to fairy mates when they grow up.

The people dread the idea of a fairy changeling being left in the cradle in place of their own lovely child; and if a wizened little thing is found there, it is sometimes taken out at night and laid in an open grave till morning, when they hope to find their own child restored, although more often nothing is found save the cold corpse of the poor outcast.

Sometimes it is said the fairies carry off the mortal child for a sacrifice, as they have to offer one every seven years to the devil in return for the power he gives them. And beautiful young girls are carried off, also, either for sacrifice or to be wedded to the fairy king.

The fairies are pure and cleanly in their habits, and they like above all things a pail of water to be set for them at night, in case they may wish to bathe.

They also delight in good wines, and are careful to repay the donor in blessings, for they are truly upright and honest. The great lords of Ireland, in ancient times, used to leave a keg of the finest Spanish wine frequently at night out on the window-sill for the fairies, and in the morning it was all gone.

Fire is a great preventative against fairy magic, for fire is the most sacred of all created things, and man alone has power over it. No animal has ever yet attained the knowledge of how to draw out the spirit of fire from the stone or the wood, where it has found a dwelling-place. If a ring of fire is made round cattle or a child's cradle, or if fire is placed under the churn, the fairies have no power to harm. And the spirit of the fire is certain to destroy all fairy magic, if it exist.

Lady Jane Francesca Agnes Wilde

The Trial by Fire

The ordeal by fire is the great test adopted by the peasants to try if a child or any one is fairy-struck. There was a man in Mayo who was bedridden for months and months, and though he ate up all the food they brought him, he never grew a bit stronger, and on Sundays when they went to mass, they locked him up and left him alone in the place with plenty of food. Now there was a fine field close by, and one Sunday, coming home from mass earlier than usual, they saw a great company of people bowling in the field, and the sick man amongst them, but at that moment he vanished away; and when the family reached home, there was the sick man lying fast asleep in his bed.

"Get up," they said, "for we have seen you bowling with the fairies, and you sha'n't eat or drink any more at our expense."

But he refused, and said he was too ill to move. Then they made down a large fire of turf and said, "Get up, or we'll lay you on the fire and break the fairy spell." And they took hold of him to burn him. Then he was frightened, and rose up and went out at the door, and they watched him till he stopped in the field where the hurlers played, and lay down there in the grass; but when they went up to him he was dead.

A man going to his work one morning early saw two women going up to a house, and one said, "There is a beautiful boy in this house, go in and hand it out to me, and we'll leave the dead child in its place." And the other went in at the window as she was told, and handed out a sleeping child, and took the dead child and laid it in the bed within. Now the man saw it was fairy work, and he went over and made the sign of the cross on the sleeping child, whereupon the two women shrieked as if they had been struck, and fled away, dropping the child on the grass. Then the man took it up gently, and put it under his coat, and went away to his wife.

"Here," he said, "take care of this child till I come back, and burn a turf beside the cradle to keep off the fairies."

When he passed by the house again, where he had seen the two women, he heard a great crying and lamentation; and he entered in and asked what ailed them.

"See here," said the mother, "my child is dead in its cradle. It died in the night, and no one near." And she wept bitterly.

"Be comforted," said the man; "this is a fairy changeling, your child is safe!" and he told her the story. "Now," he said, "if you don't believe me, just lay this dead child on the fire, and we'll see what will happen."

So she made down a good fire, and took the dead child in her arms, and laid it on the hot turf, saying, "Burn, burn, burn—if of the devil, burn; but if of God and the Saints, be safe from harm." And the child no sooner felt the fire than it sprang up the chimney with a cry and disappeared.

The Lady Witch

About a hundred years ago there lived a woman in Joyce County, of whom all the neighbours were afraid, for she had always plenty of money, though no one knew how she came by it; and the best of eating and drinking went on at her house, chiefly at night—meat and fowls and Spanish wines in plenty for all comers. And when people asked how it all came, she laughed and said, "I have paid for it," but would tell them no more.

So the word went through the county that she had sold herself to the Evil One, and could have everything she wanted by merely wishing and willing, and because of her riches they called her "The Lady Witch."

She never went out but at night, and then always with a bridle and whip in her hand; and the sound of a horse galloping was heard often far on in the night along the roads near her house.

Then a strange story was whispered about, that if a young man drank of her

Spanish wines at supper and afterwards fell asleep, she would throw the bridle over him and change him to a horse, and ride him all over the country, and whatever she touched with her whip became hers. Fowls, or butter, or wine, or the new-made cakes—she had but to wish and will and they were carried by spirit hands to her house, and laid in her larder. Then when the ride was done, and she had gathered enough through the country of all she wanted, she took the bridle off the young man, and he came back to his own shape and fell asleep; and when he awoke he had no knowledge of all that had happened, and the Lady Witch bade him come again and drink of her Spanish wines as often as it pleased him.

Now there was a fine brave young fellow in the neighbourhood, and he determined to make out the truth of the story. So he often went back and forwards, and made friends with the Lady Witch, and sat down to talk to her, but always on the watch. And she took a great fancy to him and told him he must come to supper some night, and she would give him the best of everything, and he must taste her Spanish wine.

So she named the night, and he went gladly, for he was filled with curiosity. And when he arrived there was a beautiful supper laid, and plenty of wine to drink; and he ate and drank, but was cautious about the wine, and spilled it on the ground from his glass when her head was turned away. Then he pretended to be very sleepy, and she said—

"My son, you are weary. Lie down there on the bench and sleep, for the night is far spent, and you are far from your home."

So he lay down as if he were quite dead with sleep, and closed his eyes, but watched her all the time.

And she came over in a little while and looked at him steadily, but he never stirred, only breathed the more heavily.

Then she went softly and took the bridle from the wall, and stole over to fling it over his head; but he started up, and, seizing the bridle, threw it over the woman, who was immediately changed into a spanking grey mare. And he led her out and jumped on her back and rode away as fast as the wind till he came to the forge.

65

"Ho, smith," he cried, "rise up and shoe my mare, for she is weary after the journey."

And the smith got up and did his work as he was bid, well and strong. Then the young man mounted again, and rode back like the wind to the house of the Witch; and there he took off the bridle, and she immediately regained her own form, and sank down in a deep sleep.

But as the shoes had been put on at the forge without saying the proper form of words, they remained on her hands and feet, and no power on earth could remove them.

So she never rose from her bed again, and died not long after of grief and shame. And not one in the whole country would follow the coffin of the Lady Witch to the grave; and the bridle was burned with fire, and of all her riches nothing was left but a handful of ashes, and this was flung to the four points of earth and the four winds of heaven; so the enchantment was broken and the power of the Evil One ended.

Ethna the Bride

The fairies, as we know, are greatly attracted by the beauty of mortal women, and Finvarra the king employs his numerous sprites to find out and carry off when possible the prettiest girls and brides in the country. These are spirited away by enchantment to his fairy palace at Knockma in Tuam, where they remain under a fairy spell, forgetting all about the earthly life and soothed to passive enjoyment, as in a sweet dream, by the soft low melody of the fairy music, which has the power to lull the hearer into a trance of ecstasy.

There was once a great lord in that part of the country who had a beautiful wife called Ethna, the loveliest bride in all the land. And her husband was so proud of her that day after day he had festivals in her honour; and from morning till night his castle was filled with lords and ladies, and nothing but music and dancing and feasting and hunting and pleasure was thought of.

One evening while the feast was merriest, and Ethna floated through the dance in her robe of silver gossamer clasped with jewels, more bright and beautiful than the stars in heaven, she suddenly let go the hand of her partner and sank to the floor in a faint.

They carried her to her room, where she lay long quite insensible; but towards the morning she woke up and declared that she had passed the night in a beautiful palace, and was so happy that she longed to sleep again and go there in her dreams. And they watched by her all day, but when the shades of evening fell dark on the castle, low music was heard at her window, and Ethna again fell into a deep trance from which nothing could rouse her.

Then her old nurse was set to watch her; but the woman grew weary in the silence and fell asleep, and never awoke till the sun had risen. And when she looked towards the bed, she saw to her horror that the young bride had disappeared. The whole household was roused up at once, and search made everywhere, but no trace of her could be found in all the castle, nor in the gardens, nor in the park. Her husband sent messengers in every direction, but to no purpose—no one had seen her; no sign of her could be found, living or dead.

Then the young lord mounted his swiftest steed and galloped right off to Knockma, to question Finvarra, the fairy king, if he could give any tidings of the bride, or direct him where to search for her; for he and Finvarra were friends, and many a good keg of Spanish wine had been left outside the window of the castle at night for the fairies to carry away, by order of the young lord. But he little dreamed now that Finvarra himself was the traitor; so he galloped on like mad till he reached Knockma, the hill of the fairies.

And as he stopped to rest his horse by the fairy rath, he heard voices in the air above him, and one said—

"Right glad is Finvarra now, for he has the beautiful bride in his palace at last; and never more will she see her husband's face."

"Yet," answered another, "if he dig down through the hill to the centre of the earth, he would find his bride; but the work is hard and the way is difficult, and Finvarra has more power than any mortal man."

"That is yet to be seen," exclaimed the young lord. "Neither fairy, nor devil, nor Finvarra himself shall stand between me and my fair young wife;" and on the instant he sent word by his servants to gather together all the workmen and labourers of the country round with their spades and pickaxes, to dig through the hill till they came to the fairy palace.

And the workmen came, a great crowd of them, and they dug through the hill all that day till a great deep trench was made down to the very centre. Then at sunset they left off for the night; but next morning when they assembled again to continue their work, behold, all the clay was put back again into the trench, and the hill looked as if never a spade had touched it—for so Finvarra had ordered; and he was powerful over earth and air and sea.

But the young lord had a brave heart, and he made the men go on with the work; and the trench was dug again, wide and deep into the centre of the hill. And this went on for three days, but always with the same result, for the clay was put back again each night and the hill looked the same as before, and they were no nearer to the fairy palace.

Then the young lord was ready to die for rage and grief, but suddenly he heard a voice near him like a whisper in the air, and the words it said were these—

"Sprinkle the earth you have dug up with salt, and your work will be safe."

On this new life came into his heart, and he sent word through all the country to gather salt from the people; and the clay was sprinkled with it that night, when the men had left off their work at the hill.

Next morning they all rose up early in great anxiety to see what had happened, and there to their great joy was the trench all safe, just as they had left it, and all the earth round it was untouched.

Then the young lord knew he had power over Finvarra, and he bade the men work on with a good heart, for they would soon reach the fairy palace now in the centre of the hill. So by the next day a great glen was cut right through deep down to the middle of the earth, and they could hear the fairy music if they put their ear close to the ground, and voices were heard round them in the air.

"See now," said one, "Finvarra is sad, for if one of those mortal men strike a blow on the fairy palace with their spades, it will crumble to dust, and fade away like the mist."

"Then let Finvarra give up the bride," said another, "and we shall be safe."

On which the voice of Finvarra himself was heard, clear like the note of a silver bugle through the hill.

"Stop your work," he said. "Oh, men of earth, lay down your spades, and at sunset the bride shall be given back to her husband. I, Finvarra, have spoken."

Then the young lord bade them stop the work, and lay down their spades till the sun went down. And at sunset he mounted his great chestnut steed and rode to the head of the glen, and watched and waited; and just as the red light flushed all the sky, he saw his wife coming along the path in her robe of silver gossamer, more beautiful than ever; and he sprang from the saddle and lifted her up before him, and rode away like the storm wind back to the castle. And there they laid Ethna on her bed; but she closed her eyes and spake no word. So day after day passed, and still she never spake or smiled, but seemed like one in a trance.

And great sorrow fell upon every one, for they feared she had eaten of the fairy food, and that the enchantment would never be broken. So her husband was very miserable. But one evening as he was riding home late, he heard voices in the air, and one of them said—

"It is now a year and a day since the young lord brought home his beautiful wife from Finvarra; but what good is she to him? She is speechless and like one dead; for her spirit is with the fairies though her form is there beside him."

Then another voice answered—

"And so she will remain unless the spell is broken. He must unloose the girdle from her waist that is fastened with an enchanted pin, and burn the girdle with fire, and throw the ashes before the door, and bury the enchanted pin in the earth; then will her spirit come back from Fairy-land, and she will once more speak and have true life."

Hearing this the young lord at once set spurs to his horse, and on reaching the castle hastened to the room where Ethna lay on her couch silent and beautiful like a waxen figure. Then, being determined to test the truth of the spirit voices, he untied the girdle, and after much difficulty extracted the enchanted pin from the folds. But still Ethna spoke no word; then he took the girdle and burned it with fire, and strewed the ashes before the door, and he buried the enchanted pin in a deep hole in the earth, under a fairy thorn, that no hand might disturb the spot. After which he returned to his young wife, who smiled as she looked at him, and held forth her hand. Great was his joy to see the soul coming back to the beautiful form, and he raised her up and kissed her; and speech and memory came back to her at that moment, and all her former life, just as if it had never been broken or interrupted; but the year that her spirit had passed in Fairy-land seemed to her but as a dream of the night, from which she had just awoke.

After this Finvarra made no further efforts to carry her off; but the deep cut in the hill remains to this day, and is called "The Fairy's Glen." So no one can doubt the truth of the story as here narrated.

The Fairies' Revenge

The fairies have a great objection to the fairy raths, where they meet at night, being built upon by mortal man. A farmer called Johnstone, having plenty of money, bought some land, and chose a beautiful green spot to build a house on, the very spot the fairies loved best.

The neighbours warned him that it was a fairy rath; but he laughed and never minded (for he was from the north), and looked at such things as mere old-wives' tales. So he built the house and made it beautiful to live in; and no people in the country were so well off as the Johnstones, so that the people said the farmer must have found a pot of gold in the fairy rath.

But the fairies were all the time plotting how they could punish the farmer for taking away their dancing ground, and for cutting down the hawthorn bush where they held their revels when the moon was full. And one day when the cows were milking, a little old woman in a blue cloak came to Mrs. Johnstone and asked her for a porringer of milk.

"Go away," said the mistress of the house, "you shall have no milk from me. I'll have no tramps coming about my place." And she told the farm servants to chase her away.

Some time after, the best and finest of the cows sickened and gave no milk, and lost her horns and teeth and finally died.

Then one day as Mrs. Johnstone was sitting spinning flax in the parlour, the same little woman in the blue cloak suddenly stood before her.

"Your maids are baking cakes in the kitchen," she said; "give me some off the griddle to carry away with me."

"Go out of this," cried the farmer's wife, angrily; "you are a wicked old wretch, and have poisoned my best cow." And she bade the farm servants drive her off with sticks.

Now the Johnstones had one only child; a beautiful bright boy, as strong as a young colt, and as full of life and merriment. But soon after this he began to grow queer and strange, and was disturbed in his sleep; for he said the fairies came round him at night and pinched and beat him, and some sat on his chest and he could neither breathe nor move. And they told him they would never leave him in peace unless he promised to give them a supper every night of a griddle cake and a porringer of milk. So to soothe the child the mother had these things laid every night on a table beside his bed, and in the morning they were gone.

But still the child pined away, and his eyes got a strange, wild look, as if he saw nothing near or around him, only something far, far away that troubled his spirit. And when they asked him what ailed him, he said the fairies carried him away to the hills every night, where he danced and danced with them till the morning, when they brought him back and laid him again in his bed.

At last the farmer and his wife were at their wits' end from grief and despair, for the child was pining away before their eyes, and they could do nothing for him to help him. One night he cried out in great agony—

"Mother! mother! send for the priest to take away the fairies, for they are killing me; they are here on my chest, crushing me to death," and his eyes were wild with terror.

Now the farmer and his wife believed in no fairies, and in no priest, but to soothe the child they did as he asked and sent for the priest, who prayed over him and sprinkled him with holy water.

The poor little fellow seemed calmer as the priest prayed, and he said the fairies were leaving him and going away, and then he sank into a quiet sleep. But when he woke in the morning he told his parents that he had a beautiful dream and was walking in a lovely garden with the angels; and he knew it was heaven, and that he would be there before night, for the angels told him they would come for him.

Then they watched by the sick child all through the night, for they saw the fever was still on him, but hoped a change would come before morning; for he now slept quite calmly with a smile on his lips.

But just as the clock struck midnight he awoke and sat up, and when his mother put her arms round him weeping, he whispered to her—"The angels are here, mother," and then he sank back, and so died.

Now after this calamity the farmer never held up his head. He ceased to mind his farm, and the crops went to ruin and the cattle died, and finally before a year and a day were over he was laid in the grave by the side of his little son; and the land passed into other hands, and as no one would live in the house it was pulled down. No one, either, would plant on the rath; so the grass grew again all over it, green and beautiful, and the fairies danced there once more in the moonlight as they used to do in the old time, free and happy; and thus the evil spell was broken for evermore.

But the people would have nothing to do with the childless mother, so she went away back to her own people, a broken-hearted, miserable woman—a warning to all who would arouse the vengeance of the fairies by interfering with their ancient rights and possessions and privileges.

Fairy Help: The Phouka

The Phouka is a friendly being, and often helps the farmer at his work if he is treated well and kindly. One day a farmer's son was minding cattle in the field when something rushed past him like the wind; but he was not frightened, for he knew it was the Phouka on his way to the old mill by the moat where the fairies met every night. So he called out, "Phouka, Phouka! show me what you are like, and I'll give you my big coat to keep you warm." Then a young bull came to him lashing his tail like mad; but Phadrig threw the coat over him, and in a moment he was quiet as a lamb, and told the boy to come to the mill that night when the moon was up, and he would have good luck.

So Phadrig went, but saw nothing except sacks of corn all lying about on the ground, for the men had fallen asleep, and no work was done. Then he lay down also and slept, for he was very tired: and when he woke up early in the morning there was all the meal ground, though certainly the men had not done it, for they still slept. And this happened for three nights, after which Phadrig determined to keep awake and watch.

Now there was an old chest in the mill, and he crept into this to hide, and just looked through the keyhole to see what would happen. And exactly at midnight six little fellows came in, each carrying a sack of corn upon his back; and after them came an old man in tattered rags of clothes, and he bade them turn the mill, and they turned and turned till all was ground.

Then Phadrig ran to tell his father, and the miller determined to watch the next night with his son, and both together saw the same thing happen.

"Now," said the farmer, "I see it is the Phouka's work, and let him work if it pleases him, for the men are idle and lazy and only sleep. So I'll pack the whole set off to-morrow, and leave the grinding of the corn to this excellent old Phouka."

After this the farmer grew so rich that there was no end to his money, for he had no men to pay, and all his corn was ground without his spending a penny. Of course the people wondered much over his riches, but he never told them about the Phouka, or their curiosity would have spoiled the luck.

Now Phadrig went often to the mill and hid in the chest that he might watch the fairies at work; but he had great pity for the poor old Phouka in his tattered clothes, who yet directed everything and had hard work of it sometimes keeping the little Phoukas in order. So Phadrig, out of love and gratitude, bought a fine suit of cloth and silk and laid it one night on the floor of the mill just where the old Phouka always stood to give his orders to the little men, and then he crept into the chest to watch.

"How is this?" said the Phouka when he saw the clothes. "Are these for me? I shall be turned into a fine gentleman."

And he put them on, and then began to walk up and down admiring himself. But suddenly he remembered the corn and went to grind as usual, then stopped and cried out—

"No, no. No more work for me. Fine gentlemen don't grind corn. I'll go out and see a little of the world and show my fine clothes." And he kicked away the old rags into a corner, and went out.

No corn was ground that night, nor the next, nor the next; all the little Phoukas ran away, and not a sound was heard in the mill. Then Phadrig grew very sorry for the loss of his old friend, and used to go out into the fields and call out, "Phouka, Phouka! come back to me. Let me see your face." But the old Phouka never came back, and all his life long Phadrig never looked on the face of his friend again. However, the farmer had made so much money that he wanted no more help; and he sold the mill, and reared up Phadrig to be a great scholar and a gentleman, who had his own house and land and servants. And in time he married a beautiful lady, so beautiful that the people said she must be daughter to the king of the fairies.

A strange thing happened at the wedding, for when they all stood up to drink the bride's health, Phadrig saw beside him a golden cup filled with wine. And no one knew how the golden cup had come to his hand; but Phadrig guessed it was the Phouka's gift, and he drank the wine without fear and made his bride drink also. And ever after their lives were happy and prosperous, and the golden cup was kept as a treasure in the family, and the descendants of Phadrig have it in their possession to this day.

The Farmer Punished
The fairies, with their free, joyous temperament and love of beauty and

luxury, hold in great contempt the minor virtues of thrift and economy, and, above all things, abhor the close, hard, niggardly nature that spends grudgingly and never gives freely. Indeed, they seem to hold it as their peculiar mission to punish such people, and make them suffer for the sins of the hard heart and niggard hand, as may be seen by the following tale:—

A farmer once lived near the Boyne, close to an old churchyard. He was very rich, and had crops and cattle, but was so hard and avaricious that the people hated him; for his habit was to get up very early in the morning and go out to the fields to watch that no one took a cabbage or a turnip, or got a cup of milk when the cows were being milked, for the love of God and the saints.

One morning, as he was out as usual by sunrise spying about the place, he heard a child crying bitterly—

"Oh, mother, mother! I am hungry. Give me something, or I'll die."

"Hush, darling," said the mother, "though the hunger is on you, wait; for the farmer's cow will be milked presently, and I'll knock down the pail so the milk will be spilt upon the ground, and you can drink your fill." [6]

When the farmer heard this he sent a stout man to watch the girl that milked, and to tie the cow's feet that she should not kick. So that time no milk was spilled upon the ground.

Next morning he went out again by sunrise, and he heard the child crying more bitterly even than before—

"Mother, mother! I am hungry. Give me to eat."

"Wait, my child," said the mother; "the farmer's maid bakes cakes to-day, and I'll make the dish to fall just as she is carrying them from the griddle. So we shall have plenty to eat this time."

Then the farmer went home and locked up the meal, and said—

"No cakes shall be baked to-day, not till the night."

But the cry of the child was in his ears, and he could not rest. So early in the morning he was out again, and bitter was the cry of the child as he passed the copse—

"Mother, mother!" it said, "I have had no milk, I have had no cake; let me lay down my head on your breast and die."

"Wait," said the mother, "some one will die before you, my darling. Let the old man look to his son, for he will be killed in battle before many days are over; and then the curse will be lifted from the poor, and we shall have food in plenty."

But the farmer laughed. "There is no war in Ireland now," he said to himself. "How then can my son be killed in battle?" And he went home to his own house, and there in the courtyard was his son cleaning his spear and sharpening his arrows. He was a comely youth, tall and slender as a young oak-tree, and his brown hair fell in long curls over his shoulders.

"Father," he said, "I am summoned by the king, for he is at war with the other kings. So give me the swiftest horse you have, for I must be off to-night to join the king's men. And see, I have my spears and arrows ready."

Now at that time in Ireland there were four great kings, and each of them had two deputies. And the king of Leinster made a great feast for the deputies, and to seven of them he gave a brooch of gold each, but to the eighth only a brooch of silver, for, he said, the man is not a prince like the others. Then the eighth deputy was angry, and he struck the king's page full in the face for handing him the brooch. On this all the knights sprang up and drew their swords, and some took one part and some another, and there was a great fight in the hall. And afterwards the four kings quarrelled, and the king of Leinster sent out messengers to bid all his people come to help him. So the farmer's son got the message as well as the others, and he made ready at once to join the battle with a proud heart for the sake of the king and a young man's love of adventure.

Then the farmer was filled with rage.

"This is the wicked work of the witch woman," he said; "but as I would not give her the milk to spill, nor the cakes when baked, so I will not give her the life of my only son."

And he took large stones and built up great walls the height of a man, round a hut, and set a great stone at the top to close it, only leaving places for a vessel of food to be handed down. And he placed the lad within the hut.

"Now," he said, "the king shall not have him, nor the king's men; he is safe from the battle and the spears of the warriors."

So the next morning he rose up quite content, and was out at sunrise as usual; and as he walked by the churchyard, he heard the child laughing. And the mother said—

"Child, you laugh by a grave. For the farmer's son will be laid in that ground before three days are over, and then the curse will be lifted from the poor. He would not let the milk be spilled, nor the cakes to be baked, but he cannot keep his son from death. The spell is on him for evil."

Then a voice said—

"But his father has walled him round in a hut with strong walls, high as a man. How then can he die in battle?"

And the woman answered—

"I climbed the hut last night and gave him nine stones, and bade him throw them one by one over his left shoulder, and each time a stone of the wall would fall down, till free space was left him to escape, and this he did; and before sunrise this morning he fled away, and has joined the king's army; but his grave is ready, and in three days he will be in this ground, for his doom is spoken."

When the farmer heard these words, he rushed like mad to the hut, and called his son by name; but no answer came. Then he climbed up and looked in through the hole at the top, but no sign of his son was there. And he wrung his hands in despair, and went home and spake no word, but sat moaning with his head buried in his hands.

And on the third day he heard the steps of men outside, and he rose up, for he knew they were bearing the body of his dead son to the door. And he went out to meet them, and there lay the corpse of the young man on the bier, pale and beautiful, struck through and through by a spear, even as he had died in battle.

And they laid him in the churchyard, just as the witch-woman had foretold, while all the people wept, for the young man was noble to look upon, and of a good and upright spirit.

But the father neither spoke nor wept. His mind was gone, and his heart was broken. And soon he lay down and died, unpitied by all; for he was hard and cruel in his life, and no man wept for him; and all the riches he had gathered by grinding down the poor melted away, and his race perished from the land, and his name was heard of no more, and no blessing rested on his memory.

The Farmer's Wife

Down in the South there lived another rich farmer and his wife, who were both of them hated by the people for their stingy, hard-hearted ways. Never a word of kindness was on their lips, and never a blessing from the poor was invoked on their heads.

One day an old woman came to the door to beg a little food—a cake from the griddle, or a few potatoes, or a handful of meal; but she was harshly refused by the farmer's wife and turned away.

Then she came back in a little while, and begged for a drink of milk, for she was faint and weary, she said, and had travelled far. This was also refused, and she was ordered to leave the place at once. But the woman still begged hard for leave to rest herself a little, and for even a drink of butter milk, for it was churning day and she knew there must be plenty in the house. Then the farmer's wife grew very angry, and said she would turn the dogs on her if she didn't go away, and that no tramp should get anything from her. On this the woman muttered some words, with her hand on the lintel of the door, and then went her way. Soon after, being much heated by the violence of her anger, the farmer's wife went to the dairy for a drink; but as she poured out the draught she saw something black in the cup, and she tried to take it out with her finger, but it always escaped her. Then, being very thirsty, she drank off the milk, and still another and another cup, and in the drinking the black object disappeared. That night, however, she felt nigh to death, for her body began to swell, and turned black all over. Medical aid was sent for, but the doctor could make out nothing of the cause or nature of the strange disease. Then the priest was summoned, and he at once, having heard the story, said there was witchcraft in it; and he proceeded to pray, and to exorcise the evil spirit in the woman. Besides this he made her be placed in a hot bath, into which he poured some holy water.

At first the woman uttered fierce cries, and said her body seemed rent and torn; but gradually she became calmer, and the blackness slowly went down from head to feet, and finally disappeared, leaving the body fair and whole, all except one hand, and this remained still as black as ink. The holy water was poured on it, and the priest prayed, but nothing would remove the devil's mark.

So the priest told her at last that the blackness would remain as a sign and token of her sins against the poor; and from that day forth to her death the mark of the evil spell remained on her, but she grew kinder to the poor, for her heart was shaken by terror. And when she came to die there was no blackness on her hand, for the tears of the poor she had succoured and befriended had washed all the devil's mark away, before the moment came when her soul was to appear before God.

The Midnight Ride: A Peasant's Tale

One evening a man called Shawn Ruadh was out looking for a red cow that had strayed away, when he heard voices round him, and one said "Get me a horse," and another cried "Get me a horse."

"And get me a horse, too," said Shawn, "since they seem so plenty, for I'd like a ride along with you," and with that he found himself on the instant mounted on a fine grey horse beside another man who rode a black horse. And they rode away and away till they came to a great city.

"Now, do you know where you are?" said the black horseman. "You are in London, and whatever you want you can have."

"Thank you kindly, my friend," said the other, "so, with your leave, I'll just have a good suit of clothes, for I'm much in want of that same. Can I have them?"

"By all means," said the black horseman; "there, go into that merchant's shop and ask for what you like, and if he refuses just throw the stone I give you on the floor and the whole place will seem on fire. But don't be frightened; only wait your good luck."

So Shawn went into the biggest shop there, and he spoke to the merchant quite stiff and proud.

"Show me the best suit of clothes you have," said he. "Never mind the price, that's of no consequence, only be very particular as to the fit."

But the shopman laughed aloud.

"We don't make clothes for beggars like you," he said. "Be off out of this."

Then Shawn threw down the stone on the floor, and immediately the whole place seemed on fire, and the merchant ran out himself and all the shopmen after him to get pails of water, and Shawn laughed when he saw them all drenched.

"Now what will you give me," said he, "if I put out the fire for you?"

"You shall have the price of the best suit of clothes in the shop," answered the merchant, "all paid down in gold; only help me to put out the fire."

So Shawn stooped down and picked up the stone, and put it quietly into his pocket, and instantly all the flames disappeared: and the merchant was so grateful that he paid him down all the gold for the clothes and more. And Shawn bid him good-night, and mounted the grey steed again quite happy in himself.

"Now," said the black horseman, "is there anything else you desire? for it is near ten o'clock, and we must be back by midnight; so just say what you would like to do."

"Well," said Shawn Ruadh, "I would like of all things to see the Pope of Rome, for two of our priests are disputing as to who is to get the parish, and I want Father M'Grath to have it, for I have a great opinion of him, and if I ask his Holiness he'll settle it all in no time and for ever."

"Come then," said the black horseman; "it is a long way to Rome, certainly, but I think we'll manage it in the two hours, and be back before twelve o'clock."

So away they rode like the wind, and in no time Shawn found himself before the great palace of the Pope; and all the grand servants with gold sticks in their hands stared at him, and asked him what he wanted.

"Just go in," said he, "and tell his Holiness that Shawn Ruadh, all the way from Ireland, is here and wants to see him very particularly."

But the servants laughed, and struck him with their gold sticks and hunted him away from the gate. Now the Pope hearing the rout looked out of the window, and seeing Shawn Ruadh he came down and asked him what he wanted.

"Just this, your Holiness," answered Shawn, "I want a letter on behalf of Father M'Grath bidding the Bishop give him the parish, and I'll wait till your Holiness writes it; and meanwhile let me have a little supper, for it's hungry I am after my long ride."

Then the Pope laughed, and told the servants to drive the fellow away, for he was evidently out of his wits.

So Shawn grew angry, and flung down the stone on the floor, and instantly all the palace seemed on fire, and the Pope ordered the grand servants to go for water; and they had to run about like mad getting pails and jugs of water, whatever they could lay hands on; and all their fine clothes were spoiled, and the beautiful gold sticks were flung away in their fright, while they took the jugs and splashed and dashed the water over each other.

Now it was Shawn's turn to laugh till his sides ached, but his Holiness looked very grave.

"Well," said Shawn, "if I put out the fire what will you do for me? Will you write that letter?"

"Ay, I will," said the Pope, "and you shall have your supper also; only help us to put out the fire, my fine fellow."

So Shawn quietly put the stone back in his pocket, and instantly all the flames disappeared.

"Now," said the Pope, "you shall have supper of the best in the palace; and I'll write a letter to the Bishop ordering him to give Father M'Grath the parish. And here, besides, is a purse of gold for yourself, and take it with my blessing."

Then he ordered all the grand servants to get supper for the excellent young man from Ireland, and to make him comfortable. So Shawn was mightily pleased, and ate and drank like a prince. Then he mounted his grey steed again, and just as midnight struck he found himself at his own door, but all alone; for the grey steed and the black horseman had both vanished. But there stood his wife crying her eyes out and in great trouble.

"O Shawn, Agra! I thought you were dead or that evil had fallen on you."

"Not a bit of it," said Shawn, "I've been supping with the Pope of Rome, and look here at all the gold I've brought home for you, my darlint."

And he put his hand in his pocket to get the purse; but lo! there was nothing there except a rough, grey stone. And from that hour to this his wife believes that he dreamed the whole story as he lay under the hay-rick, on his way home from a carouse with the boys.

However, Father M'Grath got the parish, and Shawn took good care to tell him how he had spoken up boldly for him to the Pope of Rome, and made his Holiness write the letter to the Bishop about him. And Father M'Grath was a nice gentleman, and he smiled and told Shawn he thanked him kindly for his good word.

The Leprehaun [7]

The Leprehauns are merry, industrious, tricksy little sprites, who do all the shoemaker's work and the tailor's and the cobbler's for the fairy gentry, and are often seen at sunset under the hedge singing and stitching. They know all the secrets of hidden treasure, and if they take a fancy to a person will guide him to the spot in the fairy rath where the pot of gold lies buried. It is believed that a family now living near Castlerea came by their riches in a strange way, all through the good offices of a friendly Leprehaun. And the legend has been handed down through many generations as an established fact.

There was a poor boy once, one of their forefathers, who used to drive his cart of turf daily back and forward, and make what money he could by the sale; but he was a strange boy, very silent and moody, and the people said he was a fairy changeling, for he joined in no sports and scarcely ever spoke to any one, but spent the nights reading all the old bits of books he picked up in his rambles. The one thing he longed for above all others was to get rich, and to be able to give up the old weary turf cart, and live in peace and quietness all alone, with nothing but books round him, in a beautiful house and garden all by himself.

Now he had read in the old books how the Leprehauns knew all the secret places where gold lay hid, and day by day he watched for a sight of the little cobbler, and listened for the click, click of his hammer as he sat under the hedge mending the shoes.

At last, one evening just as the sun set, he saw a little fellow under a dock leaf, working away, dressed all in green, with a cocked hat on his head. So the boy jumped down from the cart and seized him by the neck.

"Now, you don't stir from this," he cried, "till you tell me where to find the hidden gold."

"Easy now," said the Leprehaun, "don't hurt me, and I will tell you all about it. But mind you, I could hurt you if I chose, for I have the power; but I won't do it, for we are cousins once removed. So as we are near relations I'll just be good, and show you the place of the secret gold that none can have or keep except those of fairy blood and race. Come along with me, then, to the old fort of Lipenshaw, for there it lies. But make haste, for when the last red glow of the sun vanishes the gold will disappear also, and you will never find it again."

"Come off, then," said the boy, and he carried the Leprehaun into the turf cart, and drove off. And in a second they were at the old fort, and went in through a door made in the stone wall.

"Now, look round," said the Leprehaun; and the boy saw the whole ground covered with gold pieces, and there were vessels of silver lying about in such plenty that all the riches of all the world seemed gathered there.

"Now take what you want," said the Leprehaun, "but hasten, for if that door shuts you will never leave this place as long as you live."

So the boy gathered up his arms full of gold and silver, and flung them into the cart; and was on his way back for more when the door shut with a clap like thunder, and all the place became dark as night. And he saw no more of the Leprehaun, and had not time even to thank him.

So he thought it best to drive home at once with his treasure, and when he arrived and was all alone by himself he counted his riches, and all the bright yellow gold pieces, enough for a king's ransom.

And he was very wise and told no one; but went off next day to Dublin and put all his treasures into the bank, and found that he was now indeed as rich as a lord.

So he ordered a fine house to be built with spacious gardens, and he had servants and carriages and books to his heart's content. And he gathered all the wise men round him to give him the learning of a gentleman; and he became a great and powerful man in the country, where his memory is still held in high honour, and his descendants are living to this day rich and prosperous; for their wealth has never decreased though they have ever given largely to the poor, and are noted above all things for the friendly heart and the liberal hand.

*

But the Leprehauns can be bitterly malicious if they are offended, and one should be very cautious in dealing with them, and always treat them with great civility, or they will take revenge and never reveal the secret of the hidden gold.

One day a young lad was out in the fields at work when he saw a little fellow, not the height of his hand, mending shoes under a dock leaf. And he went over, never taking his eyes off him for fear he would vanish away; and when he got quite close he made a grab at the creature, and lifted him up and put him in his pocket.

Then he ran away home as fast as he could, and when he had the

Leprehaun safe in the house, he tied him by an iron chain to the hob.

"Now, tell me," he said, "where am I to find a pot of gold? Let me know the place or I'll punish you."

"I know of no pot of gold," said the Leprehaun; "but let me go that I may finish mending the shoes."

"Then I'll make you tell me," said the lad.

And with that he made down a great fire, and put the little fellow on it and scorched him.

"Oh, take me off, take me off!" cried the Leprehaun, "and I'll tell you. Just there, under the dock leaf, where you found me, there is a pot of gold. Go; dig and find."

So the lad was delighted, and ran to the door; but it so happened that his mother was just then coming in with the pail of fresh milk, and in his haste he knocked the pail out of her hand, and all the milk was spilled on the floor.

Then, when the mother saw the Leprehaun, she grew very angry and beat him. "Go away, you little wretch!" she cried. "You have overlooked the milk and brought ill-luck." And she kicked him out of the house.

But the lad ran off to find the dock leaf, though he came back very sorrowful in the evening, for he had dug and dug nearly down to the middle of the earth; but no pot of gold was to be seen.

That same night the husband was coming home from his work, and as he passed the old fort he heard voices and laughter, and one said–

"They are looking for a pot of gold; but they little know that a crock of gold is lying down in the bottom of the old quarry, hid under the stones close by the garden wall. But whoever gets it must go of a dark night at twelve o'clock, and beware of bringing his wife with him."

So the man hurried home and told his wife he would go that very night, for it was black dark, and she must stay at home and watch for him, and not stir from the house till he came back. Then he went out into the dark night alone.

"Now," thought the wife, when he was gone, "if I could only get to the quarry before him I would have the pot of gold all to myself; while if he gets it I shall have nothing."

And with that she went out and ran like the wind until she reached the quarry, and than she began to creep down very quietly in the black dark. But a great stone was in her path, and she stumbled over it, and fell down and down till she reached the bottom, and there she lay groaning, for her leg was broken by the fall.

Just then her husband came to the edge of the quarry and began to descend. But when he heard the groans he was frightened.

"Cross of Christ about us!" he exclaimed; "what is that down below? Is it evil, or is it good?"

"Oh, come down, come down and help me!" cried the woman. "It's your wife is here, and my leg is broken, and I'll die if you don't help me."

"And is this my pot of gold?" exclaimed the poor man. "Only my wife with a broken leg lying at the bottom of the quarry."

And he was at his wits' end to know what to do, for the night was so dark he could not see a hand before him. So he roused up a neighbour, and between them they dragged up the poor woman and carried her home, and laid her on the bed half dead from fright, and it was many a day before she was able to get about as usual; indeed she limped all her life long, so that the people said the curse of the Leprehaun was on her.

But as to the pot of gold, from that day to this not one of the family, father or son, or any belonging to them, ever set eyes on it. However, the little Leprehaun still sits under the dock leaf of the hedge and laughs at them as he mends the shoes with his little hammer—tick tack, tick tack—but they are afraid to touch him, for now they know he can take his revenge.

Legends of the Western Islands

In the islands off the West Coast of Ireland the inhabitants are still very primitive in their habits, and cling to their old superstitions with a fanatical fervour that makes it dangerous for any one to transgress or disregard the old customs, usages, and prejudices of the islanders.

Curses heavy and deep would fall on the head of the unbelieving stranger who dared to laugh or mock at the old traditions of the ancient pagan creed, whose dogmas are still regarded with a mysterious awe and dread, and held sacred as a revelation from heaven.

The chief islands are Aran and Innismore, the latter about nine miles long. The cattle live on the fine grass of the rocks, and turf is brought from the mainland. The views are magnificent of sea and mountain, and the islands contain a greater number of pagan and early Christian monuments than could be found in the same area in any other part of Europe.

Some of the *Duns* or forts include several acres. The walls are cyclopean, about sixteen feet thick and from eighteen to twenty feet high, with steps inside leading to the top. Amongst the monuments are cromlechs, tumuli, and pillar stones, those earliest memorials set up by humanity. The Irish call these huge stones *Bothal*, or House of God, as the Hebrews called them Bethel, or God's house.

Dun Ængus, the greatest barbaric monument of the kind in existence, stands on a cliff three hundred feet above the sea. It is a hundred and forty-two feet in diameter, and has two cyclopean walls fifteen feet thick and eighteen high. The sea front measures a thousand feet, and several acres are included within the outer wall. The roof of the dun is formed of large flagstones, and the doorway slopes, after the Egyptian fashion, up to three feet in width at the top. A causeway of sharp, upright stones jammed into the ground leads to the entrance.

This fort was the great and last stronghold of the Firbolg race, and they long held it as a refuge against the *Tuatha-de-Danann* invaders, who at that time conquered and took possession of Ireland.

All the islands were originally peopled by the Firbolg race many centuries before the Christian era, and the Irish language, as still spoken by the people, is the purest and most ancient of all the dialects of Erin. Afterwards so many Christian saints took up their abode there that the largest of the islands was called *Ara-na-naomh* (Aran of the Saints), and numerous remains of churches, cells, crosses and stone-roofed oratories, with the ruins of a round tower, testify to the long habitation of the islands by these holy men.

There is an old wooden idol on one of the Achil islands called Father Molosh—probably a corruption of Moloch. In former times offerings and sacrifices were made to it, and it was esteemed as the guardian or god of the sacred fire, and held in great reverence, though but a rude semblance of a human head. Many miracles also were performed by the tooth of St. Patrick, which fell from the saint's mouth one day when he was teaching the alphabet to the new converts. And a shrine was afterwards made for the tooth that was held in the greatest honour by the kings, chiefs, and people of Ireland.

The stupendous barbaric monuments of the islands, according to Irish antiquarians, offer the best exposition of early military architecture at present known, and are only equalled by some of those in Greece. There are also many sacred wells, and the whole region is haunted by strange, wild superstitions of fairies and demons and witches; legends filled with a weird and mystic poetry that thrill the soul like a strain of music from spirit voices coming to us from the far-off elder world. The following pathetic tale is a good specimen of these ancient island legends:—

The Bride's Death-Song

On a lone island by the West Coast there dwelt an old fisherman and his daughter, and the man had power over the water spirits, and he taught his daughter the charms that bind them to obey.

One day a boat was driven on the shore, and in it was a young handsome gentleman, half dead from the cold and the wet. The old fisherman brought him home and revived him, and Eileen the daughter nursed and watched him. Naturally the two young people soon fell in love, and the gentleman told the girl he had a beautiful house on the mainland ready for her, with plenty of everything she could desire—silks to wear and gold to spend. So they were betrothed, and the wedding day was fixed. But Dermot, the lover, said he must first cross to the mainland and bring back his friends and relations to the wedding, as many as the boat would hold.

88

Eileen wept and prayed him not to leave, or at least to take her to steer the boat, for she knew there was danger coming, and she alone could have power over the evil spirits and over the waves and the winds. But she dared not tell the secret of the spell to Dermot or it would fail, and the charm be useless for ever after.

Dermot, however, only laughed at her fears, for the day was bright and clear, and he scorned all thought of danger. So he put off from the shore, and reached the mainland safely, and filled the boat with his friends to return to the island for the wedding. All went well till they were within sight of the island, when suddenly a fierce gust of wind drove the boat on a rock, and it was upset, and all who were in it perished.

Eileen heard the cry of the drowning men as she stood watching on the beach, but could give no help. And she was sore grieved for her lover, and sang a funeral wail for him in Irish, which is still preserved by the people. Then she lay down and died, and the old man, her father, disappeared. And from that day no one has ever ventured to live on the island, for it is haunted by the spirit of Eileen. And the mournful music of her wail is still heard in the nights when the winds are strong and the waves beat upon the rocks where the drowned men lay dead.

The words of the song are very plaintive and simple, and may be translated literally—

"I a virgin and a widow mourn for my lover.
Never more will he kiss me on the lips;
The cold wave is his bridal bed,
The cold wave is his wedding shroud.
O love, my love, had you brought me in the boat
My spirit and my spells would have saved from harm.
For my power was strong over waves and wind,
And the spirits of evil would have feared me.
O love, my love, I go to meet you in heaven.
I will ask God to let me see your face.
If the fair angels give me back my lover,

I will not envy the Almighty on His throne."

The Child's Dream

The island of Innis-Sark (Shark Island) was a holy and peaceful place in old times; and so quiet that the pigeons used to come and build in a great cave by the sea, and no one disturbed them. And the holy saints of God had a monastery there, to which many people resorted from the mainland, for the prayers of the monks were powerful against sickness or evil, or the malice of an enemy.

Amongst others, there came a great and noble prince out of Munster, with his wife and children and their nurse; and they were so pleased with the island that they remained a year or more; for the prince loved fishing, and often brought his wife along with him.

One day, while they were both away, the eldest child, a beautiful boy of ten years old, begged his nurse to let him go and see the pigeons' cave, but she refused.

"Your father would be angry," she cried, "if you went without leave. Wait till he comes home, and see if he will allow you."

So when the prince returned, the boy told him how he longed to see the cave, and the father promised to bring him next day.

The morning was beautiful and the wind fair when they set off. But the child soon fell asleep in the boat, and never wakened all the time his father was fishing. The sleep, however, was troubled, and many a time he started and cried aloud. So the prince thought it better to turn the boat and land, and then the boy awoke.

After dinner the father called for the child. "Tell me now," he said, "why was your sleep troubled, so that you cried out bitterly in your dream."

"I dreamed," said the boy, "that I stood upon a high rock, and at the bottom flowed the sea, but the waves made no noise; and as I looked down I saw fields and trees and beautiful flowers and bright birds in the branches, and I longed to go down and pluck the flowers. Then I heard a voice, saying, 'Blessed are the souls that come here, for this is heaven.'

90

"And in an instant I thought I was in the midst of the meadows amongst the birds and the flowers; and a lovely lady, bright as an angel, came up to me, and said, 'What brings you here, dear child; for none but the dead come here.'

"Then she left me, and I wept for her going; when suddenly all the sky grew black, and a great troop of wild wolves came round me, howling and opening their mouths wide as if to devour me. And I screamed, and tried to run, but I could not move, and the wolves came closer, and I fell down like one dead with fright, when, just then, the beautiful lady came again, and took my hand and kissed me.

"'Fear not,' she said, 'take these flowers, they come from heaven. And I will bring you to the meadow where they grow.'

"And she lifted me up into the air, but I know nothing more; for then the boat stopped and you lifted me on shore, but my beautiful flowers must have fallen from my hands, for I never saw them more. And this is all my dream; but I would like to have my flowers again, for the lady told me they had the secret that would bring me to heaven."

The prince thought no more of the child's dream, but went off to fish next day as usual, leaving the boy in the care of his nurse. And again the child begged and prayed her so earnestly to bring him to the pigeons' cave, that at last she consented; but told him he must not go a step by himself, and she would bring two of the boys of the island to take care of him.

So they set off, the child and his little sister with the nurse. And the boy gathered wild flowers for his sister, and ran down to the edge of the cave where the cormorants were swimming; but there was no danger, for the two young islanders were minding him.

So the nurse was content, and being weary she fell asleep. And the little sister lay down beside her, and fell asleep likewise.

Then the boy called to his companions, the two young islanders, and told them he must catch the cormorants. So away they ran, down the path to the sea, hand in hand, and laughing as they went. Just then a piece of rock loosened and fell beside them, and trying to avoid it they slipped over the edge of the narrow path down a steep place, where there was nothing to hold on by except a large bush, in the middle of the way. They got hold of this, and thought they were now quite safe, but the bush was not strong enough to bear their weight, and it was torn up by the roots. And all three fell straight down into the sea and were drowned.

Now, at the sound of the great cry that came up from the waves, the nurse awoke, but saw no one. Then she woke up the little sister. "It is late," she cried, "they must have gone home. We have slept too long, it is already evening; let us hasten and overtake them, before the prince is back from the fishing."

But when they reached home the prince stood in the doorway. And he was very pale, and weeping.

"Where is my brother?" cried the little girl.

"You will never see your brother more," answered the prince. And from that day he never went fishing any more, but grew silent and thoughtful, and was never seen to smile. And in a short time he and his family quitted the island, never to return.

But the nurse remained. And some say she became a saint, for she was always seen praying and weeping by the entrance to the great sea cave. And one day, when they came to look for her, she lay dead on the rocks. And in her hand she held some beautiful strange flowers freshly gathered, with the dew on them. And no one knew how the flowers came into her dead hand. Only some fishermen told the story of how the night before they had seen a bright fairy child seated on the rocks singing; and he had a red sash tied round his waist, and a golden circlet binding his long yellow hair. And they all knew that he was the prince's son, who had been drowned in that spot just a twelvemonth before. And the people believe that he had brought the flowers from the spirit-land to the woman, and given them to her as a death sign, and a blessed token from God that her soul would be taken to heaven.

Lady Jane Francesca Agnes Wilde

The Fairy Child

An ancient woman living at Innis-Sark said that in her youth she knew a young woman who had been married for five years, but had no children. And her husband was a rough, rude fellow, and used to taunt her and beat her often, because she was childless. But in the course of time it came to pass that a man-child was born to her; and he was beautiful to look on as an angel from heaven. And the father was so proud of the child that he often stayed at home to rock the cradle, and help his wife at the work.

One day, however, as he rocked the cradle, the child looked up suddenly at him, and lo! there was a great beard on its face. Then the father cried out to his wife—

"This is not a child, but a demon! You have put an evil spell on him."

And he struck her and beat her worse than ever he had done in his life before, so that she screamed aloud for help. On this the place grew quite dark, and thunder rolled over their heads, and the door flew wide open with a great crash, and in walked two strange women, with red caps on their heads and stout sticks in their hands. And they rushed at the man, and one held his arms while the other beat him till he was nearly dead.

"We are the avengers," they said; "look on us and tremble; for if you ever beat your wife again, we will come and kill you. Kneel down now, and ask her pardon."

And when the poor wretch did so, all trembling with fright, they vanished away.

"Now," said the man, when they were gone, "this house is no fit place for me. I'll leave it for ever."

So he went his way, and troubled his wife no more.

Then the child sat up in the cradle.

"Now, mother," says he, "since that man has gone, I'll tell you what you are to do. There is a holy well near this that you have never seen, but you will know it by the bunch of green rushes that grows over the mouth. Go there and stoop down and cry out aloud three times, and an old woman will come up, and whatever you want she will give it to you. Only tell no one of the well or of the woman, or evil will come of it."

So the mother promised, and went to the well, and cried out three times; and an old woman came up, and said—

"Woman, why dost thou call me?"

And the poor mother was afraid, and answered all trembling—

"The child sent me, and I pray thee to do me good, and not evil."

"Come down, then, with me into the well," said the woman, "and have no fear."

So the mother held out her hand, and the other drew her down a flight of stone steps, and then they came to a massive closed door, and the old woman unlocked it and bade her enter. But the mother was afraid, and wept.

"Enter," said the other, "and fear nothing. For this is the gate of the king's palace, and you will see the queen of the fairies herself, for it is her son you are nursing; and the king, her husband, is with her on his golden throne. And have no fear, only ask no questions, and do as they order."

Then they entered into a beautiful hall, and the floor was of marble, and the walls were of solid gold, and a great light shone over everything, so that the eyes could hardly see for the light. Then they passed on into another room, and at the end of it, on a golden throne, sat the king of the fairies. He was very handsome, and beside him sat his queen, fair and beautiful to look upon, all clad in silver.

"This, madam, is the nurse of your son, the young prince," said the old woman.

The queen smiled, and bade the nurse to sit down, and asked her how she came to know of the place.

"My son it is who told her," said the king, looking very angry.

But the queen soothed him, and turning to one of her ladies, said—
"Bring here the other child."

Then the lady brought in an infant, and placed him in the arms of the mother.

"Take him," said the queen, "he is your own child, that we carried away, for he was so beautiful; and the boy you have at home is mine, a little elfish imp. Still, I want him back, and I have sent a man to bring him here; and you may take your own lovely child home in safety, for the fairy blessings are on him for good. And the man that beat you was not your husband at all, but our messenger, that we sent to change the children. So now go back, and you will find your own true husband at home in your own place, watching and waiting for you by day and by night."

With that the door opened, and the man who had beaten her came in; and the mother trembled and was afraid. But the man laughed, and told her not to fear, but to eat what was set before her, and then to go in peace.

So they brought her to another hall, where was a table covered with golden dishes and beautiful flowers, and red wine in crystal cups.

"Eat," they said; "this feast has been prepared for you. As to us, we cannot touch it, for the food has been sprinkled with salt."

So she ate, and drank of the red wine, and never in all her life were so many things set before her that were lovely and good. And, as was right and proper, after dinner was over, she stood up, and folded her hands together to give God thanks. But they stopped her, and drew her down.

"Hush!" they said, "that name is not to be named here."

There was an angry murmur in the hall. But just then beautiful music was heard, and singing like the singing of priests, and the poor mother was so enchanted that she fell on her face as one dead. And when she came to herself it was noonday, and she was standing by the door of her own house. And her husband came out and took her by the hand, and brought her in. And there was her child, more beautiful than ever, as handsome as a young prince.

"Where have you been all this while?" asked the husband.

"It is only an hour since I went away, to look for my child, that the fairies stole from me," she answered.

"An hour!" said the husband; "you have been three years away with your child! And when you were gone, a poor sickly thing was laid in the cradle—not as big as a mushroom, and I knew well it was a fairy changeling. But it so happened that one day, a tailor came by, and stopped to rest; and when he looked hard at the child, the ugly misshapen thing sat up quite straight in the cradle, and called out—

"'Come now, what are you looking at? Give me four straws to play with.'

"And the tailor gave him the straws. And when he got them, the child played and played such sweet music on them as if they were pipes, that all the chairs and tables began to dance; and when he grew tired, he fell back in the cradle and dropped asleep.

"'Now,' said the tailor, 'that child is not right; but I'll tell you what to do. Make down a great fire to begin with.'

"So we made the fire. Then the tailor shut the door, and lifted the unlucky little wretch out of the cradle, and sat it on the fire. And no sooner had the flames caught it, than it shrieked aloud and flew up the chimney and disappeared. And when everything was burned that belonged to it, I knew you would come back to me with our own fine boy. And now let us name the name of God, and make the sign of the Cross over him, and ill luck will never again fall on our house—no more for ever."

So the man and his wife lived happily from that day forth, and the child grew up and prospered, and was beautiful to look at and happy in his life; for the fairy blessings were on him of health, wealth, and prosperity, even as the queen of the fairies had promised to the mother.

The Doom

There was a young man of Innismore, named James Lynan, noted through all the island for his beauty and strength. Never a one could beat him at hunting or wrestling, and he was, besides, the best dancer in the whole townland. But he was bold and reckless, and ever foremost in all the wild wicked doings of the young fellows of the place.

One day he happened to be in chapel after one of these mad freaks, and the priest denounced him by name from the altar.

"James Lynan," he said, "remember my words; you will come to an ill end. The vengeance of God will fall on you for your wicked life; and by the power that is in me I denounce you as an evil liver and a limb of Satan, and accursed of all good men."

The young man turned pale, and fell on his knees before all the people, crying out bitterly, "Have mercy, have mercy; I repent, I repent," and he wept like a woman.

"Go now in peace," said the priest, "and strive to lead a new life, and I'll pray to God to save your soul."

From that day forth James Lynan changed his ways. He gave up drinking, and never a drop of spirits crossed his lips. And he began to attend to his farm and his business, in place of being at all the mad revels and dances and fairs and wakes in the island. Soon after he married a nice girl, a rich farmer's daughter, from the mainland, and they had four fine children, and all things prospered with him.

But the priest's words never left his mind, and he would suddenly turn pale and a shivering would come over him when the memory of the curse came upon him. Still he prospered, and his life was a model of sobriety and order.

One day he and his wife and their children were asked to the wedding of a friend about four miles off; and James Lynan rode to the place, the family going on their own car. At the wedding he was the life of the party as he always was; but never a drop of drink touched his lips. When evening came on, the family set out for the return home just as they had set out; the wife and children on the car, James Lynan riding his own horse. But when the wife arrived at home, she found her husband's horse standing at the gate riderless and quite still. They thought he might have fallen in a faint, and went back to search; when he was found down in a hollow not five perches from his own gate, lying quite insensible and his features distorted frightfully, as if seized while looking on some horrible vision.

They carried him in, but he never spoke. A doctor was sent for, who opened a vein, but no blood came. There he lay like a log, speechless as one dead. Amongst the crowd that gathered round was an old woman accounted very wise by the people.

"Send for the fairy doctor," she said; "he is struck."

So they sent off a boy on the fastest horse for the fairy man. He could not come himself, but he filled a bottle with a potion. Then he said—

"Ride for your life; give him some of this to drink and sprinkle his face and hands also with it. But take care as you pass the lone bush on the round hill near the hollow, for the fairies are there and will hinder you if they can, and strive to break the bottle."

Then the fairy man blew into the mouth and the eyes and the nostrils of the horse, and turned him round three times on the road and rubbed the dust off his hoofs.

"Now go," he said to the boy; "go and never look behind you, no matter what you hear."

So the boy went like the wind, having placed the bottle safely in his pocket; and when he came to the lone bush the horse started and gave such a jump that the bottle nearly fell, but the boy caught it in time and held it safe and rode on. Then he heard a cluttering of feet behind him, as of men in pursuit; but he never turned or looked, for he knew it was the fairies who were after him. And shrill voices cried to him, "Ride fast, ride fast, for the spell is cast!" Still he never turned round, but rode on, and never let go his hold of the fairy draught till he stopped at his master's door, and handed the potion to the poor sorrowing wife. And she gave of it to the sick man to drink, and sprinkled his face and hands, after which he fell into a deep sleep. But when he woke up, though he knew every one around him, the power of speech was gone from him; and from that time to his death, which happened soon after, he never uttered word more.

So the doom of the priest was fulfilled—evil was his youth and evil was his fate, and sorrow and death found him at last, for the doom of the priest is as the word of God.

Lady Jane Francesca Agnes Wilde

The Clearing from Guilt

To prove innocence of a crime a certain ancient form is gone through, which the people look on with great awe, and call it emphatically—"The Clearing." It is a fearful ordeal, and instances are known of men who have died of fear and trembling from having passed through the terrors of the trial, even if innocent. And it is equally terrible for the accuser as well as the accused.

On a certain day fixed for the ordeal the accused goes to the churchyard and carries away a skull. Then, wrapped in a white sheet, and bearing the skull in his hand, he proceeds to the house of the accuser, where a great crowd has assembled; for the news of "A Clearing" spreads like wildfire, and all the people gather together as witnesses of the ceremony. There, before the house of his accuser, he kneels down on his bare knees, makes the sign of the cross on his face, kisses the skull, and prays for some time in silence; the people also wait in silence, filled with awe and dread, not knowing what the result may be. Then the accuser, pale and trembling, comes forward and stands beside the kneeling man; and with uplifted hand adjures him to speak the truth. On which the accused, still kneeling and holding the skull in his hand, utters the most fearful imprecation known in the Irish language; almost as terrible as that curse of the Druids, which is so awful that it never yet was put into English words. The accused prays that if he fail to speak the truth all the sins of the man whose skull he holds may be laid upon his soul, and all the sins of his forefathers back to Adam, and all the punishment due to them for the evil of their lives, and all their weakness and sorrow both of body and soul be laid on him both in this life and in the life to come for evermore. But if the accuser has accused falsely and out of malice, then may all the evil rest on his head through this life for ever, and may his soul perish everlastingly.

It would be impossible to describe adequately the awe with which the assembled people listen to these terrible words, and the dreadful silence of the crowd as they wait to see the result. If nothing happens the man rises from his knees after an interval, and is pronounced innocent by the judgment of the people, and no word is ever again uttered against him, nor is he shunned or slighted by the neighbours. But the accuser is looked on with fear and dislike; he is considered unlucky, and seeing that his life is often made so miserable by the coldness and suspicion of the people, many would rather suffer wrong than force the accused person to undergo so terrible a trial as "The Clearing."

The Holy Well and the Murderer

The Well of St. Brendan, in High Island, has great virtue, but the miraculous power of the water is lost should a thief or a murderer drink of it. Now a cruel murder had been committed on the mainland, and the priest noticed the people that if the murderer tried to conceal himself in the island no one should harbour him or give him food or drink. It happened at that time there was a woman of the island afflicted with pains in her limbs, and she went to the Holy Well to make the stations and say the prayers, and so get cured. But many a day passed and still she got no better, though she went round and round the well on her knees, and recited the paters and aves as she was told.

Then she went to the priest and told him the story, and he perceived at once that the well had been polluted by the touch of some one who had committed a crime. So he bade the woman bring him a bottle of the water, and she did as he desired. Then having received the water, he poured it out, and breathed on it three times in the name of the Trinity; when, lo! the water turned into blood.

"Here is the evil," cried the priest. "A murderer has washed his hands in the well."

He then ordered her to make a fire in a circle, which she did, and he pronounced some words over it; and a mist rose up with the form of a spirit in the midst, holding a man by the arm.

"Behold the murderer," said the spirit; and when the woman looked on him she shrieked—

"It is my son! my son!" and she fainted.

100

For the year before her son had gone to live on the mainland, and there, unknown to his mother, he had committed the dreadful murder for which the vengeance of God lay on him. And when she came to herself the spirit of the murderer was still there.

"Oh, my Lord! let him go, let him go!" she cried.

"You wretched woman!" answered the priest. "How dare you interpose between God and vengeance. This is but the shadowy form of your son; but before night he shall be in the hands of the law, and justice shall be done."

Then the forms and the mist melted away, and the woman departed in tears, and not long after she died of a broken heart. But the well from that time regained all its miraculous powers, and the fame of its cures spread far and wide through all the islands.

Legends of Innis-Sark: a Woman's Curse

There was a woman of the Island of Innis-Sark who was determined to take revenge on a man because he called her by an evil name. So she went to the Saints' Well, and, kneeling down, she took some of the water and poured it on the ground in the name of the devil, saying, "So may my enemy be poured out like water, and lie helpless on the earth!" Then she went round the well backwards on her knees, and at each station she cast a stone in the name of the devil, and said, "So may the curse fall on him, and the power of the devil crush him!" After this she returned home.

Now the next morning there was a stiff breeze, and some of the men were afraid to go out fishing; but others said they would try their luck, and amongst them was the man on whom the curse rested. But they had not gone far from land when the boat was capsized by a heavy squall. The fishermen, however, saved themselves by swimming to shore; all except the man on whom the curse rested, and he sank like lead to the bottom, and the waves covered him, and he was drowned.

When the woman heard of the fate that had befallen her enemy, she ran to the beach and clapped her hands with joy and exulted. And as she stood there laughing with strange and horrid mirth, the corpse of the man she had

101

cursed slowly rose up from the sea, and came drifting towards her till it lay almost at her very feet. On this she stooped down to feast her eyes on the sight of the dead man, when suddenly a storm of wind screamed past her, and hurled her from the point of rock where she stood. And when the people ran in all haste to help, no trace of her body could be seen. The woman and the corpse of the man she had cursed disappeared together under the waves, and were never seen again from that time forth.

*

Another woman in Shark Island was considered to have an evil influence over any one she disliked. One day a man called her a devil's hag in his anger. The woman answered nothing, but that night she went to a Holy Well near the place, and kneeling down, invoked a curse in the name of the devil. Then she went round the well three times backward on her knees, and each time threw a stone in the name of the devil, saying, "So may the curse fall on his head!" Then she returned home, and told the people to wait for three days, and they would see her words had power. During this time the man was afraid to go out in his boat because of the curse. But on the third day as he was walking by the cliff he fell and broke his leg. And then every one knew that the woman had the witch-secret of evil, and she was held in much fear.

*

The most effective way of neutralizing the evil influence is to spit on the object and say, "God bless it!" But another must do it at your request, and sometimes people refuse, fearing to anger the fairies by interfering with their work, whether for good or evil. But the islanders have such faith in the anointing with spittle that they will often solicit a passing stranger to spit on the afflicted person. Indeed, a stranger is considered to have more power than a neighbour.

A woman who kept a small day-school had reason to think that her son, a fine lad of twelve years old, was bewitched, for when he had eaten up the whole dish of stirabout at supper, he asked for more. And she said—

"My son, you had enough for three men. Go to your bed and sleep."

102

But next morning he was worse and more ravenous, for he ate up all the bread that his mother had made for the scholars just as she took it from the oven, and not a single cake was left. Then she knew that witchcraft was on the boy, and she stood by the door to watch for a stranger. At last one came by, and she cried to him—

"Come in, come in, for the love of God, and spit on the face of my son!"

"Why should I spit on your son, O woman?" he answered; and he fled away, for he thought she was mad.

Then she sent for the priest, and his reverence poured holy water over him, and laid his hands upon his head while he prayed. So, after a time, the power of the witchcraft was broken, and the boy was restored to his right mind.

*

The islanders believe also that angels are constantly present amongst them, and all blessed things—the rain, and the dew, and the green crops—come from their power; but the fairies often bring sickness, and will do malicious tricks, and lame a horse, or steal the milk and butter, if they have been offended or deprived of their rights.

There are certain days on which it is not right to speak of the fairies. These days are Wednesdays and Fridays, for then they are present though invisible, and can hear everything, and lay their plans as to what they will carry off. On Friday especially their power for evil is very strong, and misfortunes are dreaded in the household. Therefore, on that day the children and cattle are strictly watched; a lighted wisp of straw is turned round the baby's head, and a quenched coal is set under the cradle and under the churn. And if the horses are restive in the stable, then the people know the fairies are riding on their backs. So they spit three times at the animal, when the fairies scamper off. This cure by the saliva is the most ancient of all superstitions, and the islanders still have the greatest faith in its mysterious power and efficacy.

*

At Innisboffin the fairies hold a splendid court, with revelry and dancing, when the moon is full; and it is very dangerous for young girls to be out at that time, for they will assuredly be carried off. And if they once hear the fairy music or drink of the fairy wine, they will never be the same again—a fate is on them, and before the year is out they will either disappear or die.

And the fairies are always on the watch for the handsome girls or children; for they look on mortals as of much higher race than themselves. And they are also glad to have the fine young men, the sons of mortal women, to assist them in their wars with each other; for there are two parties amongst the fairy spirits, one a gentle race that loves music and dancing, the other that has obtained power from the devil, and is always trying to work evil.

A young man lay down to sleep one Friday evening in summer under a hay-rick, and the fairies must have carried him off as he slept; for when he woke he found himself in a great hall, where a number of little men were at work—some spinning, some making shoes, some making spears and arrow-heads out of fish-bones and elf-stones; but all busy laughing and singing with much glee and merriment, while the little pipers played the merriest tunes.

Then an old man who sat in the corner came over, and looking very angry, told him he must not sit there idle; there were friends coming to dinner, and he must go down and help in the kitchen. So he drove the poor young fellow before him down into a great vaulted place, where a huge fire was burning, and a large pot was set over it.

"Now," said the old man, "prepare the dinner. There is the old hag we are going to eat."

And true enough, to his horror, on looking round, there was an old woman hung up by the arms, and an old man skinning her.

"Now make haste and let the water boil," said the old man; "don't you see the pot on the fire, and I am nearly ready for you to begin. The company will soon be here, and there is no time to lose, for this old hag will take a good while to boil. Cut her up into little bits, and throw her into the pot."

However, the young fellow was so frightened that he fell down on the floor speechless, and could neither move hand nor foot.

"Get up, you fool," said another old man, who seemed to be the head over all; and he laughed at him. "Do your work and never mind; this does not hurt her a bit. When she was there above in the world she was a wicked miser, hard to the world, and cruel and bitter in her words and works; so now we have her here, and her soul will never rest in peace, because we shall cut up the body in little bits, and the soul will not be able to find it, but wander about in the dark to all eternity without a body."

Then the young man knew no more till he found himself in a beautiful hall, where a banquet was laid out; but, in place of the old hag, the table was covered with fruit, and chickens, and young turkeys, and butter, and cakes fresh from the oven, and crystal cups of bright red wine.

"Now sit down and eat," said the prince, who sat at the top on a throne, with a red sash round his waist, and a gold band on his head. "Sit down with this pleasant company and eat with us; you are welcome."

And there were many beautiful ladies seated round, and grand noblemen, with red caps and sashes; and they all smiled at him and bade him eat.

"No," said the young man; "I cannot eat with you, for I see no priest here to bless the food. Let me go in peace."

"Not at least till you taste our wine," said the prince with a friendly smile.

And one of the beautiful ladies rose up and filled a crystal cup with the bright red wine, and gave it him. And when he saw it, the sight of it tempted him, and he could not help himself, but drank it all off without stopping; for it seemed to him the most delicious draught he ever had in his whole life.

But no sooner had he laid down the glass, than a noise like thunder shook the building, and all the lights went out; and he found himself alone in the dark night lying under the very same hay-rick where he had cast himself down to sleep, tired after his work. So he made his way home at last; but the taste of the fairy wine burned in his veins, and a fever was on him night and day for another draught; and he did no good, but pined away, seeking the fairy mansion, though he never found it any more. And so he died in his youth, a warning to all who eat of the fairy food, or drink of the fairy wine; for never more will they know peace or content, or be fit for their work, as in the days before the fairy spell was on them, which brings doom and death to all who fall under the fatal enchantment of its unholy power.

Legends of the Dead in the Western Islands

When young people die, either men or women, who were remarkable for beauty, it is supposed that they are carried off by the fairies to the fairy mansions under the earth, where they live in splendid palaces and are wedded to fairy queens or princes. But sometimes, if their kindred greatly desire to see them, they are allowed to visit the earth, though no enchantment has yet been discovered powerful enough to compel them to remain or resume again the mortal life.

Sometimes when the fishermen are out they meet a strange boat filled with people; and when they look on them they know that they are the dead who have been carried off by the fairies with their wiles and enchantments to dwell in the fairy palaces.

One day a man was out fishing, but caught nothing; and was just turning home in despair at his ill-luck when he suddenly saw a boat with three persons in it; and it seemed to him that they were his comrades, the very men who just a year before had been drowned in that spot, but whose bodies were never recovered, and he knew that he looked upon the dead. But the men were friendly, and called out to him—

"Cast your line as we direct, and you will have luck."

So he cast his line as they bade him, and presently drew up a fine fish.

"Now, cast again," they said, "and keep beside us, and row to shore, but do not look on us."

So he did as directed and hauled up fish after fish till his boat was full, and then he drew it up to the landing-place.

"Now," they said, "wait and see that no one is about before you land."

So the man looked up and down the shore, but saw no one; then he turned to land his fish, when, behold, the men and the second boat had vanished, and he saw them no more. However, he landed his fish with much joy and brought them all safely home, though the wise people said that if he had not turned away his head that time, but kept his eyes steadily on the men till he landed, the enchantment would have been broken that held them in fairy-land, and the dead would have been restored to the earthly life, and to their kindred in the island who mourned for them.

The Death Sign

A woman was out one day looking after her sheep in the valley, and coming by a little stream she sat down to rest, when suddenly she seemed to hear the sound of low music, and turning round, beheld at some distance a crowd of people dancing and making merry. And she grew afraid and turned her head away not to see them. Then close by her stood a young man, pale and strange looking, and she beheld him with fear.

"Who are you?" she said at last; "and why do you stand beside me?"

"You ought to know me," he replied, "for I belong to this place; but make haste now and come away, or evil will befall you."

Then she stood up and was going away with him, when the crowd left off their dancing and ran towards them crying—

"Come back; come back; come back!"

"Don't stop; don't listen," said the young man, "but follow me."

Then they both began to run, and ran on until they reached a hillock.

"Now we are safe," said he; "they can't harm us here." And when they stopped he said to her again, "Look me in the face and say if you know me now?"

"No," she answered, "you are a stranger to me."

"Look again," he said, "look me straight in the face and you will know me."

Then she looked, and knew instantly that he was a man who had been drowned the year before in the dark winter time, and the waves had never cast up his body on the shore. And she threw up her arms and cried aloud—

"Have you news of my child? Have you seen her, my fair-haired girl, that was stolen from me this day seven years. Will she come back to me never no more?"

"I have seen her," said the man, "but she will never come back, never more, for she has eaten of the fairy food and must now stay with the spirits under the sea, for she belongs to them body and soul. But go home now, for it is late, and evil is near you; and perhaps you will meet her sooner than you think."

Then as the women turned her face homeward, the man disappeared and she saw him no more.

When at last she reached the threshold of her house a fear and trembling came on her, and she called to her husband that some one stood in the doorway and she could not pass. And with that she fell down on the threshold on her face, but spake no word more. And when they lifted her up she was dead.

Kathleen

A young girl from Innis-Sark had a lover, a fine young fellow, who met his death by an accident, to her great grief and sorrow.

One evening at sunset, as she sat by the roadside crying her eyes out, a beautiful lady came by all in white, and tapped her on the cheek.

"Don't cry, Kathleen," she said, "your lover is safe. Just take this ring of herbs and look through it and you will see him. He is with a grand company, and wears a golden circlet on his head and a scarlet sash round his waist."

So Kathleen took the ring of herbs and looked through it, and there indeed was her lover in the midst of a great company dancing on the hill; and he was very pale, but handsomer than ever, with the gold circlet round his head, as if they had made him a prince.

"Now," said the lady, "here is a larger ring of herbs. Take it, and whenever you want to see your lover, pluck a leaf from it and burn it; and a great smoke will arise, and you will fall into a trance; and in the trance your lover will carry you away to the fairy rath, and there you may dance all night with him on the greensward. But say no prayer, and make no sign of the cross while the smoke is rising, or your lover will disappear for ever."

From that time a great change came over Kathleen. She said no prayer, and cared for no priest, and never made the sign of the cross, but every night shut herself up in her room, and burned a leaf of the ring of herbs as she had been told; and when the smoke arose she fell into a deep sleep and knew no more. But in the morning she told her people that, though she seemed to be lying in her bed, she was far away with the fairies on the hill dancing with her lover. And she was very happy in her new life, and wanted no priest nor prayer nor mass any more, and all the dead were there dancing with the rest, all the people she had known; and they welcomed her and gave her wine to drink in little crystal cups, and told her she must soon come and stay with them and with her lover for evermore.

Now Kathleen's mother was a good, honest, religious woman, and she fretted much over her daughter's strange state, for she knew the girl had been fairy-struck. So she determined to watch; and one night when Kathleen went to her bed as usual all alone by herself in the room, for she would allow no one to be with her, the mother crept up and looked through a chink in the door, and then she saw Kathleen take the round ring of herbs from a secret place in the press and pluck a leaf from it and burn it, on which a great smoke arose and the girl fell on her bed in a deep trance.

Now the mother could no longer keep silence, for she saw there was devil's work in it; and she fell on her knees and prayed aloud—

"O Maia, mother, send the evil spirit away from the child!"

And she rushed into the room and made the sign of the cross over the sleeping girl, when immediately Kathleen started up and screamed—

"Mother! mother! the dead are coming for me. They are here! they are here!"

And her features looked like one in a fit. Then the poor mother sent for the priest, who came at once, and threw holy water on the girl, and said prayers over her; and he took the ring of herbs that lay beside her and cursed it for evermore, and instantly it fell to powder and lay like grey ashes on the floor. After this Kathleen grew calmer, and the evil spirit seemed to have left her, but she was too weak to move or to speak, or to utter a prayer, and before the clock struck twelve that night she lay dead.

November Eve

It is esteemed a very wrong thing amongst the islanders to be about on November Eve, minding any business, for the fairies have their flitting then, and do not like to be seen or watched; and all the spirits come to meet them and help them. But mortal people should keep at home, or they will suffer for it; for the souls of the dead have power over all things on that one night of the year; and they hold a festival with the fairies, and drink red wine from the fairy cups, and dance to fairy music till the moon goes down.

There was a man of the village who stayed out late one November Eve fishing, and never thought of the fairies until he saw a great number of dancing lights, and a crowd of people hurrying past with baskets and bags, and all laughing and singing and making merry as they went along.

"You are a merry set," he said, "where are ye all going to?"

"We are going to the fair," said a little old man with a cocked hat and a gold band round it. "Come with us, Hugh King, and you will have the finest food and the finest drink you ever set eyes upon."

"And just carry this basket for me," said a little red-haired woman.

So Hugh took it, and went with them till they came to the fair, which was filled with a crowd of people he had never seen on the island in all his days. And they danced and laughed and drank red wine from little cups. And there were pipers, and harpers, and little cobblers mending shoes, and all the most beautiful things in the world to eat and drink, just as if they were in a king's palace. But the basket was very heavy, and Hugh longed to drop it, that he might go and dance with a little beauty with long yellow hair, that was laughing up close to his face.

"Well, here put down the basket," said the red-haired woman, "for you are quite tired, I see;" and she took it and opened the cover, and out came a little old man, the ugliest, most misshapen little imp that could be imagined.

"Ah, thank you, Hugh," said the imp, quite politely; "you have carried me nicely; for I am weak on the limbs—indeed I have nothing to speak of in the way of legs: but I'll pay you well, my fine fellow; hold out your two hands," and the little imp poured down gold and gold and gold into them, bright golden guineas. "Now go," said he, "and drink my health, and make yourself quite pleasant, and don't be afraid of anything you see and hear."

So they all left him, except the man with the cocked hat and the red sash round his waist.

"Wait here now a bit," says he, "for Finvarra, the king, is coming, and his wife, to see the fair."

As he spoke, the sound of a horn was heard, and up drove a coach and four white horses, and out of it stepped a grand, grave gentleman all in black and a beautiful lady with a silver veil over her face.

"Here is Finvarra himself and the queen," said the little old man; but Hugh was ready to die of fright when Finvarra asked—

"What brought this man here?"

And the king frowned and looked so black that Hugh nearly fell to the ground with fear. Then they all laughed, and laughed so loud that everything seemed shaking and tumbling down from the laughter. And the dancers came up, and they all danced round Hugh, and tried to take his hands to make him dance with them.

"Do you know who these people are; and the men and women who are dancing round you?" asked the old man. "Look well, have you ever seen them before?"

And when Hugh looked he saw a girl that had died the year before, then another and another of his friends that he knew had died long ago; and then he saw that all the dancers, men, women, and girls, were the dead in their long, white shrouds. And he tried to escape from them, but could not, for they coiled round him, and danced and laughed and seized his arms, and tried to draw him into the dance, and their laugh seemed to pierce through his brain and kill him. And he fell down before them there, like one faint from sleep, and knew no more till he found himself next morning lying within the old stone circle by the fairy rath on the hill. Still it was all true that he had been with the fairies; no one could deny it, for his arms were all black with the touch of the hands of the dead, the time they had tried to draw him into the dance; but not one bit of all the red gold, which the little imp had

111

given him, could he find in his pocket. Not one single golden piece; it was all gone for evermore.

And Hugh went sadly to his home, for now he knew that the spirits had mocked him and punished him, because he troubled their revels on November Eve—that one night of all the year when the dead can leave their graves and dance in the moonlight on the hill, and mortals should stay at home and never dare to look on them.

The Dance of the Dead

It is especially dangerous to be out late on the last night of November, for it is the closing scene of the revels—the last night when the dead have leave to dance on the hill with the fairies, and after that they must all go back to their graves and lie in the chill, cold earth, without music or wine till the next November comes round, when they all spring up again in their shrouds and rush out into the moonlight with mad laughter.

One November night, a woman of Shark Island, coming home late at the hour of the dead, grew tired and sat down to rest, when presently a young man came up and talked to her.

"Wait a bit," he said, "and you will see the most beautiful dancing you ever looked on there by the side of the hill."

And she looked at him steadily. He was very pale, and seemed sad.

"Why are you so sad?" she asked, "and as pale as if you were dead?"

"Look well at me," he answered. "Do you not know me?"

"Yes, I know you now," she said. "You are young Brien that was drowned last year when out fishing. What are you here for?"

"Look," he said, "at the side of the hill and you will see why I am here."

And she looked, and saw a great company dancing to sweet music; and amongst them were all the dead who had died as long as she could remember—men, women, and children, all in white, and their faces were pale as the moonlight.

"Now," said the young man, "run for your life; for if once the fairies bring you into the dance you will never be able to leave them any more."

But while they were talking, the fairies came up and danced round her in a circle, joining their hands. And she fell to the ground in a faint, and knew no more till she woke up in the morning in her own bed at home. And they all saw that her face was pale as the dead, and they knew that she had got the fairy-stroke. So the herb doctor was sent for, and every measure tried to save her, but without avail, for just as the moon rose that night, soft, low music was heard round the house, and when they looked at the woman she was dead.

It is a custom amongst the people, when throwing away water at night, to cry out in a loud voice, "Take care of the water;" or, literally from the Irish, "Away with yourself from the water"—for they say the spirits of the dead last buried are then wandering about, and it would be dangerous if the water fell on them.

One dark winter's night a woman suddenly threw out a pail of boiling water without thinking of the warning words. Instantly a cry was heard as of a person in pain, but no one was seen. However, the next night a black lamb entered the house, having the back all fresh scalded, and it lay down moaning by the hearth and died. Then they all knew this was the spirit that had been scalded by the woman. And they carried the dead lamb out reverently and buried it deep in the earth. Yet every night at the same hour it walked again into the house and lay down and moaned and died. And after this had happened many times, the priest was sent for, and finally, by the strength of his exorcism, the spirit of the dead was laid to rest, and the black lamb appeared no more. Neither was the body of the dead lamb found in the grave when they searched for it, though it had been laid by their own hands deep in the earth and covered with the clay.

*

Before an accident happens to a boat, or a death by drowning, low music is often heard, as if under the water, along with harmonious lamentations, and then every one in the boat knows that some young man or beautiful young girl is wanted by the fairies, and is doomed to die. The best safeguard is to have music and singing in the boat, for the fairies are so enamoured of the mortal voices and music that they forget to weave the spell till the fatal moment has passed, and then all in the boat are safe from harm.

Superstitions Concerning the Dead

Many strange spells are effected by the means of a dead man's hand—chiefly to produce butter in the churn. The milk is stirred round nine times with the dead hand, the operator crying aloud all the time, "Gather! gather! gather!" While a secret form of words is used which none but the initiated know.

*

Another use is to facilitate robberies. If a candle is placed in a dead hand, neither wind nor water can extinguish it. And if carried into a house the inmates will sleep the sleep of the dead as long as it remains under the roof, and no power on earth can wake them while the dead hand holds the candle.

*

For a mystic charm, one of the strongest known is the hand of an unbaptized infant fresh taken from the grave in the name of the Evil One.

*

A dead hand is esteemed also a certain cure for most diseases, and many a time sick people have been brought to a house where a corpse lay that the hand of the dead might be laid on them.

*

114

The souls of the dead who may happen to die abroad, greatly desire to rest in Ireland. And the relations deem it their duty to bring back the body to be laid in Irish earth. But even then the dead will not rest peaceably unless laid with their forefathers and their own people, and not amongst strangers.

A young girl happened to die of a fever while away on a visit to some friends, and her father thought it safer not to bring her home, but to have her buried in the nearest churchyard. However, a few nights after his return home, he was awakened by a mournful wail at the window, and a voice cried, "I am alone; I am alone; I am alone!" Then the poor father knew well what it meant, and he prayed in the name of God that the spirit of his dead child might rest in peace until the morning. And when the day broke he arose and set off to the strange burial ground, and there he drew the coffin from the earth, and had it carried all the way back from Cork to Mayo; and after he had laid the dead in the old graveyard beside his people and his kindred, the spirit of his child had rest, and the mournful cry was no more heard in the night.

*

The corner of a sheet that has wrapped a corpse is a cure for headache if tied round the head.

*

The ends of candles used at wakes are of great efficacy in curing burns.

*

A piece of linen wrap taken from a corpse will cure the swelling of a limb if tied round the part affected.

*

It is believed that the spirit of the dead last buried has to watch in the churchyard until another corpse is laid there; or has to perform menial offices in the spirit world, such as carrying wood and water until the next spirit comes from earth. They are also sent on messages to earth, chiefly to announce the coming death of some relative, and at this they are glad, for then their time of peace and rest will come at last.

*

If any one stumbles at a grave it is a bad omen; but if he falls and touches the clay, he will assuredly die before the year is out.

*

Any one meeting a funeral must turn back and walk at least four steps with the mourners.

*

If the nearest relative touches the hand of a corpse it will utter a wild cry if not quite dead.

*

On Twelfth Night the dead walk, and on every tile of the house a soul is sitting, waiting for your prayers to take it out of purgatory.

*

There are many strange superstitions in the western islands of Connemara. At night the dead can be heard laughing with the fairies and spinning the flax. One girl declared that she distinctly heard her dead mother's voice singing a mournful Irish air away down in the heart of the hill. But after a year and a day the voices cease, and the dead are gone for ever.

*

It is a custom in the West, when a corpse is carried to the grave, for the bearers to stop half way, while the nearest relatives build up a small monument of loose stones, and no hand would ever dare to touch or disturb this monument while the world lasts.

*

When the grave is dug, a cross is made of two spades, and the coffin is carried round it three times before being placed in the clay. Then the prayers for the dead are said, all the people kneeling with uncovered head.

The Fatal Love-Charm

A potent love-charm used by women is a piece of skin taken from the arm of a corpse and tied on the person while sleeping whose love is sought. The skin is then removed after some time, and carefully put away before the sleeper awakes or has any consciousness of the transaction. And as long as it remains in the woman's possession the love of her lover will be unchanged. Or the strip of skin is placed under the head to dream on, in the name of the Evil One, when the future husband will appear in the dream.

A young girl who was servant in the large and handsome house of a rich family tried this charm for fun, thinking she would dream of one of her fellow-servants, and next morning her mistress asked the result.

"Throth, ma'am," she answered, "there never was such a foolish trick, for it was of the master himself I was dreaming all night, and of no one else."

Soon after the lady died, and the girl, remembering her dream, watched her opportunity to tie a piece of skin taken from a corpse recently buried round the arm of her master while he slept. After this he became violently in love with the girl, though she was exceedingly ugly, and within the year he married her, his love all the while remaining fervent and unchanged.

But exactly one year and a day after her marriage her bedroom took fire by accident, and the strip of skin, which she had kept carefully hidden in her wardrobe, was burnt, along with all her grand wedding-clothes. Immediately the magic charm was broken, and the hatred of the gentleman for his low-born wife became as strong as the love he had once felt for her.

In her rage and grief at finding nothing but coldness and insult, she confessed the whole story; and, in consequence, the horror she inspired amongst the people was so great that no one would serve her with food or drink, or sit near her, or hold any intercourse with her; and she died miserably and half mad before the second year was out—a warning and a terror to all who work spells in the name of the Evil One.

The Fenian Knights: A Legend of the West

There is a fort near the Killeries in Connemara called *Lis-na-Keeran*. One day the powerful chief that lived there invited the great Fionn Ma-Coul, with his son Oscar and a band of Fenian knights, to a great banquet. But when the guests arrived they found no chairs prepared for them, only rough benches of wood placed round the table.

So Oscar and his father would take no place, but stood watching, for they suspected treachery. The knights, however, fearing nothing, sat down to the feast, but were instantly fixed to the benches so firmly by magic, that they could neither rise nor move.

Then Fionn began to chew his thumb, from which he always derived knowledge of the future, and by his magic power he saw clearly a great and terrible warrior riding fiercely towards the fort, and Fionn knew that unless he could be stopped before crossing a certain ford, they must all die, for they had been brought to Lis-na-Keeran only to be slain by their treacherous host; and unless the warrior was killed and his blood sprinkled on the Fenian knights, they must remain fixed on the wooden benches for ever.

So Oscar of the Lion heart rushed forth to the encounter. And he flung his spear at the mighty horseman, and they fought desperately till the setting of the sun. Then at last Oscar triumphed; victory was his; and he cut off the head of his adversary, and carried it on his spear all bleeding to the fort, where he let the blood drop down upon the Fenian knights that were transfixed by magic. On this they at once sprang up free and scatheless, all except one, for on him unhappily no blood had fallen, and so he remained fixed to the bench. His companions tried to drag him up by main force, but as they did so the skin of his thighs was left on the bench, and he was like to die.

Then they killed a sheep, and wrapped the fleece round him warm from the animal to heal him. So he was cured, but ever after, strange to relate, seven stone of wool were annually shorn from his body as long as he lived.

*

The manner in which Fionn learned the mystery of obtaining wisdom from his thumb was in this wise.

It happened one time when he was quite a youth that he was taken prisoner by a one-eyed giant, who at first was going to kill him, but then he changed his mind and sent him to the kitchen to mind the dinner. Now there was a great and splendid salmon broiling on the fire, and the giant said—

"Watch that salmon till it is done; but if a single blister rise on the skin you shall be killed."

Then the giant threw himself down to sleep while waiting for the dinner.

So Fionn watched the salmon with all his eyes, but to his horror saw a blister rising on the beautiful silver skin of the fish, and in his fright and eagerness he pressed his thumb down on it to flatten it; then the pain of the burn being great, he clapped the thumb into his mouth and kept it there to suck out the fire. When he drew it back, however, he found, to his surprise that he had a knowledge of all that was going to happen to him, and a clear sense of what he ought to do. And it came into his mind that if he put out the giant's eye with an iron rod heated in the fire, he could escape from the monster. So he heated the rod, and while the giant slept he plunged it into his eye, and before the horrid being recovered from the shock, Fionn escaped, and was soon back safe amongst his own people, the Fenian knights; and ever after in moments of great peril and doubt, when he put his thumb into his mouth and sucked it, the vision of the future came on him, and he could foresee clearly whatever danger lay in his path, and how to avoid it. But it was only in such extreme moments of peril that the mystic power was granted to him. And thus he was enabled to save his own life and the lives of his chosen Fenian guard when all hope seemed well-nigh gone.

Rathlin Island

There is an old ruin called Bruce's Castle on this island, and the legend runs that Bruce and his chief warriors lie in an enchanted sleep in a cave of the rock on which stands the castle, and that one day they will rise up and unite the island to Scotland.

The entrance to this cave is visible only once in seven years. A man who happened to be travelling by at the time discovered it, and entering in he found himself all at once in the midst of the heavy-handed warriors. He looked down and saw a sabre half unsheathed in the earth at his feet, and on his attempting to draw it every man of the sleepers lifted up his head and put his hand on his sword. The man being much alarmed fled from the cave, but he heard voices calling fiercely after him: "Ugh! ugh! Why could we not be left to sleep?" And they clanged their swords on the ground with a terrible noise, and then all was still, and the gate of the cave closed with a mighty sound like a clap of thunder.

The Strange Guests

A company of strangers came one day to Rathlin island and the people distrusted them, but pretended to be friendly, and invited them to a feast, meaning to put an end to them all when they came unarmed to the festival, and the drink flowed freely. So the strangers came, but each man as he sat down drew his knife and stuck it in the table before him ere he began to eat. When the islanders saw their guests so well prepared, they were afraid; and the feast passed off quietly.

The next morning early, the strangers sailed away before any one was aware on the island; but on the table where each guest had sat, a piece of silver was found, covering the hole made by the knife. So the islanders rejoiced, and determined never again to plot evil against the wayfaring guests; but to be kind and hospitable to all wanderers for the sake of the Holy Mother, who had sent them to the island to bring good luck to the people. But they never saw the strangers more.

The islanders have great faith in the power of the Virgin Mary, for our Lord Himself told St. Bridget that His mother had a throne in heaven near His own; and whatever she asked of God it was granted, especially if it was any grace or favour for the Irish people, because He held them in great esteem on account of their piety and good works.

The Dead Soldier

There is an island in the Shannon, and if a mermaid is seen sitting on the rocks in the sunshine, the people know that a crime has been committed somewhere near; for she never appears but to announce ill-luck, and she has a spite against mortals, and rejoices at their misfortunes.

One day a young fisherman was drawn by the current towards the island, and he came on a long streak of red blood, and had to sail his boat through it till he reached the rocks where the mermaid was seated; and then the boat went round and round as in a whirlpool, and sank down at last under the waves.

Still he did not lose consciousness. He looked round and saw that he was in a beautiful country, with tall plants growing all over it; and the mermaid came and sang sweetly to him, and offered him wine to drink, but he would not taste it, for it was red like blood. Then he looked down, and to his horror he saw a soldier lying on the floor with his throat cut; and all round him was a pool of blood, and he remembered no more till he found himself again in his boat drifting against a hurricane, and suddenly he was dashed upon a rock, where his friends who were in search of him found him, and carried him home. There he heard a strange thing: a soldier, a deserter from the Athlone Barracks, being pursued had cut his throat and flung himself over the bridge into the river; and this was the very man the young fisher had seen lying a corpse in the mermaid's cave. After this he had no peace or comfort till he went to the priest, who exorcised him and gave him absolution; and then the wicked siren of the rocks troubled him no more, though she still haunts the islands of the Shannon and tries to lure victims to their death.

The Three Gifts

A great, noble-looking man called one night at a cottage, and told the woman that she must come away with him then and there on the instant, for his wife wanted a nurse for her baby. And so saying, before she could answer, he swung her up on his great black horse on a pillion behind him. And she sat wondering at his tall, shadowy form, for she could see the moonlight through him.

"Do not fear," he said, "and no harm will happen to you. Only ask no questions whatever happens, and drink no wine that may be offered to you."

On reaching the palace she saw the most beautiful ladies going about all covered with jewels, and she was led into a chamber hung with silk and gold, and lace as fine as cobwebs; and there on a bed supported by crystal pillars lay the mother, lovely as an angel, and her little baby beside her. And when

121

the nurse had dressed the baby and handed it to the mother, the lady smiled and offered her wine; "for then," she said, "you will never leave us, and I would love to have you always near me."

But the woman refused, though she was sorely tempted by the beautiful bright red wine.

"Well, then," said the lord and master, "here are three gifts, and you may take them away in safety, for no harm will come to you by them. A purse, never to be opened, but while you have it, you will never want money; a girdle, and whoso wears it will never be slain in battle; and an herb that has power to cure all diseases for seven generations."

So the woman was put again upon the horse with her three gifts, and reached her home safely. Then, from curiosity, the first thing she did was to open the purse, and behold, there was nothing in it but some wild flowers. On seeing this, she was so angry that she flung away the herb, "for they were only making a fool of me," she said, "and I don't believe one word of their stories." But the husband took the belt and kept it safe, and it went down in the family from father to son; and the last man who wore it was out in all the troubles of '98, and fought in every one of the battles, but he never got hurt or wound. However, after his death, no one knew what became of the belt; it was never seen more.

*

A woman was carried off one night to a fairy palace to attend one of the beautiful fairy ladies who lay sick on her golden bed. And as she was going in at the gate a man whispered to her, "Eat no food, and take no money from the fairies; but ask what you like and it will be granted." So when the fairy lady was well, she bade the nurse ask what she pleased. The woman answered, "I desire three things for my sons and their race—luck in fishing, luck in learning, and luck in gambling," which things were granted—and to this day the family are the richest, the wisest, and the luckiest in the whole neighbourhood. They win at every game, and at every race, but always by fair play and without cheating; and not the priest himself can beat them at book learning. And every one knows that the power comes to them from the fairy gift, though good luck comes with it and not evil; and all the work of their hands has prospered through every generation since the day of the Three Wishes.

The Fairies as Fallen Angels

The islanders, like all the Irish, believe that the fairies are the fallen angels who were cast down by the Lord God out of heaven for their sinful pride. And some fell into the sea, and some on the dry land, and some fell deep down into hell, and the devil gives to these knowledge and power, and sends them on earth where they work much evil. But the fairies of the earth and the sea are mostly gentle and beautiful creatures, who will do no harm if they are let alone, and allowed to dance on the fairy raths in the moonlight to their own sweet music, undisturbed by the presence of mortals. As a rule, the people look on fire as the great preservative against witchcraft, for the devil has no power except in the dark. So they put a live coal under the churn, and they wave a lighted wisp of straw above the cow's head if the beast seems sickly. But as to the pigs, they take no trouble, for they say the devil has no longer any power over them now. When they light a candle they cross themselves, because the evil spirits are then clearing out of the house in fear of the light. Fire and Holy Water they hold to be sacred, and are powerful; and the best safeguard against all things evil, and the surest test in case of suspected witchcraft.

The Fairy Changeling

One evening, a man was coming home late, and he passed a house where two women stood by a window, talking.

"I have left the dead child in the cradle as you bid me," said one woman, "and behold here is the other child, take it and let me go;" and she laid down an infant on a sheet by the window, who seemed in a secret sleep, and it was draped all in white.

"Wait," said the other, "till you have had some food, and then take it to the fairy queen, as I promised, in place of the dead child that we have laid in the cradle by the nurse. Wait also till the moon rises, and then you shall have the payment which I promised."

They then both turned from the window. Now the man saw that there was some devil's magic in it all. And when the women turned away he crept up close to the open window and put his hand in and seized the sleeping child and drew it out quietly without ever a sound. Then he made off as fast as he could to his own home, before the women could know anything about it, and handed the child to his mother's care. Now the mother was angry at first, but when he told her the story, she believed him, and put the baby to sleep—a lovely, beautiful boy with a face like an angel.

Next morning there was a great commotion in the village, for the news spread that the first-born son of the great lord of the place, a lovely, healthy child, died suddenly in the night, without ever having had a sign of sickness. When they looked at him in the morning, there he laid dead in his cradle, and he was shrunk and wizened like a little old man, and no beauty was seen on him any more. So great lamentation was heard on all sides, and the whole country gathered to the wake. Amongst them came the young man who had carried off the child, and when he looked on the little wizened thing in the cradle he laughed. Now the parents were angry at his laughter, and wanted to turn him out.

But he said, "Wait, put down a good fire," and they did so.

Then he went over to the cradle and said to the hideous little creature, in a loud voice before all the people—

"If you don't rise up this minute and leave the place, I will burn you on the fire; for I know right well who you are, and where you came from."

At once the child sat up and began to grin at him; and made a rush to the door to get away; but the man caught hold of it and threw it on the fire. And the moment it felt the heat it turned into a black kitten, and flew up the chimney and was seen no more.

Then the man sent word to his mother to bring the other child, who was found to be the true heir, the lord's own son. So there was great rejoicing, and the child grew up to be a great lord himself, and when his time came, he ruled well over the estate; and his descendants are living to this day, for all things prospered with him after he was saved from the fairies.

Fairy Wiles

When the fairies steal away a beautiful mortal child they leave an ugly, wizened little creature in its place. And these fairy changelings grow up malicious and wicked, and have voracious appetites. The unhappy parents often try the test of fire for the child, in this wise—placing it in the centre of the cabin, they light a fire round it, and fully expect to see it changed into a sod of turf. But if the child survives the ordeal it is accepted as one of the family, though very grudgingly; and it is generally hated by all the neighbours for its impish ways. But the children of the Sidhe and a mortal mother are always clever and beautiful, and specially excel in music and dancing. They are, however, passionate and wilful, and have strange, moody fits, when they desire solitude above all things, and seem to hold converse with unseen spiritual beings.

Fine young peasant women are often carried off by the fairies to nurse their little fairy progeny. But the woman is allowed to come back to her own infant after sunset. However, on entering the house, the husband must at once throw holy water over her in the name of God, when she will be restored to her own shape. For sometimes she comes with a hissing noise like a serpent; then she appears black, and shrouded like one from the dead; and, lastly, in her own shape, when she takes her old place by the fire and nurses her baby; and the husband must ask no questions, but give her food in silence. If she falls asleep the third night, all will be well, for the husband at once ties a red thread across the door to prevent the fairies coming in to carry her off, and if the third night passes over safely the fairies have lost their power over her for evermore.

Shaun-Mor: A Legend of Innis-Sark

The islanders believe firmly in the existence of fairies who live in the caves by the sea—little men about the height of a sod of turf, who come out of the fissures of the rocks and are bright and merry, wearing green jackets and red caps, and ready enough to help any one they like, though often very malicious if offended or insulted.

There was an old man on the island called Shaun-Mor, who said that he had often travelled at night with the little men and carried their sacks for them; and in return they gave him strange fairy gifts and taught him the secret of power, so that he could always triumph over his enemies; and even as to the fairies, he was as wise as any of them, and could fight half a dozen of them together if he were so minded, and pitch them into the sea or strangle them with seaweed. So the fairies were angered at his pride and presumption, and determined to do him a malicious turn, just to amuse themselves when they were up for fun. So one night when he was returning home, he suddenly saw a great river between him and his house.

"How shall I get across now?" he cried aloud; and immediately an eagle came up to him.

"Don't cry, Shaun-Mor," said the eagle, "but get on my back and I'll carry you safely."

So Shaun-Mor mounted, and they flew right up ever so high, till at last the eagle tumbled him off by the side of a great mountain in a place he had never seen before.

"This is a bad trick you have played me," said Shaun; "tell me where I am now?"

"You are in the moon," said the eagle, "and get down the best way you can, for now I must be off; so good-bye. Mind you don't fall off the edge. Good-bye," and with that the eagle disappeared.

Just then a cleft in the rock opened, and out came a man as pale as the dead with a reaping-hook in his hand.

"What brings you here?" said he. "Only the dead come here," and he looked fixedly at Shaun-Mor so that he trembled like one already dying.

"O your worship," he said, "I live far from here. Tell me how I am to get down, and help me I beseech you."

"Ay, that I will," said the pale-faced man. "Here is the help I give you," and with that he gave him a blow with the reaping-hook which tumbled Shaun right over the edge of the moon; and he fell and fell ever so far till luckily he came in the midst of a flock of geese, and the old gander that was leading stopped and eyed him.

"What are you doing here, Shaun-Mor?" said he, "for I know you well. I've often seen you down in Shark. What will your wife say when she hears of your being out so late at night, wandering about in this way. It is very disreputable, and no well brought up gander would do the like, much less a man; I am ashamed of you, Shaun-Mor."

"O your honour," said the poor man, "it is an evil turn of the evil witches, for they have done all this; but let me just get up on your back, and if your honour brings me safe to my own house I shall be for ever grateful to every goose and gander in the world as long as I live."

"Well then, get up on my back," said the bird, fluttering its wings with a great clatter over Shaun; but he couldn't manage at all to get on its back, so he caught hold of one leg, and he and the gander went down and down till they came to the sea.

"Now let go," said the gander, "and find your way home the best way you can, for I have lost a great deal of time with you already, and must be away;" and he shook off Shaun-Mor, who dropped plump down into the sea, and when he was almost dead a great whale came sailing by, and flapped him all over with its fins. He knew no more till he opened his eyes lying on the grass in his own field by a great stone, and his wife was standing over him drenching him with a great pail of water, and flapping his face with her apron.

And then he told his wife the whole story, which he said was true as gospel, but I don't think she believed a word of it, though she was afraid to let on the like to Shaun-Mor, who affirms to this day that it was all the work of the fairies, though wicked people might laugh and jeer and say he was drunk.

The Cave Fairies

The Tuatha-de-Danann

It is believed by many people that the cave fairies are the remnant of the ancient Tuatha-de-Dananns who once ruled Ireland, but were conquered by the Milesians.

These Tuatha were great necromancers, skilled in all magic, and excellent in all the arts as builders, poets, and musicians. At first the Milesians were going to destroy them utterly, but gradually were so fascinated and captivated by the gifts and power of the Tuatha that they allowed them to remain and to build forts, where they held high festival with music and singing and the chant of the bards. And the breed of horses they reared could not be surpassed in the world—fleet as the wind, with the arched neck and the broad chest and the quivering nostril, and the large eye that showed they were made of fire and flame, and not of dull, heavy earth. And the Tuatha made stables for them in the great caves of the hills, and they were shod with silver and had golden bridles, and never a slave was allowed to ride them. A splendid sight was the cavalcade of the Tuatha-de-Danann knights. Seven-score steeds, each with a jewel on his forehead like a star, and seven-score horsemen, all the sons of kings, in their green mantles fringed with gold, and golden helmets on their head, and golden greaves on their limbs, and each knight having in his hand a golden spear.

And so they lived for a hundred years and more, for by their enchantments they could resist the power of death.

Edain the Queen

Now it happened that the king of Munster one day saw a beautiful girl bathing, and he loved her and made her his queen. And in all the land was no woman so lovely to look upon as the fair Edain, and the fame of her beauty came to the ears of the great and powerful chief and king of the Tuatha-de-Danann, Midar by name. So he disguised himself and went to the court of the king of Munster, as a wandering bard, that he might look on the beauty of Edain. And he challenged the king to a game of chess.

"Who is this man that I should play chess with him?" said the king.

"Try me," said the stranger; "you will find me a worthy foe."

Then the king said—"But the chess-board is in the queen's apartment, and I cannot disturb her."

However, when the queen heard that a stranger had challenged the king to chess, she sent her page in with the chess-board, and then came herself to greet the stranger. And Midar was so dazzled with her beauty, that he could not speak, he could only gaze on her. And the queen also seemed troubled, and after a time she left them alone.

"Now, what shall we play for?" asked the king.

"Let the conqueror name the reward," answered the stranger, "and whatever he desires let it be granted to him."

"Agreed," replied the monarch.

Then they played the game and the stranger won.

"What is your demand now?" cried the king. "I have given my word that whatever you name shall be yours."

"I demand the Lady Edain, the queen, as my reward," replied the stranger. "But I shall not ask you to give her up to me till this day year." And the stranger departed.

Now the king was utterly perplexed and confounded, but he took good note of the time, and on that night just a twelvemonth after, he made a great feast at Tara for all the princes, and he placed three lines of his chosen warriors all round the palace, and forbade any stranger to enter on pain of death. So all being secure, as he thought, he took his place at the feast with the beautiful Edain beside him, all glittering with jewels and a golden crown on her head, and the revelry went on till midnight. Just then, to his horror, the king looked up, and there stood the stranger in the middle of the hall, but no one seemed to perceive him save only the king, He fixed his eyes on the queen, and coming towards her, he struck the golden harp he had in his hand and sang in a low sweet voice—

"O Edain, wilt thou come with me
To a wonderful palace that is mine?
White are the teeth there, and black the brows,
And crimson as the mead are the lips of the lovers.
"O woman, if thou comest to my proud people,
'Tis a golden crown shall circle thy head,
Thou shalt dwell by the sweet streams of my land,
And drink of the mead and wine in the arms of thy lover."

Then he gently put his arm round the queen's waist, and drew her up from her royal throne, and went forth with her through the midst of all the guests, none hindering, and the king himself was like one in a dream, and could neither speak nor move. But when he recovered himself, then he knew that the stranger was one of the fairy chiefs of the Tuatha-de-Danann who had carried off the beautiful Edain to his fairy mansion. So he sent round messengers to all the kings of Erin that they should destroy all the forts of the hated Tuatha race, and slay and kill and let none live till the queen, his young bride, was brought back to him. Still she came not. Then the king out of revenge ordered his men to block up all the stables where the royal horses of the Dananns were kept, that so they might die of hunger; but the horses were of noble blood, and no bars or bolts could hold them, and they broke through the bars and rushed out like the whirlwind, and spread all over the country. And the kings, when they saw the beauty of the horses, forgot all about the search for Queen Edain, and only strove how they could seize and hold as their own some of the fiery steeds with the silver hoofs and golden bridles. Then the king raged in his wrath, and sent for the chief of the Druids, and told him he should be put to death unless he discovered the place where the queen lay hid. So the Druid went over all Ireland, and searched, and made spells with oghams, and at last, having carved four oghams on four wands of a hazel-tree, it was revealed to him that deep down

130

in a hill in the very centre of Ireland, Queen Edain was hidden away in the enchanted palace of Midar the fairy chief.

Then the king gathered a great army, and they circled the hill, and dug down and down till they came to the very centre; and just as they reached the gate of the fairy palace, Midar by his enchantments sent forth fifty beautiful women from the hillside, to distract the attention of the warriors, all so like the queen in form and features and dress, that the king himself could not make out truly, if his own wife were amongst them or not. But Edain, when she saw her husband so near her, was touched by love of him in her heart, and the power of the enchantment fell from her soul, and she came to him, and he lifted her up on his horse and kissed her tenderly, and brought her back safely to his royal palace of Tara, where they lived happily ever after.

*

But soon after the power of the Tuatha-de-Danann was broken for ever, and the remnant that was left took refuge in the caves where they exist to this day, and practise their magic, and work spells, and are safe from death until the judgment day.

The Royal Steed

Of the great breed of splendid horses, some remained for several centuries, and were at once known by their noble shape and qualities. The last of them belonged to a great lord in Connaught, and when he died, all his effects being sold by auction, the royal steed came to the hammer, and was bought up by an emissary of the English Government, who wanted to get possession of a specimen of the magnificent ancient Irish breed, in order to have it transported to England.

But when the groom attempted to mount the high-spirited animal, it reared, and threw the base-born churl violently to the ground, killing him on the spot.

Then, fleet as the wind, the horse galloped away, and finally plunged into the lake and was seen no more. So ended the great race of the mighty Tuatha-de-Danann horses in Ireland, the like of which has never been seen since in

131

all the world for majesty and beauty.

*

Sometimes the cave fairies make a straight path in the sea from one island to another, all paved with coral, under the water; but no one can tread it except the fairy race. Fishermen coming home late at night, on looking down, have frequently seen them passing and re-passing—a black band of little men with black dogs, who are very fierce if any one tries to touch them.

There was an old man named Con, who lived on an island all alone, except for a black dog who kept him company. Now all the people knew right well that he was a fairy king, and could walk the water at night like the other fairies. So they feared him greatly, and brought him presents of cakes and fowls, for they were afraid of him and of his evil demon, the dog. For often, men coming home late have heard the steps of this dog and his breathing quite close to them, though they could not see him; and one man nearly died of fright, and was only saved by the priest who came and prayed over him.

But the cave fairies can assume many forms.

One summer's evening, a young girl, the daughter of the man who owned the farm, was milking the cows in the yard, when three beautiful ladies, all in white, suddenly appeared, and asked her for a drink of milk. Now the girl knew well that milk should not be given away without using some precaution against fairy wiles, so she hesitated, fearing to bring ill-luck on the cows.

"Is that the way you treat us?" said one of the ladies, and she slapped the girl on the face.

"But, you'll remember us," said the second lady, and she took hold of the girl's thumb and twisted it out of joint.

"And your lover will be false to you," said the third, and with that she turned the girl's mantle crooked, the back to the front.

Then the first lady took a vessel and milked the cow, and they all drank of the milk as much as they wanted; after which they turned to the girl and bade her beware of again offending the spirits of the cave, for they were very powerful, and would not let her off so easily another time.

The poor girl fainted from fright, and was found quite senseless when they

132

came to look for her; but the white ladies had disappeared. Though the story must have been true, just as she told it when she came to her senses, for not a drop of milk was left in the pail, nor could a drop more be got from the cows all that evening.

Evil Spells

Cathal the King

It is said by the wise women and fairy doctors that the roots of the elder tree, and the roots of an apple tree that bears red apples, if boiled together and drunk fasting, will expel any evil living thing or evil spirit that may have taken up its abode in the body of a man.

But an evil charm to produce a living thing in the body can also be made, by pronouncing a certain magic and wicked spell over the food or drink taken by any person that an enemy wishes to injure.

One should therefore be very cautious in accepting anything to eat from a person of known malicious tongue and spiteful heart, or who has an ill will against you, for poison lies in their glance and in the touch of their hands; and an evil spell is in their very presence, and on all they do, say, or touch.

Cathal, king of Munster, was the tallest and handsomest of all the kings of Erin, and he fell deeply in love with the beautiful sister of Fergus, king of Ulster; and the lovers were happy in their love and resolved on marriage. But Fergus, King of the North, had a mortal hatred to Cathal, King of the South, and wished, in secret, to prevent the marriage. So he set a watch over his sister, and by this means found out that she was sending a basket of the choicest apples to her lover, by the hands of a trusty messenger. On this Fergus managed to get hold of the basket of fruit from the messenger; and he changed them secretly for another lot of apples, over which he worked an evil spell. Furnished with these the messenger set out for Cashel, and presented them to Cathal the king, who, delighted at this proof of love from his princess, began at once to eat the apples. But the more he ate, the more he longed for them, for a wicked spell was on every apple. When he had eaten

133

them all up, he sent round the country for more, and ate, and ate, until there was not an apple left in Cashel, nor in all the country round.

Then he bade his chieftains go forth and bring in food to appease his appetite; and he ate up all the cattle and the grain and the fruit, and still cried for more; and had the houses searched for food to bring to him. So the people were in despair, for they had no more food, and starvation was over the land.

Now a great and wise man, the chief poet of his tribe, happened to be travelling through Munster at that time, and hearing of the king's state, he greatly desired to see him, for he knew there was devil's work in the evil spell. So they brought him to the king, and many strong invocations he uttered over him, and many powerful incantations, for poets have a knowledge of mysteries above all other men; until finally, after three days had passed, he announced to the lords and chiefs that on that night, when the moon rose, the spell would be broken, and the king restored to his wonted health. So all the chiefs gathered round in the courtyard to watch; but no one was allowed to enter the room where the king lay, save only the poet. And he was to give the signal when the hour had come and the spell was broken.

So as they watched, and just as the moon rose, a great cry was heard from the king's room, and the poet, flinging open the door, bade the chiefs enter; and there on the floor lay a huge dead wolf, who for a whole year had taken up his abode in the king's body; but was now happily cast forth by the strong incantations of the poet.

After this the king fell into a deep sleep, and when he arose he was quite well, and strong again as ever, in all the pride of his youth and beauty. At this the people rejoiced much, for he was greatly loved, and the poet who had restored him was honoured above all men in the land; for the king himself took off the golden torque from his own neck, and placed it on that of the poet, and he set him at his right hand at the feast.

Now a strange thing happened just at this time; for Fergus, King of the North, fell ill, and wasted away to a shadow, and of all the beautiful meats and wines they set before him he could taste nothing. So he died before a year had passed by; and then Cathal the king wedded his beloved princess, and they lived happily through many years.

The Poet's Malediction

The imprecations of the poets had often also a mysterious and fatal effect.

King Breas, the pagan monarch, was a fierce, cruel, and niggardly man, who was therefore very unpopular with the people, who hate the cold heart and the grudging hand.

Amongst others who suffered by the king's inhospitality, was the renowned Carbury the poet, son of Eodain, the great poetess of the Tuatha-de-Danann race; she who chanted the song of victory when her people conquered the Firbolgs, on the plains of Moytura; and the stone that she stood on, during the battle, in sight of all the warriors, is still existing, and is pointed out as the stone of Eodain, the poetess, with great reverence, even to this day.

It was her son, Carbury the poet, who was held in such high honour by the nation, that King Breas invited him to his court, in order that he might pronounce a powerful malediction over the enemy with whom he was then at war.

Carbury came on the royal summons, but in place of being treated with the distinction due to his high rank, he was lodged and fed so meanly that the soul of the poet raged with wrath; for the king gave him for lodgement only a small stone cell without fire or a bed; and for food he had only three cakes of meal without any flesh meat or sauce, and no wine was given him, such wine as is fit to light up the poet's soul before the divine mystic spirit of song can awake in its power within him. So very early the next morning, the poet rose up and departed, with much rage in his heart. But as he passed the king's house he stopped, and in place of a blessing, pronounced a terrible malediction over Breas and his race, which can still be found in the ancient books of Ireland, commencing thus—

"Without fire, without bed, on the surface of the floor!

Without meat, without fowl, on the surface of the dish.

Three little dishes and no flesh thereon,

A cell without bed, a dish without meat, a cup without wine,
Are these fit offerings from a king to a poet?
May the king and his race be three times accursed for ever and for ever!"

Immediately three large blisters rose on the king's forehead, and remained there as a sign and mark of the poet's vengeance.

And from that day forth to his death, which happened not long after, the reign of Breas was a time of sore trouble and disaster, for he was three times defeated by his enemies, and from care and sorrow a grievous disease fell on him; for though hungry he could not swallow any food; and though all the meat and wine of the best was set before him, yet his throat seemed closed, and though raging with hunger yet not a morsel could pass his lips; and so he died miserably, starved in the midst of plenty, and accursed in all things by the power and malediction of the angry poet.

Drimial Agus Thorial
(A WICKED SPELL.)

When a girl wishes to gain the love of a man, and to make him marry her, the dreadful spell is used called *Drimial Agus Thorial*. At dead of night, she and an accomplice go to a churchyard, exhume a newly-buried corpse, and take a strip of the skin from the head to the heel. This is wound round the girl as a belt with a solemn invocation to the devil for his help.

After she has worn it for a day and a night she watches her opportunity and ties it round the sleeping man whose love she desires; during which process the name of God must not be mentioned.

When he awakes the man is bound by the spell; and is forced to marry the cruel and evil harpy. It is said the children of such marriages bear a black mark round the wrist, and are known and shunned by the people, who call them "sons of the devil."

An Irish Adept of the Islands

Some persons, even at the present day amongst the peasants, have strange gifts and a knowledge of the hidden mysteries, but they can only impart this knowledge when they know that death is on them, and then it must be to a female, to an unmarried man, or to a childless woman, for these are the most susceptible to the mysterious power by which miracles can be worked.

A man now living at Innis-Sark has this strange and mystic gift. He can heal diseases by a word, even at a distance, and his glance sees into the very heart, and reads the secret thoughts of men. He never touched beer, spirits, or meat, in all his life, but has lived entirely on bread, fruit, and vegetables. A man who knew him thus describes him—"Winter and summer his dress is the same, merely a flannel shirt and coat. He will pay his share at a feast, but neither eats nor drinks of the food and drink set before him. He speaks no English, and never could be made to learn the English tongue, though he says it might be used with great effect to curse one's enemy. He holds a burial-ground sacred, and would not carry away so much as a leaf of ivy from a grave. And he maintains that the people are right in keeping to their ancient usages, such as never to dig a grave on a Monday; and to carry the coffin three times round the grave, following the course of the sun, for then the dead rest in peace. Like the people, also, he holds suicides as accursed; for they believe that all the dead who have been recently buried turn over on their faces if a suicide is laid amongst them.

"Though well off he never, even in his youth, thought of taking a wife, nor was he ever known to love a woman. He stands quite apart from life, and by this means holds his power over the mysteries. No money will tempt him to impart this knowledge to another, for if he did he would be struck dead—so he believes. He would not touch a hazel stick, but carries an ash wand, which he holds in his hand when he prays, laid across his knees, and the whole of his life is devoted to works of grace and charity."

Though now an old man he has never had a day's sickness. No one has ever seen him in a rage, nor heard an angry word from his lips but once; and then being under great irritation, he recited the Lord's Prayer backwards, as an imprecation on his enemy. Before his death he will reveal the mystery of his power, but not till the hand of death is on him for certain.

The May Festival

There were four great festivals held in Ireland from the most ancient pagan times, and these four sacred seasons were February, May, Midsummer, and November. May was the most memorable and auspicious of all; then the Druids lit the *Baal-Tinne*, the holy, goodly fire of Baal, the Sun-god, and they drove the cattle on a path made between two fires, and singed them with the flame of a lighted torch, and sometimes they cut them to spill blood, and then burnt the blood as a sacred offering to the Sun-god.

The great feast of Bel, or the Sun, took place on May Eve; and that of Samhain, or the Moon, on November Eve; when libations were poured out to appease the evil spirits, and also the spirits of the dead, who come out of their graves on that night to visit their ancient homes.

The Phœnicians, it is known, adored the Supreme Being under the name of Bel-Samen, and it is remarkable that the peasants in Ireland, wishing you good luck, say in Irish, "The blessing of Bel, and the blessing of Samhain, be with you," that is, of the sun and of the moon.

These were the great festivals of the Druids, when all domestic fires were extinguished, in order to be re-lit by the sacred fire taken from the temples, for it was deemed sacrilege to have any fires kindled except from the holy altar flame.

St. Patrick, however, determined to break down the power of the Druids; and, therefore, in defiance of their laws, he had a great fire lit on May Eve, when he celebrated the paschal mysteries; and henceforth Easter, or the Feast of the Resurrection, took the place of the Baal festival.

The Baal fires were originally used for human sacrifices and burnt-offerings of the first-fruits of the cattle; but after Christianity was established the children and cattle were only passed between two fires for purification from sin, and as a safeguard against the power of the devil.

The Persians also extinguished the domestic fires on the Baal festival, the 21st of April, and were obliged to re-light them from the temple fires, for which the priests were paid a fee in silver money. A fire kindled by rubbing two pieces of wood together was also considered lucky by the Persians; then water was boiled over the flame, and afterwards sprinkled on the people and on the cattle. The ancient Irish ritual resembles the Persian in every particular, and the Druids, no doubt, held the traditional worship exactly as brought from the East, the land of the sun and of tree worship and well worship.

May Day, called in Irish *Là-Beltaine*, the day of the Baal fires, was the festival of greatest rejoicing held in Ireland. But the fairies have great power at that season, and children and cattle, and the milk and butter, must be well guarded from their influence. A spent coal must be put under the churn, and another under the cradle; and primroses must be scattered before the door, for the fairies cannot pass the flowers. Children that die in April are supposed to be carried off by the fairies, who are then always on the watch to abduct whatever is young and beautiful for their fairy homes.

Sometimes on the 1st of May, a sacred heifer, snow white, appeared amongst the cattle; and this was considered to bring the highest good luck to the farmer. An old Irish song that alludes to the heifer, may be translated thus—

"There is a cow on the mountain,
A fair white cow;
She goes East and she goes West,
And my senses have gone for love of her;
She goes with the sun and he forgets to burn,
And the moon turns her face with love to her,
My fair white cow of the mountain."

The fairies are in the best of humours upon May Eve, and the music of the fairy pipes may be heard all through the night, while the fairy folk are dancing upon the rath. It is then they carry off the young people to join their revels; and if a girl has once danced to the fairy music, she will move ever after with such fascinating grace, that it has passed into a proverb to say of a good dancer, "She has danced to fairy music on the hill."

At the great long dance held in old times on May Day, all the people held hands and danced round a great May-bush erected on a mound. The circle sometimes extended for a mile, the girls wearing garlands, and the young men carrying wands of green boughs, while the elder people sat round on the grass as spectators, and applauded the ceremony. The tallest and strongest young men in the county stood in the centre and directed the movements, while the pipers and harpers, wearing green and gold sashes, played the most spirited dance tunes.

The oldest worship of the world was of the sun and moon, of trees, wells, and the serpent that gave wisdom. Trees were the symbol of knowledge, and the dance round the May-bush is part of the ancient ophite ritual. The Baila also, or waltz, is associated with Baal worship, where the two circling motions are combined; the revolution of the planet on its own axis, and also round the sun.

In Italy, this ancient festival, called *Calendi Maggio*, is celebrated in the rural districts much in the Irish way. Dante fell in love at the great May Day festival, held in the Portinari Palace. The Sclavonic nations likewise light sacred fires, and dance round a tree hung with garlands on May Day. This reverence for the tree is one of the oldest superstitions of humanity and the most universal, and the fires are a relic of the old pagan worship paid to the Grynian Apollo—fire above all things being held sacred by the Irish as a safeguard from evil spirits. It is a saying amongst them, "Fire and salt are the two most sacred things given to man, and if you give them away on May Day, you give away your luck for the year." Therefore no one will allow milk, or fire, or salt, to be carried away from the house on that day; and if people came in and asked for a lighted sod, they would be driven away with curses, for their purpose was evil.

The witches, however, make great efforts to steal the milk on May morning, and if they succeed, the luck passes from the family, and the milk and butter for the whole year will belong to the fairies. The best preventative is to scatter primroses on the threshold; and the old women tie bunches of primroses to the cows' tails, for the evil spirits cannot touch anything guarded by these flowers, if they are plucked before sunrise, not else. A piece of iron, also, made red hot, is placed upon the hearth; any old iron will do, the older the better, and branches of whitethorn and mountain ash are wreathed round the doorway for luck. The mountain ash has very great and mysterious qualities. If a branch of it be woven into the roof, that house is safe from fire for a year at least, and if a branch of it is mixed with the timber of a boat, no storm will upset it, and no man in it will be drowned for a twelvemonth certain. To save milk from witchcraft, the people on May morning cut and peel some branches of the mountain ash, and bind the twigs round the milk pails and the churn. No witch or fairy will then be able to steal the milk or butter. But all this must be done *before sunrise*. However, should butter be missed, follow the cow to the field, and gather the clay her hoof has touched; then, on returning home, place it under the churn with a live coal and a handful of salt, and your butter is safe from man or woman, fairy or fiend, for that year. There are other methods also to preserve a good supply of butter in the churn; a horse-shoe tied on it; a rusty nail from a coffin driven into the side; a cross made of the leaves of veronica placed at the bottom of the milk pail; but the mountain ash is the best of all safeguards against witchcraft and devil's magic. Without some of these precautions the fairies will certainly overlook the churn, and the milk and butter, in consequence, will fail all through the year, and the farmer suffer great loss. Herbs gathered on May Eve have a mystical and strong virtue for curing disease; and powerful potions are made then by the skilful herb women and fairy doctors, which no sickness can resist, chiefly of the yarrow, called in Irish "the herb of seven needs" or cures, from its many and great virtues. Divination is also practised to a great extent by means of the yarrow. The girls dance round it singing—

"Yarrow, yarrow, yarrow,
I bid thee good morrow,
And tell me before to-morrow
Who my true love shall be."

The herb is then placed under the head at night, and in dreams the true lover will appear. Another mode of divination for the future fate in life is by snails. The young girls go out early before sunrise to trace the path of the snails in the clay, for always a letter is marked, and this is the initial of the true lover's name. A black snail is very unlucky to meet first in the morning, for his trail would read *death*; but a white snail brings good fortune. A white lamb on the right hand is also good; but the cuckoo is ominous of evil. Of old the year began with the 1st of May, and an ancient Irish rhyme says—

"A white lamb on my right side,
So will good come to me;
But not the little false cuckoo
On the first day of the year."

Prophecies were also made from the way the wind blew on May mornings. In '98 an old man, who was drawing near to his end and like to die, inquired from those around him—

"Where did you leave the wind last night?" (May Eve.)

They told him it came from the north.

"Then," he said, "the country is lost to the Clan Gael; our enemies will triumph. Had it been from the south, we should have had the victory; but now the Sassenach will trample us to dust." And he fell back and died.

Ashes are often sprinkled on the threshold on May Eve; and if the print of a foot is found in the morning, turned inward, it betokens marriage; but if turned outward, death. On May Eve the fairy music is heard on all the hills, and many beautiful tunes have been caught up in this way by the people and the native musicians.

About a hundred years ago a celebrated tune, called *Moraleana*, was learnt by a piper as he traversed the hills one evening; and he played it perfectly, note by note, as he heard it from the fairy pipes; on which a voice spoke to him and said that he would be allowed to play the tune *three times* in his life before all the people, but never a fourth, or a doom would fall on him. However, one day he had a great contest for supremacy with another piper, and at last, to make sure of victory, he played the wonderful fairy melody; when all the people applauded and declared he had won the prize by reason

142

of its beauty, and that no music could equal his. So they crowned him with the garland; but at that moment he turned deadly pale, the pipes dropped from his hand, and he fell lifeless to the ground. For nothing escapes the fairies; they know all things, and their vengeance is swift and sure.

It is very dangerous to sleep out in the open air in the month of May, for the fairies are very powerful then, and on the watch to carry off the handsome girls for fairy brides, and the young mothers as nurses for the fairy babies; while the young men are selected as husbands for the beautiful fairy princesses.

A young man died suddenly on May Eve while he was lying asleep under a hay-rick, and the parents and friends knew immediately that he had been carried off to the fairy palace in the great moat of Granard. So a renowned fairy man was sent for, who promised to have him back in nine days. Meanwhile he desired that food and drink of the best should be left daily for the young man at a certain place on the moat. This was done, and the food always disappeared, by which they knew the young man was living, and came out of the moat nightly for the provisions left for him by his people.

Now on the ninth day a great crowd assembled to see the young man brought back from Fairyland. And in the midst stood the fairy doctor performing his incantations by means of fire and a powder which he threw into the flames that caused a dense grey smoke to arise. Then, taking off his hat, and holding a key in his hand, he called out three times in a loud voice, "Come forth, come forth, come forth!" On which a shrouded figure slowly rose up in the midst of the smoke, and a voice was heard answering, "Leave me in peace; I am happy with my fairy bride, and my parents need not weep for me, for I shall bring them good luck, and guard them from evil evermore."

Then the figure vanished and the smoke cleared, and the parents were content, for they believed the vision, and having loaded the fairy-man with presents, they sent him away home.

May-Day Superstitions

The marsh marigold is considered of great use in divination, and is called "the shrub of Beltaine." Garlands are made of it for the cattle and the doorposts to keep off the fairy power. Milk also is poured on the threshold, though none would be given away; nor fire, nor salt—these three things being sacred. There are many superstitions concerning May-time. It is not safe to go on the water the first Monday in May. Hares found on May morning are supposed to be witches, and should be stoned.

If the fire goes out on May morning it is considered very unlucky, and it cannot be re-kindled except by a lighted sod brought from the priest's house. And the ashes of this blessed turf are afterwards sprinkled on the floor and the threshold of the house. Neither fire, nor water, nor milk, nor salt should be given away for love or money, and if a wayfarer is given a cup of milk, he must drink it in the house, and salt must be mixed with it. Salt and water as a drink is at all times considered a potent charm against evil, if properly prepared by a fairy doctor and the magic words said over it.

One day in May a young girl lay down to rest at noontide on a fairy rath and fell asleep—a thing of great danger, for the fairies are strong in power during the May month, and are particularly on the watch for a mortal bride to carry away to the fairy mansions, for they love the sight of human beauty. So they spirited away the young sleeping girl, and only left a shadowy resemblance of her lying on the rath. Evening came on, and as the young girl had not returned, her mother sent out messengers in all directions to look for her. At last she was found on the fairy rath, lying quite unconscious, like one dead.

They carried her home and laid her on her bed, but she neither spoke nor moved. So three days passed over. Then they thought it right to send for the fairy doctor. At once he said that she was fairy struck, and he gave them a salve made of herbs to anoint her hands and her brow every morning at sunrise, and every night when the moon rose; and salt was sprinkled on the threshold and round her bed where she lay sleeping. This was done for six days and six nights, and then the girl rose up suddenly and asked for food.

They gave her to eat, but asked no questions, only watched her that she should not quit the house. And then she fixed her eyes on them steadily and said—

"Why did you bring me back? I was so happy. I was in a beautiful palace where lovely ladies and young princes were dancing to the sweetest music; and they made me dance with them, and threw a mantle over me of rich gold; and now it is all gone, and you have brought me back, and I shall never, never see the beautiful palace more."

Then the mother wept and said—

"Oh, child, stay with me, for I have no other daughter, and if the fairies take you from me I shall die."

When the girl heard this, she fell on her mother's neck and kissed her, and promised that she would never again go near the fairy rath while she lived, for the fairy doctor told her that if ever she lay down there again and slept, she would never return alive to her home any more.

Festivals

Candlemas

Candlemas day, the 2nd of February, used to be held in the old pagan times as a kind of saturnalia, with dances and torches and many unholy rites. But these gave occasion to so much ill conduct that in the ninth century the Pope abolished the festival, and substituted for it the Feast of the Purification of the Blessed Virgin, when candles were lit in her honour. Hence the name of Candlemas.

Whitsuntide

Whitsuntide is a very fatal and unlucky time. Especially beware of water then, for there is an evil spirit in it, and no one should venture to bathe, nor to sail in a boat for fear of being drowned; nor to go a journey where water has to be crossed. And everything in the house must be sprinkled with holy water at Whitsuntide to keep away the fairies, who at that season are very active and malicious, and bewitch the cattle, and carry off the young children, and come up from the sea to hold strange midnight revels, when they kill with their fairy darts the unhappy mortal who crosses their path and pries at their mysteries.

Whitsuntide Legend of the Fairy Horses

There was a widow woman with one son, who had a nice farm of her own close to a lake, and she took great pains in the cultivation of the land, and her corn was the best in the whole country. But when nearly ripe, and just fit for cutting, she found to her dismay that every night it was trampled down and cruelly damaged; yet no one could tell by what means it was done.

So she set her son to watch. And at midnight he heard a great noise and a rushing of waves on the beach, and up out of the lake came a great troop of horses, who began to graze the corn and trample it down madly with their hoofs.

When he told all this to his mother she bade him watch the next night also, but to take several of the men with him furnished with bridles, and when the horses rose from the lake they were to fling the bridles over as many as they could catch.

Now at midnight there was the same noise heard again, and the rush of the waves, and in an instant all the field was filled with the fairy horses, grazing the corn and trampling it down. The men pursued them, but only succeeded in capturing one, and he was the noblest of the lot. The rest all plunged back into the lake. However, the men brought home the captured horse to the widow, and he was put in the stable and grew big and strong, and never another horse came up out of the lake, nor was the corn touched after that night of his capture. But when a year had passed by the widow said it was a shame to keep so fine a horse idle, and she bade the young man, her son, take him out to the hunt that was held that day by all the great gentry of the country, for it was Whitsuntide.

And, in truth, the horse carried him splendidly at the hunt, and every one admired both the fine young rider and his steed. But as he was returning

146

home, when they came within sight of the lake from which the fairy steed had risen, he began to plunge violently, and finally threw his rider. And the young man's foot being unfortunately caught in the stirrup, he was dragged along till he was torn limb from limb, while the horse still continued galloping on madly to the water, leaving some fragment of the unhappy lad after him on the road, till they reached the margin of the lake, when the horse shook off the last limb of the dead youth from him, and plunging into the waves disappeared from sight.

The people reverently gathered up the remains of the dead, and erected a monument of stones over the lad in a field by the edge of the lake; and every one that passes by still lays a stone and says a prayer that the spirit of the dead may rest in peace.

The phantom horses were never seen again, but the lake has an evil reputation even to this day amongst the people; and no one would venture a boat on it after sundown at Whitsuntide, or during the time of the ripening of the corn, or when the harvest is ready for the sickle, for strange sounds are heard at night, like the wild galloping of a horse across the meadow, along with the cries as of a man in his death agony.

November Spells

The ancient Irish divided the year into summer and winter—*Samrath* and *Gheimrath*; the former beginning in May, the latter in November, called also *Sam-fuim* (summer end). At this season, when the sun dies, the powers of darkness exercise great and evil influence over all things. The witch-women say they can then ride at night through the air with Diana of the Ephesians, and Herodias, and others leagued with the devil; and change men to beasts; and ride with the dead and cover leagues of ground on swift spirit-horses. Also on November Eve, by certain incantations, the dead can be made to appear and answer questions; but for this purpose blood must be sprinkled on the dead body when it rises; for it is said the spirits love blood. The colour excites them and gives them for the time the power and the semblance of life. Divination by fire, by earth, and by water, is also largely practised; but, as an ancient writer has observed, "All such divinations are accursed, for they are worked by the power of the fallen angels, who give knowledge only through malice, and to bring evil on the questioner. Neither should times and seasons be held lucky or unlucky, nor the course of the moon, nor the death of the sun, nor the so-called Egyptian days; for all things are blessed to a Christian. And this is the doctrine of the Holy Church, which all men should take to heart.... But a prayer to God, written fine, may be worn tyed round the neck, for this is done in a holy spirit, and is not against the ordinances of the Church."

The scapular here alluded to is a piece of cloth on which the name of Mary is written on one side and I.H.S. on the other. It preserves against evil spirits, and is a passport to heaven, and ensures against the pains of hell; for the Blessed Virgin takes the wearer under her especial care. It is placed in a little silk bag and worn tied round the neck, and is left upon the dead in their coffin for the angels to see at the resurrection. The scapular is never given to an evil liver, so it is a sign both of a pious life here and a blessed life hereafter.

November Eve

All the spells worked on November Eve are performed in the name of the devil, who is then forced to reveal the future fate of the questioner. The most usual spell is to wash a garment in a running brook, then hang it on a thorn bush, and wait to see the apparition of the lover, who will come to turn it. But the tricks played on this night by young persons on each other have often most disastrous consequences. One young girl fell dead with fright when an apparition really came and turned the garment she had hung on the bush. And a lady narrates that on the 1st of November her servant rushed into the room and fainted on the floor. On recovering, she said that she had played a trick that night in the name of the devil before the looking-glass; but what she had seen she dared not speak of, though the remembrance of it would never leave her brain, and she knew the shock would kill her. They tried to laugh her out of her fears, but the next night she was found quite dead, with her features horribly contorted, lying on the floor before the looking-glass, which was shivered to pieces.

Another spell is the building of the house. Twelve couples are taken, each being made of two holly twigs tied together with a hempen thread; these are all named and stuck round in a circle in the clay. A live coal is then placed in the centre, and whichever couple catches fire first will assuredly be married. Then the future husband is invoked in the name of the Evil One to appear and quench the flame.

On one occasion a dead man in his shroud answered the call, and silently drew away the girl from the rest of the party. The fright turned her brain, and she never recovered her reason afterwards. The horror of that apparition haunted her for ever, especially as on November Eve it is believed firmly that the dead really leave their graves and have power to appear amongst the living.

*

A young girl in a farmer's service was in the loft one night looking for eggs when two men came into the stable underneath, and through a chink in the boards she could see them quite well and hear all they said. To her horror she found that they were planning the murder of a man in the neighbourhood who was suspected of being an informer, and they settled how they would get rid of the body by throwing it into the Shannon. She crept home half dead with fright, but did not venture to tell any one what she had heard. Next day, however, the news spread that the man was missing, and it was feared he was murdered. Still the girl was afraid to reveal what she knew, though the ghost of the murdered man seemed for ever before her. Finally she could bear the place no longer, and, giving up her situation, she went to another village some miles off and took service. But on November Eve, as she was washing clothes in the Shannon, the dead body of the murdered man arose from the water and floated towards her, until it lay quite close to her feet. Then she knew the hand of God was in it, and that the spirit of the dead would not rest till he was avenged. So she went and gave information, and on her evidence the two murderers were convicted and executed.

*

If the cattle fall sick at this season, it is supposed that some old fairy man or woman is lying hid about the place to spy out the doings of the family and work some evil spells.

A farmer had a splendid cow, the pride of his farm, but suddenly it seemed ailing and gave no milk, though every morning it went and stood quite patiently under an old hawthorn-tree as if some one were milking her. So the man watched the time, and presently the cow came of herself and stood under the hawthorn, when a little old wizened woman came forth from the trunk of the tree, milked the cow, and then retreated into the tree again. On this the farmer sent at once for a fairy doctor, who exorcised the cow and gave it a strong potion, after which the spell was broken and the cow was restored to its usual good condition and gave the milk as heretofore.

*

The fairies also exercise a malign influence by making a path through a house, when all the children begin to pine and a blight falls on the family.

A farmer who had lost one son by heart disease (always a mysterious malady to the peasants) and another by gradual decay, consulted a wise fairy woman as to what should be done, for his wife also had become delicate and weak. The woman told him that on November Eve the fairies had made a road through the house, and were going back and forward ever since, and whatever they looked upon was doomed. The only remedy was to build up the old door and open another entrance. This the man did, and when the witch-women came as usual in the morning to beg for water or milk or meal they found no door, and were obliged to turn back. After this the spell was taken off the household, and they all prospered without fear of the fairies.

A Terrible Revenge
The fairies often take a terrible revenge if they are ever slighted or offended. A whole family once came under their ban because a fairy woman had been refused admittance into the house. The eldest boy lost his sight for some

time, and though he recovered the use of his eyes yet they always had a strange expression, as if he saw some terrible object in the distance that scared him. And at last the neighbours grew afraid of the family, for they brought ill-luck wherever they went, and nothing prospered that they touched.

There were six children, all wizened little creatures with withered old faces and thin crooked fingers. Every one knew they were fairy changelings, and the smith wanted to put them on the anvil, and the wise women said they should be passed through the fire; but destiny settled the future for them, for one after another they all pined away and died, and the ban of the fairies was never lifted from the ill-fated house till the whole family lay in the grave.

Midsummer

The Baal Fires and Dances

This season is still made memorable in Ireland by lighting fires on every hill, according to the ancient pagan usage, when the Baal fires were kindled as part of the ritual of sun-worship, though now they are lit in honour of St. John. The great bonfire of the year is still made on St. John's Eve, when all the people dance round it, and every young man takes a lighted brand from the pile to bring home with him for good luck to the house.

In ancient times the sacred fire was lighted with great ceremony on Midsummer Eve; and on that night all the people of the adjacent country kept fixed watch on the western promontory of Howth, and the moment the first flash was seen from that spot the fact of ignition was announced with wild cries and cheers repeated from village to village, when all the local fires began to blaze, and Ireland was circled by a cordon of flame rising up from every hill. Then the dance and song began round every fire, and the wild hurrahs filled the air with the most frantic revelry.

Many of these ancient customs are still continued, and the fires are still lighted on St. John's Eve on every hill in Ireland. When the fire has burned down to a red glow the young men strip to the waist and leap over or through the flames; this is done backwards and forwards several times, and he who braves the greatest blaze is considered the victor over the powers of evil, and is greeted with tremendous applause. When the fire burns still lower, the young girls leap the flame, and those who leap clean over three times back and forward will be certain of a speedy marriage and good luck in after life, with many children. The married women then walk through the lines of the burning embers; and when the fire is nearly burnt and trampled down, the yearling cattle are driven through the hot ashes, and their back is singed with a lighted hazel twig. These hazel rods are kept safely afterwards, being considered of immense power to drive the cattle to and from the watering places. As the fire diminishes the shouting grows fainter, and the song and the dance commence; while professional story-tellers narrate tales of fairy-land, or of the good old times long ago, when the kings and princes of Ireland dwelt amongst their own people, and there was food to eat and wine to drink for all comers to the feast at the king's house. When the crowd at length separate, every one carries home a brand from the fire, and great virtue is attached to the lighted *brone* which is safely carried to the house without breaking or falling to the ground. Many contests also arise amongst the young men; for whoever enters his house first with the sacred fire brings the good luck of the year with him.

On the first Sunday in Midsummer all the young people used to stand in lines after leaving chapel, to be hired for service—the girls holding white hands, the young men each with an emblem of his trade. The evening ended with a dance and the revelry was kept up until the dawn of the next day, called "Sorrowful Monday," because of the end of the pleasure and the frolic.

The Fairy Doctress

But all this time the fairies were not idle; for it was at this very season of dances and festivals, when the mortals around them were happiest, that Finvarra the king and his chosen band were on the watch to carry off the prettiest girls to the fairy mansions.

There they kept them for seven years, and at the end of that time, when they grew old and ugly, they were sent back, for the fairies love nothing so much as youth and beauty. But as a compensation for the slight put on them, the women were taught all the fairy secrets and the magical mystery that lies in herbs, and the strange power they have over diseases. So by this means the women became all-powerful, and by their charms or spells or potions could kill or save as they chose.

There was a woman of the islands greatly feared, yet respected by the people for her knowledge of herbs, which gave her power over all diseases. But she never revealed the nature of the herb, and always gathered the leaves herself at night and hid them under the eaves of the house. And if the person who carried the herb home let it fall to the ground by the way, it lost its power; or if they talked of it or showed it to any one, all the virtue went out of it. It was to be used secretly and alone, and then the cure would be perfected without fail.

One time, a man who was told of this came over from the mainland in a boat with two other men to see the fairy woman; for he was lame from a fall and could do no work.

Now the woman knew they were coming, for she had a knowledge of all things through the power of divination she had learned from the fairies, and could see and hear though no man told her. So she went out and prepared the herb, and made a salve and brewed a potion, and had all ready for the man and his friends.

When they appeared she stood at the door and cried, "Enter! This is the lucky day and hour; have no fear, for you will be cured by the power that is in me, and by the herb I give you."

Then the man bowed down before her, and said, "Oh, mother, this is my case." And he told her, that being out one day on the mountains, he slipped and fell on his face. A mere slight fall, but when he rose up his leg was powerless though no bone seemed broken.

"I know how it happened," she said. "You trod upon a fairy herb under which the fairies were resting, and you disturbed them and broke in the top of their dwelling, so they were angry and struck you on the leg and lamed you out of spite. But my power is greater than theirs. Do as I tell you and you will soon be cured."

So she gave him the salve and the bottle of potion, and bade him take it home carefully and use it in silence and alone, and in three days the power of the limb would come back to him.

Then the man offered her silver; but she refused.

"I do not sell my knowledge," she said, "I give it. And so the strength and the power remain with me."

On this the men went their way. But after three days a message came from the man to say that he was cured. And he sent the wise woman a handsome present also; for a gift works no evil, though to sell the sacred power and mysteries of knowledge for money would be fatal; for then the spirit of healing that dwelt in the woman would have fled away and returned no more.

Marriage Rites

In old times in Ireland it was thought right and proper to seem to use force in carrying off the bride to her husband. She was placed on a swift horse before the bridegroom, while all her kindred started in pursuit with shouts and cries. Twelve maidens attended the bride, and each was placed on horseback behind the young men who rode after the bridal pair. On arriving at her future home, the bride was met on the threshold by the bridegroom's mother, who broke an oaten cake over her head as a good augury of plenty in the future. In the mountains where horses cannot travel, the bridal party walk in procession; the young men carrying torches of dried bogwood to light the bride over the ravines, for in winter the mountain streams are rapid and dangerous to cross.

The Celtic ceremonial of marriage resembles the ancient Greek ritual in many points. A traveller in Ireland some fifty years ago, before politics had quite killed romance and ancient tradition in the hearts of the people, thus describes a rustic marriage festival which he came on by chance one evening in the wilds of Kerry:—

A large hawthorn tree that stood in the middle of a field near a stream was hung all over with bits of coloured stuff, while lighted rush candles were placed here and there amongst the branches, to symbolize, no doubt, the new life of brightness preparing for the bridal pair. Then came a procession of boys marching slowly with flutes and pipes made of hollow reeds, and one struck a tin can with a stick at intervals, with a strong rhythmical cadence. This represented the plectrum. Others rattled slates and bones between their fingers, and beat time, after the manner of the Crotolistrai—a rude attempt at music, which appears amongst all nations of the earth, even the most savage. A boy followed, bearing a lighted torch of bogwood. Evidently he was Hymen, and the flame of love was his cognizance. After him came the betrothed pair hand-in-hand, a large square canopy of black stuff being held over their heads; the emblem, of course, of the mystery of love, shrouded and veiled from the prying light of day.

Behind the pair followed two attendants bearing high over the heads of the young couple a sieve filled with meal; a sign of the plenty that would be in their house, and an omen of good luck and the blessing of children.

A wild chorus of dancers and singers closed the procession; the chorus of the epithalamium, and grotesque figures, probably the traditional fauns and satyrs, nymphs and bacchanals, mingled together with mad laughter and shouts and waving of green branches.

The procession then moved on to a bonfire, evidently the ancient altar; and having gone round it three times, the black shroud was lifted from the bridal pair, and they kissed each other before all the people, who shouted and waved their branches in approval.

Then the preparations for the marriage supper began, on which, however, the traveller left them, having laid some money on the altar as an offering of good-will for the marriage future. At the wedding supper there was always plenty of eating and drinking, and dancing and the feast were prolonged till near morning, when the wedding song was sung by the whole party of friends standing, while the bride and bridegroom remained seated at the head of the table. The chorus of one of these ancient songs may be thus literally translated from the Irish—

"It is not day, nor yet day,
It is not day, nor yet morning;
It is not day, nor yet day,
For the moon is shining brightly."

Another marriage song was sung in Irish frequently, each verse ending with the lines—

"There is sweet enchanting music, and the golden harps are ringing;
And twelve comely maidens deck the bride-bed for the bride."

A beautiful new dress was presented to the bride by her husband at the marriage feast; at which also the father paid down her dowry before the assembled guests; and all the place round the house was lit by torches when night came on, and the song and the dance continued till daylight, with much speech-making and drinking of poteen. All fighting was steadily avoided at a wedding; for a quarrel would be considered a most unlucky omen. A wet day was also held to be very unlucky, as the bride would assuredly weep for sorrow throughout the year. But the bright warm sunshine was hailed joyfully, according to the old saying—

"Happy is the bride that the sun shines on;
But blessed is the corpse that the rain rains on."

The Dead

There are many strange superstitions concerning the dead. The people seem to believe in their actual presence, though unseen, and to have a great fear and dread of their fatal and mysterious power.

If a person of doubtful character dies, too bad for heaven, too good for hell, they imagine that his soul is sent back to earth, and obliged to obey the order of some person who bids him remain in a particular place until the Day of Judgment, or until another soul is found willing to meet him there, and then they may both pass into heaven together, absolved.

An incident is related that happened in the County Galway, concerning this superstition.

Lady Jane Francesca Agnes Wilde

A gentleman of rank and fortune, but of a free and dissipated life, became the lover of a pretty girl, one of the tenant's daughters. And the girl was so devoted to him that perhaps he might have married her at last; but he was killed suddenly, when out hunting, by a fall from his horse.

Some time after, the girl, coming home late one evening, met the ghost of her lover, at a very lonesome part of the road. The form was the same as when living, but it had no eyes. The girl crossed herself, on which the ghost disappeared.

Again she met the same apparition at night, and a third time, when the ghost stood right before her in the path, so that she could not pass. Then she spoke, and asked in the name of God and the good angels, why he appeared to her; and he answered, that he could not rest in his grave till he had received some command from her, which he was bound to obey.

"Then," she said, "go stand by the gate of heaven till the Judgment Day, and look in at the blessed dead on their thrones, but you may not enter. This is my judgment on your soul."

On this the ghost sighed deeply and vanished, and was seen no more. But the girl prayed earnestly that she soon might meet her lover at the gate of heaven, whither she had sent him, that so both might enter together into the blessed land. And thus it happened; for by that day year she was carried to her grave in the churchyard, but her soul went forth to meet her lover, where he waited for her by the gate of heaven; and through her love he was absolved, and permitted to enter within the gate before the Judgment Day.

*

It was considered disrespectful to the dead to take a short cut when carrying the coffin to the grave.

*

In the Islands, when a person is dying, they place twelve lighted rushes round the bed. This, they say, is to prevent the devil coming for the soul; for nothing evil can pass a circle of fire. They also forbid crying for the dead until three hours have passed by, lest the wail of the mourners should waken the dogs who are waiting to devour the souls of men before they can reach the throne of God.

*

It is a very general custom during some nights after a death to leave food outside the house—a griddle cake, or a dish of potatoes. If it is gone in the morning, the spirits must have taken it; for no human being would touch the food left for the dead.

*

The great and old families of Ireland consider it right to be buried with their kindred, and are brought from any distance, however remote, to be laid in the ancient graveyard of the race.

A young man of family having died far away, from fever, it was thought advisable not to bring him home, but to bury him where he died. However, on the night of the funeral a phantom hearse with four black horses stopped at the churchyard. Some men then entered with spades and shovels and dug a grave, after which the hearse drove away. But next morning no sign of the grave was to be found, except a long line marked out, the length of a man's coffin.

*

It is unlucky and a bad omen to carry fire out of a house where any one is ill. A gentleman one day stopped at a cabin to get a light for his cigar, and having wished good morning in the usual friendly fashion, he took a stick from the fire, blew it into a blaze, and was walking away, when the woman of the house rose up fiercely and told him it was an evil thing to take fire away when her husband was dying. On looking round he saw a wretched skeleton lying on a bed of straw; so he flung back the stick at once, and fled from the place, leaving his blessing in the form of a silver offering, to neutralize the evil of the abducted fire.

*

After the priest has left a dying person, and confession has been made, all the family kneel round the bed reciting the Litany for the Dying, and holy water is sprinkled over the room until the soul departs.

Then they all rise and begin the mournful death-wail in a loud voice; and by this cry all the people in the village know the exact moment of the death, and each one that hears it utters a prayer for the departing soul.

At the wake the corpse is often dressed in the habit of a religious order. A cross is placed in the hands and the scapular on the breast. Candles are lighted all round in a circle, and the friends and relatives arrange themselves in due order, the nearest of kin being at the head. At intervals they all stand up and intone the death-wail, rocking back and forward over the dead, and reciting his virtues; while the widow and orphans frequently salute the corpse with endearing epithets, and recall the happy days they spent together.

When the coffin is borne to the grave each person present helps to carry it a little way; for this is considered a mode of showing honour to the dead. The nearest relatives take the front handles first; then after a little while they move to the back and others take their place, until every person in turn has borne the head of the coffin to the grave—for it would be dishonourable to the dead to omit this mark of respect.

As the coffin is lowered into the grave the death-cry rises up with a loud and bitter wail, and the excitement often becomes so great that women have fallen into hysterics; and at one funeral a young girl in her agony of grief jumped into her father's grave and was taken up insensible.

The Wake Orgies

From ancient times the wakes, or funeral games, in Ireland were held with many strange observances carried down by tradition from the pagan era. Some of the rites, however, were so revolting and monstrous that the priesthood used all their influence to put them down. The old funeral customs, in consequence, have now been discontinued almost entirely amongst the people, and the ancient traditional usages are unknown to the new generation, though the elders of the village can yet remember them. An old man still living thus described to an inquiring antiquary and lover of folk-lore, his experience of the ceremonial of a wake at which he had been present in the South of Ireland, when he was quite a youth, some fifty years before.

"One dark winter's night, about seven o'clock, a large party of us," he said, "young men and women, perhaps thirty or more, set out across the mountain to attend a wake at the house of a rich farmer, about three miles off. All the young men carried lighted torches, for the way was rugged and dangerous; and by their light we guided the women as best we could over the deep clefts and across the rapid streams, swollen by the winter's rain. The girls took off their shoes and stockings and walked barefoot, but where the water was heavy and deep the men carried them across in their arms or on their backs. In this way we all arrived at last at the farmhouse, and found a great assemblage in the large barn, which was hung throughout with branches of evergreen and festoons of laurel and holly.

"At one end of the barn, on a bed decorated with branches of green leaves, lay the corpse, an old woman of eighty, the mother of the man of the house. He stood by the head of the dead woman, while all the near relatives had seats round. Then the mourning women entered and sat down on the ground in a circle, one in the centre cloaked and hooded, who began the chant or funeral wail, all the rest joining in chorus. After an interval there would come a deep silence; then the chant began again, and when it was over the women rose up and went out, leaving the place free for the next comers, who acted a play full of ancient symbolic meaning. But, first, whisky was served round, and the pipers played; for every village had sent their best player and singer to honour the wake.

"When a great space was cleared in the centre of the barn, the first set of players entered. They wore masks and fantastic garments, and each carried a long spear and a bit of plaited straw on the arm for a shield. At once they began to build a fort, as it were, marking out the size with their spears, and using some rough play with the spectators. While thus engaged a band of enemies appeared, also masked and armed. And now a great fight began and many prisoners were taken; but to save slaughter a horn was blown, and a fight demanded between the two best champions of the hostile forces. Two of the finest young men were then selected and placed at opposite ends of the barn, when they ran a tilt against one another with their spears, uttering fierce, loud cries, and making terrible demonstrations. At length one fell down as if mortally wounded; then all the hooded women came in again and keened over him, a male voice at intervals reciting his deeds, while the pipers played martial tunes. But on its being suggested that perhaps he was not dead at all, an herb doctor was sent for to look at him; and an aged man with a flowing white beard was led in, carrying a huge bundle of herbs. With these he performed sundry strange incantations, until finally the dead man sat up and was carried off the field by his comrades, with shouts of triumph. So ended the first play.

"Then supper was served and more whisky drunk, after which another play was acted of a different kind. A table was set in the middle of the barn, and two chairs, while all the people, about a hundred or more, gathered round in a circle. Then two men, dressed as judges, took their seats, with guards beside them, and called on another man to come forth and address the people. On this a young man sprang on the table and poured forth an oration in Irish, full of the most grotesque fun and sharp allusions, at which the crowd roared with laughter. Then he gave out a verse like a psalm, in gibberish Irish, and bade the people say it after him. It ran like this, being translated—

"'Yellow Macauly has come from Spain,
He brought sweet music out of a bag,
Sing *See-saw, Sulla Vick Dhau,*
Sulla, Sulla Vick Dhau righ.'
(That is, Solomon, son of David the King.)

"If any one failed to repeat this verse after him he was ordered to prison by the judges, and the guards seized him to cut off his head; or if any one laughed the judge sentenced him, saying in Irish, 'Seize that man, he is a pagan: he is mocking the Christian faith. Let him die!'

"After this the professional story-teller was in great force, and held the listeners enchained by the wonders of his narration and the passionate force of his declamation. So the strange revelry went on, and the feasting and the drinking, till sunrise, when many of the guests returned to their homes, but others stayed with the family till the coffin was lifted for the grave."

*

Full details of these strange wake orgies can seldom be obtained, for the people are afraid of the priesthood, who have vehemently denounced them. Yet the peasants cling to them with a mysterious reverence, and do not see the immorality of many of the wake practices. They accept them as mysteries, ancient usages of their forefathers, to be sacredly observed, or the vengeance of the dead would fall on them.

According to all accounts an immense amount of dramatic talent was displayed by the actors of these fantastic and symbolic plays. An intelligent peasant, who was brought to see the acting at the Dublin theatre, declared on his return: "I have now seen the great English actors, and heard plays in the English tongue, but poor and dull they seemed to me after the acting of our own people at the wakes and fairs; for it is a truth, the English cannot make us weep and laugh as I have seen the crowds with us when the players played and the poets recited their stories."

The Celts certainly have a strong dramatic tendency, and there are many peasant families in Ireland who have been distinguished for generations as bards and actors, and have a natural and hereditary gift for music and song.

On the subject of wake orgies, a clever writer observes that they are evidently a remnant of paganism, and formed part of those Druidic rites meant to propitiate the evil spirits and the demons of darkness and doom; for the influence of Druidism lasted long after the establishment of Christianity. The Druid priests took shelter with the people, and exercised a powerful and mysterious sway over them by their magic spells. Druid practices were known to exist down to the time of the Norman invasion in the twelfth century, and even for centuries after; and to this Druidic influence may be traced the sarcasms on Christianity which are occasionally introduced into the mystery plays of the wake ceremonial. As in the one called "Hold the Light," where the passion of the Lord Christ is travestied with grotesque imitation. The same writer describes the play acted at wakes called "The Building of the Ship," a symbolic rite still older than Druidism, and probably a remnant of the primitive Arkite worship. This was followed by a scene called "Drawing the Ship out of the Mud." It was against these two plays that the anathemas of the Church were chiefly directed, in consequence of their gross immorality, and they have now entirely ceased to form any portion of the wake ceremonial of Ireland. Hindu priests would recognize some of the ceremonies as the same which are still practised in their own temples; and travellers have traced a similarity also in these ancient usages to the "big canoe games" of the Mandan Indians.

In the next play, the Hierophant, or teacher of the games, orders all the men out of the room; a young girl is then dressed with a hide thrown over her, and horns on her head, to simulate a cow, while her maidens form a circle and slowly dance round her to music, on which a loud knocking is heard at the door. "Who wants to enter?" asks the Hierophant. He is answered, "The guards demand admittance for the bull who is without." Admittance is refused, and the maidens and the cow affect great alarm. Still the knocking goes on, and finally the door is burst open and the bull enters. He also is robed with a hide and wears horns, and is surrounded by a band of young men as his guards. He endeavours to seize the cow, who is defended by her maidens, forming the dramatic incidents of the play. A general mock fight now takes place between the guards and the maidens, and the scene ends with uproarious hilarity and the capture of the cow.

There are other practices mentioned by writers on the subject, who trace in the Irish observances a tradition of the Cabyric rites, and also a striking similarity to the idolatrous practices of Hindustan as described in the "Asiatic Researches," and in Moore's "Hindu Pantheon."

It is remarkable also that in the Polynesian Islands the funeral rites were accompanied by somewhat similar ceremonies. These the early missionaries viewed with horror, and finally succeeded in extirpating them.

These ancient funeral rites have now disappeared in Ireland; still the subject remains one of intense interest to the ethnologist and antiquary, who will find in the details indications of the oldest idolatries of the world, especially of that primitive religion called Arkite, as in the dramatic performance called "The Building of the Ship," where one man prostrates himself on the ground as the ship, while two others sit head and foot to represent the prow and stern. This ship drama is, perhaps, a fragment of the earliest tradition of humanity represented by a visible symbol to illustrate the legend of the Deluge.

The Ancient Mysteries

Ireland, from its remote position and immunity from Roman conquest, remained longer in the possession of the Druidic mysteries than any other nation of Europe. Besides, the early missionaries adopted no intolerant measures against the ancient creed; no persecutions are recorded. The sacred trees were not cut down, nor the sacrificial stones destroyed; but the holy wells and the antique monuments were sanctified by association with a saint's name and history, and from being objects of pagan idolatry became shrines of prayer and centres of holy worship, where enlightened men preached the new gospel of light, purity, and love to an awe-struck, wondering multitude.

To this tolerant policy, as Mr. Windell, the learned antiquary, remarks, may be attributed the strong endurance of Druidic superstitions and usages in Ireland. Much also is due to the peculiar and truly Oriental tenacity with which the Irish at all times have clung to the customs and traditions of their forefathers. The belief in a fairy race ever present amongst them and around them, is one of these ineffaceable superstitions which the people still hold with a faith as fervent as those of the first Aryan tribes who wandered westward from the mystic East, where all creeds, symbols, and myths had their origin.

Many other broken fragments of the early ritual of the world can also still be traced in the popular superstitions and usages of the people. The sun and moon with the mysterious powers of nature were the first gods of humanity. Astarte, Ashtaroth, and Isis were all the same moon-goddess under different names, and all were represented by the symbol of the horned cow. The Egyptians typified the sun and moon, Osiris and Isis, as the ox and the cow; and these symbols were still used at the Irish wake ceremonial until very recently: for the Druids also worshipped the sun and moon and the winds, and venerated trees, fountains, rivers, and pillar stones, like their Persian ancestry. But the Irish considered the east wind demoniacal, the Druidic wind of accursed power. They called it "The Red Wind," "A wind that blasts the trees and withers men is that Red Wind," according to a bard.

The Hindus had their triad of Brahm , Vishnu, and Siva, representing the sun at morning, noon, and evening; so the Irish Druids had their triad of Baal, Budh, and Grian, and they called the May festival *Lá Budha na Baal tinne* (the day of Buddha of the Baal fires). Chrishna was another Hindu name for the sun, and the Irish had Crias, a name for the sun likewise.

The Hindus had their cattle, or cow festival in spring, when they walked round the animals with great ceremony, always going westward, while they flung garlands on their horns. So in Ireland there was also a procession, when the cows were decorated with vervain and the rowan, and were sprinkled with the *Sgaith-an-Tobar* (the purity of the well), that is, the first water drawn from a sacred well after midnight on May Eve. This was considered an effective antidote to witchcraft, and whoever succeeded in being first at the well, cast into it a tuft of grass, called *Cuisheag grass*, to show that the *Sgaith-an-Tobar* had been abstracted. So also the Hindus esteem the *Cusha grass* as sacred, and cast it into their wells for a like purpose. The ceremonial of wreathing the horns of the cows was in honour of the moon, the wife of the Sun-god, whose emblem, as we know, all through the East, as in Ireland, was the horned cow.

Many and strange, indeed, are the analogies between the practices of the Egyptians, Hindus, Persians, and the Irish; and the legend may, after all, have some truth in it which brings the first Colonists of Ireland from Egypt, and makes the first Queen of Erin a daughter of Pharaoh. The ancient war-cry of the Irish clans was *Pharrah!* a word that has no significance in the Irish language, but which is supposed by some antiquarians to be the same as *Phi-Ra*, the sun—the regal title of the Egyptian kings, by which they were invoked by the warriors as they rushed into battle.

The ancient funeral ceremonies of Egypt can be still seen and studied at the wake of an Irish peasant; especially in that singular symbol, when a man and a woman appeared, one bearing the head of an ox, the other that of a cow at the funeral games; a custom which has now lost all its meaning, but which originally, no doubt, represented Isis and Osiris waiting to receive the soul of the dead.

The Persians held that fire and water were the most sacred of all things and so did the Irish; hence their reverence for the waters of purification at the holy wells. And as the heathen passed their children and cattle through the fire to Moloch, so the Irish performed the same rite at the Baal festival, when the young men leaped through the flames, and the cattle were driven through the hot embers. Fire was held to be the visible symbol of the invisible God, endowed with mystic cleansing powers, and the ascending flame was thought to be a divine spirit dwelling in the substance ignited. For this reason the Irish made a circle of fire round their children and their cattle to guard them from evil, holding the belief that no evil spirit could pass this special emblem of divinity.

But even in matters less divine there was a similarity between the Persian and Irish usages. The Persian Magi made a considerable revenue from the sacred fire; for each devotee paid a silver coin for the ember carried away from the holy temple, to light the home fire on the day of the Sun-festival. And fire was also a source of wealth to the Druid priests; each person being obliged to buy it from them on the great day of Baal. Therefore it was a sin to give away fire on that day; and the habit of borrowing it to light the home fire was denounced as fatal and unlucky. The true reason being that to borrow the sacred element was to injure the priestly revenue. Yet this ancient ordinance is still religiously observed in Ireland; and even to this day no peasant would venture to give away fire or milk on May Day, for fear of the worst consequences to the giver; while any one who came to borrow a lighted brand would be looked on as an emissary of Satan.

The sacred fire of Tara (*Tamhair-na-Righ*, Tara of the Kings) was only lit every three years, and then with great ceremony. The sun's rays were concentrated by means of a brazen lens, on some pieces of dried wood, and from this alone were all the sacred fires in Ireland kindled in the holy places.

Lady Jane Francesca Agnes Wilde

At the present time, if a peasant has to light a fire in the house on May morning, which does not often happen, as the custom is to keep the fire burning all night, a lighted sod taken from the priest's house is esteemed of great virtue and sacredness, just as in old time a lighted brand from the altar of Baal was used to light the domestic fire.

The sacred fire was also obtained from the friction of wood, or the striking of stones; and it was supposed that the spirits of fire dwelt in these objects, and when the priest invoked them to appear, they brought good luck to the household for the coming year; but if invoked by other hands on that special day their influence was malific.

The migration of races can be clearly traced by their superstitions. The oldest seem to have come from Persia and Egypt; while mutilated, though still authentic portions of the old-world ritual can still be found all along the Mediterranean, marking the westward progress of the primitive nations, till the last wave found a resting-place on our own far-distant shores, washed by the waters of the Atlantic.

Assyria was the teacher of Egypt; Egypt of Greece; and Greece of Europe; and little seems to have been lost during the progress of sixty centuries. The old myths still remain at the base of all thought and all creeds; broken fragments of the primal faith; shadowy traditions of some great human life that once was real and actual, or of some great event that changed the destiny of nations, and the echo of which still vibrates through the legends, the songs, the poetry, and the usages of every people on the face of the earth.

Persia, Egypt, India, the Teuton, and the Celt, have all the same primal ideas in their mythology, and the same instincts of superstition; and the signs to which past ages have given a mystic meaning still come to us laden with a fateful significance, even in this advanced era of culture and the triumph of reason.

We still cannot help believing that prophecies come in the night, for the mystical and prophetic nature of dreams is confirmed by the personal experience of almost every human being; and few are found brave enough, even amongst the educated classes, lightly to break through a traditional usage on which all the ages have set the seal of good or ill luck.

Superstition, or the belief in unseen, mysterious, spiritual influences, is an instinct of human nature. A vague, shadowy, formless belief, certainly, yet ineradicable. We feel that our dual humanity, the material as well as the psychical, holds some strange and mystic relation with an unseen spiritual world, though we cannot define the limits, nor bring it under a law.

Before the written word existed, the people strove to express their creed and history in symbols. Divine nations, like the Greeks, made the symbols beautiful, and these the uncultured tribes may afterwards have distorted into grotesque and rude imitations; but the same idea can be traced through all forms by which humanity has tried to represent history, nature, and God.

And the old Pagan customs of the early world seem to have an enduring vitality, and to have become fixed, even in the usages of the enlightened nineteenth century. The Persian Magi and the Druid priest exacted a tribute of the firstlings of the flock as a burnt-offering to the Sun-god on the day of his festival; so in modern times, we sacrifice a lamb at Easter and an ox at Christmas, retaining the pagan rite while we honour the Christian legend. The Christmas-tree is still lighted to guide the Sun-god back to life; and the spotted cake, anciently made in his honour, of corn and fruit, still finds its place on our tables, as the plum pudding of civilization, even as its primitive prototype was laid on the sacred altars of the Persians as an offering of gratitude to the Lord of Light and Life.

The widespread range of the same traditional customs and superstitions amongst all peoples and through every age is a most interesting study, as showing the primitive unity of the human race and the subsequent divergence of the nations, even as recorded in the Biblical narrative; but it would be endless to follow the lines of affinity that run through all the creeds, legends, usages and superstitions of the world. Thus the Algonquil Indians, according to Mr. Leland, held the ash-tree and the elm as sacred and mystical, because these trees were made human. Of the ash was made man, of the elm, woman.

So in the Edda, we read of the mighty ash-tree whose summit reaches to heaven, and whose roots go down to hell. Two fountains sprang from beneath it—one the knowledge of all that is; the other of all that shall be. And out of the wood man was created.

The Irish also hold the ash-tree as all-powerful against witchcraft; therefore branches of it were wreathed rounds the horns of the cattle, and round the child's cradle to keep off evil influence; while in all their weird tales of the fairy dances with the dead, the mortals drawn into their company are infallibly safe if they get possession of a branch of the ash-tree, and hold it safely till out of reach of the evil spell.

The alder is another of the mystical trees of Ireland, held sacred, as in Persia, on account of its possessing strange mysterious properties and powers to avert evil; and the hawthorn likewise was sacred to the Irish fairies, therefore a libation of milk was poured over the roots on May Day, as the Hindus poured milk on the earth round the sacred tree as an offering to the manes of the dead.

In the Transylvanian legends and superstitions, of which Madame Gerard has recently given an interesting record, many will be found identical with the Irish; such as these—Friday is the most unlucky day of all the week; evil spirits are strongest between sunset and midnight; it is ill-luck to have your path crossed by a hare; on entering a strange house sit down a moment, or a death will happen; spitting is at all times most efficacious against the influence of the devil; an infant's nails should be bitten, not cut; never rock an empty cradle; the robin and the swallow bring luck; never kill a spider; the crow and a black hen are ominous of evil. The dead are only in a trance; they hear everything but can make no sign. The Irish also believe that the dead are allowed at certain times to visit their living kindred. A whirlwind denotes that a devil is dancing with a witch; so the Irish believe that the fairies are rushing by in the whirlwind intent on carrying off some mortal victim to the fairy mansions; and the only help is to fling clay at the passing wind, when the fairies will be obliged to drop the mortal child, or the beautiful young girl they have abducted.

But the Roumanians are a mixed race—Greek, Slav, Teuton, Gypsey—and many of their superstitions are dark and gloomy, especially those relating to vampires, wolves, and terrible demons, evil spirits, and fearful witches. The Irish legends rarely deal with anything terrible or revolting. They circle, in general, round the mythus of the fairy, a bright and beautiful creation, only living for pleasure, music, and the dance, and rarely malignant or ill-natured, except when their dancing grounds are interfered with, or when they are not treated with proper generous consideration in the matter of wine.

The strange dance practised at Midsummer in Ireland round the Baal fires can clearly be traced from the East to Erin; and in its origin was evidently a religious symbol and rite. The Greeks practised it from the most ancient times. It was called the Pyrrhic dance—from *pur* fire—and simulated the windings of a serpent.

The *Syrtos*, the great national dance of the Ægean Islands, so well described by Mr. Bent in his interesting book on the Cyclades, also resembles the winding of a serpent. The dancers hold hands and circle round in tortuous curves precisely as in Ireland, where the line of dancers with joined hands, always moving from east to west, extends sometimes for a mile in length. It was probably a mystic dance symbolic of the path of the sun, though the esoteric meaning has now been entirely lost; part of the primal range of ideas out of which man first formed a religion and ritual of worship.

Many other practices and superstitions of the Greek islanders strongly resemble the Irish. The Nereids of the Ægean play the part of the Irish fairies, and are as capricious though often more malignant. If a child grows wan and weak the Nereids have struck it; and it is laid naked for a night on the altar steps to test the truth of the suspicion. If the poor child dies under the trial, then it certainly was bewitched by the evil spirits, and the parents are well content to be rid of the unholy thing.

The funeral wail over the dead also closely resembles the Irish, when the hired mourning women sit round the corpse, tear their hair, beat their breast and rock to and fro, intoning in a monotone chant the praises of the deceased, the cries at times rising to a scream, in a frenzy of grief and despair.

The islanders likewise use many charms and incantations like the Irish, while the old women amongst them display wonderful knowledge of the mystic nature and power of herbs, and are most expert in the cure of disease. It is indeed remarkable that, amongst all primitive tribes and nations, women have always shown the highest skill in the treatment of disease, and have been rightly accounted the best doctors, and the most learned in mystic medicinal lore.

The Marquis of Lorne, in his graphic and instructive "Canadian Pictures," speaks of the wonderful skill of the Indian women, and the remarkable cures effected by the squaws through their knowledge of the varied properties of herbs. The Indians also have a sweating bath for the sick, such as was used by the ancient Irish. A bath is made by stones covered over with branches; hot water is then poured on the stones, and the patient crouches over the heated vapour evolved until a violent perspiration is produced, which carries off the disease, or the pains in the members, without fail. The sweating bath of the Irish was made quite on the same principles, and is the most effective cure known for pains in the bones and feverish disorders. It is still used in the Western Islands. "The Sweating House," as it is called, is made of rough stones with a narrow entrance, through which the patient creeps on all-fours; when inside, however, he can stand up. A peat fire is kindled, and divesting himself of all clothing, he undergoes the process of sweating in a profuse perspiration as he lies on the stone floor. The place is heated like a baker's oven, but there is sufficient ventilation kept up by means of chinks and apertures through the stone work of the walls.

The cures effected by this process are marvellous. As the people say of it themselves, "Any disease that has a hold on the bones can't stand before it no time at all, at all."

The Power of the Word

The belief in the malific influence of the Evil Eye pervades all the Greek islands, and the same preventive measures are used as in Ireland. An old woman is employed to spit three times at the person affected, if she is a person learned in the mysteries and accounted wise. Salt and fire are also used as safeguards, precisely as the Irish peasant employs them to guard his cattle and children from the evil influence. But no superstition is more widely spread; it seems to pervade all the world, and to be instinctive to humanity. The educated are as susceptible to it as the illiterate, and no nerves are strong enough, apparently, to resist the impression made by an envious, malicious glance, for a poison that blights and withers seems to emanate from it. Reason appeals in vain; the feelings cannot be overcome that the presence and glance of some one person in a room can chill all the natural flow of spirits, while the presence of another seems to intensify all our mental powers, and transform us for the moment into a higher being.

But a malific power, stronger even than the glance of the Evil Eye, was exercised by the Bards of Erin: whom they would they blessed, but whom they would they also banned; and the poet's malison was more dreaded and was more fatal than any other form of imprecation—for the bard had the mystic prophet power: he could foresee, and he could denounce. And no man could escape from the judgment pronounced by a poet over one he desired to injure; for the poet had the knowledge of all mysteries and was Lord over the secrets of life by the power of The Word. Therefore poets were emphatically called the tribe of *Duars*, that is, THE MEN OF THE WORD; for by a word the poets could produce deformities in those they disliked, and make them objects of scorn and hateful in the sight of other men.

The Poet and the King

Nuadhé, the celebrated poet, is remembered in history by a memorable exercise of his malific power, and the punishment that fell on him in consequence; for Heaven is just, and even a bard cannot escape the penalty due for sin.

He was nephew to Caer, the king of Connaught, who reared him with all kindness and gentleness as his own son. But by an evil fate the wife of Caer the king loved the young man; and she gave him a silver apple in proof of her love, and further promised him the kingdom and herself if he could overthrow Caer and make the people depose him from the sovranty.

"How can I do this?" answered Nuadhé, "for the king has ever been kind to me."

"Ask him for some gift," said the queen, "that he will refuse, and then put a blemish on him for punishment, that so he can be no longer king;" for no one with a blemish was ever suffered to reign in Erin.

"But he refuses me nothing," answered Nuadhé.

"Try him," said the queen. "Ask of him the dagger he brought from Alba, for he is under a vow never to part with it."

So Nuadhé went to him, and asked for the dagger that came out of Alba as a gift.

"Woe is me!" said the king. "This I cannot grant; for I am under a solemn vow never to part with it, or give it to another."

Then the poet by his power made a satire on him, and this was the form of the imprecation—

"Evil death, and a short life
Be on Caer the king!
Let the spears of battle wound him,
Under earth, under ramparts, under stones,
Let the malediction be on him!"

And when Caer rose up in the morning he put his hand to his face and found it was disfigured with three blisters, a white, a red, and a green. And when he saw the blemish he fled away filled with fear that any man should see him, and took refuge in a fort with one of his faithful servants, and no one knew where he lay hid.

So Nuadhé took the kingdom and held it for a year, and had the queen to wife. But then grievous to him was the fate of Caer, and he set forth to search for him.

And he was seated in the king's own royal chariot, with the king's wife beside him, and the king's greyhound at his feet, and all the people wondered at the beauty of the charioteer.

Now Caer was in the fort where he had found shelter, and when he saw them coming he said—

"Who is this that is seated in my chariot in the place of the champion, and driving my steeds?"

But when he saw that it was Nuadhé he fled away and hid himself for shame.

Then Nuadhé drove into the fort in the king's chariot, and loosed the dogs to pursue Caer. And they found him hid under the flagstone behind the rock even where the dogs tracked him. And Caer fell down dead from shame on beholding Nuadhé, and the rock where he fell flamed up and shivered into fragments, and a splinter leaped up high as a man, and struck Nuadhé on the eyes, and blinded him for life. Such was the punishment decreed, and just and right was the vengeance of God upon the sin of the poet.

The Sidhe Race

The Sidhe dwell in the Sifra, or fairy palace of gold and crystal, in the heart of the hill, and they have been given youth, beauty, joy, and the power over music, yet they are often sad; for they remember that they were once angels in heaven though now cast down to earth, and though they have power over all the mysteries of Nature, yet they must die without hope of regaining heaven, while mortals are certain of immortality. Therefore this one sorrow darkens their life, a mournful envy of humanity; because, while man is created immortal, the beautiful fairy race is doomed to annihilation.

One day a great fairy chief asked Columb-Kille if there were any hope left to the Sidhe that one day they would regain heaven and be restored to their ancient place amongst the angels. But the saint answered that hope there was none; their doom was fixed, and at the judgment-day they would pass through death into annihilation; for so had it been decreed by the justice of God.

On hearing this the fairy chief fell into a profound melancholy, and he and all his court sailed away from Ireland, and went back to their native country of Armenia, there to await the coming of the terrible judgment-day, which is fated to bring the fairy race certain death on earth, without any hope of regaining heaven.

The West of Ireland is peculiarly sacred to ancient superstitions of the Sidhe race. There is a poetry in the scenery that touches the heart of the people; they love the beautiful glens, the mountains rising like towers from the sea, the islands sanctified by the memory of a saint, and the green hills where Finvarra holds his court. Every lake and mountain has its legend of the spirit-land, some holy traditions of a saint, or some historic memory of a national hero who flourished in the old great days when Ireland had native chiefs and native swords to guard her; and amongst the Western Irish, especially, the old superstitions of their forefathers are reverenced with a solemn faith and fervour that is almost a religion. Finvarra the king is still believed to rule over all the fairies of the west, and *Onagh* is the fairy queen. Her golden hair sweeps the ground, and she is robed in silver gossamer all glittering as if with diamonds, but they are dew-drops that sparkle over it.

The queen is more beautiful than any woman of earth, yet Finvarra loves the mortal women best, and wiles them down to his fairy palace by the subtle charm of the fairy music, for no one who has heard it can resist its power, and they are fated to belong to the fairies ever after. Their friends mourn for them as dead with much lamentation, but in reality they are leading a joyous life down in the heart of the hill, in the fairy palace with the silver columns and the crystal walls.

Yet sometimes they are not drawn down beneath the earth, but remain as usual in the daily life, though the fairy spell is still on them; and the young men who have once heard the fairy harp become possessed by the spirit of music which haunts them to their death, and gives them strange power over the souls of men. This was the case with Carolan, the celebrated bard. He acquired all the magic melody of his notes by sleeping out on a fairy rath at night, when the fairy music came to him in his dreams; and on awaking he played the airs from memory. Thus it was that he had power to madden men to mirth, or to set them weeping as if for the dead, and no one ever before or since played the enchanting fairy music like Carolan, the sweet musician of Ireland.

There was another man also who heard the fairy music when sleeping on a rath, and ever after he was haunted by the melody day and night, till he grew mad and had no pleasure in life, for he longed to be with the fairies again that he might hear them sing. So one day, driven to despair by the madness of longing, he threw himself from the cliff into the mountain lake near the fairy rath, and so died and was seen no more.

In the Western Islands they believe that the magic of fairy music is so strong that whoever hears it cannot choose but follow the sound, and the young girls are drawn away by the enchantment, and dance all night with Finvarra the king, though in the morning they are found fast asleep in bed, yet with a memory of all they had heard and seen; and some say that, while with the fairies, the young women learn strange secrets of love potions, by which they can work spells and dangerous charms over those whose love they desire, or upon any one who has offended and spoken ill of them.

It is a beautiful idea that the Irish airs, so plaintive, mournful, and tear-compelling, are but the remembered echoes of that spirit music which had power to draw souls away to the fairy mansions, and hold them captive by the sweet magic of the melody.

Music

Music formed the chief part of education in ancient Ireland as in Greece, where the same word signified a song and a law. Laws, religion, sciences, and history were all taught in music to the Irish people by the *Ollamhs*, or learned men. The Poets chanted the *Ros-Catha*, or song of battle, to incite the warriors to deeds of bravery. The Bards recited the deeds of the chiefs, or pleasant tales of love, at the festivals, and struck the harp to sustain the voice. The Brehons intoned the law in a recitative or monotone chant, seated on an eminence in the open air, while all the people were gathered round to listen. The Senachie chanted the history, genealogies, and traditions of the tribe, and the female mourners were instructed by the poets in the elegiac measure, or funeral wail over the dead.

The poet-power was also believed to confer the gift of prophecy; and no great expedition was undertaken by the tribe without the advice and sanction of the bard, and especially of the poet-priestess of the tribe. Thus Ethna the poetess stood on a high stone at the battle of Moytura, and gave inspiration by her chants to the warriors of the Tuatha-de-Dananns, and stimulated their courage by her prophecies of victory; and the stone she stood on is in existence to this day on the plain of the battle, and is still called by the people "the Stone of the Prophetess."

Poet Inspiration: Eodain the Poetess

The *Leanan-Sidhe*, or the spirit of life, was supposed to be the inspirer of the poet and singer, as the *Ban-Sidhe* was the spirit of death, the foreteller of doom.

The Leanan-Sidhe sometimes took the form of a woman, who gave men valour and strength in the battle by her songs. Such was Eodain the poetess, by whom Eugene, king of Munster, gained complete victory over his foes. But afterwards he gave himself up to luxury and pleasure, and went away to Spain, where he remained nine years, and took to wife the daughter of the king of Spain. At the end of that time he returned to Ireland with a band of Spanish followers. But he found his kingdom plundered and ruined, and the revellers and drunkards were feasting in his banquet hall, and wasting his revenues for their pleasures while the people starved. And the whole nation despised the king, and would not hear his words when he sat down in his golden chair to give just judgment for iniquity. Then Eugene the king, in his

177

deep sorrow and humiliation, sent for Eodain the poetess to come and give him counsel. So Eodain came to him, and upheld him with her strong spirit, for she had the power within her of the poet and the prophet, and she said—

"Arise now, O king, and govern like a true hero, and bring confusion on the evil workers. Be strong and fear not, for by strength and justice kings should rule."

And Eugene the king was guided by her counsel and was successful. And he overthrew his enemies and brought back peace and order to the land. For the strength of the Leanan-Sidhe was in the words of Eodain, the power of the spirit of life which is given to the poet and the prophet, by which they inspire and guide the hearts of men.

The Banshee

The Banshee means, especially, the woman of the fairy race, from *van*, "the Woman—the Beautiful;" the same word from which comes *Venus*. Shiloh-Van was one of the names of Buddha—"the son of the woman;" and some writers aver that in the Irish—*Sullivan* (Sulli-van), may be found this ancient name of Buddha.

As the Leanan-Sidhe was the acknowledged *spirit of life*, giving inspiration to the poet and the musician, so the Ban-Sidhe was the *spirit of death*, the most weird and awful of all the fairy powers.

But only certain families of historic lineage, or persons gifted with music and song, are attended by this spirit; for music and poetry are fairy gifts, and the possessors of them show kinship to the spirit race—therefore they are watched over by the spirit of life, which is prophecy and inspiration; and by the spirit of doom, which is the revealer of the secrets of death.

Sometimes the Banshee assumes the form of some sweet singing virgin of the family who died young, and has been given the mission by the invisible powers to become the harbinger of coming doom to her mortal kindred. Or she may be seen at night as a shrouded woman, crouched beneath the trees, lamenting with veiled face; or flying past in the moonlight, crying bitterly: and the cry of this spirit is mournful beyond all other sounds on earth, and betokens certain death to some member of the family whenever it is heard in the silence of the night.

*

The Banshee even follows the old race across the ocean and to distant lands; for space and time offer no hindrance to the mystic power which is selected and appointed to bear the prophecy of death to a family. Of this a well-authenticated instance happened a few years ago, and many now living can attest the truth of the narrative.

A branch of the ancient race of the O'Gradys had settled in Canada, far removed, apparently, from all the associations, traditions, and mysterious influences of the old land of their forefathers.

But one night a strange and mournful lamentation was heard outside the house. No word was uttered, only a bitter cry, as of one in deepest agony and sorrow, floated through the air.

Inquiry was made, but no one had been seen near the house at the time, though several persons distinctly heard the weird, unearthly cry, and a terror fell upon the household, as if some supernatural influence had overshadowed them.

Next day it so happened that the gentleman and his eldest son went out boating. As they did not return, however, at the usual time for dinner, some alarm was excited, and messengers were sent down to the shore to look for them. But no tidings came until, precisely at the exact hour of the night when the spirit-cry had been heard the previous evening, a crowd of men were seen approaching the house, bearing with them the dead bodies of the father and the son, who had both been drowned by the accidental upsetting of the boat, within sight of land, but not near enough for any help to reach them in time.

Thus the Ban-Sidhe had fulfilled her mission of doom, after which she disappeared, and the cry of the spirit of death was heard no more.

*

At times the spirit-voice is heard in low and soft lamenting, as if close to the window.

Not long ago an ancient lady of noble lineage was lying near the death-hour in her stately castle. One evening, after twilight, she suddenly unclosed her eyes and pointed to the window, with a happy smile on her face. All present looked in the direction, but nothing was visible. They heard, however, the sweetest music, low, soft, and spiritual, floating round the house, and at times apparently close to the window of the sick room.

Many of the attendants thought it was a trick, and went out to search the grounds; but nothing human was seen. Still the wild plaintive singing went on, wandering through the trees like the night wind—a low, beautiful music that never ceased all through the night.

Next morning the noble lady lay dead; then the music ceased, and the lamentation from that hour was heard no more.

*

There was a gentleman also in the same country who had a beautiful daughter, strong and healthy, and a splendid horsewoman. She always followed the hounds, and her appearance at the hunt attracted unbounded admiration, as no one rode so well or looked so beautiful.

One evening there was a ball after the hunt, and the young girl moved through the dance with the grace of a fairy queen.

But that same night a voice came close to the father's window, as if the face were laid close to the glass, and he heard a mournful lamentation and a cry; and the words rang out on the air—

"In three weeks death; in three weeks the grave—dead—dead—dead!"

Three times the voice came, and three times he heard the words; but though it was bright moonlight, and he looked from the window over all the park, no form was to be seen.

Next day, his daughter showed symptoms of fever, and exactly in three weeks, as the Ban-Sidhe had prophesied, the beautiful girl lay dead.

The night before her death soft music was heard outside the house, though

180

no word was spoken by the spirit-voice, and the family said the form of a woman crouched beneath a tree, with a mantle covering her head, was distinctly visible. But on approaching, the phantom disappeared, though the soft, low music of the lamentation continued till dawn.

Then the angel of death entered the house with soundless feet, and he breathed upon the beautiful face of the young girl, and she rested in the sleep of the dead, beneath the dark shadows of his wings.

Thus the prophecy of the Banshee came true, according to the time foretold by the spirit-voice.

Queen Maeve

A remarkable account is given in the Bardic Legends of a form that appeared to Maeve, queen of Connaught, on the eve of battle.

Suddenly there stood before the queen's chariot, a tall and beautiful woman. She wore a green robe clasped with a golden bodkin, a golden fillet on her head, and seven braids for the Dead of bright gold were in her hand. Her skin was white as snow that falls in the night; her teeth were as pearls; her lips red as the berries of the mountain ash; her golden hair fell to the ground; and her voice was sweet as the golden harp-string when touched by a skilful hand.

"Who art thou, O woman?" asked the queen, in astonishment.

"I am Feithlinn, the fairy prophetess of the Rath of Cruachan," she answered.

"'Tis well, O Feithlinn the prophetess," said Maeve; "but what dost thou foresee concerning our hosts?"

"I foresee bloodshed; I foresee power; I foresee defeat!" answered the prophetess.

"My couriers have brought me good tidings!" said the queen; "my army is strong, my warriors are well prepared. But speak the truth, O prophetess; for my soul knows no fear."

"I foresee bloodshed; I foresee victory!" answered the prophetess the second time.

"But I have nothing to fear from the Ultonians," said the queen, "for my couriers have arrived, and my enemies are under dread. Yet, speak the truth, O prophetess, that our hosts may know it."

"I foresee bloodshed; I foresee conquest; I foresee *death!*" answered the prophetess, for the third time.

"To me then it belongs not, thy prophecy of evil," replied the queen, in anger.

"Be it thine, and on thy own head."

And even as she spoke the prophet maiden disappeared, and the queen saw her no more.

But it so happened that, some time afterwards, Queen Maeve was cruelly slain by her own kinsman, at Lough Rea by the Shannon, to avenge the assistance she had given in war to the king of Ulster; there is an island in the lake where is shown the spot where the great queen was slain, and which is still known to the people as—*the stone of the dead queen.*

Maeve, the great queen of Connaught, holds a distinguished place in Bardic Legends. When she went to battle, it is said, she rode in an open car, accompanied by four chariots—one before, another behind, and one on each side—so that the golden *assion* on her head and her royal robes should not be defiled by the dust of the horses' feet, or the foam of the fiery steeds; for all the sovereigns of Ireland sat crowned with a diadem in battle, as they drove in their war-chariots, as well as in the festal and the public assemblies.

Death Signs

In one Irish family a cuckoo always appears before a death. A lady who arrived on a visit at a house observed one morning a cuckoo perched on the window-sill, but she felt no alarm, for there was no sickness in the family. Next day, however, one of the sons was carried home dead. He had been thrown from his horse when hunting, and killed on the spot.

In another family a mysterious sound is heard like the crashing of boards, and a rush of wind seems to pass through the house, yet nothing is broken or disturbed. The death of an officer in the Crimea was in this way announced to his family, for the news came immediately after the warning sound, and then they knew that the rush of the wind was the spirit of the dead which had passed by them, but without taking any visible form.

The Hartpole Doom

There is a tradition concerning the Hartpole family of Shrule Castle in the Queen's County (called the castle on the bloody stream, from the sanguinary deeds of the owner) that every male member of the family is doomed and fated to utter three screeches terrible to hear when dying. As to the origin of this doom the story goes that Sir Richard Hartpole about 300 years ago, in the time of the Elizabethan wars, committed many savage acts against the Irish, he being an upholder of the English faction.

One day a priest named O'More, having come to the castle on some friendly mission, the savage Hartpole ordered his retainers to seize him and hang him up in the courtyard.

"Good God!" exclaimed the priest. "Give me at least a moment to pray!"

"Go then," said Hartpole, "you may pray."

The priest kneeled down apart from the crowd. But Hartpole grew impatient, and ordered him to rise.

"You have prayed long enough," he said, "prepare for death."

And when the priest heard the order for his death, and saw the man approach to seize him, he swayed from right to left and gave three fearful screams.

"Why do you screech?" asked the tyrant.

"So shall you scream, and all your descendants in your last agony," exclaimed O'More, "as a sign of the doom upon your race. You have murdered my people, you are now going to take my life; but I lay the curse of God on you and yours—your property shall pass away; your race shall perish off the earth; and by the three death screeches all men shall know that you and your posterity are accursed."

The words of O'More only made the tyrant more furious, and the priest was hung at once in the courtyard before the eyes of Hartpole. But the prophecy of doom was fulfilled—the property perished, the castle became a ruin. The last Hartpole died miserably of want and hunger, and the whole race finally has become extinct.

Superstitions

The two great festivals of the ancient Irish were *Lá Baal Tinné*, or May Day (sacred to the Sun), and *Lá Samnah*, or November Eve (sacred to the Moon).

*

Food should be left out on November Eve for the dead, who are then wandering about. If the food disappears, it is a sign that the spirits have taken it, for no mortal would dare to touch or eat of the food so left.

*

Never turn your head to look if you fancy you hear footsteps behind you on that night; for the dead are walking then, and their glance would kill.

*

In November a distaff is placed under the head of a young man at night to make him dream of the girl he is destined to marry.

*

If a ball of worsted is thrown into a lime-kiln and wound up till the end is caught by invisible hands, the person who winds it calls out, "Who holds the ball?" and the answer will be the name of the future husband or wife. But the experiment must be made only at midnight, and in silence and alone.

*

Whitsuntide is a most unlucky time; horses foaled then will grow up dangerous and kill some one.

*

A child born at Whitsuntide will have an evil temper, and may commit a murder.

Lady Jane Francesca Agnes Wilde

*

Beware also of water at Whitsuntide, for an evil power is on the waves and the lakes and the rivers, and a boat may be swamped and men drowned unless a bride steers; then the danger ceases.

*

To turn away ill-luck from a child born at that time, a grave must be dug and the infant laid in it for a few minutes. After this process the evil spell is broken, and the child is safe.

*

If any one takes ill at Whitsuntide there is great danger of death, for the evil spirits are on the watch to carry off victims, and no sick person should be left alone at this time, nor in the dark. Light is a great safeguard, as well as fire, against malific influences.

*

In old times at Whitsuntide blood was poured out as a libation to the evil spirits; and the children and cattle were passed through two lines of fire.

*

On May morning the Skellig rocks go out full sail to meet the opposite rocks, which advance half way to meet them, and then slowly retire like retreating ships.

*

At Midsummer the fairies try to pass round the Baal fires in a whirlwind in order to extinguish them, but the spirits may be kept off by throwing fire at them. Then the young men are free to leap over the burning embers and to drive the cattle through the flames, while coals of fire must also be passed three times over and three times under the body of each animal.

*

Foot-worship was a homage to Buddha, and it was also a Christian ceremony to wash the feet of the saints. The Irish had many superstitions about foot-water, and no woman was allowed to wash her feet in the sacred wells though the lavation was permitted to men.

*

If a child is fairy-struck, give it a cup of cold water in the name of Christ and make the sign of the cross over it.

*

On St. Martin's Day when blood is spilt, whoever is signed with the blood is safe, for that year at least, from disease.

*

For the Evil Eye, a piece cut from the garment of the evil-eyed, burned to tinder and ground to powder, must be given to the person under the baneful spell, while his forehead is anointed with spittle thrice. So the Greeks spat three times in the face of the evil-eyed to break the spell.

*

Pass a red-hot turf three times over and under the body of an animal supposed to be fairy-struck, singeing the hair along the back. This drives off the fairies.

*

The Irish always went westward round a holy well, following the course of the sun, and creeping on their hands and knees. So did the ancient Persians when offering homage at the sacred fountains.

*

Red-haired people were held to be evil and malicious and unlucky, probably because Typhon, the evil principle, was red; and therefore a red heifer was sacrificed to him by the Egyptians.

*

In the mystic, or snake dance, performed at the Baal festival, the gyrations of the dancers were always westward, in the track of the sun, for the dance was part of the ancient ritual of sun worship.

The Fairy Rath

The ancient rath, or fort, or liss, generally enclosed about half an acre, and had two or more ramparts, formed by the heads of the tribe for defence. But when the race of the chieftains died out, then the Sidhe crowded into the forts, and there held their councils and revels and dances; and if a man put his ear close to the ground at night he could hear the sweet fairy music rising up from under the earth.

The rath ever after is sacred to the fairies, and no mortal is allowed to cut down a tree that grows on it, or to carry away a stone. But dangerous above all would it be to build on a fairy rath. If a man attempted such a rash act, the fairies would put a blast on his eyes, or give him a crooked mouth; for no human hand should dare to touch their ancient dancing grounds.

It is not right, the people say, to sing or whistle at night that old air, "The pretty girl milking her cow;" for it is a fairy tune, and the fairies will not suffer a mortal to sing their music while they are dancing on the grass. But if a person sleeps on the rath the music will enter into his soul, and when he awakes he may sing the air he has heard in his dreams.

In this way the bards learned their songs, and they were skilled musicians, and touched the harp with a master hand, so that the fairies often gathered round to listen, though invisible to mortal eyes.

Fairy Nature

The *Siodh-Dune*, or the Mount of Peace, is also a favourite resort of the fairies. It is an ancient, sacred place, where the Druids in old time used to retire to pray, when they desired solitude; and the fairies meet there every seven years to perform the act of lamentation and mourning for having been cast out of heaven.

Earth, lake, and hill are peopled by these fantastic, beautiful gods of earth; the wilful, capricious child-spirits of the world. The Irish seem to have created this strange fairy race after their own image, for in all things they strangely resemble the Irish character.

The Sidhe passionately love beauty and luxury, and hold in contempt all the mean virtues of thrift and economy. Above all things they hate the close, niggard hand that gathers the last grain, and drains the last drop in the milk-pail, and plucks the trees bare of fruit, leaving nothing for the spirits who wander by in the moonlight. They like food and wine to be left for them at night, yet they are very temperate; no one ever saw an intoxicated fairy.

But people should not sit up too late; for the fairies like to gather round the smouldering embers after the family are in bed, and drain the wine-cup, and drink the milk which a good housewife always leaves for them, in case the fairies should come in and want their supper. A vessel of pure water should also be left for them to bathe in, if they like. And in all things the fairies are fond of being made much of, and flattered and attended to; and the fairy blessing will come back in return to the giver for whatever act of kindness he has done to the spirits of the hill and the cave. Some unexpected good fortune or stroke of luck will come upon his house or his children; for the fairy race is not ungrateful, and is powerful over man both for good and evil.

Therefore be kind to the wayfarer, for he may be a fairy prince in disguise, who has come to test the depth of your charity, and of the generous nature that can give liberally out of pure love and kindliness to those who are in need, and not in hope of a reward.

If treated well, the fairies will discover the hidden pot of gold, and reveal the mysteries of herbs, and give knowledge to the fairy women of the mystic spells that can cure disease, and save life, and make the lover loved.

All they ask in return is to be left in quiet possession of the rath and the hill and the ancient hawthorn trees that have been theirs from time immemorial, and where they lead a joyous life with music and dance, and charming little suppers of the nectar of flowers, down in the crystal caves, lit by the diamonds that stud the rocks.

But some small courtesies they require. Never drain your wine-glass at a feast, nor the poteen flask, nor the milk-pail; and never rake out all the fire at night, it looks mean, and the fairies like a little of everything going, and to have the hearth comfortable and warm when they come in to hold a council after all the mortal people have gone to bed. In fact, the fairies are born aristocrats, true ladies and gentlemen, and if treated with proper respect are never in the least malignant or ill-natured.

All the traditions of the fairies show that they love beauty and splendour, grace of movement, music and pleasure; everything, in fact, that is artistic, in contradistinction to violent, brutal enjoyment. Only an Aryan people, therefore, could have invented the Sidhe race.

Irish Nature

The Irish show their Aryan descent by the same characteristics as the Fairy race, for they also love everything that is artistic—the fascinations of life, beauty of form, music, poetry, song, splendour, and noble pleasures. Their kings in ancient times were elected for their personal beauty as much as for their chivalrous qualities. No man with a blemish or a deformity was allowed to reign. Then, their appreciation of intellect proved the value they set on the spiritual and ideal above the material and the brutal. The poet ranked next to the princes of the land. His person was sacred in battle; he was endowed with an estate, so that his soul might be free from sordid cares; and his robe of many colours, and the golden circlet on his brow at the festivals, showed his claim and right to rank next to royalty, and to sit at the right hand of the king. Poetry, learning, music, oratory, heroism, and splendour of achievement—these were the true objects of homage and admiration amongst the ancient Irish.

There was nothing brutal in their ideal of life; no hideous images or revolting cruelties; and the beautiful and graceful Sidhe race, with their plaintive music and soft melancholy, and aspirations for a lost heaven, is the expression in a graceful and beautiful symbol of the instinctive tendencies of the Irish nature to all that is most divine in human intellect, and soft and tender in human emotion.

Ireland is a land of mists and mystic shadows; of cloud-wraiths on the purple mountains; of weird silences in the lonely hills, and fitful skies of deepest gloom alternating with gorgeous sunset splendours. All this fantastic caprice of an ever-varying atmosphere stirs the imagination, and makes the Irish people strangely sensitive to spiritual influences. They see visions and dream dreams, and are haunted at all times by an ever-present sense of the supernatural. One can see by the form of the Irish head—a slender oval, prominent at the brows and high in the region of veneration, so different from the globular Teutonic head—that the people are enthusiasts, religious, fanatical; with the instincts of poetry, music, oratory, and superstition far stronger in them than the logical and reasoning faculties. They are made for worshippers, poets, artists, musicians, orators; to move the world by passion, not by logic. Scepticism will never take root in Ireland; infidelity is impossible to the people. To believe fanatically, trust implicitly, hope infinitely, and perhaps to revenge implacably—these are the unchanging and ineradicable characteristics of Irish nature, of Celtic nature, we may say; for it has been the same throughout all history and all ages. And it is these passionate qualities that make the Celt the great motive force of the world, ever striving against limitations towards some vision of ideal splendour; the restless centrifugal force of life, as opposed to the centripetal, which is ever seeking a calm quiescent rest within its appointed sphere.

The very tendency to superstition, so marked in Irish nature, arises from an instinctive dislike to the narrow limitations of common sense. It is characterized by a passionate yearning towards the vague, the mystic, the invisible, and the boundless infinite of the realms of imagination. Therefore the *Daine-Sidhe*, the people of the fairy mansions, have an irresistible attraction for the Irish heart. Like them, the Irish love youth, beauty, splendour, lavish generosity, music and song, the feast and the dance. The mirth and the reckless gaiety of the national temperament finds its true exponent in the mad pranks of the *Phouka* and the *Leprehaun*, the merry spirits that haunt the dells and glens, and look out at the wayfarer from under the dock-leaf with their glittering eyes. The inspiration that rises to poetry under the influence of excitement is expressed by the belief in the *Leanan-Sidhe*, who gives power to song; while the deep pathos of Irish nature finds its fullest representation in the tender, plaintive, spiritual music of the wail and lamentation of the *Ban-Sidhe*.

Legends of Animals

There are no traces in Irish legend of animal worship, but many concerning the influence of animals upon human life, and of their interference with human affairs.

The peasants believe that the domestic animals know all about us, especially the dog and the cat. They listen to everything that is said; they watch the expression of the face, and can even read the thoughts. The Irish say it is not safe to ask a question of a dog, for he may answer, and should he do so the questioner will surely die.

The position of the animal race in the life scheme is certainly full of mystery. Gifted with extraordinary intelligence, yet with dumb souls vainly struggling for utterance, they seem like prisoned spirits in bondage, suffering the punishment, perhaps, for sin in some former human life, and now waiting the completion of the cycle of expiation that will advance them again to the human state.

The three most ancient words in the Irish language are, it is said, *Tor*, a tower; *Cu*, a hound, and *Bo*, a cow. The latter word is the same as is found in the Greek *Bosphorus*, and in the nomenclature of many places throughout Europe.

Concerning Dogs

Some very weird superstitions exist in Ireland concerning the howlings of dogs. If a dog is heard to howl near the house of a sick person, all hope of his recovery is given up, and the patient himself sinks into despair, knowing that his doom is sealed. But the Irish are not alone in holding this superstition. The Egyptians, Hebrews, Greeks, and Romans all looked on the howling of the dog as ominous. The very word *howling* may be traced in the Latin *ululu*, the Greek *holuluzo*, the Hebrew *hululue*, and the Irish *ulluloo*. In Ireland the cry raised at the funeral ceremony was called the *Caoin*, or keen, probably from χυων, a dog. And this doleful lamentation was also common to other nations of antiquity. The Hebrews, Greeks, and Romans had their hired mourners, who, with dishevelled hair and mournful cadenced hymns, led on the melancholy parade of death. Thus the Trojan women keened over Hector, the chorus being led by the beautiful Helen herself.

The howling of the dog was considered by these nations as the first note of the funeral dirge and the signal that the coming of death was near.

But the origin of the superstition may be traced back to Egypt, where dogs and dog-faced gods were objects of worship; probably because Sirius, the Dog-star, appeared precisely before the rising of the Nile, and thereby gave the people a mystic and supernatural warning to prepare for the overflow.

The Romans held that the howling of dogs was a fatal presage of evil, and it is noted amongst the direful omens that preceded the death of Cæsar. Horace also says that Canidia by her spells and sorceries could bring ghosts of dogs from hell; and Virgil makes the dog to howl at the approach of Hecate.

It is remarkable that when dogs see spirits (and they are keenly sensitive to spirit influence) they never bark, but only howl. The Rabbins say that "when the Angel of Death enters a city the dogs do howl. But when Elias appears then the dogs rejoice and are merry." And Rabbi Jehuda the Just states, that once upon a time when the Angel of Death entered a house the dog howled and fled; but being presently brought back he lay down in fear and trembling, and so died.

This strange superstition concerning the howling of dogs, when, as is supposed, they are conscious of the approach of the Spirit of Death, and see him though he is shrouded and invisible to human eyes, may be found pervading the legends of all nations from the earliest period down to the present time; for it still exists in full force amongst all classes, the educated, as well as the unlettered peasantry; and to this day the howling of a dog where a sick person is lying is regarded in Ireland in all grades of society with pale dismay as a certain sign of approaching death.

The Irish may have obtained the superstition through Egypt, Phœnicia, or Greece, for it is the opinion of some erudite writers that the Irish wolf-dog (*Canis gracius Hibernicus*) was descended from the dogs of Greece.

It is strange and noteworthy that although the dog is so faithful to man, yet it is never mentioned in the Bible without an expression of contempt; and Moses in his code of laws makes the dog an unclean animal, probably to deter the Israelites from the Egyptian worship of this animal. It was the lowest term of offence—"Is thy servant a dog?" False teachers, persecutors, Gentiles, unholy men, and others sunk in sin and vileness were called dogs; while at the same time the strange prophetic power of these animals was universally acknowledged and recognized.

The Romans sacrificed a dog at the Lupercalia in February. And to meet a dog with her whelps was considered in the highest degree unlucky. Of all living creatures the name of "dog" applied to any one expressed the lowest form of insult, contempt, and reproach. Yet, of all animals, the dog has the noblest qualities, the highest intelligence, and the most enduring affection for man.

*

The Irish wolf-dog had a lithe body, a slender head, and was fleet as the wind. The form of the animal is produced constantly in Irish ornamentation, but the body always terminates in endless twisted convolutions. The great Fionn Ma-Coul had a celebrated dog called "Bran," who is thus described in the bardic legends: "A ferocious, small-headed, white-breasted, sleek-haunched hound; having the eyes of a dragon, the claws of a wolf, the vigour of a lion, and the venom of a serpent."

In the same poem Fionn himself is described in highly ornate bardic language, as he leads the hound by a chain of silver attached to a collar of gold: "A noble, handsome, fair-featured Fenian prince; young, courteous, manly, puissant; powerful in action; the tallest of the warriors; the strongest of the champions; the most beautiful of the human race."

Bran, like his master, was gifted in a remarkable degree with the foreknowledge of evil, and thus he was enabled to give his young lord many warnings to keep him from danger.

Once, when victory was not for the Fenian host, Bran showed the deepest sorrow.

"He came to Fionn, wet and weary, and by this hand," says the chronicler, "his appearance was pitiful. He lay down before the chief, and cried bitterly and howled.

"'Tis likely, my dog,' saith Fionn, 'that our heads are in great danger this day.'"

Another time, the Fenian host having killed a huge boar, Ossian, the bard and prophet, ordered it to be burnt as of demon race. Bran, hearing this, went out readily and knowingly, and he brings in three trees in his paw; no one knew from whence; but the trees were put into the fire and the great pig was burnt, and the ashes of the beast were cast into the sea.

The Fenian princes generally went to the hunt accompanied altogether by about three thousand hounds; Bran leading, the wisest and fleetest of all. The chiefs formed a goodly army, a thousand knights or more—each wearing a silken shirt and a *chotan* of fine silk, a green mantle and fine purple cloak over to protect it; a golden diademed helmet on the head, and a javelin in each man's hand.

Once, a chief, being jealous of the splendour of the Fenian princes, became their bitter enemy, and set himself to curse Bran above all hounds in the land.

But Fionn answered, "If thou shouldest curse Bran, my wise, intelligent dog, not a room east or west in thy great mansion but I will burn with fire."

So Bran rested on the mountain with Fionn, his lord and master, and was safe from harm.

Yet, so fate decreed, Bran finally met his death by means of a woman. One day a snow-white hart, with hoofs that shone like gold, was scented on the hill, and all the hounds pursued, Bran leading. Hour after hour passed by, and still the hart fled on, the hounds following, till one by one they all dropped off from weariness, and not one was left save Bran. Then the hart headed for the lake, and reaching a high cliff, she plunged from it straight down into the water; the noble hound leaped in at once after her, and seized the hart as she rose to the surface; but at that instant she changed into the form of a beautiful lady, and laying her hand upon the head of Bran, she drew him down beneath the water, and the beautiful lady and Fionn's splendid hound disappeared together and were seen no more. But in memory of the event the cliff from which he leaped is called Coegg-y-Bran; while the lake and the castle beside it are called *Tiernach Bran* (the lordship of Bran) to this day. So the name and memory of Fionn's hound, and his wisdom and achievements are not forgotten by the people; and many dogs of the chase are still called after him, for the name is thought to bring luck to the hunter and sportsman. But the *Cailleach Biorar* (the Hag of the Water) is held in much dread, for it is believed that she still lives in a cave on the hill, and is ready to work her evil spells whenever opportunity offers, and her house is shown under the cairn, also the beaten path she traversed to the lake. Many efforts have been made to drain the lake, but the Druid priestess, the Hag of the Water, always interferes, and casts some spell to prevent the completion of the work. The water of the lake has, it is said, the singular property of turning the hair a silvery white; and the great Fionn having once bathed therein, he emerged a withered old man, and was only restored to youth by means of strong spells and incantations.

*

In Cormac's Glossary there is an interesting account of how the first lapdog came into Ireland, for the men of Britain were under strict orders that no lapdog should be given to the Gael, either of solicitation or of free will, for gratitude or friendship.

Now it happened that Cairbré Musc went to visit a friend of his in Britain, who made him right welcome and offered him everything he possessed, save only his lapdog, for that was forbidden by the law. Yet this beautiful lapdog was the one only possession that Cairbré coveted, and he laid his plans cunningly to obtain it.

There was a law at that time in Britain to this effect: "Every criminal shall be given as a forfeit for his crime to the person he has injured."

Now Cairbré had a wonderful dagger, around the haft of which was an adornment of silver and gold. It was a precious jewel, and he took fat meat and rubbed it all over the haft, with much grease. Then he set it before the lapdog, who began to gnaw at the haft, and continued gnawing all night till the morning, so that the haft was spoiled and was no longer beautiful.

Then on the morrow, Cairbré made complaint that his beautiful dagger was destroyed, and he demanded a just recompense.

"That is indeed fair," said his friend, "I shall pay a price for the trespass."

"I ask no other price," said Cairbré, "than what the law of Britain allows me, namely, the criminal for his crime."

So the lapdog was given to Cairbré, and it was called ever after *Mug-Eimé*, the slave of the haft, which name clung to it because it passed into servitude as a forfeit for the trespass.

Now when Cairbré brought it back to Erin with him, all the kings of Ireland began to wrangle and contend for possession of the lapdog, and the contention at last ended in this wise—it was agreed that the dog should abide for a certain time in the house of each king. Afterwards the dog littered, and each of them had a pup of the litter, and from this stock descends every lapdog in Ireland from that time till now.

After a long while the lapdog died, and the bare skull being brought to the blind poet Maer to try his power of divination, he at once exclaimed, through the prophetic power and vision in him, "O Mug-Eimé! this is indeed the head of Mug-Eimé, the slave of the haft, that was brought into Ireland and given over to the fate of a bondsman, and to the punishment of servitude as a forfeit."

*

The word hound entered into many combinations as a name for various animals. Thus the rabbit was called, "the hound of the brake;" the hare was the "brown hound;" the moth was called "the hound of fur," owing to the voracity with which it devoured raiment. And the otter is still called by the Irish *Madradh-Uisgue* (the dog of the water).

The names of most creatures of the animal kingdom were primitive, the result evidently of observation. Thus the hedgehog was named "the ugly little fellow." The ant was the "slender one." The trout, *Breac*, or "the spotted," from the skin. And the wren was called "the Druid bird," because if any one understood the chirrup, they would have a knowledge of coming events as foretold by the bird.

Concerning Cats

Cats have been familiar to the human household from all antiquity, but they were probably first domesticated in Egypt, where, so far back as two thousand years ago, a temple was dedicated to the goddess of cats—Bubastis Pasht—represented with a cat's head. The Greeks had this feline pet of the house from Egypt, and from Greece the cat race, such as we have it now, was disseminated over Europe. It was a familiar element in Greek household life, and if anything was broken, according to Aristophanes, the phrase went then as now, "The cat did it." But cats were never venerated in Greece with religious adoration as in Egypt, the only country that gave them Divine honour, and where, if a cat died, the whole family shaved off their eyebrows in token of mourning.

The Irish have always looked on cats as evil and mysteriously connected with some demoniacal influence. On entering a house the usual salutation is, "God save all here, except the cat." Even the cake on the griddle may be blessed, but no one says, "God bless the cat."

It is believed that the devil often assumes the form of these animals. The familiar of a witch is always a black cat; and it is supposed that black cats have powers and faculties quite different from all other of the feline tribe. They are endowed with reason, can understand conversations, and are quite able to talk if they considered it advisable and judicious to join in the conversation. Their temperament is exceedingly unamiable, they are artful, malignant, and skilled in deception, and people should be very cautious in caressing them, for they have the venomous heart and the evil eye, and are ever ready to do an injury. Yet the liver of a black cat has the singular power to excite love when properly administered. If ground to powder and infused into potion, the recipient is fated to love passionately the person who offers it and has worked the charm.

An instance of this is narrated as having happened not very long ago. A farmer's daughter, a pretty coquette, attracted the attention of the young squire of the place. But though he was willing to carry on a flirtation, the young gentleman had no idea of debasing his proud lineage by an alliance. Yet a marriage was exactly what the girl desired, and which she was determined to accomplish. So she and a friend, an accomplice, searched the village till they found a black cat, black as night, with only three white hairs on the breast. Him they seized, and having tied up the animal in a bag, they proceeded to throw him from one to the other over a low wall, till the poor beast was quite dead. Then at midnight they began their unholy work. The liver and heart were extracted in the name of the Evil One, and then boiled down until they became so dry that they could easily be reduced to a powder, which was kept for use when opportunity offered. This soon came; the young squire arrived one evening as usual, to pay a visit to the pretty Nora, and began to make love to the girl with the ordinary amount of audacity and hypocrisy. But Nora had other views, so she made the tea by her little fire in a *black* teapot, for this was indispensable, and induced her lover to stay and partake of it with her, along with a fresh griddle cake. Then cunningly she infused the powder into his cup and watched him as he drank the tea with feverish anxiety. The result was even beyond her hopes. A violent and ardent passion seemed suddenly to have seized the young man, and he not only made earnest love to the pretty Nora, but offered her his hand in marriage, vowing that he would kill himself if she refused to become his lawful bride. To avoid such a catastrophe, Nora gently yielded to his request, and from that evening they were engaged. Daily visits followed from the young squire, and each time that he came Nora took care to repeat the charm of the love powder, so that the love was kept at fever heat, and finally the wedding day was fixed.

The family of the young squire were, however, not quite contented, especially as rumours of witchcraft and devil's dealings were bruited about the neighbourhood. And on the very eve of the marriage, just as the young man was pouring forth his vows of eternal love to the bride expectant, the door was burst open, and a body of men entered, headed by the nearest relations of the squire, who proceeded at once to belabour the young bridegroom with hazel sticks in the most vigorous manner. In vain the bride tried to interpose. She only drew the blows on herself, and finally the young man was carried away half stunned, lifted into the carriage and driven straight home, where he was locked up in his own room, and not allowed to hold any communication with the bride elect.

The daily doses of the powder having thus ceased, he began to recover from the love madness, and finally the fever passed away. And he looked back with wonder and horror on the fatal step he had so nearly taken. Now he saw there was really witchcraft in it, which the power of the hazel twigs had completely broken. And the accomplice having confessed the sorcery practised on him by Nora and herself, he hated the girl henceforth as much as he had once loved her.

And after a little he went away on foreign travel, and remained abroad for three years. When he returned, he found that Nora had degenerated into a withered little witch-faced creature, who was shunned by every one, and jeered at for the failure of her wicked spells, which had all come to nothing, though she had the Evil One himself to aid her; for such is the fate of all who deal in sorcery and devil's magic, especially with the help of Satan's chief instrument of witchcraft—the black cat.

*

But there is a certain herb of more power even than the cat's liver to produce love. Though what this herb is, only the adept knows and can reveal. The influence it exercises lasts, it is said, for twenty-one years, and then ceases and cannot be renewed.

A gentleman, now living, once ate of this herb, which was given to him by his wife's serving-maid, and in consequence he was fated to love the girl for the specified time. Not being then able to endure his wife's presence, he sent her away from the house, and devoted himself exclusively to the servant. Nineteen years have now passed by, and the poor lady is still waiting patiently to the end of the twenty-one years, believing that the witch-spell will then cease, and that her husband's love will be hers once more. For already he has been inquiring after her and his children, and has been heard lamenting the madness that forced him to drive them from the house for the sake of the menial, who usurped his wife's place by means of some wicked sorcery which he had no power to resist.

The King of the Cats

A most important personage in feline history is the King of the Cats. He may be in your house a common looking fellow enough, with no distinguishing mark of exalted rank about him, so that it is very difficult to verify his genuine claims to royalty. Therefore the best way is to cut off a tiny little bit of his ear. If he is really the royal personage, he will immediately speak out and declare who he is; and perhaps, at the same time, tell you some very disagreeable truths about yourself, not at all pleasant to have discussed by the house cat.

A man once, in a fit of passion, cut off the head of the domestic pussy, and threw it on the fire. On which the head exclaimed, in a fierce voice, "Go tell your wife that you have cut off the head of the King of the Cats; but wait! I shall come back and be avenged for this insult," and the eyes of the cat glared at him horribly from the fire.

And so it happened; for that day year, while the master of the house was playing with a pet kitten, it suddenly flew at his throat and bit him so severely that he died soon after.

A story is current also, that one night an old woman was sitting up very late spinning, when a knocking came to the door. "Who is there?" she asked. No answer; but still the knocking went on. "Who is there?" she asked a second time. No answer; and the knocking continued. "Who is there?" she asked the third time, in a very angry passion.

Then there came a small voice—"Ah, Judy, agrah, let me in, for I am cold and hungry; open the door, Judy, agrah, and let me sit by the fire, for the night is cold out here. Judy, agrah, let me in, let me in!"

The heart of Judy was touched, for she thought it was some small child that had lost its way, and she rose up from her spinning, and went and opened the door—when in walked a large black cat with a white breast, and two white kittens after her.

They all made over to the fire and began to warm and dry themselves, purring all the time very loudly; but Judy said never a word, only went on spinning.

Then the black cat spoke at last—"Judy, agrah, don't stay up so late again, for the fairies wanted to hold a council here to-night, and to have some supper, but you have prevented them; so they were very angry and determined to kill you, and only for myself and my two daughters here you would be dead by this time. So take my advice, don't interfere with the fairy hours again, for the night is theirs, and they hate to look on the face of a mortal when they are out for pleasure or business. So I ran on to tell you, and now give me a drink of milk, for I must be off."

And after the milk was finished the cat stood up, and called her daughters to come away.

"Good-night, Judy, agrah," she said. "You have been very civil to me, and I'll not forget it to you. Good-night, good-night."

With that the black cat and the two kittens whisked up the chimney; but Judy looking down saw something glittering on the hearth, and taking it up she found it was a piece of silver, more than she ever could make in a month

201

by her spinning, and she was glad in her heart, and never again sat up so late to interfere with the fairy hours, but the black cat and her daughters came no more again to the house.

The Demon Cat

The cat of the foregoing legend had evidently charming manners, and was well intentioned; but there are other cats of evil and wicked ways, that are, in fact, demons or witches, who assume the cat-form, in order to get easy entrance to a house, and spy over everything.

There was a woman in Connemara, the wife of a fisherman, and as he always had very good luck, she had plenty of fish at all times stored away in the house ready for market. But to her great annoyance she found that a great cat used to come in at night and devour all the best and finest fish. So she kept a big stick by her and determined to watch.

One day, as she and a woman were spinning together, the house suddenly became quite dark; and the door was burst open as if by the blast of the tempest, when in walked a huge black cat, who went straight up to the fire, then turned round and growled at them.

"Why, surely this is the devil!" said a young girl, who was by, sorting the fish.

"I'll teach you how to call me names," said the cat; and, jumping at her, he scratched her arm till the blood came. "There now," he said, "you will be more civil another time when a gentleman comes to see you." And with that he walked over to the door and shut it close to prevent any of them going out, for the poor young girl, while crying loudly from fright and pain, had made a desperate rush to get away.

Just then a man was going by, and hearing the cries he pushed open the door and tried to get in, but the cat stood on the threshold and would let no one pass. On this, the man attacked him with his stick, and gave him a sound blow; the cat, however, was more than his match in the fight, for it flew at him and tore his face and hands so badly that the man at last took to his heels and ran away as fast as he could.

"Now it's time for my dinner," said the cat, going up to examine the fish that was laid out on the tables. "I hope the fish is good to-day. Now don't disturb me, nor make a fuss; I can help myself." With that he jumped up and began to devour all the best fish, while he growled at the woman.

"Away, out of this, you wicked beast!" she cried, giving it a blow with the tongs that would have broken its back, only it was a devil; "out of this! No fish shall you have to-day."

But the cat only grinned at her, and went on tearing and spoiling and devouring the fish, evidently not a bit the worse for the blow. On this, both the women attacked it with sticks, and struck hard blows enough to kill it, on which the cat glared at them, and spit fire; then making a leap, it tore their hands and arms till the blood came, and the frightened women rushed shrieking from the house.

But presently the mistress returned, carrying with her a bottle of holy water; and looking in, she saw the cat still devouring the fish, and not minding. So she crept over quietly and threw the holy water on it without a word. No sooner was this done than a dense black smoke filled the place, through which nothing was seen but the two red eyes of the cat, burning like coals of fire. Then the smoke gradually cleared away, and she saw the body of the creature burning slowly till it became shrivelled and black like a cinder, and finally disappeared. And from that time the fish remained untouched and safe from harm, for the power of the Evil One was broken, and the demon cat was seen no more.

*

Cats are very revengeful, and one should be very careful not to offend them. A lady was in the habit of feeding the cat from her own table at dinner, and no doubt giving it choice morsels; but one day there was a dinner party, and pussy was quite forgotten. So she sulked and plotted revenge; and that night, after the lady was in bed, the cat, who had hid herself in the room, sprang at the throat of her friend and mistress, and bit her so severely that in a week the lady died of virulent blood poisoning.

*

Yet it is singular that the blood of the black cat is esteemed of wonderful power when mixed with herbs, for charms; and also of great efficacy in potions for the cure of disease; but three drops of the blood are sufficient, and it is generally obtained by nipping off a small piece of the tail.

Cat Nature

The observation of cats is very remarkable, and also their intense curiosity. They examine everything in a house, and in a short time know all about it as well as the owner. They are never deceived by stuffed birds, or any such weak human delusions. They fathom it all at one glance, and then turn away with apathetic indifference, as if saying, in cat language—"We know all about it."

A favourite cat in a gentleman's house was rather fond of nocturnal rambles and late hours, perhaps copying his master, but no matter what his engagements were the cat always returned regularly next morning precisely at nine o'clock, which was the breakfast hour, and *rang the house bell* at the hall door. This fact was stated to me on undoubted authority; and, in truth, there is nothing too wonderful to believe about the intellect of cats; no matter what strange things may be narrated of them, nothing should be held improbable or impossible to their intelligence.

But cats are decidedly malific; they are selfish, revengeful, treacherous, cunning, and generally dangerous. The evil spirit in them is easily aroused. It is an Irish superstition that if you are going a journey, and meet a cat, you should turn back. But the cat must meet you on the road, not simply be in the house; and it must look you full in the face. Then cross yourself and turn back; for a witch or a devil is in your path.

It is believed also that if a black cat is killed and a bean placed in the heart, and the animal afterwards buried, the beans that grow from that seed will confer extraordinary power; for if a man places one in his mouth, he will become invisible, and can go anywhere he likes without being seen.

Cats have truly something awful in them. According to the popular belief they know everything that is said, and can take various shapes through their demoniac power. A cat once lived in a farmer's family for many years, and

understood both Irish and English perfectly. Then the family grew afraid of
it, for they said it would certainly talk some day. So the farmer put it into a
bag, determined to get rid of it on the mountains. But on the way he met a
pack of hounds, and the dogs smelt at the bag and dragged it open, on which
the cat jumped out; but the hounds were on it in a moment, and tore the
poor animal to pieces. However, before her death she had time to say to the
farmer in very good Irish—"It is well for you that I must die to-day, for had I
lived I meant to have killed you this very night." These were the last dying
words of the cat uttered in her death agonies, before the face of many
credible witnesses, so there can be no doubt on the matter.

Cats were special objects of mysterious dread to the ancient Irish. They
believed that many of them were men and women metamorphosed into cats
by demoniacal power. Cats also were the guardians of hidden treasure, and
had often great battles among themselves on account of the hidden gold;
when a demon, in the shape of the chief cat, led on the opposing forces on
each side, and compelled all the cats in the district to take part in the
conflict.

The Druidical or royal cat, the chief monarch of all the cats in Ireland, was
endowed with human speech and faculties, and possessed great and singular
privileges. "A slender black cat, wearing a chain of silver," so it is described.

There is a legend that a beautiful princess, a king's daughter, having gone
down to bathe one day, was there enchanted by her wicked stepmother, who
hated her; and by the spell of the enchantment she was doomed to be one
year a cat, another a swan, and another an otter; but with the privilege of
assuming her natural shape one day in each year, under certain conditions.
It is to be regretted that we have no account as to the mode in which the
Princess Faithlean exercised her brief enjoyment of human rights; for the
narration would have had a mystic and deep psychological interest if the fair
young victim had only retained during all her transformations the memory
of each of her successive incarnations as the cat, the swan, and the otter.

This abnormal mode of existence, however, was not unusual amongst the
Irish. Fionn himself had a wife who for seven years was alive by day and dead

by night; and the Irish Princess Zeba, being enchanted by her wicked stepfather, the king of Munster, died and came to life again each alternate year.

All nations seem to have appreciated the mysterious and almost human qualities of cat nature; the profound cunning, the impertinent indifference, the intense selfishness, yet capable of the most hypocritical flatteries when some point has to be gained. Their traits are not merely the product of brute instinct with unvarying action and results, but the manifestation of a calculating intellect, akin to the human. Then their grace and flexile beauty make them very attractive; while the motherly virtues of the matron cat are singularly interesting as a study of order, education, and training for the wilful little kitten, quite on the human lines of salutary discipline. Humboldt declared that he could spend a whole day with immense profit and advantage to himself as a philosopher, by merely watching a cat with her kittens, the profound wisdom of the mother and the incomparable grace of the children. For cats are thoroughly well-bred, born aristocrats; never abrupt, fussy, or obtrusive like the dog, but gentle, grave, and dignified in manner. Cats never run, they glide softly, and always with perfect and beautiful curves of motion; and they express their affection, not violently, like the dog, but with the most graceful, caressing movements of the head.

Their intellect also is very remarkable, they easily acquire the meaning of certain words, and have a singular and exact knowledge of hours.

Mr. St. George Mivart, in his interesting and exhaustive work on cats, has devoted a whole chapter to the psychology of the cat; in which he shows that the race possesses evident mental qualities and peculiar intelligence, with also a decided and significant language of sounds and gestures to express the emotions of the cat mind. The highly reflective and observant nature of the cat is also admirably described in that very clever novel called "The Poison Tree," recently translated from the Bengalee. There the house-cat is drawn with the most lifelike touches, as she sits watching the noble and beautiful lady at work on her embroidery, while her little child is playing beside her with all the pretty toys scattered over the carpet: "The cat's disposition was grave: her face indicated much wisdom, and a heart devoid of fickleness. She evidently was thinking—'the condition of human creatures is frightful; their minds are ever given to sewing of canvas, playing with dolls, or some such silly employment; their thoughts are not turned to good works, such as providing suitable food for cats. What will become of them hereafter!' Then, seeing no means by which the disposition of mankind could be improved, the cat, heaving a sigh, slowly departs."

Seanchan the Bard and the King of the Cats

There is an amusing legend preserved in Ossianic tradition of the encounter between Seanchan, the celebrated chief poet of Ireland, and the King of all the Cats, who dwelt in a cave near Clonmacnoise.

In ancient Ireland the men of learning were esteemed beyond all other classes; all the great ollaves and professors and poets held the very highest social position, and took precedence of the nobles, and ranked next to royalty. The leading men amongst them lived luxuriously in the great Bardic House; and when they went abroad through the country they travelled with a train of minor bards, fifty or more, and were entertained free of cost by the kings and chiefs, who considered themselves highly honoured by the presence of so distinguished a company at their court. If the receptions were splendid and costly, the praise of the entertainer was chanted by all the poets at the feast; but if any slight were offered, then the Ard-Filé poured forth his stinging satire in such bitter odes, that many declared they would sooner die than incur the anger of the poets or be made the subject of their scathing satire.

All the learned men and professors, the ollaves of music, poetry, oratory, and of the arts and sciences generally, formed a great Bardic Association, who elected their own president, with the title of Chief Poet of all Ireland, and they also elected chief poets for each of the provinces. Learned women, likewise, and poetesses, were included in the Bardic Association, with distinct and recognized privileges, both as to revenue and costly apparel. Legal enactments even were made respecting the number of colours allowed to be worn in their mantles—the poet being allowed six colours, and the poetess five in her robe and mantle; the number of colours being a distinct recognition and visible sign of rank, and therefore very highly esteemed. But, in time, as a consequence of their many and great privileges, the pride and insolence of the learned class, the ollamhs, poets, and poetesses, became so insufferable, that even the kings trembled before them. This is shown in the Ossianic tale, from which we may gather that Seanchan the Bard, when entertained at the court of King Guaire, grew jealous of the attention paid to the nobles while he was present. So he sulked at the festival, and made himself eminently disagreeable, as will be seen by the following legend:—

When Seanchan, the renowned Bard, was made *Ard-Filé*, or Chief Poet of Ireland, Guaire, the king of Connaught, to do him honour, made a great feast for him and the whole Bardic Association. And all the professors went to the king's house, the great ollaves of poetry and history and music, and of the arts and sciences; and the learned, aged females, Grug and Grag and Grangait; and all the chief poets and poetesses of Ireland, an amazing number. But Guaire the king entertained them all splendidly, so that the ancient pathway to his palace is still called "The Road of the Dishes."

And each day he asked, "How fares it with my noble guests?" But they were all discontented, and wanted things he could not get for them. So he was very sorrowful, and prayed to God to be delivered from "the learned men and women, a vexatious class."

Still the feast went on for three days and three nights. And they drank and made merry. And the whole Bardic Association entertained the nobles with the choicest music and professional accomplishments.

But Seanchan sulked and would neither eat nor drink, for he was jealous of the nobles of Connaught. And when he saw how much they consumed of the best meats and wine, he declared he would taste no food till they and their servants were all sent away out of the house.

And when Guaire asked him again, "How fares my noble guest, and this great and excellent people?" Seanchan answered, "I have never had worse days, nor worse nights, nor worse dinners in my life." And he ate nothing for three whole days.

Then the king was sorely grieved that the whole Bardic Association should be feasting and drinking while Seanchan, the chief poet of Erin, was fasting and weak. So he sent his favourite serving-man, a person of mild manners and cleanliness, to offer special dishes to the bard.

"Take them away," said Seanchan; "I'll have none of them."

"And why, oh, Royal Bard?" asked the servitor.

"Because thou art an uncomely youth," answered Seanchan. "Thy grandfather was chip-nailed—I have seen him; I shall eat no food from thy hands."

Then the king called a beautiful maiden to him, his foster daughter, and said, "Lady, bring thou this wheaten cake and this dish of salmon to the illustrious poet, and serve him thyself." So the maiden went.

But when Seanchan saw her he asked: "Who sent thee hither, and why hast thou brought me food?"

"My lord the king sent me, oh, Royal Bard," she answered, "because I am comely to look upon, and he bade me serve thee with food myself."

"Take it away," said Seanchan, "thou art an unseemly girl, I know of none more ugly. I have seen thy grandmother; she sat on a wall one day and pointed out the way with her hand to some travelling lepers. How could I touch thy food?" So the maiden went away in sorrow.

And then Guaire the king was indeed angry, and he exclaimed, "My malediction on the mouth that uttered that! May the kiss of a leper be on Seanchan's lips before he dies!"

Now there was a young serving-girl there, and she said to Seanchan, "There is a hen's egg in the place, my lord, may I bring it to thee, oh, Chief Bard?"

"It will suffice," said Seanchan; "bring it that I may eat."

But when she went to look for it, behold the egg was gone.

"Thou hast eaten it," said the bard, in wrath.

"Not so, my lord," she answered; "but the mice, the nimble race, have carried it away."

"Then I will satirize them in a poem," said Seanchan; and forthwith he chanted so bitter a satire against them that ten mice fell dead at once in his presence.

"'Tis well," said Seanchan; "but the cat is the one most to blame, for it was her duty to suppress the mice. Therefore I shall satirize the tribe of the cats, and their chief lord, Irusan, son of Arusan. For I know where he lives with his wife Spit-fire, and his daughter Sharp-tooth, with her brothers, the Purrer and the Growler. But I shall begin with Irusan himself, for he is king, and answerable for all the cats."

And he said—"Irusan, monster of claws, who strikes at the mouse, but lets it go; weakest of cats. The otter did well who bit off the tips of thy progenitor's ears, so that every cat since is jagged-eared. Let thy tail hang down; it is right, for the mouse jeers at thee."

Now Irusan heard these words in his cave, and he said to his daughter, Sharp-tooth: "Seanchan has satirized me, but I will be avenged."

"Nay, father," she said, "bring him here alive, that we may all take our revenge."

"I shall go then and bring him," said Irusan; "so send thy brothers after me."

Now when it was told to Seanchan that the King of the Cats was on his way to come and kill him, he was timorous, and besought Guaire and all the nobles to stand by and protect him. And before long a vibrating, impressive, impetuous sound was heard, like a raging tempest of fire in full blaze. And when the cat appeared he seemed to them of the size of a bullock; and this was his appearance—rapacious, panting, jagged-eared, snub-nosed, sharp-toothed, nimble, angry, vindictive, glare-eyed, terrible, sharp-clawed. Such was his similitude. But he passed on amongst them, not minding till he came to Seanchan; and him he seized by the arm and jerked him up on his back, and made off the way he came before any one could touch him; for he had no other object in view but to get hold of the poet.

Now Seanchan, being in evil plight, had recourse to flattery. "Oh, Irusan," he exclaimed, "how truly splendid thou art, such running, such leaps, such strength, and such agility! But what evil have I done, oh, Irusan, son of

Arusan? spare me, I entreat. I invoke the saints between thee and me, oh, great King of the Cats."

But not a bit did the cat let go his hold for all this fine talk, but went straight on to Clonmacnoise where there was a forge; and St. Kieran happened to be there standing at the door.

"What!" exclaimed the saint; "is that the Chief Bard of Erin on the back of a cat? Has Guaire's hospitality ended in this?" And he ran for a red-hot bar of iron that was in the furnace, and struck the cat on the side with it, so that the iron passed through him, and he fell down lifeless.

"Now my curse on the hand that gave that blow!" said the bard, when he got upon his feet.

"And wherefore?" asked St. Kieran.

"Because," answered Seanchan, "I would rather Irusan had killed me, and eaten me every bit, that so I might bring disgrace on Guaire for the bad food he gave me; for it was all owing to his wretched dinners that I got into this plight."

And when all the other kings heard of Seanchan's misfortunes, they sent to beg he would visit their courts. But he would have neither kiss nor welcome from them, and went on his way to the bardic mansion, where the best of good living was always to be had. And ever after the kings were afraid to offend Seanchan.

So as long as he lived he had the chief place at the feast, and all the nobles there were made to sit below him, and Seanchan was content. And in time he and Guaire were reconciled; and Seanchan and all the ollamhs, and the whole Bardic Association, were feasted by the king for thirty days in noble style, and had the choicest of viands and the best of French wines to drink, served in goblets of silver. And in return for his splendid hospitality the Bardic Association decreed, unanimously, a vote of thanks to the king. And they praised him in poems as "Guaire the Generous," by which name he was ever after known in history, for the words of the poet are immortal.

The Bards

The Irish kings in ancient times kept up splendid hospitality at their respective courts, and never sat down to an entertainment, it was said, without a hundred nobles at least being present. Next in rank and superb living to the royal race came the learned men, the ollamhs and poets; they were placed next the king, and above the nobles at the festivals, and very gorgeous was the appearance of the Ard-Filé on these occasions, in his white robes clasped with golden brooches, and a circlet of gold upon his head; while by his side lay the golden harp, which he seized when the poetic frenzy came upon him, and swept the chords to songs of love, or in praise of immortal heroes. The queen alone had the privilege to ask the poet to recite at the royal banquets, and while he declaimed, no man dared to interrupt him by a single word.

A train of fifty minor bards always attended the chief poet, and they were all entertained free of cost wherever they visited, throughout Ireland, while the Ard-Filé was borne on men's shoulders to the palace of the king, and there presented with a rich robe, a chain, and a girdle of gold. Of one bard, it is recorded that the king gave him, in addition, his horse and armour, fifty rings to his hand, one thousand ounces of pure gold, and his chess-board.

The game of chess is frequently referred to in the old bardic tales; and chess seems to have been a favourite pastime with the Irish from the most remote antiquity. The pieces must have been of great size, for it is narrated that the great Cuchullen killed a messenger who had told him a lie, by merely flinging a chessman at him, which pierced his brain. The royal chess-board was very costly and richly decorated. One is described in a manuscript of the twelfth century: "It was a board of silver and pure gold, and every angle was illuminated with precious stones. And there was a man-bag of woven brass wire." But the ancestors of the same king had in their hall a chess-board with the pieces formed of the *bones of their hereditary enemies.*

The dress of the bards added to their splendour, for the Brehon laws enacted that the value of the robes of the chief poet should be five milch cows, and that of the poetess three cows; the queen's robes being of the value of seven cows, including a diadem and golden veil, and a robe of scarlet silk, embroidered in divers colours. The scions of the royal house had also the right to seven colours in their mantle; while the poet was allowed six, and the poetess five—the number of colours being a sign of dignity and rank.

Learning was always highly esteemed in Ireland, and in ancient Erin the *literati* ranked next to the kings.

The great and wise *Ollamh-Fodla*, king of Ireland in Druidic times, built and endowed a college at Tara, near the royal palace, which was called *Mur-Ollamh*, "the Wall of the Learned." All the arts and sciences were represented there by eminent professors, the great ollaves of music, history, poetry, and oratory; and they lived and feasted together, and formed the great Bardic Association, ruled over by their own president, styled the Ard-Filé, or chief poet of Ireland, from *Filidecht* (philosophy or the highest wisdom); for the poets, above all men, were required to be pure and free from all sin that could be a reproach to learning. From them was demanded—

"Purity of hand,
Purity of mouth,
Purity of learning,
Purity of marriage;"

and any ollamh that did not preserve these four purities lost half his income and his dignity, the poet being esteemed not only the highest of all men for his learning and intellect, but also as being the true revealer of the supreme wisdom.

Music was sedulously taught and cultivated at the college of the ollamhs; for all the ancient life of Ireland moved to music.

The Brehons seated on a hill intoned the laws to the listening people; the Senachies chanted the genealogies of the kings; and the Poets recited the deeds of the heroes, or sang to their gold harps those exquisite airs that still enchant the world, and which have been wafted down along the centuries, an echo, according to tradition, of the soft, pathetic, fairy music, that haunted the hills and glens of ancient Ireland.

The chief poet was required to know by heart four hundred poems, and the minor bards two hundred. And they were bound to recite any poem called for by the kings at the festivals. On one occasion a recitation was demanded of the legend of the *Taine-bo-Cuailne*, or The Great Cattle Raid, of which Maeve, queen of Connaught, was the heroine, but none of the bards knew it. This was felt to be a great disgrace, and Seanchan and the bards set forth to traverse Ireland in search of the story of the Taine, under *Geasa*, or a solemn oath, not to sleep twice in the same place till it was found.

At length it was revealed to them that only the dead Fergus-Roy knew the poem, and forthwith they proceeded to his grave, and fasted and prayed for three days, while they invoked him to appear. And on their invocation Fergus-Roy uprose in awful majesty, and stood in his grave clothes before them, and recited the Taine from beginning to end to the circle of listening bards. Then, having finished, he descended again into the grave, and the earth closed over him.

During this expedition, Guaire the Generous took charge of all the wives and the poetesses of the Bardic Association, so as they should not trouble the bards while on their wanderings in search of the ballad of the Taine. Yet they do not seem to have been great feeders, these learned ladies; for it is related of one of them, Brigit the poetess, that although she only ate one hen's egg at a meal, yet she was called "Brigit of the great appetite."

It was on their return from the search for the Taine that the bards decreed a vote of thanks to Guaire the king.

In order to keep up the dignity of the great bardic clan, an income was paid by the State to each of the professors and poets according to his eminence; that of the chief poet being estimated by antiquarians at about five thousand a year of our money, for the lofty and learned Bardic Association disdained commerce and toil. The Fileas lived only on inspiration and the hospitality of their royal and noble patrons, which they amply repaid by laudatory odes and sonnets. But, if due homage were denied them, they denounced the ungenerous and niggard defaulter in the most scathing and bitter satires. Of one chief it is recorded that he absolutely went mad and died in consequence of the malignant poems that were made on him by a clever satirical bard.

Lady Jane Francesca Agnes Wilde

At last the Brehons found it necessary to take cognizance of this cruel and terrible implement of social torture, and enactments were framed against it, with strict regulations regarding the quality and justice of the satires poured out by the poets on those who had the courage to resist their exactions and resent their insolence. Finally, however, the ollamhs, poets, and poetesses became so intolerable that the reigning king of Ireland about the seventh century made a great effort to extirpate the whole bardic race, but failed; they were too strong for him, though he succeeded in, at least, materially abridging their privileges, lessening their revenues, and reducing their numbers; and though they still continued to exist as the Bardic Association, yet they never afterwards regained the power and dignity which they once held in the land, before their pride and insolent contempt of all classes who were not numbered amongst the ollamhs and fileas, had aroused such violent animosity. The Brehon laws also decreed, as to the distraint of a poet, that his horsewhip be taken from him, "as a warning that he is not to make use of it until he renders justice." Perhaps by the horsewhip was meant the wand or staff which the poets carried, made of wood, on which it is conjectured they may have inscribed their verses in the Ogham character.

The Brehons seem to have made the most minute regulations as to the life of the people, even concerning the domestic cats. In the *Senchas Mor* (The Great Antiquity) it is enacted that the cat is exempt from liability for eating the food which he finds in the kitchen, "owing to negligence in taking care of it." But if it were taken from the security of a vessel, then the cat is in fault, and he may safely be killed. The cat, also, is exempt from liability for injuring an idler in catching mice while mousing; but *half-fines* are due from him for the profitable worker he may injure, and the excitement of his mousing takes the other half. For the distraint of a dog, a stick was placed over his trough in order that he be not fed. And there was a distress of two days for a black and white cat if descended from the great champion, which was taken from the ship of Breasal Breac, in which were white-breasted black cats; the same for the lapdog of a queen.

215

King Arthur and the Cat

While on the subject of cats, the curious and interesting legend of "King Arthur's Fight with the Great Cat" should not be passed over; for though not exactly Irish, yet it is at least Celtic, and belongs by affinity to our ancient race. It is taken from a prose romance of the fifteenth century, entitled, "Merlin; or, The Early Life of King Arthur," recently edited, from the unique Cambridge Manuscript, by Mr. Wheatly.

Merlin told the king that the people beyond the Lake of Lausanne greatly desired his help, "for there repaireth a devil that destroyeth the country. It is a cat so great and ugly that it is horrible to look on." For one time a fisher came to the lake with his nets, and he promised to give our Lord the first fish he took. It was a fish worth thirty shillings; and when he saw it so fair and great, he said to himself softly, "God shall not have this; but I will surely give Him the next." Now, the next was still better, and he said, "Our Lord may wait yet awhile; but the third shall be His without doubt." So he cast his net, but drew out only a little kitten, as black as any coal.

And when the fisher saw it he said he had need of it at home for rats and mice; and he nourished it and kept it in his house till it strangled him and his wife and children. Then the cat fled to a high mountain and destroyed and slew all that came in his way, and was great and terrible to behold.

When the king heard this he made ready and rode to the Lac de Lausanne and found the country desolate and void of people, for neither man nor woman would inhabit the place for fear of the cat.

And the king was lodged a mile from the mountain, with Sir Gawvain and Merlin and others. And they clomb the mountain, Merlin leading the way. And when they were come up, Merlin said to the king, "Sir, in that rock liveth the cat;" and he showed him a great cave, large and deep, in the mountain.

"And how shall the cat come out?" said the king.

"That shall ye see hastily," quoth Merlin; "but look you, be ready to defend, for anon he will assail you."

"Then draw ye all back," said the king, "for I will prove his power."

And when they withdrew, Merlin whistled loud, and the cat leaped out of the cave, thinking it was some wild beast, for he was hungry and fasting; and he ran boldly to the king, who was ready with his spear, and thought to smite him through the body. But the fiend seized the spear in his mouth and broke it in twain.

Then the king drew his sword, holding his shield also before him. And as the cat leaped at his throat, he struck him so fiercely that the creature fell to the ground; but soon was up again, and ran at the king so hard that his claws gripped through the hauberk to the flesh, and the red blood followed the claws.

Now the king was nigh falling to earth; but when he saw the red blood he was wonder-wrath, and with his sword in his right hand and his shield at his breast, he ran at the cat vigorously, who sat licking his claws, all wet with blood. But when he saw the king coming towards him, he leapt up to seize him by the throat, as before, and stuck his fore-feet so firmly in the shield that they stayed there; and the king smote him on the legs, so that he cut them off to the knees, and the cat fell to the ground.

Then the king ran at him with his sword; but the cat stood on his hind-legs and grinned with his teeth, and coveted the throat of the king, and the king tried to smite him on the head; but the cat strained his hinder feet and leaped at the king's breast, and fixed his teeth in the flesh, so that the blood streamed down from breast and shoulder.

Then the king struck him fiercely on the body, and the cat fell head downwards, but the feet stayed fixed in the hauberk. And the king smote them asunder, on which the cat fell to the ground, where she howled and brayed so loudly that it was heard through all the host, and she began to creep towards the cave; but the king stood between her and the cave, and when she tried to catch him with her teeth he struck her dead.

Then Merlin and the others ran to him and asked how it was with him.

"Well, blessed be our Lord!" said the king, "for I have slain this devil; but, verily, I never had such doubt of myself, not even when I slew the giant on the mountain; therefore I thank the Lord."

217

(This was the great giant of St. Michael's Mount, who supped all the season on seven knave children chopped in a charger of white silver, with powder of precious spices, and goblets full plenteous of Portugal wine.)

"Sir," said the barons, "ye have great cause for thankfulness."

Then they looked on the feet that were left in the shield and in the hauberk, and said, "Such feet were never seen before!" And they took the shield and showed it to the host with great joy.

So the king let the shield be with the cat's feet; but the other feet he had laid in a coffin to be kept. And the mountain was called from that day, "The Mountain of the Cat," and the name will never be changed while the world endureth.

Concerning Cows

The most singular legends of Ireland relate to bulls and cows, and there are hundreds of places all commencing with the word *Bo* (one of the most ancient words in the Irish language), which recall some mystic or mythical story of a cow, especially of a white heifer, which animal seems to have been an object of the greatest veneration from all antiquity.

In old times there arose one day a maiden from the sea, a beautiful Berooch, or mermaid, and all the people on the Western Coast of Erin gathered round her and wondered at her beauty. And the great chief of the land carried her home to his house, where she was treated like a queen.

And she was very gentle and wise, and after some time she acquired the language, and could talk to the people quite well in their own Irish tongue, to their great delight and wonder. Then she informed them that she had been sent to their country by a great spirit, to announce the arrival in Ireland of the three sacred cows—*Bo-Finn*, *Bo-Ruadh*, and *Bo-Dhu*—the white, the red, and the black cows, who were destined to fill the land with the most splendid cattle, so that the people should never know want while the world lasted.

This was such good news that the people in their delight carried the sea-maiden from house to house in procession, in order that she might tell it herself to every one; and they crowned her with flowers, while the musicians

218

went before her, singing to their harps.

After dwelling with them a little longer she asked to be taken back to the sea, for she had grown sad at being away so long from her own kindred. So, on May Eve, a great crowd accompanied her down to the strand, where she took leave of them, telling them that on that day year they should all assemble at the same place to await the arrival of the three cows. Then she plunged into the sea and was seen no more.

However, on that day year all the people of Ireland assembled on the shore to watch, as they had been directed by the beautiful sea-maiden; and all the high cliffs and all the rocks were covered with anxious spectators from the early dawn. Nor did they wait in vain. Exactly at noon the waves were stirred with a mighty commotion, and three cows rose up from the sea—a white, a red, and a black—all beautiful to behold, with sleek skins, large soft eyes, and curved horns, white as ivory. They stood upon the shore for a while, looking around them. Then each one went in a different direction, by three roads; the black went south, the red went north, and the milk-white heifer—the *Bo-Finn*—crossed the plain of Ireland to the very centre, where stood the king's palace. And every place she passed was named after her, and every well she drank at was called *Lough-na-Bo*, or *Tober-Bo-Finn* (the well of the white cow), so her memory remains to this day.

In process of time the white heifer gave birth to twins, a male and female calf, and from them descended a great race, still existing in Ireland; after which the white cow disappeared into a great cave by the sea, the entrance to which no man knows. And there she remains, and will remain, in an enchanted sleep, until the true king of Eire, the lord of Ireland, shall come to waken her; but the lake near the cave is still known as *Lough-na-Bo-banna* (the lake of the snow-white cow). Yet some say that it was the king's daughter was carried off by enchantment to the cave, in the form of a cow, and she will never regain her form until she sleeps on the summit of each of the three highest mountains in Ireland; but only the true king of Eire can wake her from her sleep, and bring her to "the rock of the high place," when she will be restored at last to her own beautiful form.

Another legend says that a red-haired woman struck the beautiful Bo-Finn with her staff, and smote her to death; and the roar which the white cow gave in dying was heard throughout the whole of Ireland, and all the people trembled. This is evidently an allegory. The beautiful Bo-Finn—the white cow—is Ireland herself; and the red-haired woman who smote her to death was Queen Elizabeth, "in whose time, after her cruel wars, the cry of the slaughtered people was heard all over the land, and went up to heaven for vengeance against the enemies of Ireland; and the kingdom was shaken as by an earthquake, by the roar of the oppressed against the tyrant."

The path of the white cow across Ireland is marked by small rude stone monuments, still existing. They show the exact spot where she rested each night and had her bed, and the adjoining lands have names connected with the tradition—as, "The plain of the Fenian cows;" "The hill of worship;" "The pool of the spotted ox," called after him because he always waited to drink till the white cow came, for they were much attached to each other.

There are also Druid stones at one resting-place, with Ogham marks on them. Some time ago an endeavour was made to remove and carry off the stones of one of the monuments; but the man who first put a spade in the ground was "struck," and remained bedridden for seven years.

The plain of the death of the *Bo-banna* (the white cow), where she gave the roar that shook all Ireland is called "the plain of lamentation." It never was tilled, and never will be tilled. The people hold it as a sacred spot, and until recently it was the custom to have dances there every Sunday. But these old usages are rapidly dying out; for though meant originally as mystic ceremonies, yet by degrees they degenerated to such licentious revelry that the wrath of the priesthood fell on them, and they were discontinued.

There is a holy well near "the plain of lamentation," called *Tobar-na-Bo* (the well of the white cow); and these ancient names, coming down the stream of time from the far-off Pagan era, attest the great antiquity of the legend of the coming to Ireland of the mystic and beautiful *Bo-Finn*.

There is another legend concerning the arrival of the three cows—the white, the red, and the black—which is said to be taken from the Book of Enoch.

Four cows sprang at once from the earth—two white, a red, and a black—and one of the four went over to the white cow and taught it a mystery. And it trembled and became a man, and this was the first man that appeared in Erin. And the man fashioned a ship and dwelt there with the cows while a deluge covered the earth. And when the waters ceased, the red and the black cows went their way, but the white remained.

The story is supposed by Bryant to be a literal rendering of some ancient hieroglyph, descriptive of the three races of mankind, and of the dispersion of the primal human family.

Fairy Wiles

The fairies are very desirous to abduct handsome cows and carry them off to the fairy palace under the earth; and if a farmer happens to find one of his stock ailing or diseased, the belief is that the fairies have carried off the real good animal, and sent an old wizened witch to take the form of the farmer's cow. It is therefore to neutralize the fairy spells that the cattle are driven through the fire on St. John's Eve; and other devices are employed—a bunch of primroses is very effective tied on the tail, or a hot coal run down the cow's back to singe the hair.

One evening a boy was driving home his father's cows when a fairy blast arose in the form of a whirlwind of dust, on which the cows took fright, and one of them ran upon a fairy rath. The boy followed to turn her back, when he was met and stopped by an old witch-woman.

"Let her alone, Alanna," she cried, "she is on our ground now, and you can't take her away. So just run home and tell your father that on this day twelvemonth the cow will be restored to him, and bring a fine young calf along with her. But the fairies want her badly now, for our beautiful queen down there is fretting her life out for want of some milk that has the scent of the green grass in it and of the fresh upper air. Now don't fret, Alanna, but trust my words. There, take yon hazel stick and strike the cow boldly three times on the head, that so the way may be clear we have to travel."

With that the boy struck the animal as he was desired, for the old witch-woman was so nice and civil that he liked to oblige her, and immediately after she and the cow vanished away as if they had sunk into the earth.

However, the father minded the time, and when that day year came round he sent his son to the fairy rath to see if the witch had kept her promise, and there truly was the cow standing quite patiently, and a fine white calf by her side. So there were great rejoicings when he brought them home, for the fairies had kept their promise and behaved honourably, as indeed they always do when properly treated and trusted.

*

Not but that the fairies will do wicked things sometimes, and, above all, steal the milk when they get a chance, or skim the cream off the milk crocks.

A farmer had a fine cow that was the pride of his farm and gave splendid milk, but suddenly the animal seemed ailing and queer; for she gave no milk, but went every morning and stood under the old hawthorn-tree quite quietly as if some one were milking her.

So the man watched the place at milking time, and as usual down the field came the cow and took up her position close under the old hawthorn. Then the farmer beheld the trunk of the tree open, and out of the cleft came a little witch-woman all in red, who milked the cow in a vessel she had with her, and then she retreated into the tree again.

Here was devil's work in earnest, so thought the farmer, and he hastened off for the greatest fairy doctor in the country. And when he came the cow was singed all along its back with a live coal; and then an incantation was said over it, but no one heard the words the fairy doctor uttered; after this he gave the animal a strong potion to drink, but no one knew the herbs of which it was made. However, the next day the cow was quite restored, and gave her milk as heretofore, and the spell was broken for ever and ever, after they had drawn a circle round the old hawthorn-tree with a red-hot piece of iron taken from the hearth; for neither witch nor fairy can pass a circle of fire.

The Dead Hand

Witchcraft is sometimes practised by the people to produce butter in the churn, the most efficacious being to stir the milk round with the hand of a dead man, newly taken from the churchyard; but whoever is suspected of this practice is looked upon with great horror and dread by the neighbours.

A woman of the mainland got married to a fine young fellow of one of the islands. She was a tall, dark woman who seldom spoke, and kept herself very close and reserved from every one. But she minded her business; for she had always more butter to bring to market than any one else, and could therefore undersell the other farmers' wives. Then strange rumours got about concerning her, and the people began to whisper among themselves that something was wrong, and that there was witchcraft in it, especially as it was known that whenever she churned she went into an inner room off the kitchen, shut the door close, and would allow no one to enter. So they determined to watch and find out the secret, and one day a girl from the neighbourhood, when the woman was out, got in through a window and hid herself under the bed, waiting there patiently till the churning began.

At last in came the woman, and having carefully closed the door began her work with the milk, churning in the usual way without any strange doings that might seem to have magic in them. But presently she stopped, and going over to a box unlocked it, and from this receptacle, to the girl's horror, she drew forth the hand of a dead man, with which she stirred the milk round and round several times, going down on her knees and muttering an incantation all the while.

Seven times she stirred the milk with the dead hand, and seven times she went round the churn on her knees muttering some strange charm. After this she rose up and began to gather the butter from the churn with the dead hand, filling a pail with as much butter as the milk of ten cows. When the pail was quite full she dipped the dead hand three times in the milk, then dried it and put it back again in the box.

The girl, as soon as she could get away unperceived, fled in horror from the room, and spread the news amongst the people. At once a crowd gathered round the house with angry cries and threats to break open the door to search for the dead hand.

At last the woman appeared calm and cold as usual, and told them they were taking a deal of trouble about nothing, for there was no dead hand in the house. However, the people rushed in and searched, but all they saw was a huge fire on the hearth, though the smell of burning flesh was distinctly perceptible, and by this they knew that she had burnt the dead hand. Yet this did not save her from the vengeance of the neighbours. She was shunned by every one; no one would eat with her, or drink with her, or talk to her, and after a while she and her husband quitted the island and were never more heard of.

However, after she left and the butter was brought to the market, all the people had their fair and equal rights again, of which the wicked witchcraft of the woman had defrauded them for so long, and there was great rejoicing in the island over the fall and punishment of the wicked witch of the dead hand.

The Wicked Widow

The evil spells over milk and butter are generally practised by women, and arise from some feeling of malice or envy against a prosperous neighbour. But the spell will not work unless some portion of the milk is first given by consent. The people therefore are very reluctant to give away milk, unless to some friend that they could not suspect of evil. Tramps coming in to beg for a mug of milk should always be avoided, they may be witches in disguise; and even if milk is given, it must be drunk in the house, and not carried away out of it. In every case the person who enters must give a hand to the churn, and say, "God bless all here."

A young farmer, one of the fine handsome fellows of the West, named Hugh Connor, who was also well off and rich, took to wife a pretty young girl of the village called Mary, one of the Leydons, and there was no better girl in all the country round, and they were very comfortable and happy together. But Hugh Connor had been keeping company before his marriage with a young widow of the place, who had designs on him, and was filled with rage when Mary Leydon was selected for Connor's bride, in place of herself. Then a desire for vengeance rose up in her heart, and she laid her plans accordingly. First she got a fairy woman to teach her some witch secrets and spells, and then by great pretence of love and affection for Mary Connor, she got frequent admission to the house, soothing and flattering the young wife; and on churning days she would especially make it a point to come in and offer a helping hand, and if the cakes were on the griddle, she would sit down to watch and turn them. But it so happened that always on these days the cakes were sure to be burned and spoiled, and the butter would not rise in the churn, or if any did come, it was sour and bad, and of no use for the market. But still the widow kept on visiting, and soothing, and flattering, till Mary Connor thought she was the very best friend to her in the whole wide world, though it was true that whenever the widow came to the house something evil happened. The best dish fell down of itself off the dresser and broke; or the rain got in through the roof, and Mary's new cashmere gown, a present that had come to her all the way from Dublin, was quite ruined and spoiled. But worse came, for the cow sickened, and a fine young brood of turkeys walked straight into the lake and got drowned. And still worst of all, the picture of the Blessed Virgin Mother, that was pinned up to the wall, fell down one day, and was blown into the fire and burned.

After this, what luck could be on the house? and Mary's heart sank within her, and she fairly broke down, and cried her very life out in a torrent of tears.

Now it so happened that an old woman with a blue cloak, and the hood of it over her head, a stranger, was passing by at the time, and she stepped in and asked Mary kindly what ailed her. So Mary told her all her misfortunes, and how everything in the house seemed bewitched for evil.

"Now," said the stranger, "I see it all, for I am wise, and know the mysteries. Some one with the Evil Eye comes to your house. We must find out who it is."

Then Mary told her that the nearest friend she had was the widow, but she was so sweet and kind, no one could suspect her of harm.

"We'll see," said the stranger, "only do as I bid you, and have everything ready when she comes."

"She will be here soon," said Mary, "for it is churning day, and she always comes to help exactly at noon."

"Then I'll begin at once; and now close the door fast," said the stranger.

And with that, she threw some herbs on the fire, so that a great smoke arose. Then she took all the plough irons that were about, and one of them she drove into the ground close beside the churn, and put a live coal beside it; and the other irons she heated red-hot in the fire, and still threw on more herbs to make a thick smoke, which Mary thought smelt like the incense in the church. Then with a hot iron rod from the fire, the strange woman made the sign of the cross on the threshold, and another over the hearth. After which a loud roaring was heard outside, and the widow rushed in crying out that a hot stick was running through her heart, and all her body was on fire. And then she dropped down on the floor in a fit, and her face became quite black, and her limbs worked in convulsions.

"Now," said the stranger, "you see who it is put the Evil Eye on all your house; but the spell has been broken at last. Send for the men to carry her back to her own house, and never let that witch-woman cross your threshold again."

After this the stranger disappeared, and was seen no more in the village.

Now when all the neighbours heard the story, they would have no dealings with the widow. She was shunned and hated; and no respectable person would be seen talking to her, and she went by the name of the Evil Witch. So her life was very miserable, and not long after she died of sheer vexation and spite, all by herself alone, for no one would go near her; and the night of the wake no one went to offer a prayer, for they said the devil would be there in person to look after his own. And no one would walk with her coffin to the grave, for they said the devil was waiting at the churchyard gate for her; and they firmly believe to this day that her body was carried away on that night from the graveyard by the powers of darkness. But no one ventured to test the truth of the story by opening the coffin, so the weird legend remains still unsolved.

But as for Hugh Connor and the pretty Mary, they prospered after that in all things, and good luck and the blessing of God seemed to be evermore on them and their house, and their cattle, and their children. At the same time, Mary never omitted on churning days to put a red-hot horse-shoe under the churn according as the stranger had told her, who she firmly believed was a good fairy in disguise, who came to help her in the time of her sore trouble and anxiety.

The Butter Mystery

There were two brothers who had a small farm and dairy between them, and they were honest and industrious, and worked hard to get along, though they had barely enough, after all their labour, just to keep body and soul together.

One day while churning, the handle of the dash broke, and nothing being near to mend it, one of the brothers cut off a branch from an elder-tree that grew close to the house, and tied it to the dash for a handle. Then the churning went on, but to their surprise, the butter gathered so thick that all the crocks in the house were soon full, and still there was more left. The same thing went on every churning day, so the brothers became rich, for they could fill the market with their butter, and still had more than enough for every buyer.

At last, being honest and true men, they began to fear that there was witchcraft in it, and that they were wronging their neighbours by abstracting their butter, and bringing it to their own churn in some strange way. So they both went off together to a great fairy doctor, and told him the whole story, and asked his advice.

"Foolish men," he said to them, "why did you come to me? for now you have broken the spell, and you will never have your crocks filled with butter any more. Your good fortune has passed away, for know the truth now. You were not wronging your neighbours; all was fair and just that you did, but this is how it happened. Long ago, the fairies passing through your land had a dispute and fought a battle, and having no arms, they flung lumps of butter at each other, which got lodged in the branches of the elder-tree in great quantities, for it was just after May Eve, when butter is plenty. This is the butter you have had, for the elder-tree has a sacred power which preserved it until now, and it came down to you through the branch you cut for a handle to the dash. But the spell is broken now that you have uttered the mystery, and you will have no more butter from the elder-tree."

Then the brothers went away sorrowful, and never after did the butter come beyond the usual quantity. However, they had already made so much money that they were content. And they stocked their farm, and all things prospered with them, for they had dealt uprightly in the matter, and the blessing of the Lord was on them.

Concerning Birds

In all countries superstitions of good or evil are attached to certain birds. The raven, for instance, has a wide-world reputation as the harbinger of evil and ill-luck. The wild geese portend a severe winter; the robin is held sacred, for no one would think of harming a bird who bears on his breast the blessed mark of the blood of Christ; while the wren is hunted to death with intense and cruel hate on St. Stephen's Day.

The Magpie

There is no Irish name for the Magpie. It is generally called *Francagh*, a Frenchman, though no one knows why. Many queer tales are narrated of this bird, arising from its quaint ways, its adroit cunning and habits of petty larceny. Its influence is not considered evil, though to meet one alone in the morning when going a journey is an ill omen, but to meet more than one

magpie betokens good fortune, according to the old rhyme which runs thus—
"One for Sorrow,
Two for Mirth,
Three for Marriage,
Four for a Birth."

The Wren

The wren is mortally hated by the Irish; for on one occasion, when the Irish troops were approaching to attack a portion of Cromwell's army, the wrens came and perched on the Irish drums, and by their tapping and noise aroused the English soldiers, who fell on the Irish troops and killed them all. So ever since the Irish hunt the wren on St. Stephen's Day, and teach their children to run it through with thorns and kill it whenever it can be caught. A dead wren was also tied to a pole and carried from house to house by boys, who demanded money; if nothing was given the wren was buried on the door-step, which was considered a great insult to the family and a degradation.

The Raven and Water Wagtail

If ravens come cawing about a house it is a sure sign of death, for the raven is Satan's own bird; so also is the water wagtail, yet beware of killing it, for it has three drops of the devil's blood in its little body, and ill-luck ever goes with it, and follows it.

The Cuckoo and Robin Redbreast

It is very unlucky to kill the cuckoo or break its eggs, for it brings fine weather; but most unlucky of all things is to kill the robin redbreast. The robin is God's own bird, sacred and holy, and held in the greatest veneration because of the beautiful tradition current amongst the people, that it was the robin plucked out the sharpest thorn that was piercing Christ's brow on the cross; and in so doing the breast of the bird was dyed red with the Saviour's blood, and so has remained ever since a sacred and blessed sign to preserve the robin from harm and make it beloved of all men.

Ancient Legends of Ireland

Concerning Living Creatures

The Cricket
The crickets are believed to be enchanted. People do not like to express an exact opinion about them, so they are spoken of with great mystery and awe, and no one would venture to kill them for the whole world. But they are by no means evil; on the contrary, the presence of the cricket is considered lucky, and their singing keeps away the fairies at night, who are always anxious, in their selfish way, to have the whole hearth left clear for themselves, that they may sit round the last embers of the fire, and drink the cup of milk left for them by the farmer's wife, in peace and quietness. The crickets are supposed to be hundreds of years old, and their talk, could we understand it, would no doubt be most interesting and instructive.

The Beetle
The beetle is not killed by the people for the following reason: they have a tradition that one day the chief priests sent messengers in every direction to look for the Lord Jesus, and they came to a field where a man was reaping, and asked him—

"Did Jesus of Nazareth pass this way?"

"No," said the man, "I have not seen him."

"But I know better," said a little clock running up, "for He was here to-day and rested, and has not long gone away."

"That is false," said a great big black beetle, coming forward; "He has not passed since yesterday, and you will never find Him on this road; try another."

So the people kill the clock because he tried to betray Christ; but they spare the beetle and will not touch him, because he saved the Lord on that day.

The Hare
Hares are considered unlucky, as the witches constantly assume their form in order to gain entrance to a field where they can bewitch the cattle. A man

230

once fired at a hare he met in the early morning, and having wounded it, followed the track of the blood till it disappeared within a cabin. On entering he found Nancy Molony, the greatest witch in all the county, sitting by the fire, groaning and holding her side. And then the man knew that she had been out in the form of a hare, and he rejoiced over her discomfiture.

Still it is not lucky to kill a hare before sunrise, even when it crosses your path; but should it cross *three* times, then turn back, for danger is on the road before you.

A tailor one time returning home very late at night from a wake, or better, very early in the morning, saw a hare sitting on the path before him, and not inclined to run away. As he approached, with his stick raised to strike her, he distinctly heard a voice saying, "Don't kill it." However, he struck the hare three times, and each time heard the voice say, "Don't kill it." But the last blow knocked the poor hare quite dead; and immediately a great big weasel sat up, and began to spit at him. This greatly frightened the tailor who, however, grabbed the hare, and ran off as fast as he could. Seeing him look so pale and frightened, his wife asked the cause, on which he told her the whole story; and they both knew he had done wrong, and offended some powerful witch, who would be avenged. However, they dug a grave for the hare and buried it; for they were afraid to eat it, and thought that now perhaps the danger was over. But next day the man became suddenly speechless, and died off before the seventh day was over, without a word evermore passing his lips; and then all the neighbours knew that the witch-woman had taken her revenge.

The Weasel

Weasels are spiteful and malignant, and old withered witches sometimes take this form. It is extremely unlucky to meet a weasel the first thing in the morning; still it would be hazardous to kill it, for it might be a witch and take revenge. Indeed one should be very cautious about killing a weasel at any time, for all the other weasels will resent your audacity, and kill your chickens when an opportunity offers. The only remedy is to kill one chicken yourself, make the sign of the cross solemnly three times over it, then tie it to a stick hung up in the yard, and the weasels will have no more power for evil, nor the witches who take their form, at least during the year, if the stick is left standing; but the chicken may be eaten when the sun goes down.

*

A goose is killed on St. Michael's Day because the son of a king, being then at a feast, was choked by the bone of a goose; but was restored by St. Patrick. Hence the king ordered a goose to be sacrificed every year on the anniversary of the day to commemorate the event, and in honour of St. Michael.

*

A fowl is killed on St. Martin's Day, and the blood sprinkled on the house. In Germany a black cock is substituted.

*

A crowing hen, a whistling girl, and a black cat, are considered most unlucky. Beware of them in a house.

*

If a cock comes on the threshold and crows, you may expect visitors.

*

To see three magpies on the left hand when on a journey is unlucky; but two on the right hand is a good omen.

*

If you hear the cuckoo on your right hand you will have luck all the year after.

*

Whoever kills a robin redbreast will never have good luck were they to live a thousand years.

*

A water wagtail near the house betokens bad news on its way to you.

*

If the first lamb of the season is born black, it foretells mourning garments for the family within the year.

*

Lady Jane Francesca Agnes Wilde

It is very lucky for a hen and her chickens to stray into your house. Also it is good to meet a white lamb in the early morning with the sunlight on its face.

*

It is unlucky to meet a magpie, a cat, or a lame woman when going a journey. Or for a cock to meet a person in the doorway and crow before him—then the journey should be put off.

*

If one magpie comes chattering to your door it is a sign of death; but if two prosperity will follow. For a magpie to come to the door and look at you is a sure death-sign, and nothing can avert the doom.

*

A flight of rooks over an army betokens defeat; if over a house, or over people when driving or walking, death will follow.

*

It is very unlucky to ask a man on his way to fish where he is going. And many would turn back, knowing that it was an evil spell.

*

When a swarm of bees suddenly quits the hive it is a sign that death is hovering near the house. But the evil may be averted by the powerful prayers and exorcism of the priest.

*

The shoe of a horse or of an ass nailed to the door-post will bring good luck; because these animals were in the stall when Christ was born, and are blessed for evermore. But the shoe must be found, not given, in order to bring luck.

*

In whatever quarter you are looking when you first hear the cuckoo in the season, you will be travelling in that direction before the year is over.

*

It was the privilege of the chief bards to wear mantles made of birds' plumage. A short cape flung on the shoulders made of mallards' necks and crests must have been very gorgeous in effect, glittering like jewels, when the torch-light played on the colours at the festivals.

The Properties of Herbs and their Use in Medicine

The Irish, according to the saying of a wise man of the race, are the last of the 305 great Celtic nations of antiquity spoken of by Josephus, the Jewish historian; and they alone preserve inviolate the ancient venerable language, minstrelsy, and Bardic traditions, with the strange and mystic secrets of herbs, through whose potent powers they can cure disease, cause love or hatred, discover the hidden mysteries of life and death, and dominate over the fairy wiles or the malific demons.

The ancient people used to divine future events, victory in wars, safety in a dangerous voyage, triumph of a projected undertaking, success in love, recovery from sickness, or the approach of death; all through the skilful use of herbs, the knowledge of which had come down to them through the earliest traditions of the human race. One of these herbs, called the *Fairy-plant*, was celebrated for its potent power of divination; but only the adepts knew the mystic manner of its preparation for use.

There was another herb of which a drink was made, called *the Bardic potion*, for the Bards alone had the secret of the herb, and of the proper mode of treatment by which its mystic power could be revealed. This potion they gave their infant children at their birth, for it had the singular property of endowing the recipient with a fairy sweetness of voice of the most rapturous and thrilling charm. And instances are recorded of men amongst the Celtic Bards, who, having drunk of this potion in early life, were ever after endowed with the sweet voice, like fairy music, that swayed the hearts of the hearers as they chose to love or war, joy or sadness, as if by magic influence, or lulled them into the sweet calm of sleep. Such, according to the Bardic legends, was the extraordinary power of voice possessed by the great Court Minstrel of Fionn Ma-Coul, who resided with the great chief at his palace of Almhuin, and always sat next him at the royal table.

The virtue of herbs is great, but they must be gathered at night, and laid in the hand of a dead man to hold. There are herbs that produce love, and herbs that produce sterility; but only the fairy doctor knows the secrets of their power, and he will reveal the knowledge to no man unless to an adept. The wise women learn the mystic powers from the fairies, but how they pay for the knowledge none dare to tell.

The fairy doctors are often seized with trembling while uttering a charm, and look round with a scared glance of terror, as if some awful presence were beside them. But the people have the most perfect faith in the herb-men and wise women, and the faith may often work the cure.

There are seven herbs of great value and power; they are ground ivy, vervain, eyebright, groundsel, foxglove, the bark of the elder-tree, and the young shoots of the hawthorn.

Nine balls of these mixed together may be taken, and afterwards a potion made of bog-water and salt, boiled in a vessel, with a piece of money and an elf-stone. The elf-stone is generally found near a rath; it has great virtues, but being once lifted up by the spade it must never again touch the earth, or all its virtue is gone. (This elf-stone is in reality only an ancient stone arrow-head.)

*

The *Mead Cailleath*, or wood anemone, is used as a plaister for wounds.

*

The hazel-tree has many virtues. It is sacred and powerful against devils' wiles, and has mysteries and secret properties known to the wise and the adepts. The ancient Irish believed that there were fountains at the head of the chief rivers of Ireland, over each of which grew nine hazel-trees that at certain times produced beautiful red nuts. These nuts fell on the surface of the water, and the salmon in the river came up and ate of them, which caused the red spots on the salmon. And whoever could catch and eat one of these salmon would be indued with the sublimest poetic intellect. Hence the phrase current amongst the people: "Had I the net of science;" "Had I eaten of the salmon of knowledge." And this supernatural knowledge came to the great Fionn through the touch of a salmon, and made him foreknow all events.

*

Of all herbs the yarrow is the best for cures and potions. It is even sewn up in clothes as a preventive of disease.

*

The *Liss-more*, or great herb, has also strong healing power, and is used as a charm.

*

There is an herb, also, or fairy grass, called the *Faud Shaughran*, or the "stray sod," and whoever treads the path it grows on is compelled by an irresistible impulse to travel on without stopping, all through the night, delirious and restless, over bog and mountain, through hedges and ditches, till wearied and bruised and cut, his garments torn, his hands bleeding, he finds himself in the morning twenty or thirty miles, perhaps, from his own home. And those who fall under this strange influence have all the time the sensation of flying and are utterly unable to pause or turn back or change their career. There is, however, another herb that can neutralize the effects of the *Faud Shaughran*, but only the initiated can utilize its mystic properties.

Another grass is the *Fair-Gortha*, or the "hunger-stricken sod," and if the hapless traveller accidentally treads on this grass by the road-side, while passing on a journey, either by night or day, he becomes at once seized with the most extraordinary cravings of hunger and weakness, and unless timely relief is afforded he must certainly die.

*

When a child is sick a fairy woman is generally sent for, who makes a drink for the patient of those healing herbs of which she only has the knowledge. A childless woman is considered to have the strongest power over the secrets of herbs, especially those used for the maladies of children.

*

There is an herb, grown on one of the western islands off the coast of Connemara, which is reported to have great and mystic power. But no one will venture to pronounce its name. If it is desired to know for certain whether one lying sick will recover, the nearest relative must go out and look for the herb just as the sun is rising. And while holding it in the hand, an ancient form of incantation must be said. If the herb remains fresh and green the patient will certainly recover; but if it wither in the hand while the words of the incantation are said over it, then the sick person is doomed. He will surely die.

*

It was from their great knowledge of the properties of herbs that the Tuatha-de-Dananns obtained the reputation of being sorcerers and necromancers. At the great battle of Moytura in Mayo, fought about three thousand years ago, Dianecht, the great, wise Druid physician to the army, prepared a bath of herbs and plants in the line of the battle, of such wonderful curative efficacy that the wounded who were plunged into it came out whole, it being a sovereign remedy for all diseases. But the king of the Tuatha having lost his hand in the combat, the bath had no power to heal him. So Dianecht made him a silver hand, and the monarch was ever after known in history as *Nuad Airgeat lamh* (Nuad of the silver hand).

*

All herbs pulled on May Day Eve have a sacred healing power, if pulled in the name of the Holy Trinity; but if in the name of Satan, they work evil. Some herbs are malific if broken by the hand. So the plant is tied to a dog's foot, and when he runs it breaks, without a hand touching it, and may be used with safety.

A man pulled a certain herb on May Eve to cure his son who was sick to death. The boy recovered, but disappeared and was never heard of after, and the father died that day year. He had broken the fatal herb with the hand and so the doom fell on him.

Another man did the like, and gave the herb to his son to eat, who immediately began to bark like a dog, and so continued till he died.

*

The fatal herbs have signs known only to the fairy doctors, who should always be consulted before treating the sick in the family.

There are *seven* herbs that nothing natural or supernatural can injure; they are vervain, John's-wort, speedwell, eyebright, mallow, yarrow, and self-help. But they must be pulled at noon on a bright day, near the full of the moon, to have full power.

It is firmly believed that the herb-women who perform curses receive their knowledge from the fairies, who impart to them the mystical secrets of herbs and where to find them; but these secrets must not be revealed except on the death-bed, and then only to the eldest of the family. Many mysterious rites are practised in the making and the giving of potions; and the messenger who carries the draught to the sufferer must never look behind him nor utter a word till he hands the medicine to the patient, who instantly swallows a cup of the mixture before other hands have touched it.

A celebrated doctor in the south was an old woman, who had lived seven years with the fairies. She performed wonderful cures, and only required a silver tenpence to be laid on her table for the advice given and for the miraculous herb potion.

A Love Potion

Some of the country people have still a traditional remembrance of very powerful herbal remedies, and love potions are even now frequently in use. They are generally prepared by an old woman; but must be administered by the person who wishes to inspire the tender passion. At the same time, to give a love potion is considered a very awful act, as the result may be fatal, or at least full of danger.

A fine, handsome young man, of the best character and conduct, suddenly became wild and reckless, drunken and disorderly, from the effect, it was believed, of a love potion administered to him by a young girl who was passionately in love with him. When she saw the change produced in him by her act, she became moody and nervous, as if a constant terror were over her, and no one ever saw her smile again. Finally, she became half deranged, and after a few years of a strange, solitary life, she died of melancholy and despair. This was said to be "The Love-potion Curse."

Lady Jane Francesca Agnes Wilde

Love Dreams

The girl who wishes to see her future husband must go out and gather certain herbs in the light of the full moon of the new year, repeating this charm—

"Moon, moon, tell unto me
When my true love I shall see?
What fine clothes am I to wear?
How many children shall I bear?
For if my love comes not to me
Dark and dismal my life will be."

Then the girl, cutting three pieces of clay from the sod with a black-hafted knife, carries them home, ties them up in the left stocking with the right garter, places the parcel under her pillow, and dreams a true dream of the man she is to marry and of all her future fate.

To Cause Love

Ten leaves of the hemlock dried and powdered and mixed in food or drink will make the person you like to love you in return. Also keep a sprig of mint in your hand till the herb grows moist and warm, then take hold of the hand of the woman you love, and she will follow you as long as the two hands close over the herb. No invocation is necessary; but silence must be kept between the two parties for ten minutes, to give the charm time to work with due efficacy.

Medical Superstitions and Ancient Charms

The healing art in all the early stages of a nation's life, and amongst all primitive tribes, has been associated with religion. For the wonderful effects produced by certain herbs and modes of treatment were believed by the simple and unlettered people to be due to supernatural influence acting in a mystic and magical manner on the person afflicted.

The medicine men were therefore treated with the profoundest awe and respect. And the medicine women came in also for their share of veneration

239

and often of superstitious dread; for their mysterious incantations were supposed to have been taught to them by fairies and the spirits of the mountain.

The Irish from the most remote antiquity were devoted to mystical medicine, and had a remarkable knowledge of cures and remedies for disease, obtained through the power and action of herbs on the human frame.

The physicians of the pagan era formed a branch of the Druid priesthood, and were treated with distinguished honour. They had special places assigned to them at the royal banqueting table at Tara, and a certain revenue was secured to them that they might live honourably.

When in attendance on a patient the doctor was entitled by law to his diet, along with four of his pupils; but if he failed to cure from deficiency of skill, he was obliged to refund the fees and pay back all the expenses of his keep; a measure which no doubt greatly stimulated the serious attention of the learned ollamhs of healing to the case in hand.

So great, indeed, was the importance attached to the healing art in Ireland, that even prior to the Christian era, a building of the nature of an hospital was erected at Tara, near to the palace of the king. This was called "The House of Sorrow," and the sick and wounded were provided there with all necessary care.

On one occasion it is recorded that a great chief and prince out of Munster was brought to "The House of Sorrow" to be treated of wounds received in battle, but the attendant, through treachery, placed poison in the wounds, and then closed them so carefully that there was no external sign, though the groans of the wounded man were terrible to hear. Then the learned Fioneen was sent for, "the prophetic physician," as he was called, from his great skill in diagnosis; and when he arrived with three of his pupils at the hospital they found the chief lying prostrate, groaning in horrible agony.

"What groan is that?" asked the master of the first pupil.

"It is from a poisoned barb," he answered.

"And what groan is that?" asked the master, of the second pupil.

"It is from a hidden reptile," he answered.

"And what groan is that?" asked Fioneen of the third pupil.

"It is from a poisoned seed," he answered.

Then Fioneen set to work, and having cauterized the wounds with red hot irons, the poisonous bodies were extracted from beneath the skin, and the chief was healed.

In later times the Irish physicians were much celebrated for their learning, and numerous Irish medical manuscripts are in existence, both in Ireland and England, and are also scattered through the public libraries of the continent. They are chiefly written in Latin, with a commentary in Irish, and show a thorough knowledge on the part of the writers of the works of Hippocrates, Galen, Aristotle, and others as celebrated. For after the introduction of Christianity Latin was much cultivated in the Irish schools, and the priests and physicians not only wrote, but could converse fluently in Latin, which language became the chief medium of communication between them and the learned men of the continent. But the most ancient mode of procedure amongst the Irish ollamhs and adepts was of a medico-religious character; consisting of herb cures, fairy cures, charms, invocations, and certain magical ceremonies. A number of these cures have been preserved traditionally by the people, and form a very interesting study of early medical superstitions, as they have been handed down through successive generations; for the profession of a physician was hereditary in certain families, and the accumulated lore of centuries was transmitted carefully from father to son by this custom and usage.

*

Many of the ancient cures and charms are strange and mystic, and were accompanied by singular mysterious forms, which no doubt in many cases aided the cure; especially amongst a people so imaginative and susceptible to spiritual influences as the Irish. Others show a fervent faith and have a pathetic simplicity of expression, such as we find in "The Charm against Sorrow," and others, from the original Irish, of equal pathos and tenderness, to be quoted further on. The utterance evidently of a people of deep, almost sublime, faith in the Divine power of the Ruler of the world, and of the ever-present ministration of saints and angels to humanity.

Every act of the Irish peasant's life has always been connected with the belief in unseen spiritual agencies. The people live in an atmosphere of the supernatural, and nothing would induce them to slight an ancient form or break through a traditional usage. They believe that the result would be something awful; too terrible to be spoken of save in a whisper, should the customs of their forefathers be lightly interfered with.

In the Western Islands especially, the old superstitions that have come down from the ancient times are observed with the most solemn reverence, and the people in fact, as to their habits and ideas, remain much the same as St. Patrick left them fourteen hundred years ago. The swift currents of thought that stir the great centres of civilization and impel the human intellect on its path of progress, have never reached them; all the waves of the centuries drift by their shores and leave them unchanged.

It is therefore in the islands and along the western coast that one gathers most of those strange legends, charms, mysteries, and world-old superstitions which have lingered longer in Ireland than in any other part of Europe.

Many of those included in the following selection were narrated by the peasants, either in Irish, or in the expressive Irish-English, which still retains enough of the ancient idiom to make the language impressively touching and picturesque. The ancient charms which have come down by tradition from a remote antiquity are peculiarly interesting from their deep human pathos, blended with the sublime trust in the Divine invisible power, so characteristic of the Irish temperament in all ages. A faith that believes implicitly, trusts devoutly, and hopes infinitely; when the soul in its sorrow turns to heaven for the aid which cannot be found on earth, or given by earthly hands. The following charms from the Irish express much of this mingled spirit of faith and hope:—

Against Sorrow

A charm set by Mary for her Son, before the fair man and the turbulent woman laid Him in the grave.

The charm of Michael with the shield;

Of the palm-branch of Christ;

Of Bridget with her veil.

The charm which God set for Himself when the divinity within Him was darkened.

A charm to be said by the cross when the night is black and the soul is heavy with sorrow.

A charm to be said at sunrise, with the hands on the breast, when the eyes are red with weeping, and the madness of grief is strong.

A charm that has no words, only the silent prayer.

To Win Love

"O Christ, by your five wounds, by the nine orders of angels, if this woman is ordained for me, let me hold her hand now, and breathe her breath. O my love, I set a charm to the top of your head; to the sole of your foot; to each side of your breast, that you may not leave me nor forsake me. As a foal after the mare, as a child after the mother, may you follow and stay with me till death comes to part us asunder. AMEN."

Another.

A charm of most desperate love, to be written with a raven's quill in the blood of the ring finger of the left hand.

"By the power that Christ brought from heaven, mayest thou love me, woman! As the sun follows its course, mayest thou follow me. As light to the eye, as bread to the hungry, as joy to the heart, may thy presence be with me, O woman that I love, till death comes to part us asunder."

For the Night-Fire (the Fever)

"God save thee, Michael, archangel! God save thee!"

"What aileth thee, O man?"

"A headache and a sickness and a weakness of the heart. O Michael, archangel, canst thou cure me, O angel of the Lord?"

"May three things cure thee, O man. May the shadow of Christ fall on thee!

May the garment of Christ cover thee! May the breath of Christ breathe on thee! And when I come again thou wilt be healed."

These words are said over the patient while his arms are lifted in the form of a cross, and water is sprinkled on his head.

For a Pain in the Side

"God save you, my three brothers, God save you! And how far have ye to go, my three brothers?"

"To the Mount of Olivet, to bring back gold for a cup to hold the tears of Christ."

"Go, then. Gather the gold; and may the tears of Christ fall on it, and thou wilt be cured, both body and soul."

These words must be said while a drink is given to the patient.

For the Measles

"'The child has the measles,' said John the Baptist.

"'The time is short till he is well,' said the Son of God.

"'When?' said John the Baptist.

"'Sunday morning, before sunrise,' said the Son of God."

This is to be repeated three times, kneeling at a cross, for three mornings before sunrise, and the child will be cured by the Sunday following.

For the Mad Fever

Three stones must be charmed by the hands of a wise fairy doctor, and cast by his hand, saying as he does so—

"The first stone I cast is for the head in the mad fever; the second stone I cast is for the heart in the mad fever; the third stone I cast is for the back in the mad fever.

"In the name of the Trinity, let peace come. AMEN."

Against Enemies

Three things are of the Evil One—

An evil eye;

An evil tongue;

An evil mind.

Three things are of God; and these three are what Mary told to her Son, for she heard them in heaven—

The merciful word;

The singing word;

And the good word.

May the power of these three holy things be on all the men and women of Erin for evermore.

To Extract a Thorn

"The briar that spreads, the thorn that grows, the sharp spike that pierced the brow of Christ, give you power to draw this thorn from the flesh, or let it perish inside; in the name of the Trinity. AMEN."

To Cause Hatred Between Lovers

Take a handful of clay from a new-made grave, and shake it between them, saying—

"Hate ye one another! May ye be as hateful to each other as sin to Christ, as bread eaten without blessing is to God."

For Love

This is a charm I set for love; a woman's charm of love and desire; a charm of God that none can break—

"You for me, and I for thee and for none else; your face to mine, and your head turned away from all others."

This is to be repeated three times secretly, over a drink given to the one beloved.

How to Have Money Always

Kill a black cock, and go to the meeting of three cross-roads where a murderer is buried. Throw the dead bird over your left shoulder then and there, after nightfall, in the name of the devil, holding a piece of money in your hand all the while. And ever after, no matter what you spend, you will always find the same piece of money undiminished in your pocket.

For the Great Worm [8]

"I kill a hound. I kill a small hound. I kill a deceitful hound. I kill a worm, wherein there is terror; I kill all his wicked brood. Seven angels from Paradise will help me, that I may do valiantly, and give no more time to the worm to live than while I recite this prayer. AMEN."

For Sore Eyes

"Take away the pain, O Mary, mother, and scatter the mist from the eyes. For all power is given to the mother of Christ to give light to the eyes, and to drive the red mist back to the billows whence it came."

For Pains in the Body

Rub the part affected with flax and tow, heated in the fire, repeating in Irish—

"In the name of a rough man and a mild woman, and of the Lamb of God, be healed from your pains and your sins. So be it. AMEN."

This custom refers to the tradition that one day the Lord Christ, being weary, asked leave to rest in a house, but was refused by the master of the house, a rough, rude man. Then the wife, being a mild woman, had pity on the wayfarer, and brought Him in to rest, and gave Him a cup of water to drink, and spake kindly to Him. After which the man was suddenly taken with severe pains, and seemed like to die in his agony.

On this Christ called for some flax and tow, and, breathing on it, placed it on the part affected, by which means the man was quite healed. And then the Lord Christ went His way, but not before the man had humbly asked pardon for his rudeness to a stranger.

The tradition of this cure has remained ever since, and a hot plaster of flax and tow is used by the peasantry invariably for all sudden pains, and found to be most efficacious as a cure.

Lady Jane Francesca Agnes Wilde

Against Drowning

"May Christ and His saints stand between you and harm.
Mary and her Son.
St. Patrick with his staff.
Martin with his mantle.
Bridget with her veil.
Michael with his shield.
And God over all with His strong right hand."

In Time of Battle

"O Mary, who had the victory over all women, give me victory now over my enemies, that they may fall to the ground, as wheat when it is mown."

For the Red Rash

"Who will heal me from the red, thirsty, shivering cold disease that came from the foreigner, and kills people with its poisonous pain?" "The prayer of Mary to her Son, the prayer of Columbkill to God; these will heal thee. AMEN."

Another.

Say this oration three times over the patient, making the sign of the cross each time—

"Bridget, Patrick, Solomon, and the great Mary, banish this redness off you."

Then take butter, breathe on it quite close, and give it to the person to chafe himself therewith.

To ascertain if he will recover, put a handful of yarrow in his hand while he is sleeping; if it is withered in the morning he will die; but if it remains fresh the disease will leave him.

To Tame a Horse

Whisper the Creed in his right ear on a Friday, and again in his left ear on a Wednesday. Do this weekly till he is tamed; for so he will be.

A Very Ancient Charm Against Wounds or Poisons

"The poison of a serpent, the venom of the dog, the sharpness of the spear, doth not well in man. The blood of one dog, the blood of many dogs, the blood of the hound of Fliethas—these I invoke. It is not a wart to which my spittle is applied. I strike disease; I strike wounds. I strike the disease of the dog that bites, of the thorn that wounds, of the iron that strikes. I invoke the three daughters of Fliethas against the serpent. Benediction on this body to be healed; benediction on the spittle; benediction on him who casts out the disease. In the name of God. Amen."

For a Sore Breast

To be said in Irish, while a piece of butter is rubbed over the breast—

"O Son, see how swelled is the breast of the woman! O, you that bore a Son, look at it yourself! O Mary! O King of Heaven, let this woman be healed! Amen."

For a Wound

Close the wound tightly with the two fingers, and repeat these words slowly—

"In the name of the Father, Son, and Holy Mary. The wound was red, the cut was deep, and the flesh was sore; but there will be no more blood, and no more pain, till the blessed Virgin Mary bears a child again."

For the Evil Eye

This is a charm Mary gave to St. Bridget, and she wrote it down, and hid it in the hair of her head, without deceit—

"If a fairy, or a man, or a woman hath overlooked thee, there are three greater in heaven who will cast all evil from thee into the great and terrible sea. Pray to them, and to the seven angels of God, and they will watch over thee. Amen."

For St. Anthony's Fire

"The fire of earth is hot, and the fire of hell is hotter; but the love of Mary is above all. Who will quench the fire? Who will heal the sick? May the fire of God consume the Evil One! AMEN."

How to Go Invisible

Get a raven's heart, split it open with a black-hafted knife; make three cuts and place a black bean in each cut. Then plant it, and when the beans sprout put one in your mouth and say—

"By virtue of Satan's heart,
And by strength of my great art,
I desire to be invisible."

And so it will be as long as the bean is kept in the mouth.

For Pains

"I kill the evil; I kill the worm in the flesh, the worm in the grass. I put a venomous charm in the murderous pain. The charm that was set by Peter and Paul; the charm that kills the worm in the flesh, in the tooth, in the body."

This oration to be said three times, while the patient is rubbed with butter on the place of the pain.

Another.

A happy mild charm, a charm which Christ discovered. The charm that kills the worm in the flesh.

"May Peter take, may Paul take, may Michael take, the pain away, the cruel pain that kills the back and the life, and darkens the eyes."

This oration written, and tied to a hare's foot, is always to be worn by the person afflicted, hung round the neck.

For a Sprain

In the Western Isles the following charm is used for a sprain—

A strand of black wool is wound round and round the ankle, while the operator recites in a low voice—

249

"The Lord rade and the foal slade,
He lighted and He righted;
Set joint to joint and bone to bone,
And sinew unto sinew.
In the name of God and the Saints,
Of Mary and her Son,
Let this man be healed. AMEN."

A similar charm was used in Germany in the tenth century, according to Jacob Grimm.

To Cause Love

Golden butter on a new-made dish, such as Mary set before Christ. This to be given in the presence of a mill, of a stream, and the presence of a tree; the lover saying softly—

"O woman, loved by me, mayest thou give me thy heart, thy soul and body. AMEN."

For the Bite of a Mad Dog

An oration which Colum-Cille set to a wound full of poison—"Arise, O Carmac, O Clunane, through Christ be thou healed. By the hand of Christ he thou healed in blood, in marrow, and in bone. AMEN."

This oration to be pronounced over a man or a woman, a horse or a cow, but never over a hog or a dog. The wound to be rubbed with butter during the oration.

For Toothache

Go to a graveyard; kneel upon any grave; say three paters and three aves for the soul of the dead lying beneath. Then take a handful of grass from the grave, chew it well, casting forth each bite without swallowing any portion. After this process the sufferer, were he to live a hundred years, will never have toothache any more.

Another.

The patient must vow a vow to God, the Virgin, and the new moon, never to comb his hair on a Friday, in remembrance of relief should he be cured; and whenever or wherever he first sees the moon he must fall on his knees and say five prayers in gratitude for the cure, even if crossing a river at the time.

Another.

Carry in your pocket the two jaw-bones of a haddock; for ever since the miracle of the loaves and fishes these bones are an infallible remedy against toothache, and the older they are the better, as nearer the time of the miracle.

Also this charm is to be sewn on the clothes—

"As Peter sat on a marble stone,
The Lord came to him all alone,
'Peter, Peter, what makes you shake?'
'O Lord and Master, it is the toothache.'
Then Christ said, 'Take these for My sake,
And never more you'll have toothache.'"

To avoid toothache never shave on a Sunday.

For Freckles

Anoint a freckled face with the blood of a bull, or of a hare, and it will put away the freckles and make the skin fair and clear. Also the distilled water of walnuts is good.

For a Burn

There is a pretty secret to cure a burn without a scar: "Take sheep's suet and the rind of the elder-tree, boil both together, and the ointment will cure a burn without leaving a mark."

For the Memory

The whitest of frankincense beaten fine, and drunk in white wine, wonderfully assisteth the memory, and is profitable for the stomach also.

For the Falling Sickness

Take a hank of grey yarn, a lock of the patient's hair, some parings of his nails, and bury them deep in the earth, repeating, in Irish, as a burial service, "Let the great sickness lie there for ever. By the power of Mary and the soul of Paul, let the great sickness lie buried in the clay, and never more rise out of the ground. AMEN."

If the patient, on awaking from sleep, calls out the name of the person who uttered these words, his recovery is certain.

If a person crosses over the patient while he is in a fit, or stands between him and the fire, then the sickness will cleave to him and depart from the other that was afflicted.

For Chin-Cough

A griddle cake made of meal, to be given, not bought or made; but a cake *given* of love or of charity, not for begging; a cake given freely, with a prayer and a blessing; and from the breakfast of a man and his wife who had the same name before marriage; this is the cure.

*

The touch of a piebald horse. Even a piebald horse pawing before the door helps the cure.

*

The child to be passed seven times under and over an ass while a red string is tied on the throat of the patient.

*

Nine hairs from the tail of a black cat, chopped up and soaked in water, which is then swallowed, and the cough will be relieved.

"One day when out snipe shooting," a gentleman writes, "I saw a horrid-looking insect staring up at me. I called to a man close by, and asked him the name of it. He told me it was called the *Thordall*, and was reckoned a great cure for the *chin-cough*; for if any one got it safe in a bottle and kept it prisoner till it died, the disease would go away from the patient. It was just the time to try the cure, for my child was laid up with the epidemic. So I bottled my friend and daily examined the state of his health. It lasted for a fortnight, and at the end of that time the child had quite recovered, and the horrible-looking insect creature lay dead."

For Rheumatism

The operator makes passes, like the mesmerist, over the member affected by the rheumatic pain, never touching the part, but moving his hand slowly over it at some distance, while he mutters a form of words in a low voice.

For a Stye on the Eyelid

Point a gooseberry thorn at it nine times, saying, "Away, away, away!" and the stye will vanish presently and disappear.

To Cure Warts

On meeting a funeral, take some of the clay from under the feet of the men who bear the coffin and apply it to the wart, wishing strongly at the same time that it may disappear; and so it will be.

For a Stitch in the Side

Rub the part affected with unsalted butter, and make the sign of the cross seven times over the place.

For Weak Eyes

A decoction of the flowers of daisies boiled down is an excellent wash, to be used constantly.

For Water on the Brain

Cover the head well with wool, then place oil-skin over, and the water will be drawn up out of the head. When the wool is quite saturated the brain will be free and the child cured.

For Hip Disease

Take three green stones, gathered from a running brook, between midnight and morning, while no word is said. In silence it must be done. Then uncover the limb and rub each stone several times closely downwards from the hip to the toe, saying in Irish—

"Wear away, wear away,
There you shall not stay,
Cruel pain—away, away."

For the Mumps

Wrap the child in a blanket, take it to the pigsty, rub the child's head to the back of a pig, and the mumps will leave it and pass from the child to the animal.

Another.

Take nine black stones gathered before sunrise, and bring the patient with a rope round his neck to a holy well—not speaking all the while. Then cast in three stones in the name of God, three in the name of Christ, and three in the name of Mary. Repeat this process for three mornings and the disease will be cured.

For Epilepsy

Take nine pieces of young elder twig; run a thread of silk of three strands through the pieces, each piece being an inch long. Tie this round the patient's neck next the skin. Should the thread break and the amulet fall, it must be buried deep in the earth and another amulet made like the first, for if once it touches the ground the charm is lost.

Another.

Take nine pieces of a dead man's skull, grind them to powder, and then mix with a decoction of wall rue. Give the patient a spoonful of this mixture every morning fasting, till the whole potion is swallowed. None must be left, or the dead man would come to look for the pieces of his skull.

For Depression of Heart

When a person becomes low and depressed and careless about everything, as if all vital strength and energy had gone, he is said to have got a fairy blast.

And blast-water must be poured over him by the hands of a fairy doctor while saying, "In the name of the saint with the sword, who has strength before God and stands at His right hand." Great care being taken that no portion of the water is profaned. Whatever is left after the operation, must be poured on the fire.

For the Fairy Dart

Fairy darts are generally aimed at the fingers, causing the joints to swell and grow red and inflamed. An eminent fairy-woman made the cure of fairy darts her speciality, and she was sent for by all the country round, and was generally successful. But she had no power unless *asked* to make the cure, and she took no reward at the time; not till the patient was cured, and the dart extracted. The treatment included a great many prayers and much anointing with a salve, of which she only had the secret. Then she proceeded to extract the dart with great solemnity, working with a small instrument, on the point of which she finally produced the dart. This proved to be a bit of flax artfully laid under the skin by the malicious fairies, causing all the evil, and of course on seeing the flax no one could doubt the power of the operator, and the grateful patient paid his fee.

Various Superstitions and Cures

There is a book, a little book, and the house which has it will never be burned; the ship that holds it will never founder; the woman who keeps it in her hand will be safe in childbirth. But none except a fairy man knows the name of the book, and he will not reveal it for love or money; only on his death-bed will he tell the secret of the name to the one person he selects.

The adepts and fairy doctors keep their mysteries very secret, and it is not easy to discover the word of a charm, for the operator loses his power if the words are said without the proper preliminaries, or if said by a profane person without faith, for the operator should not have uttered the mystery in the hearing of one who would mock, or treat the matter lightly; therefore he is punished.

Some years ago an old man lived in Mayo who had great knowledge of charms, and of certain love philtres that no woman could resist. But before his death he enclosed the written charms in a strong iron box, with directions that no one was to dare to open it except the eldest son of an eldest son in a direct line from himself.

Some people pretend that they have read the charms; and one of them has the strange power to make every one in the house begin to dance, and they can never cease dancing till another spell has been said over them.

But the guardian of the iron box is the only one who knows the magic secret of the spell, and he exacts a good price before he utters it, and so reveals or destroys the witchcraft of the dance.

*

The juice of deadly night-shade distilled, and given in a drink, will make the person who drinks believe whatever you will to tell him, and choose him to believe.

*

A bunch of mint tied round the wrist is a sure remedy for disorders of the stomach.

*

A sick person's bed must be placed north and south, not cross ways.

*

Nettles gathered in a churchyard and boiled down for a drink have the power to cure dropsy.

*

The touch from the hand of a seventh son cures the bite of a mad dog. This is also an Italian superstition.

*

The hand of a dead man was a powerful incantation, but it was chiefly used by women. The most eminent fairy women always collected the mystic herbs for charms and cures by the light of a candle held by a dead man's hand at midnight or by the full moon.

*

Lady Jane Francesca Agnes Wilde

When a woman first takes ill in her confinement, unlock instantly every press and drawer in the house, but when the child is born, lock them all up again at once, for if care is not taken the fairies will get in and hide in the drawers and presses, to be ready to steal away the little mortal baby when they get the opportunity, and place some ugly, wizened changeling in the cradle beside the poor mother. Therefore every key should be turned, every lock made fast; and if the fairies are hidden inside, let them stay there until all danger is over for the baby by the proper precautions being taken, such as a red coal set under the cradle, and a branch of mountain ash tied over it, or of the alder-tree, according to the sex of the child, for both trees have mystic virtues, probably because of the ancient superstition that the first man was created from an alder-tree, and the first woman from the mountain ash.

The fairies, however, are sometimes successful in carrying off a baby, and the mother finds in the morning a poor weakly little sprite in the cradle in place of her own splendid child. But should the mortal infant happen to grow up ugly, the fairies send it back, for they love beauty above all things; and the fairy chiefs greatly desire a handsome mortal wife, so that a handsome girl must be well guarded, or they will carry her off. The children of such unions grow up beautiful and clever, but are also wild, reckless and extravagant. They are known at once by the beauty of their eyes and hair, and they have a magic fascination that no one can resist, and also a fairy gift of music and song.

*

If a person is bitten by a dog, the dog must be killed, whether mad or not, for it might become mad; then, so also would the person who had been touched by the saliva of the animal.

*

If, by accident, you find the back tooth of a horse, carry it about with you as long as you live, and you will never want money; but it must be found by chance.

*

When a family has been carried off by fever, the house where they died may be again inhabited with safety if a certain number of sheep are driven in to sleep there for three nights.

*

An iron ring worn on the fourth finger was considered effective against rheumatism by the Irish peasantry from ancient times.

*

Paralysis is cured by stroking, but many forms and mystic incantations are also used during the process; and only certain persons have the power in the hands that can effect a cure by the magic of the stroke.

*

The seed of docks tied to the left arm of a woman will prevent her being barren.

*

A spoonful of *aqua vitæ* sweetened with sugar, and a little grated bread added, that it may not annoy the brain or the liver, will preserve from lethargy and apoplexy and all cold diseases.

*

The juice of carrots boiled down is admirable for purifying the blood.

*

Clippings of the hair and nails of a child tied up in a linen cloth and placed under the cradle will cure convulsions.

*

Tober Maire (Mary's well), near Dundalk, has a great reputation for cures. And thousands used to visit it on Lady Day for weak eyesight, and the lowness of heart. Nine times they must go round the well on their knees, always westward. Then drink a cup of the water, and not only are they cured of their ailment, but are as free from sin as the angels in heaven.

*

When children are pining away, they are supposed to be fairy-struck; and the juice of twelve leaves of foxglove may be given: also in cases of fever the same.

*

258

Lady Jane Francesca Agnes Wilde

A bunch of mint tied round the wrist keeps off infection and disease.

*

There is a well near the Boyne where King James washed his sword after the battle, and ever since the water has power to cure the king's evil.

*

When a seventh son is born, if an earth-worm is put into the infant's hand and kept there till it dies, the child will have power to charm away all diseases.

*

The ancient arrowheads, called elf-stones by the people, are used as charms to guard the cattle.

*

It is not safe to take an unbaptized child in your arms without making the sign of the cross over it.

*

It is unlucky to give a coal of fire out of the house before the child is baptized. And a piece of iron should be sewn in the infant's clothes, and kept there till after the baptism.

*

Take a piece of bride-cake and pass it three times through a wedding-ring, then sleep on it, and you will see in a dream the face of your future spouse.

*

It is unlucky to accept a lock of hair, or a four-footed beast from a lover.

*

People ought to remember that egg-shells are favourite retreats of the fairies, therefore the judicious eater should always break the shell after use, to prevent the fairy sprite from taking up his lodgment therein.

*

Finvarra, the king of the fairies of the west, keeps up the most friendly relations with most of the best families of Galway, especially with the Kirwans of Castle Hacket, for Finvarra is a gentleman, every inch of him, and the Kirwans always leave out kegs of wine for him at night of the best Spanish wine. And in return, it is said, the wine vaults at Castle Hacket are never empty, though the wine flows freely for all comers.

*

If a living worm is put into the hand of a child before he is baptized, and kept there till the worm is dead, that child will have power in after life to cure all diseases to which children are subject.

*

After being cured from a sickness, take an oath never to comb the hair on a Friday, that so the memory of the grace received may remain by this sign till your death. Or whenever you first see the new moon, kneel down and say an ave and a pater; this also is for memory of grace done.

*

People born in the morning cannot see spirits or the fairy world; but those born at night have power over ghosts, and can see the spirits of the dead.

*

Unbaptized children are readily seized by the fairies. The best preventive is a little salt tied up in the child's dress when it is laid to sleep in the cradle.

*

If pursued at night by an evil spirit, or the ghost of one dead, and you hear footsteps behind you, try and reach a stream of running water, for if you can cross it, no devil or ghost will be able to follow you.

*

If a chair fall as a person rises, it is an unlucky omen.

*

The fortunate possessor of the four-leaved shamrock will have luck in gambling, luck in racing, and witchcraft will have no power over him. But he must always carry it about his person, and never give it away, or even show it to another.

*

A purse made from a weasel's skin will never want for money; but the purse must be found, not given or made.

*

260

If a man is ploughing, no one should cross the path of the horses.

*

It is unlucky to steal a plough, or take anything by stealth from a smith's forge.

*

When yawning make the sign of the cross instantly over the mouth, or the evil spirit will make a rush down and take up his abode within you.

*

Never give away water before breakfast, nor milk while churning is going on.

*

A married woman should not walk upon graves, or her child will have a club-foot. If by accident she treads on a grave she must instantly kneel down, say a prayer, and make the sign of the cross on the sole of her shoe three times over.

*

Never take an infant in your arms, nor turn your head to look at it without saying, "God bless it." This keeps away the fatal influence of the Evil Eye.

*

If a bride steers a boat on the day of her marriage, the winds and the waves have no power over it, be the tempest ever so fierce or the stream ever so rapid.

*

Do not put out a light while people are at supper, or there will be one less at the table before the year is out.

*

Never give any salt or fire while churning is going on. To upset the salt is exceedingly unlucky and a bad omen; to avert evil gather up the salt and fling it over the right shoulder into the fire, with the left hand.

*

If you want a person to win at cards, stick a crooked pin in his coat.

*

The seventh son of a seventh son has power over all diseases, and can cure them by laying on of hands; and a son born after his father's death has power over fevers.

*

There is one hour in every day when whatever you wish will be granted, but no one knows what that hour is. It is all a chance if we come on it. There is also one hour in the day when ghost-seers can see spirits—but only one—at no other time have they the power, yet they never know the hour, the coming of it is a mystery.

*

In some parts of Ireland the people, it is said, on first seeing the new moon, fall on their knees and address her in a loud voice with the prayer: "O moon; leave us well as thou hast found us!"

*

It is unlucky to meet a cat, a dog, or a woman, when going out first in the morning; but unlucky above all is it to meet a woman with red hair the first thing in the morning when going on a journey, for her presence brings ill-luck and certain evil.

*

It is unlucky to pass under a hempen rope; the person who does so will die a violent death, or is fated to commit an evil act in after life, so it is decreed.

*

The cuttings of your hair should not be thrown where birds can find them; for they will take them to build their nests, and then you will have headaches all the year after.

*

The cause of a club-foot is this—The mother stood on a cross in a churchyard before her child was born—so evil came.

*

To cure fever, place the patient on the sandy shore when the tide is coming in, and the retreating waves will carry away the disease and leave him well.

Lady Jane Francesca Agnes Wilde

*

To make the skin beautiful, wash the face in May dew upon May morning just at sunrise.

*

If the palm of the hand itches you will be getting money; if the elbow, you will be changing beds; if the ear itches and is red and hot, some one is speaking ill of you.

*

If three drops of water are given to an infant before it is baptized, it will answer the first three questions put to it.

*

To know the name of the person you are destined to marry, put a snail on a plate of flour—cover it over and leave it all night; in the morning the initial letter of the name will be found traced on the flour by the snail.

*

If one desires to know if a sick person will recover, take nine smooth stones from the running water; fling them over the right shoulder, then lay them in a turf fire to remain untouched for one night. If the disease is to end fatally the stones in the morning will emit a clear sound like a bell when struck together.

*

A whitethorn stick is a very unlucky companion on a journey; but a hazel switch brings good luck and has power over the devil.

*

A hen that crows is very unlucky and should be killed; very often the hen is stoned, for it is believed that she is bewitched by the fairies.

*

It is asserted that on Christmas morning the ass kneels down in adoration of Christ, and if a person can manage to touch the cross on the back of the animal at that particular moment the wish of his heart will be granted, whatever it may be.

*

When taking possession of a new house, every one should bring in some present, however trifling, but nothing should be taken away, and a prayer should be said in each corner of your bedroom, and some article of your clothing be deposited there at the same time.

To Find Stolen Goods
Place two keys on a sieve, in the form of a cross. Two men hold the sieve, while a third makes the sign of the cross on the forehead of the suspected party, and calls out his name loudly, three times over. If innocent, the keys remain stationary; but if guilty, the keys revolve slowly round the sieve, and then there is no doubt as to who is the thief.

A Prayer Against the Plague
"O Star of Heaven, beloved of the Lord, drive away the foul constellation that has slain the people with the wound of dreadful death. O Star of the Sea, save us from the poison-breath that kills, from the enemy that slays in the night. AMEN."

A Blessing
"O aged old woman of the grey locks, may eight hundred blessings twelve times over be on thee! Mayest thou be free from desolation, O woman of the aged frame! And may many tears fall on thy grave."

A Cure For Cattle
Take nine leaves of the male crowfoot, plucked on a Sunday night; bruise them on a stone that never was moved since the world began, and never can be moved. Mix with salt and spittle, and apply the plaster to the ear of the sick beast. Repeat this three times for a man, and twice for a horse.

A Charm For Safety
Pluck ten blades of yarrow, keep nine, and cast the tenth away for tithe to the spirits. Put the nine in your stocking, under the heel of the right foot,

when going a journey, and the Evil One will have no power over you.

An Elixir of Potency
(From a Manuscript of Date 1770.)

Two ounces of cochineal, one ounce of gentian root, two drachms of saffron, two drachms of snakeroot, two drachms of salt of wormwood, and the rind of ten oranges. The whole to be steeped in a quart of brandy, and kept for use.

For the Bite of a Mad Dog

Six ounces of rue, four ounces of garlic, two ounces of Venice treacle, and two ounces of pewter filings. Boil for two hours in a close vessel, in two quarts of ale, and give a spoonful fasting each morning till the cure is effected. The liquor is to be strained before use.

Dreams

Never tell your dreams fasting, and always tell them first to a woman called Mary.

*

To dream of a hearse with white plumes is a wedding; but to dream of a wedding is grief, and death will follow.

*

To dream of a woman kissing you is deceit; but of a man, friendship; and to dream of a horse is exceedingly lucky.

*

To dream of a priest is bad; even to dream of the devil is better. Remember, also, either a present or a purchase from a priest is unlucky.

Fairy Doctors

The fairy doctors are generally females. Old women, especially, are considered to have peculiar mystic and supernatural power. They cure chiefly by charms and incantations, transmitted by tradition through many generations; and by herbs, of which they have a surprising knowledge.

The fairies have an aversion to the sight of blood; and the peasants, therefore, have a great objection to being bled, lest "the good people" would be angry. Besides, they have much more faith in charms and incantations than in any dispensary doctor that ever practised amongst them.

Charms by Crystals

The charms by crystals are of great antiquity in Ireland—a mode of divination, no doubt, brought from the East by the early wandering tribes. Many of these stones have been found throughout the country, and are held in great veneration. They are generally globular, and appear to have been originally set in royal sceptres or sacred shrines. A very ancient crystal globe of this kind, with miraculous curative powers, is still to be seen at Currahmore, the seat of the Marquis of Waterford, and it is believed to have been brought from the Holy Land by one of the Le Poers, who had it as a gift from Godfrey de Bouillon. The ball is of rock crystal, a little larger than an orange, and is circled round the middle by a silver band. It is still constantly borrowed by the people to effect cures upon cattle suffering from murrain or other distempers. This is done by placing the ball in a running stream, through which the cattle are driven backwards and forwards many times.

The peasants affirm that the charm never fails in success, and the belief in its miraculous powers is so widespread that people from the most distant parts of Ireland send to Currahmore to borrow it. Even to this day the faith in its magic power continues unabated, and requests for the loan come from every quarter. The Marquis of Waterford leaves it in the care of his steward, and it is freely lent to all comers; but to the credit of the people it may be noted, that the magic crystal is always brought back to Currahmore with the most scrupulous care. [9]

Alectromancia

Should a person be bewitched by an evil neighbour, he must take two black cocks, lay a charm over the head of one and let it loose; but the other must be boiled down, feathers and all, and eaten. Then the malice of the neighbour will have no effect on him or his.

Ancient Egypt and Greece had likewise superstitions on the subject of sacrificing a cock. Even the last words of Socrates had reference to this subject. It is remarkable also that in the Christian legend it was a cock that testified indignantly by his crowing against Peter's treachery and cowardice, and aroused in him the remorse that was evidenced by his tears.

Fairy Power

It is on Fridays that the fairies have the most power to work evil; therefore Friday is an unlucky day to begin work, or to go on a journey, or to have a wedding; for the spirits are then present everywhere, and hear and see everything that is going on, and will mar and spoil all they can, just out of malice and jealousy of the mortal race.

It is then they strike cattle with their elfin arrows, lame a horse, steal the milk, and carry off the handsome children, leaving an ugly changeling in exchange, who is soon known to be a fairy sprite by its voracious appetite, without any natural increase in growth.

This superstition makes the peasant-women often very cruel towards weakly children; and the trial by fire is sometimes resorted to in order to test the nature of the child who is suspected of being a changeling. For this purpose a fairy woman is usually sent for, who makes a drink for the little patient of certain herbs of whose power she alone has the secret knowledge; and a childless woman is considered the best to make the potion. Should there be no improvement in the child after the treatment with herbs, then the witch-women sometimes resort to terrible measures to test the fairy nature of the sufferer.

A child who was suspected of being a changeling, because he was wasted and thin and always restless and fretful, was ordered by the witch-woman to be placed for three nights on a shovel outside the door from sunset to sunrise, during which time he was given foxglove to chew, and cold water was flung over him to banish the fire-devil. The screams of the child at night were frightful, calling on his mother to come and take him in; but the fairy doctor told the mother not to fear; the fairies were certainly tormenting him, but by the third night their power would cease, and the child would be quite restored. However, on the third night the poor little child lay dead.

Omens and Superstitions

Auguries and prophecies of coming fate may also be obtained from the flight of birds, the motion of the winds, from sneezing, dreams, lots, and the signs from a verse of the Psalter or Gospels. The peasantry attach great importance to the first verses of St. John's Gospel, and maintain that when the cock crows in the morning he is repeating these verses (from the 1st to the 14th), and if we understood the language of animals and birds, we could often hear them quoting these same verses.

*

A charm against sickness is an amulet worn round the neck, enclosing a piece of paper, on which is written the first three verses of St. John's Gospel.

Omens That Forbode Evil

To stick a penknife in the mast of a boat when sailing is most unlucky.

To meet a man with red hair, or a woman with a red petticoat, the first thing in the morning.

To kill the robin redbreast.

To pass a churn and not give a helping hand.

To meet a funeral and not go back three steps with it.

To have a hare cross your path before sunrise.

To take away a lighted sod on May days or churning days; for fire is the most sacred of all things, and you take away the blessing from the house along with it.

*

The Irish are very susceptible to omens. They say, "Beware of a childless woman who looks fixedly at your child."

*

Fire is the holiest of all things. Walk three times round a fire on St. John's

Eve, and you will be safe from disease for all that year.

*

It is particularly unlucky to meet a red-haired man the first thing in the morning. There is a tradition that Judas Iscariot had red hair, and it is from this the superstitious dread of the evil interference of a red-haired man may have originated.

*

Never begin work on a Friday.
Never remove from a house or leave a situation on Saturday.
Never begin to make a dress on Saturday, or the wearer will die within the year.
Never mend a rent in a dress while on, or evil and malicious reports will be spread about you.

*

Some days are unlucky to certain families—as Tuesday to the Tudors. Henry VIII., Edward, Mary, and Elizabeth all died upon a Tuesday.

*

To throw a slipper after a party going a journey is lucky. Also to breakfast by candle-light on Christmas morning.

*

It is fatal at a marriage to tie a knot in a red handkerchief, and only an enemy would do it. To break the spell the handkerchief should be burned.

*

The first days of the year and of the week are the luckiest. Never begin a journey on a Friday or Saturday, nor move from your residence, nor change a situation. Never cut out a dress or begin to make it on a Friday, nor fix a marriage, for of all days the fairies have the most malific power on a Friday. They are present then, and hear all that is said, therefore beware of speaking ill of them, for they will work some evil if offended.

*

Never pay away money on the first Monday of the year, or you will lose your luck in gaining money all the year after.

*

Presents may be given on New Year's Day, but no money should be paid away.

*

Those who marry in autumn will die in spring.

*

The yew-tree, the ash, and the elder-tree were sacred. The willow has a mystery in it of sound. The harp of King Brian-Boru was made of willow-wood.

*

When a servant leaves her place, if her mistress gives her a piece of bread let her put by some of it carefully, for as long as she has it good luck will follow her.

To Attract Bees

Gather foxglove, raspberry leaves, wild marjorum, mint, camomile, and valerian; mix them with butter made on May Day, and let the herbs also be gathered on May Day. Boil them all together with honey; then rub the vessel into which the bees should gather, both inside and out, with the mixture; place it in the middle of a tree, and the bees will soon come. Foxglove or "fairy fingers" is called "the great herb" from its wondrous properties.

Superstitions of the Islands

Concerning the Dead

It is ill luck when going with a funeral to meet a man on a white horse. No matter how high the rank of the rider may be, the people must seize the reins and force him to turn back and join the procession at least for a few yards.

*

The three most powerful divinations are by fire, by water, and by clay. These are the three great powers—the power that ascends, which is fire; the power that falls, which is water; and the power that lies level on the earth, and has the mystery of the dead, which is clay.

*

If a short cut should be taken while carrying a corpse to the grave the dead will be disturbed in the coffin, for it is a slight and an insult to the corpse.

*

When a death was expected it was usual to have a good deal of bread ready baked in the house in order that the evil spirits might be employed eating it, and so let the soul of the dying depart in peace. Twelve candles stuck in clay should also be placed round the dying.

*

If two funerals meet at the same churchyard, the last corpse that enters will have to supply the dead with water till the next corpse arrives.

*

Never take a child in your arms after being at a wake where a corpse was laid out unless you first dip your hands in holy water.

*

The moment the soul leaves the body the evil spirits try to seize it, but the guardian angel fights against them, and those around must pray earnestly that the angel may conquer. After death the body must not be disturbed, nor should the funeral chant be raised for one hour.

*

There are many superstitions prevalent in the Western Islands which are implicitly believed and acted on. Fishermen when going to sea must always enter the boat by the right side, no matter how inconvenient.

*

A coal of fire thrown after the fisherman brings him good fortune.

*

A sick person must not be visited on a Friday, nor by any person who has just quitted a wake and looked upon the dead. The hair and nails of a sick person must not be cut till after recovery.

*

If a corpse falls to the ground the most fatal events will happen to the family.

*

The lid must not be nailed on the coffin of a new-born child, or the mother that bore it will never have another.

The Coastguard's Fate

One day a coastguard man was out in his boat with some of the islanders when a terrible storm arose with thunder and lightning. The poor people fell on their knees and prayed devoutly, but the man laughed at them, called them fools and cowards, and said he also could make lightning and thunder as well as the God they were praying to. So he immediately prepared a small cannon he had on board, and set a match to the powder and fired it off. But before the echo died away a stream of lightning passed over him, and he fell dead in the boat a blackened corpse—a dreadful sign of the vengeance of heaven on his blasphemous daring.

Relics

If a false oath is taken upon a relic the vengeance of God falls upon the swearer, and the doom that few can bear and live rests upon him and upon all his descendants even to the seventh generation. They are shunned by the people, and looked upon as unlucky and accursed. There are some living even now from whom the curse of the past is not lifted, because the seventh generation has not yet passed by.

Legends of the Saints

St. Patrick

Many saints in old time used to come and take up their abode in the wild desolate Western Islands for the rest and sanctity of solitude, and innumerable evidences of their presence still remain in the ancient ruins of the so-called cells or churches built in the rudest form, but always placed in a picturesque locality beside a well, which ever since has been held sacred, and no woman is allowed to wash her feet in the water.

In one of these islands is a stone bed called "The Bed of the Holy Ghost," and many people go from the mainland to lie a night in this bed, though the sea is always rough and dangerous, believing that it heals all diseases, and it brings good luck to all, and to women the blessing of children.

If the lark sings on St. Bridget's Day it is a good omen, and a sign of fine weather. And whoever hears it the first thing in the morning will have good luck in all he does for that whole day. St. Bridget was granted by the Lord to have every second Sunday fine so that she might preach to the converts that came to her.

Then St. Patrick greatly desired that his day should also be fine so that the people might gather together in remembrance of him, and this also was granted. So from that time forth the Saints' Day, the 17th of March, is always fine, for so it was decreed from the ancient times when he was upon earth.

On St. Patrick's Day it is the usage in the islands to affix large crosses made of straw and flowers on the door-posts, and a black cock is sacrificed in honour of the saint, though no one can tell why it is considered necessary that blood should be spilt, except that the idea of sacrifice is found in all religions and rituals of worship. At first the object most loved or most prized was sacrificed—a child, or a costly jewel. Then the human sacrifice began to be replaced by the offering of an animal, who was made the medium of expiation. And the god was satisfied so that blood was spilled to purify from sin.

It is remarkable that relics of this ancient ritual of sacrifice can still be found even in the enlightened households of this advanced nineteenth century. An ox is still slaughtered at Christmas, though Baal is forgotten; and a lamb is sacrificed at Easter, as the Druids offered the firstlings of the flock to the Sun-god; while a goose is slain on St. Michael's Day as a burnt-offering to the saint.

The Well of the Book

When St. Patrick was one time amongst the Pagan Irish they grew very fierce and seemed eager to kill him. Then his life being in great danger, he kneeled down before them and prayed to God for help and for the conversion of their souls. And the fervour of the prayer was so great that as the saint rose up the mark of his knees was left deep in the stone, and when the people saw the miracle they believed.

Now when he came to the next village the people said if he performed some wonder for them they also would believe and pray to his God. So St. Patrick drew a great circle on the ground and bade them stand outside it; and then he prayed, and lo! the water rushed up from the earth, and a well pure and bright as crystal filled the circle. And the people believed and were baptized.

The well can be seen to this day, and is called *Tober-na-Lauer* (The Well of the Book), because St. Patrick placed his own prayer-book in the centre of the circle before the water rose.

St. Patrick and the Serpent

There is a lake in one of the Galtee mountains where there is a great serpent chained to a rock, and he may be heard constantly crying out, "O Patrick, is the *Luan*, or Monday, long from us?" For when St. Patrick cast this serpent into the lake he bade him be chained to the rock till *La-an-Luan* (The Day of Judgment). But the serpent mistook the word, and thought the saint meant *Luan*, Monday.

So he still expects to be freed from one Monday to another, and the clanking of his chains on that day is awful to hear as he strives to break them and get free.

In another lake there is a huge-winged creature, it is said, which escaped the power of St. Patrick, and when he gambols in the water such storms arise that no boat can withstand the tumult of the waves.

St. Patrick and the Princesses

One day the two daughters of the King of Meath, named Ethna and Fedalma, went down to the river to bathe, and there they beheld St. Patrick and his band of converts all draped in white robes, for they were celebrating morning prayers. And the princesses seeing strange men in white garments thought they were of the race of the male fairies, the *Daine-Sidhe*. And they questioned them. Then St. Patrick expounded the truth to them, and the maidens asked him many questions: "Who is your God? Is He Handsome? Are His daughters as handsome as we are? Is He rich? Is He young or aged? Is He to die, or does He live for ever?"

Now St. Patrick having satisfied them on all these points the maidens, Ethna and Fedalma, were baptized, and became zealous workers for the Christian cause.

The Poison Cup

St. Patrick went on to Tara, and there he lit the Paschal fire and celebrated the Easter mysteries. But the Druids were wroth, for it was against their ordinances for any fire to be lit until the chief Druid himself had kindled the sacred fire. Therefore they sought to poison St. Patrick, and a cupful of poison was given him by one of the Druids; but the danger was revealed to him, and thereupon he pronounced certain words over the liquor, and whoever pronounceth these words over poison shall receive no injury from it. He also then composed the prayer, "In nomine Dei Patris," and recited it over the cup of poison.

*

The number of companions with whom St. Patrick travelled through the country was seven score and ten, and before his time only three classes of persons were allowed to speak in public in Erin—the chronicler, to relate events; the poet, to eulogize and satirize; and the Brehon, to pass judgment according to the law. But after St. Patrick's arrival every utterance of the three professions was subject to "the men of the white language"—that is, the Gospel—and only such utterances were allowed as did not clash with the Gospel.

Divination

In ancient Pagan times in Ireland the poets were supposed to possess the gift of prophecy, and by certain means could throw themselves into a state in which they had lucid vision of coming events. This state, called *Imbas for Osna*, was produced by incantations and the offering of the flesh of a red pig, a dog, or a cat to their idols. Then the poet, laying the two palms of his hands on his two cheeks, lay down and slept; his idol gods being beside him. And when he awoke he could see all things and foretell all things. He could make verses with the ends of his fingers, and repeat the same without studying, and in this way proved his right to be chief poet at the court of the king. Also he laid his staff upon the head of a person, and thus he found out his name, and the name of his father and mother, and all unknown things that were proposed to him. And this prophetic power was also obtained by *Imbas for Osna*, though a different kind of offering was made to the idol.

But Patrick abolished these practices, and declared that whoever used them should enjoy neither heaven nor earth; and he substituted for them the *Corus Cerda* (the Law of Poetry), in which no offering was made to demons; for the profession of the poet, he said, was pure, and should not be subject to the power of the devil. He left to the poets, however, the gift of extemporaneous recital, because it was acquired through great knowledge and diligent study, but all other rites he strictly forbade to the poets of Erin.

The Blind Poet

As a proof of the magnetic, lucid vision obtained by the great ollamhs of poetry, it is recorded of the blind poet, Louad Dall, that his attendants having brought him the skull of an animal found upon the strand, they asked him to declare its history. And thereupon placing the end of his wand upon the skull, he beheld with the inner vision, and said—

"The tempestuous waters have destroyed Breccan, and this is the skull of his lapdog; and but little of greatness now remains, for Breccan and his people have perished in the waves."

And this was "divination by the staff"—a power possessed only by the chief poets, and by none else.

The Story of Breccan

The story of Breccan is related in Cormac's Glossary. He was a merchant who traded between Ireland and Scotland with fifty corracles. Now there was a great whirlpool at Rathlin Island caused by the meeting of the seas, and they formed a caldron vast enough to swallow all Ireland. And it happened on a time that Breccan and all his corracles were lost and engulfed in this caldron. Not a man was left to tell the tale of how or where they had perished. Thus it was that the skull of a small animal being discovered on the beach, it was brought to the blind poet, who laying his staff on it obtained the inner vision by which he revealed the fate of Breccan and his fifty corracles.

Bardic Privileges

Now St. Patrick left the poets all their rights of divination by wisdom, and all their ancient rights over story-telling with the music of the harp, three hundred and fifty stories being allowed to the chief poet. He also secured just judgments for their professional rights; so that if land was mentioned in their songs as having been walled and trenched by them, that was considered to be sufficient legal evidence of title to the soil.

But what they received of St. Patrick was better, he affirmed, than all the evil rites to devils which they had abandoned; along with the profane practice of magic by the two palms, called *Imbas for Osna*, by which lucid vision and the spirit of prophecy was supposed to come on them after invocations to idols and demons—all of which evil practices St. Patrick abolished, but left to the poets the skilled hand in music and the fluent tongue in recitation; for which none can equal the Bards of Ireland throughout all the world.

*

The ogham writing on the poet's staff is mentioned in very old manuscripts as in use in the Pagan period, before St. Patrick's time, though no specimen of ogham writing has yet been found of earlier date than the Christian era.

St. Patrick introduced Latin and the Latin letters, which superseded ogham. And after his time Latin was taught very generally in the Irish schools.

St. Patrick also confirmed as right and proper for observance, whatever was just in the Brehon laws, so as it was not at variance with the law of Christ, for the people had been guided by the Brehon laws from all antiquity, and it was not easy to overthrow them. Besides, many or most of them were framed with strict regard to justice and morality.

When St. Patrick was dying, an angel of the Lord was sent to him, who announced to the great and holy saint that God had granted this favour to his prayers—namely, that his jurisdiction over the Church was ordained to be for ever at Armagh; and that Patrick, as the Apostle of Ireland, should be the judge of all the Irish at the last day, and none other, according to the promise made to the other apostles, "Ye shall sit upon twelve thrones judging the tribes of Israel."

St. Ciaron

This eminent saint died at the early age of thirty-three; and it is said that his death was caused by the prayers of the other saints of Ireland, who were jealous of his power and fame for sanctity. St. Ciaron knowing that death was coming upon him, composed a verse which has been preserved as an appeal against the cruel fate that ended his life while he was yet in his prime. And the pathos of the quatrain is very tender and natural—

"I ask is it right, O King of Stars,
To reap a cornfield before it is ripe?
It is eating fruit before the time,
It is plucking the blossom from a hazel when it is white."

St. Martin

St. Martin was a bad man before his conversion, and, above all, was exceedingly close-fisted, as they say, to the poor; giving nothing and grasping all. So he was very rich but hated by every one.

One day, when going out, he charged the servant to have a fine batch of loaves ready made and baked by the time he returned. While she was kneading the dough in came a poor man and begged for some as he was hungry; but she told him she dare not give away anything or the master would beat her. Still the poor man begged the harder, and at last she gave him dough enough for a couple of loaves. However, when the girl's back was turned, he threw the dough into the oven and went his way without a word.

Now when the dough was ready, the girl opened the oven to put in the loaves, but, behold, it was already quite full of baked bread, and would hold no more. So when Martin came home she told him all the truth; and his heart smote him, and he cried out, "An Angel of the Lord has been here; God has sent His messenger to rebuke me of my sins!" And he ran out to search for the man along the road, and at last saw him a great way off. Then Martin flung off his coat that he might run the faster; and when he came up to the man he fell on his knees before him on the ground, and cried out, "Oh, my Lord, I repent me of my sins; pray to God for me, for I know you are His angel." And from that moment Martin's heart was changed, and the devil left him; and he became a true saint and servant of God, and, above all, the saint and patron of the poor.

Nevertheless, St. Bridget was offended with St. Martin, because she thought he did not receive her with sufficient hospitality and consideration. Perhaps some of the old stinginess of nature still clung to him. And she thus pronounced her malediction over him—

"Oh, little man, the sea-wave shall come up over thy house, and thy name shall lie in ashes, while my name and fame shall be glorious all over the world."

And this was fulfilled; for the sea actually broke in and covered the saint's dwelling; and the house of St. Martin can still be seen low down beneath the waves, but if any one tries to reach it the house fades away into the mist and is seen no more.

There is an old superstition still observed by the people, that blood must be spilt on St. Martin's Day; so a goose is killed, or a black cock, and the blood is sprinkled over the floor and on the threshold. And some of the flesh is given to the first beggar that comes by, in the name and in honour of St. Martin.

In the Arran Isles St. Martin's Day is observed with particular solemnity, and it was held necessary, from ancient times, to spill blood on the ground in honour of the saint. For this purpose a cock was sacrificed; but if such could not be procured people have been known to cut their finger in order to draw blood, and let it fall upon the earth. The custom arose in this way:—St. Martin, having given away all his goods to the poor, was often in want of food, and one day he entered a widow's house and begged for something to eat. The widow was poor, and having no food in the house, she sacrificed her young child, boiled it, and set it before the saint for supper. Having eaten, and taken his departure, the woman went over to the cradle to weep for her lost child; when lo! there he was, lying whole and well, in a beautiful sleep, as if no evil had ever happened to him; and to commemorate this miracle and from gratitude to the saint, a sacrifice of some living thing is made yearly in his honour. The blood is poured or sprinkled on the ground, and along the door-posts, and both within and without the threshold, and at the four corners of each room in the house.

For this symbol of purification by blood the rich farmers sacrifice a sheep; while the poorer people kill a black cock or a white hen, and sprinkle the blood according to ancient usage. Afterwards the whole family dine upon the sacrificial victim.

In some places it was the custom for the master of the house to draw a cross on the arm of each member of the family and mark it out in blood. This was a very sacred sign which no fairy or evil spirit, were they ever so strong, could overcome; and whoever was signed with the blood was safe.

There is a singular superstition forbidding work of a certain kind to be done on St. Martin's Day, the 11th of November. No woman should spin on that day; no miller should grind his corn, and no wheel should be turned. And this custom was long held sacred, and is still observed in the Western Islands.

Lady Jane Francesca Agnes Wilde

St. Bridget

At one time a certain leper came to St. Bridget to beg a cow from her.

"Which would you prefer?" said the holy Bridget, "to be healed of your disease or to have the cow?"

"I would be healed," he answered.

Then she touched him, and he became whole and went away rejoicing.

After this Bridget's fame spread all over Ireland; and a man of the Britons, and his son, came to be healed; but she was at Mass, and sent to them to wait till Mass was over.

Now the Britons are a hasty people, and the man said, "You healed your own people yesterday and you shall heal us to-day."

Then Bridget came forth and prayed over them, and they were healed.

Another time, two lepers came to beg, and Bridget said, "I have but this one cow—take it between you and go in peace."

But one leper was proud, and made answer: "I shall divide my goods with no man. Give me the cow and I shall go."

And she gave it to him.

Then the other leper said, "Give me your prayers, holy Bridget, I ask no more."

And she gave him her blessing. And as he turned to depart a man came in, and offered a cow as a present to the holy woman.

"Now the Lord has blessed you," she said to the humble leper. "Take this cow and depart to your home."

So the man drove the cow before him, and presently came up with the proud leper just at the ford of the river. "Cross you first," said the proud leper, "there is not room for two," and the humble leper crossed in safety with his cow; but when the other entered the ford, the river rose, and he and his cow were carried away and drowned, for the blessing of St. Bridget was not on him.

Another time, two lepers came to be healed, and Bridget ordered one of them to wash the other; which he did, and the man was healed.

"Now," she said, "do to your comrade as he has done to you; wash him with water that he may be made clean of his leprosy."

"Oh, veiled woman," he answered, "why should I, that am clean now in body and limb, touch this filthy leper of the blue-grey skin? Ask me not to do this thing."

Then Bridget took water and washed the leper herself. Immediately the other who had been healed, cried out, "A fire is raging under my skin;" and the disease came again on him worse than ever. Thus was he punished for his pride.

The lark is sacred to St. Bridget because its song woke her every morning to prayers, when she had service for the women who were her converts.

The influence of St. Bridget remains a permanent power in Ireland even to this day, and she is much feared by the enemy of souls and the ill-doer. When Earl Strongbow was dying, he affirmed that he saw St. Bridget approaching his bed, and she struck him on the foot, and the wound she gave him mortified, and of this he died. This happened six hundred years after Bridget's death.

St. Bridget, throughout her long life, held the highest position and dignity in the Irish Church. She erected a temple in Kildare, ordained bishops, and was head and chief of all the sacred virgins.

She also held equal rank with the archbishop; if he had an episcopal chair (*cathedra episcopalis*), so St. Bridget had a virginal chair (*cathedra puellaris*), and was pre-eminent above all the abbesses of Ireland, or of the Scots, for sanctity and power.

St. Kieran

St. Kieran, also, did good service five hundred years after his death; for when a great chief and his band plundered Clonmacnoise and carried off the jewels from the shrine, the spirit of St. Kieran was seen in the doorway, crosier in hand, striking at the plunderers; and when they fled to their boat, St. Kieran raised up a strong wind that drove back the boat, and finally the chief robber was taken and put to death, having first confessed his crime, and testified as to St. Kieran's wrath against him.

Lady Jane Francesca Agnes Wilde

St. Kevin

It is related of St. Kevin that after he had been seven years at Glendalough, a weariness of life came over him, and a longing to hear the voice of man once more. Then Satan came to him in the form of an angel, bright and beautiful, and persuaded him that he should quit the valley and travel abroad and see the world, while yet his youth was left to him. And St. Kevin was near yielding to the words of the tempter, when fortunately St. Munna came by that way, and he at once saw through the trick, and showed to St. Kevin that the advice was from the devil, and not from God. And St. Kevin promised St. Munna that he would never leave the valley till his death. However, God, not willing that the saint should eat his heart away in idleness, bade him build a monastery on the east of the lake, the place where the resurrection was to be; and he sent his angel to show him the exact spot.

But St. Kevin, when he saw the place so wild and rude, could not help telling the friendly angel that it was very rugged and difficult to build on; and the stones were heavy and hard to be moved. Then the angel, to prevent any difficulty in the building, rendered the stones light and easy to move, and so the work of building went on to the glory of God; and St. Kevin rejoiced in the task set before him.

And the monk who tells the story adds, that from that day in all the place which the angel appointed for the building, there is now no stone that cannot be lightly moved and easily worked all through the valley of Glendalough.

Christian Legends

The Round Tower of Clonmacnoise was never finished, for the monks objected to the price demanded by the chief mason; and one day that he was at the top of the tower, they said he should never come down till he lowered the price; and they removed the scaffolding.

Then he said, "It is easier to pull down than to build a tower," and he began to cast down stone by stone, so that he could descend in safety.

On this the monks grew alarmed, and prayed him to desist and the price should be paid; so he came down at their request, but would never again lay hand to the work, so the tower remains unfinished to this day.

The first bells ever used in all Ireland were hung at Clonmacnoise, but the people of Athlone, being jealous, came at night to steal the bells, and succeeded in carrying them away in a boat. However, before they got out of sight of the church, the boat went down, and the bells were never recovered, though the river was dragged from Athlone to Shannon Bridge.

At the seven churches of Clonmacnoise is to be seen the great cross of St. Kieran, beautifully carved of a stone not common to the country, called the Grecian stone, and if a woman can clasp the cross round with her arms she will never die in childbirth.

At a pattern held there one time, a soldier from Athlone shot off the hand of a figure of St. Kieran, which was over the grand entrance, but returning home he fell from the boat, and was drowned in the very spot where the bells went down a hundred years before.

*

At Saints' Island, in the Shannon, the ruins of a monastery, which was destroyed by King John, may still be seen. When the monks, broken-hearted and beggared, were leaving their beautiful home, one of them knelt down and prayed to God for forgiveness of his enemies. Immediately a well of pure water sprang up where the monk had knelt; and the water even to this day is held by the people to have the power to cure all diseases, if the soul of the patient, as he drinks of the well, is free from all malice and the desire of revenge upon those who may have injured him.

Swearing Stones and Relics

The Cremave

In the old churchyard of the monastery at Saints' Island, there is an ancient black marble flagstone; and the monks gave it power as *A Revealer of Truth*, and it is called the *Cremave*, or Swearing Stone.

Any one suspected of sin or crime is brought here from the country round, and if the accused swears falsely, the stone has the power to set a mark upon him and his race for seven generations. But if no mark appears then he is known to be innocent; and as long as the world lasts, the stone is to have this power, for so the monks decreed; and with many holy and mystic ceremonies they gave it consecration, as the "Revealer of Truth." And though the English burned the monastery and defaced the altar and carried off the holy vessels, yet they had no power over the Cremave, or Swearing Stone, which remains to this day.

Many years ago, so runs the tale, a murder was committed in the neighbourhood, and a certain man being suspected as the murderer, he was forced to go to the "clearing stone"; for the people said, "If he is innocent, the Cremave will clear him; and if guilty, let him suffer for his crime."

So, on the appointed day, he went with his friends and the accuser to the Swearing Stone; and there he was met by the priest, who adjured him to speak the truth in presence of all the people and before the face of God.

The man laid his hand upon the stone, and solemnly swore that he was innocent; but instantly his right arm was shrivelled up, his feet failed, and he was carried home a miserable cripple, and so remained to the end of his life.

Some weeks after a daughter was born to him, who bore across her forehead the impress of a bloody hand; and every one of his descendants have some strange mark, by which the people know that the race is accursed to the seventh generation; after which time the doom will be lifted, and the expiation made for the crime and the perjury will be considered sufficient by the Lord in heaven, who will then grant to the race pardon and grace at last.

Relics For Clearing From Guilt

Another relic held in reverence for swearing on by an accused person is St. Finian's Dish. This was found about one hundred and fifty years ago, buried in the ruins of an old abbey. It is of silver with stones set in it, which, the people say, are the eyes of Christ looking at them while they swear. And when the dish is shaken a rattling noise is heard, which they believe is made by the Virgin Mary's bones that are enclosed therein.

Should a false oath be taken on the relic, the perjurer will at once be stricken by disease, and die before the year is out. And so great is the terror inspired by this belief, that men have fainted from fear when brought up to swear on it. This is done by placing the hand on the cross that is engraved in the centre of the dish, while the two eyes of Christ are fixed on the swearer who comes for clearance from guilt.

*

The *Ghar-Barra*, or Crosier of St. Barry, is also a holy relic once overlaid with gold, on which it was the custom to take a clearing oath; as the people held it in great reverence, and nothing was more dreaded than the consequence of a false oath on the *Ghar-Barra*. Once a man who swore falsely thereon had his mouth turned awry, and it so remained to his life's end, a proof of the saint's hatred for the sin of perjury. The relic is kept covered carefully with green cloth, and whoever is brought to take a clearing oath thereon must first lay down a small piece of silver for the guardian of the shrine.

Innis-Murry

At Innis-Murry, Sligo, there is a large table-stone supported on eight perpendicular stones as a pedestal. And on the table are seventy-three stones, from five to twenty inches in circumference, which have been lying there from the most ancient times; for to remove them would be at the peril of one's life.

On these seventy-three stones all the anathematic spirit of the island is concentrated. If the islanders suffer any injury, real or supposed, they come and turn these stones, uttering a malediction over their enemy, and should he be guilty he will assuredly die, or suffer some calamity before the year is out.

A Scripture reader, having boldly taken away one of these stones to show the folly of the superstition, was obliged to restore it and to quit the island, or his life would not have been safe.

There is another stone on the island where alone can fires be lighted, should all the domestic fires become extinct, and the spark must be struck from the stone itself.

Innis-Murry is a desolate spot, rarely visited; the approach is so dangerous on account of the sunken rocks. The crops are scanty, and the soil is poor and light, growing only a short herbage of a spiral and sharp kind. Neither scythe nor sickle could be used in the entire island. Meal is unknown, and dairy produce scarcely to be had, as the grass can only support a few sheep; but the islanders have fish in abundance, crabs, lobsters, and mackerel especially.

A traveller, who visited the island about fifty years ago, describes the manners and mode of living as most primitive; but the women have the reputation of being exceedingly virtuous, and the households are happy and well conducted. At that time a rude stone image was venerated by the people, called "Father Molosh," but supposed to be an ancient pagan idol, probably Moloch. The priest, however, has since had it destroyed.

Mysteries of Fairy Power

The Evil Stroke

Some persons are possessed naturally with the power of the Evil Stroke, but it is not considered at all so unlucky as the Evil Eye; for the person who has it does not act from intentional malice but from necessity, from a force within him which acts without his will, and often to his deep regret: as in hurling matches, where a chance stroke of his may do serious injury, and even the dust of the earth raised by his foot has blinded his opponent for a week.

One day a young man, while wrestling with another in play at a fair, where they met by chance, struck him on the arm, which immediately became fixed and powerless as stone. His friends brought him home, but nothing would restore the power of the arm or bring back the life; so after he had lain in this state for three days his family sent for the young man who had struck him, to ask for his help. When he came and saw the arm stiff as stone, he anointed it all over with spittle, making also the sign of the cross; and after some time the arm began to move again with life, and finally was quite restored. But the young man of the Evil Stroke was so dismayed at this proof of the strange power in him, that he would never again join in sports for fear of some unlucky accident.

The power, however, is sometimes very useful, as in the case of attack from a bull or a ferocious dog; for a touch from the hand of a person possessing the Evil Stroke at once quells the madness in the animal, who will crouch down trembling with fear, and become as incapable of doing injury as if suddenly and powerfully mesmerized.

But the power does not come by volition, only at intervals; and the person possessing it does not himself know the moment when it can be effectively exercised.

Women, also, have the mysterious gift of this strange occult force, and one young girl was much dreaded in the country in consequence; for anything struck by her, beast or man, became instantly paralyzed, as if turned to stone. One day, at a hurling match, she threw a lump of clay at the winner in anger, because her own lover had failed to win the prize. Immediately the young victor fell down stunned and lifeless, and was so carried home to his mother. Then they sent in all haste for the young girl to restore him to consciousness; but she was so frightened at her own evil work that she went and hid herself. Finding it then impossible to bring her, his friends sent for the fairy doctor, who, by dint of many charms and much stroking, at last restored the young man to life. The girl, however, was in such dread of the curses of the mother, that she fled, and took service in a distant part of the country. And all the people rejoiced much over her departure from amongst them.

Yet it was considered lucky in some ways to have a fairy-stricken child in the house, for the fairies generally did a good turn by the family to compensate for the evil. And so there was always plenty of butter in the churn, and the cattle did not sicken wherever there was a stricken child.

*

It is also lucky to employ a half-simpleton about the farm, and to be kind to the deaf and dumb, and other afflicted creatures. No one in Ireland would harm them or turn them out of their way, and they always get food and drink for the asking, without any payment being thought of or accepted.

The Changeling

A woman was one night lying awake while her husband slept, when the door suddenly opened and a tall dark man entered, of fierce aspect, followed by an old hag with a child in her arms—a little, misshapen, sickly-looking little thing. They both sat down by the fire to warm themselves, and after some time the man looked over at the cradle that stood beside the mother's bed with her boy in it, and kept his eyes on it for several minutes. Then he rose, and when the mother saw him walking over direct to the cradle, she fainted and knew no more.

When she came to herself she called to her husband, and bade him light a candle; this he did, on which the old hag in the corner rose up at once and blew it out. Then he lit it a second time, and it was blown out; and still a third time he lit the candle, when again it was blown out, and a great peal of laughter was heard in the darkness.

On this the man grew terribly angry, and taking up the tongs he made a blow at the hag; but she slipped away, and struck him on the arm with a stick she held in her hand. Then he grew more furious, and beat her on the head till she roared, when he pushed her outside and locked the door.

After this he lit the candle in peace; but when they looked at the cradle, lo! in place of their own beautiful boy, a hideous little creature, all covered with hair, lay grinning at them. Great was their grief and lamentation, and both the man and his wife wept and wailed aloud for the loss of their child, and the cry of their sorrow was bitter to hear.

Just then the door suddenly opened, and a young woman came in, with a scarlet handkerchief wound round her head.

"What are you crying for," she asked, "at this time of night, when every one should be asleep?"

"Look at this child in the cradle," answered the man, "and you will cease to wonder why we mourn and are sad at heart." And he told her all the story.

When the young woman went over to the cradle and looked at the child, she laughed, but said nothing.

"Your laughter is stranger than our tears," said the man. "Why do you laugh in the face of our sorrows?"

"Because," she said, "this is my child that was stolen from me to-night; for I am one of the fairy race, and my people, who live under the fort on the hill, thought your boy was a fine child, and so they changed the babies in the cradle; but, after all, I would rather have my own, ugly as he is, than any mortal child in the world. So now I'll tell you how to get back your own son, and I'll take away mine at once. Go to the old fort on the hill when the moon is full, and take with you three sheaves of corn and some fire, and burn them one after the other. And when the last sheaf is burning, an old man will come up through the smoke, and he will ask you what it is you desire. Then tell him you must have your child back, or you will burn down the fort, and leave no dwelling-place for his people on the hill. Now, the fairies cannot stand against the power of fire, and they will give you back your child at the mere threat of burning the fort. But mind, take good care of him after, and tie a nail from a horse-shoe round his neck, and then he will be safe."

With that the young woman took up the ugly little imp from the cradle in her arms, and was away before they could see how she got out of the house.

Next night, when the moon was full, the man went to the old fort with the three sheaves of corn and the fire, and burned them one after the other; and as the second was lighted there came up an old man and asked him what was his desire.

"I must have my child again that was stolen," he answered, "or I'll burn down every tree on the hill, and not leave you a stone of the fort where you can shelter any more with your fairy kindred."

Then the old man vanished, and there was a great silence, but no one appeared.

On this the father grew angry, and he called out in a loud voice, "I am lifting the third sheaf now, and I'll burn and destroy and make desolate your dwelling-place, if my child is not returned."

Then a great tumult and clamour was heard in the fort, and a voice said, "Let it be. The power of the fire is too strong for us. Bring forth the child."

And presently the old man appeared, carrying the child in his arms.

"Take him," he said. "By the spell of the fire, and the corn you have conquered. But take my advice, draw a circle of fire, with a hot coal this night, round the cradle when you go home, and the fairy power cannot touch him any more, by reason of the fire."

So the man did as he was desired, and by the spell of fire and of corn the child was saved from evil, and he grew and prospered. And the old fort stands to this day safe from harm, for the man would allow no hand to move a stone or harm a tree; and the fairies still dance there on the rath, when the moon is full, to the music of the fairy pipes, and no one hinders them.

The Fairy Doctor

If a healthy child suddenly droops and withers, that child is fairy-struck, and a fairy doctor must be at once called in. Young girls also, who fall into rapid decline, are said to be fairy-struck; for they are wanted in Fairy-land as brides for some chief or prince, and so they pine away without visible cause till they die.

The other malign influences that act fatally on life are the Wind and the Evil Eye. The evil power of the Wind is called a fairy-blast; while, of one suffering from the Evil Eye, they say he has been "overlooked."

The fairy doctor must pronounce from which of these three causes the patient is suffering. The fairy-stroke, or the fairy-blast, or the Evil Eye; but he must take no money for the opinion given. He is paid in some other way; by free gracious offerings in gratitude for help given.

A person who visited a great fairy doctor for advice, thus describes the process of cure at the interview:—

"The doctor always seems as if expecting you, and had full knowledge of your coming. He bids you be seated, and after looking fixedly on your face for

291

some moments, his proceedings begin. He takes three rods of witch hazel, each three inches long, and marks them separately, 'For the Stroke,' 'For the Wind,' 'For the Evil Eye.' This is to ascertain from which of these three evils you suffer. He then takes off his coat, shoes, and stockings; rolls up his shirt sleeves, and stands with his face to the sun in earnest prayer. After prayer he takes a dish of pure water and sets it by the fire, then kneeling down, he puts the three hazel rods he had marked into the fire, and leaves them there till they are burned black as charcoal. All the time his prayers are unceasing; and when the sticks are burned, he rises, and again faces the sun in silent prayer, standing with his eyes uplifted and hands crossed. After this he draws a circle on the floor with the end of one of the burned sticks, within which circle he stands, the dish of pure water beside him. Into this he flings the three hazel rods, and watches the result earnestly. The moment one sinks he addresses a prayer to the sun, and taking the rod out of the water he declares by what agency the patient is afflicted. Then he grinds the rod to powder, puts it in a bottle which he fills up with water from the dish, and utters an incantation or prayer over it, in a low voice, with clasped hands held over the bottle. But what the words of the prayer are no one knows, they are kept as solemn mysteries, and have been handed down from father to son through many generations, from the most ancient times. The potion is then given to be carried home, and drunk that night at midnight in silence and alone. Great care must be taken that the bottle never touches the ground; and the person carrying it must speak no word, and never look round till home is reached. The other two sticks he buries in the earth in some place unseen and unknown. If none of the three sticks sink in the water, then he uses herbs as a cure. Vervain, eyebright, and yarrow are favourite remedies, and all have powerful properties known to the adept; but the words and prayers he utters over them are kept secret, and whether they are good or bad, or addressed to Deity or to a demon, none but himself can tell."

These are the visible mysteries of the fairy doctor while working out his charms and incantations. But other fairy doctors only perform the mysteries in private, and allow no one to see their mode of operation or witness the act of prayer.

If a potion is made up of herbs it must be paid for in silver but charms and incantations are never paid for, or they would lose their power. A present, however, may be accepted as an offering of gratitude.

The Poet's Spell

A very ancient story, as old as the tenth century, is narrated, and firmly believed by the people, that once on a time when the reapers were at work, a fine handsome young married woman, who was in the field with them, suddenly fell down dead. This caused a great fear and consternation, especially as it was asserted that just before the fatal event, a fairy blast had passed over the field, carrying a cloud of dust and stones with it; and there could be no doubt but that the fairies had rushed by in the cloud, and struck the woman dead as they passed.

Then her people sent for the great wise poet of the tribe, who was reputed to have the power by his song to break the strongest fairy spells: and he chanted low music over her, and uttered mystic incantations, the words of which no man heard; but after a while the woman unclosed her eyes and rose up, restored to life.

When they questioned her, she told them all she knew.

"In sickness I was," she said, "and I appeared to be dead, for I could neither speak nor move, till the song of the poet gave me power. Then the life rose up in me again, and the strength, and I was healed."

Charm for the Fairy Stroke

There is a very ancient and potent charm which may be tried with great effect in case of a suspected fairy-stroke.

Place three rows of salt on a table in three lines, three equal measures to each row. The person performing the spell then encloses the rows of salt with his arm, leaning his head down over them, while he repeats the Lord's Prayer three times over each row—that is, nine times in all. Then he takes the hand of the one who has been fairy-struck, and says over it, "By the power of the

Father, and of the Son, and of the Holy Spirit, let this disease depart, and the spell of the evil spirits be broken! I adjure, I command you to leave this man [naming him]. In the name of God I pray; in the name of Christ I adjure; in the name of the Spirit of God I command and compel you to go back and leave this man free! AMEN! AMEN! AMEN!"

The Farmer's Fate

The peasants have the greatest dread of the fairy-stroke, and consider it the most dangerous indication of fairy hostility. When a person is struck, he becomes wholly insensible to external things, as if his soul had been taken out of him and carried away.

A farmer once began to build a barn on a fairy circle, to the great horror of the neighbours, who warned him of the danger; but he only laughed at their nonsense, and built and finished his barn on the fairy rath.

However, riding home one evening after sunset, he was suddenly "struck," and fell insensible to the ground. They carried him home and laid him on his bed, where he lay for several days, his eyes fixed and staring without any motion of the eyelids, and no indication of life remaining, except his colour which never changed.

All the doctors came and looked at him, but could do nothing. There was no fracture nor injury of any kind to his frame; so the doctors shook their heads and went their way, saying they would call again in a day or two. But the family objected to delay, and sent at once for the great fairy doctor of the district. The moment he came he threw herbs on the fire, when a fragrant smell filled the room like church incense. Then he pounded some herbs and mixed a liquid with them, but what the herbs were, no one knew. And with this mixture he touched the brow and the lips and the hands of the man, and sprinkled the rest over his insensible form. After this he told them to keep silence round him for two hours, when he would return and finish the cure. And so it happened, for in two hours the life came back to the man, though he could not speak. But strength came gradually; and by the next day he rose up, and said he had dreamed a dream, and heard a voice saying to him, "Pull down the barn, for ill-luck is on it." Accordingly he gave orders to his men, and every stick and stone was carried away, and the fairy rath left free again for the fairies to dance on, as in the olden time, when they were the gods of the earth, long before men came to dispute their rights, and take possession of their ancient pleasure grounds—an indignity no high-spirited fairy could calmly endure. For in their councils they had decreed that the fairy rath, at least, should be sacred for all time, and woe to the man who builds his house thereon. An evil fate is on him and on the house for evermore. Down it must come, or the evil spell will never be lifted. There is no hope for it, for the most dangerous and subtle of all enemies is an angry fairy.

Nor should the paths even be crossed by work of human hand, which the fairies traverse from one palace to another. Their line of march must not be impeded. Finvarra and his men would resent such a gross insult to the royal fairy rights, and severely punish the audacious and offending mortal. Not even the Grand Jury would be allowed to interfere, for if they did, every man of them would be demolished in some way or other by fairy power.

The Fairy Rath

The fairies, beside being revengeful, are also very arrogant, and allow no interference with their old-established rights.

There is a rath in the Queen's County, only four yards in diameter, but held so sacred as the fairies' dancing ground that no one dared to remove a handful of earth from the mound; and at night the sweetest low music may be heard floating round the hill, as if played by silver bagpipes.

One evening a boy lay down on the rath to listen to the music, and, without thinking, began to gather up balls of the clay and fling them hither and thither in sport, when suddenly he was struck down by a violent blow and became senseless.

There he was found by his people, who went to search for him; and when he came to himself he bleated like a calf, and it was a long time before he recovered his reason, for the power of the fairies is great, and none can resist it.

The Holy Wells

There is no superstition stronger in Ireland than a belief in the curative power of the sacred wells that are scattered over the country; fountains of health and healing which some saint had blessed, or by which some saint had dwelt in the far-off ancient times. But well-worship is even older than Christianity. It is part of the early ritual of humanity, brought from the Eastern lands by the first Aryan tribes who migrated westward, passing along from the Mediterranean to the Atlantic shores.

The Delphic oracle in its origin was nothing more than a holy well, shadowed by trees, on which were hung the votive offerings of the praying peasants, long before the rival kings brought to the sacred spot their votive tributes of silver and gold, and crowns of precious stones.

In Ireland the beautiful, picturesque, and tree-shadowed wells of the country were held sacred by the Druid priests, as is evident from the many remarkable Druidical remains that have been found in their vicinity—ruins of temples and pillar-stones, and stones with strange carvings. Much also of the ancient Druidic ceremonial has been preserved by the people, such as the symbolic dances, the traditions of sun-worship, and other pagan rites, which were incorporated into the Christian ritual of well-worship by the early converts, and are still retained, though, through the lapse of ages, they have entirely lost their original significance, and are now only practised as ancient customs, for which the Irish have great reverence, as having come down to them from their forefathers. The ceremonial is the same at all these places of devout pilgrimage. The pilgrims go round the well a certain number of times, either three or nine, creeping on their hands and knees, but always from east to west, following the apparent motion of the sun, and reciting paters and aves all the time. At the close of each round they build up a small pile of stones; for at the last day the angels will reckon these stones, and he who has said the most prayers will have the highest place in heaven, each saint keeping count for his own votaries. The patient then descends the broken steps to the well and, kneeling down, bathes his forehead and hands in the water, after which oblation the pain or disease he suffered from will be gradually removed, and depart from him for evermore.

At some wells there is often a rude stone monument of the ancient times, and the eyes of the pilgrim must be kept steadily fixed on it while reciting the prayers.

Whenever a white-thorn or an ash-tree shadows the place, the well is held to be peculiarly sacred; and on leaving, having first drunk of the water, the patient ties a votive offering to the branches—generally a coloured handkerchief or a bright red strip cut from a garment; and these offerings are never removed. They remain for years fluttering in the wind and the rain, just as travellers have described the votive offerings on the sacred trees that shadow the holy wells of Persia. They are signs and tokens of gratitude to the patron saint, and are meant to show the devil that he has no longer power to harm the praying pilgrim, or torment him with pains and aches as heretofore. It is not supposed that the water of the well has any natural medicinal properties. The curative efficacy is wholly due to the observance of the ritual in honour of the saint, whose spirit and influence is still over the well, by which he lived, and of which he drank while living on the earth.

The White Stones

At many of the wells quantities of beautiful white stones are found that glitter in the sun, and these are highly esteemed by the pilgrims to build up their prayer monuments.

One day some women were eagerly collecting these stones, after each round of praying, in order to build up a monument; when suddenly a strain of soft, exquisite music seemed to rise up from the water and float by them. In their joy and wonder the women clapped their hands and laughed aloud, when instantly the music ceased and the pile of stones fell down. By which sign they knew that they should not have laughed while the angels were singing; and they fell on their knees and prayed.

*

A holy well once lost all its power because a murder had been committed near it; and another because it was cursed by a priest in consequence of the immorality that prevailed at the patterns.

The Sacred Trout

The water of the sacred well must never be used for household purposes—cooking, washing, or the like. But after the well was cursed by the priest, and the tents were struck, and no pattern was held there any longer, it lost all its sanctity, and was no longer held sacred by the people, who began to fill their pails, and carry the water away home for cooking and household use; while also they all washed their clothes down at the well, just as if no sanctity had ever been in the water.

However, one day a woman having put down a pot of water to boil, found that no amount of fire would heat it. Still it remained ice-cold, as if just drawn from the well. So she looked carefully into the pot, and there beheld the Sacred Speckled Trout sailing round and round quite contented and happy. On seeing this, she knew that the curse was lifted from the well, and she ran and told the priest. His reverence having seen the Sacred Trout with his own eyes, ordered it to be carried back to the well, the water of which at once regained all its sacred powers by the blessing of the priest; and he gave the people leave thenceforth to hold their pattern there, so as they behaved themselves like decent, God-fearing Christians for the future. But the water was not allowed to be carried away any more to their houses for household purposes; the desecration of the holy water of a sacred well being strictly forbidden as dangerous and unlucky.

St. Augustine's Well

At a holy well in the south, dedicated to St. Augustine, the friars began to build a convent. And during all the hours of work bells were heard ringing sweetly and voices singing; but one day a woman came and washed her feet in the water of the well, and thereupon all the bells ceased and the singing stopped, and the work could not go on. So the friars chose another site, and they drew a circle round it, within which no woman was to set her foot; and after this the bells began to ring again and the voices sang, and the work went on safely till the convent was completed in the name of God and St. Augustine; but no woman during all that time ever set foot on the holy ground.

The Grilled Trout

In Sligo there is a well called *Tober-na-alt*, beautifully shadowed by trees, the branches of which are thickly hung with all sorts of votive offerings from those who have been cured by the water; and miracle-men attended, who professed to heal diseases by charms, prayers, and incantations.

A man who had been born blind once recited his experiences there. "Oh, Christians, look on me! I was blind from my birth and saw no light till I came to the blessed well; now I see the water and the speckled trout down at the bottom, with the white cross on his back. Glory be to God for the cure." And when the people heard that he could really see the speckled trout, of course they all believed in the miracle. For a tradition exists that a sacred trout has lived there from time immemorial, placed in the well by the saint who first sanctified the water. Now there was an adventurous man who desired much to get possession of this trout, and he watched it till at last he caught it asleep. Then he carried it off and put it on the gridiron. The trout bore the grilling of one side very patiently; but when the man tried to turn it on the fire, the trout suddenly jumped up and made off as hard as it could back to the well, where it still lives, and can be seen at times by those who have done proper penance and paid their dues to the priest, with one side all streaked and marked brown by the bars of the gridiron, which can never be effaced.

Legend of Neal-Mor

There is a great hole or well near the river Suir, always filled with water, whose depth no man has yet fathomed. Near it is a castle, which in old times belonged to a powerful chief called *Neal-mor*. One day while his servants were saving the hay, a violent tempest of wind and rain came on, which quite destroyed the crop. Then Neal-mor was filled with rage, and he mounted his horse and drew his sword, and rode forth to the field; and there he challenged the Lord God Himself to battle. And he swung his sword round his head and struck at the air, as if he would kill and slay the Great Invisible Spirit. On which suddenly a strange thing happened, for a great whirlwind arose and the earth opened, and Neal-mor, still astride on his horse and with his sword in his hand, was lifted high up into the air and then cast down alive into the great hole, called *Poul-mor*, which may be seen to this day, and the castle is still standing by the margin. But no trace of Neal-mor or his steed was ever again beheld. They perished utterly by the vengeance of God.

But some time after his disappearance, a rude stone figure seated on a horse, was cast up out of the earth; and then all men knew the fate of the terrible chief who had braved the wrath of God, for here was his image and the sign of his destruction. The stone figure is still preserved at the castle, and tradition says that if it were removed, the whole castle would crumble to pieces in a single night and be cast into the *Poul-mor*.

St. John's Well

At St. John's well, County Cork, there is a large stone, believed to be the real true head of John the Baptist, grown hard and solid from time and the action of the elements. And the stone has certainly a rude resemblance to a human head.

Suspected persons are brought to swear on it for a clearing from guilt; for it is held in high reverence. Compacts are also made there, which are held inviolate, for no one who swears with his hand on the stone, would ever dream of breaking the oath, and each person present as witness scratches a cross on the surface with a sharp piece of slate.

A number of pagan remains are in the vicinity, but they are now held in reverence as places of Christian sanctity.

Some time ago an ancient stone image was dug up from the earth, which antiquarians pronounced to be a pagan idol, probably the Irish Siva. This was at first consecrated as Saint Gobnath, but afterwards the priest destroyed the image with his own hands.

All the paths round the well are marked deep by the lines of praying pilgrims who go round it on their knees. And there are piles of the little stones that mark the prayers of the penitents, all ready for the angels to count. Most of the stones are of pure quartz, white and glistening, and these are highly esteemed.

The Well of Fionn Ma-Coul

The ancient churches and cells of the saints were generally placed in the vicinity of a well, which then became sanctified and endowed with miraculous healing power. Or the well may have been held sacred by the Druids, and the scene of their pagan rites; therefore selected by the saint specially as his dwelling-place, so that he might bring it under the fosterage and holy influence of Christianity.

The grave of the great Fionn was laid by a celebrated well in the County Cork, and it is certain that a massive human jawbone was found there not long ago, far exceeding in size the bones of the present race of men. This jawbone was sent to London to be inspected by the learned philosophers, but was never returned—a great and grievous wrong to the renowned Irish chief, for no doubt the mighty Fionn will want it badly at the last day, when he is gathering up his bones to appear before the Lord.

St. Seenan's Well

There is a place on the shore of Scattery Island, where, according to the most ancient tradition, a sacred well once existed, with miraculous curative powers. But no one could ever discover the place, for at high water the sea covered every point up to the edge of the land, and the shifting sand made all efforts to find the locality of the well vain and fruitless.

But one day a young man who was lame in both legs from the effects of a fall, and much disabled in consequence, was going along the shore with some companions, when he suddenly sank up to his waist in the sand. With much difficulty, and after a long while, his comrades managed to haul him up, when to their amazement they found that his legs were now quite straight, and he stood up before them four inches taller than before he sank down into the sand.

So at once they knew that the sacred well must have worked the cure, and they dug and dug and cleared away the sand, till at last they came on some ancient steps, and down below lay the well, clear and fresh, and untouched by the salt of the sea, the holy well of St. Seenan, that their fathers and forefathers had vainly looked for.

Now there was great rejoicing in the country when the news spread; and all the people from far and near who had pains and ailments rushed off to the well and drank of the waters and poured libations of it over their persons, wherever the pain or the disease lay, and in a short time wonderful cures were effected. So next day still greater crowds arrived to try their good luck. But when they came to the place, not a vestige of the well could be found. The sand and the sea had covered all, and from that day to this the holy well of St. Seenan has never been seen by mortal eyes.

Kil-na-Greina

Tober Kil-na-Greina (the well of the fountain of the sun) was discovered only about eighty years ago, by a strange chance in the County Cork.

The land was a desolate marsh, no one built on it, and nothing grew on it or near it. But a large grey stone lay there, with a natural hollow in the centre that would hold about a gallon of water, and close by were the remains of an old pagan fort.

One day, the farmer who owned the land carried off this great grey stone to use as a drinking trough for his cattle. But not long after all the cattle grew sick, and then all the children sickened, so the farmer said there was ill luck in the business, and he carried back the stone to its old place, on which all the household recovered their health. Thereupon the farmer began to think there must be something wonderful and mysterious in the locality, so he had the marsh thoroughly drained, after which process they came upon an ancient stone circle, and in the midst was a well of beautiful fresh water. Some people said there was writing on the stones, and strange carvings; but it was generally believed to be a Druid temple and oracle, for there was a

302

tradition that a woman called the *Ban-na-Naomha* (the nymph of the well) had once lived there—and that she had the gift of prophecy, and uttered oracles to those who sought her at the shrine by the well; and there was a little wooden image of her, also, that used to speak to the people—so it was said and believed. It is certain, however, that a pagan temple once existed there, for which reason St. Patrick cursed the land and turned it into a marsh, and the well was hidden for a thousand years, according to St. Patrick's word.

On the discovery of the well the whole country flocked to it for cures. Tents were erected and a pattern was organized, which went on for some years with great success, and many authentic instances are recorded of marvellous miracles performed there.

The ritual observed was very strict at the beginning, three draughts of water were taken by the pilgrims, the number of drinks three, the number of rounds on their knees were three, thus making the circuit of the well nine times. After each round the pilgrim laid a stone on the ancient altar in the Druid circle, called "the well of the sun," and these stones, named in Irish "the stones of the sun," are generally pure white, and about the size of a pigeon's egg. They have a beautiful appearance after rain when the sun shines on them, and were doubtless held sacred to the sun in pagan times. The angels will reckon these stones at the last day, but each particular saint will take charge of his own votaries and see that the stones are properly counted, for each man will receive forgiveness according to their number.

But gradually the revelry at the pattern gave occasion for so much scandal, that the priest denounced the well from the altar, along with all the wickedness it fostered and encouraged. Still the people would not give up the pattern, and the drinking, and dancing, and gambling, and fighting went on worse than ever, until one day a man was killed. After this a curse seemed to have fallen on the place. The well lost all its miraculous powers, no cures were effected; the maimed, the halt, and the blind prayed before it, and went the rounds, and piled the stones as usual, but no help came, and worst sign of all, a great pagan stone on which a cross had been erected, fell down of its own accord, and the cross lay shattered on the ground. Then all the people knew that the curse of blood and of St. Patrick was indeed over the well; so it was deserted, and the tents were struck, and no pattern was ever held there any more, for the virtue of healing had gone from "the fountain of the sun," and never has come back to it through all the years.

Even the *Ban-Naomha*, the nymph of the fountain, who used to manifest herself occasionally to the regenerate under the form of a trout, disappeared at the same time, and though she may be heard of at other sacred wells, was never again seen by the devout pilgrims who watched for her appearance at the *Tober-kil-na-Greina*.

The Well of Worship

At *Tober Mire*, the well of the field of worship, County Cork, there are also many pagan monuments, and it is evident that the vicinity was one of the strongholds of the Druids in ancient times, where they had a temple, a burial-ground, and stones for sacrifice: a much larger population existed also round the temple than can now be numbered in the same locality.

The Bride's Well

Near the last-named well is the Bride's Well, *Tober Breda* (the holy well of St. Bridget). There is a stone oratory here of fabulous antiquity, with a doorway fashioned after the Egyptian model, sloping towards the top; also an ancient white-thorn covered with votive offerings, amongst which one may see many a long lock of the splendid dark hair of the Irish southern women, who adopt this antique traditional symbol of self-sacrifice to show their gratitude to the patron saint.

St. Bridget took the name of the pagan goddess Brighita in order to destroy and obliterate the idolatrous rites and transfer the devotion of the people to the Christian ceremonies, and *Tober-Breda* is now considered of the highest sanctity, being under the special patronage of St. Bridget.

The Irish Fakir

Many of the professional prayer-men, or Fakirs, resort to the *Tober-Breda* during the pattern, and manage to obtain gifts and contributions and all sorts of excellent things in exchange for their prayers from the rich farmers and young girls, to whom they promise good luck, and perhaps also a lover who will be handsome and young.

These Irish Fakirs, or sacred fraternity of beggars, lead a pleasant, thoroughly idle life. They carry a wallet and a staff, and being looked on as holy men endowed with strange spiritual gifts, they are entirely supported by the voluntary gifts of the people, who firmly believe in the mysterious efficacy of their prayers and blessings and prognostics of luck.

One of these Fakirs towards the end of his life was glad to find shelter in the poor-house. He was then eighty years of age, but a tall, erect old man, with flowing white beard and hair, keen eyes, and of the most venerable aspect.

A gentleman who saw him there, being much struck with his dignified and remarkable appearance, induced him to tell the story of his life, which was marked by several strange and curious incidents.

He said he was a farmer's son, but from his earliest youth hated work, and only liked to spend the long summer day lying on the grass gazing up into the clouds dreaming and thinking where they were all sailing to, and longing to float away with them to other lands.

Meanwhile his father raged and swore and beat him, often cruelly, because he would not work. But all the same, he could not bring himself to be digging from morning to night, and herding cattle, and keeping company only with labourers.

So when he was about twenty he formed a plan to run away; for, he thought, if the stupid old Fakirs who are lame and blind and deaf find people ready to support them, all for nothing, might not he have a better chance for getting board and lodging without work, since he had youth and health and could tell them stories to no end of the great old ancient times.

So one night he quitted his father's house secretly, and went forth on his travels into the wide world, only to meet bitter disappointment and rude repulse, for the farmers would have nothing to say to him, nor the farmers' wives. Every one eyed him with suspicion. "Why," they said, "should a great stalwart young fellow over six feet high go about the country begging? He was a tramp and meant no good." And they chased him away from their grounds.

Then he thought he would disguise himself as a regular Fakir; so he got a long cloak, and took a wallet and a staff, and hid his raven black hair under a close skull cap, and tried to look as old as he could.

But the regular Fakirs soon found him out, and their spite and rage was great, for all of them were either lame of a leg or blind of an eye, and they said; "Why should this great broad-shouldered young fellow with the black eyes come and take away our chances of living, when he ought to be able to work and earn enough to keep himself without robbing us of our just rights?" And they grumbled and snarled at him like so many dogs, and set people to spy on him and watch him.

Still he was determined to try his luck on every side: so he went to all the stations round about and prayed louder and faster than any pilgrim or Fakir amongst the whole lot.

But wherever he went he saw a horrible old hag for ever following him. Her head was wrapped up in an old red shawl, and nothing was seen of her face except two eyes, that glared on him like coals of fire whichever way he turned. And now, in truth, his life became miserable to him because of this loathsome hag. So he went from station to station to escape her; but still she followed him, and the sound of her stick on the ground was ever after him like the hammering of a nail into his coffin, for he felt sure he would die of the torment and horror.

At last he thought he would try *Tobar-Breda* for his next station, as it was several miles off and she might not be able to follow him so far. So he went, and not a sign of her was to be seen upon the road. This rejoiced his heart, and he kneeled down at the well and was saying his prayers louder and faster than ever when he looked up, and there, kneeling right opposite to him at the other side of the road, was the detestable old witch. But she took no notice of him, only went on saying her prayers and telling her beads as if no one were by.

306

Presently, however, she stooped down to wash her face in the well, and, as she threw up the water with her hands, she let the red shawl slip down over her shoulders, and then the young man beheld to his astonishment a beautiful young girl before him with a complexion like the lily and the rose, and soft brown hair falling in showers of curls over her snow-white neck.

He had only a glimpse for a moment while she cast the water in her face, and then she drew the red shawl again over her head and shoulders and was the old hag once more that had filled him with horror. But that one glimpse was enough to make his heart faint with love; and now for the first time she turned her burning eyes full on him, and kept them fixed until he seemed to swoon away in an ecstacy of happiness, and knew nothing more till he found her seated beside him, holding his hand in hers, and still looking intently on his face with her glittering eyes.

"Come away," she whispered; "follow me. We must leave this crowd of pilgrims. I have much to say to you."

So he rose up, and they went away together to a secluded spot, far from the noise and tumult of the station. Then she threw off the shawl, and took the bandage from her face, and said, "Look on me. Can you love me? I have followed you day by day for love of you. Can you love me in return, and join your fate to mine? I have money enough for both, and I'll teach you the mysteries by which we can gain more."

And from that day forth they two travelled together all over the country; and they practised many strange mysteries and charms, for Elaine, his wife, was learned in all the secrets of herb lore. And the people paid them well for their help and knowledge, so that they never wanted anything, and lived like princes, though never an evil act was done by their hands, nor did a word of strife ever pass between them.

Thus they lived happily for many years, till an evil day came when Elaine was struck by sickness, and she died.

Then the soul of the man seemed to die with her, and all his knowledge left him, and sad and weary, and tired of all things, he finally came to end his days in the poor-house, old, poor, and broken-hearted. Yet still he had the bearing of one born for a higher destiny, and the noble dignity as of a discrowned king.

Such was the strange story told to the gentleman by the aged Fakir in the poor-house, a short time before his death.

Sacred Trees

The large old hawthorns, growing singly in a field or by an ancient well, are considered very sacred; and no one would venture to cut them down, for the fairies dance under the branches at night, and would resent being interfered with.

There is a Holy Stone in an island of the Shannon, called St. Patrick's Stone. It is shadowed by an aged hawthorn, the perfume of which can be scented far off on the mainland in the flowering season. At the top of this stone is a large hollow, always filled with water by the rain or the dew, which is kept from evaporation by the heavy shadows of the branching hawthorn. It is believed that the water of this hollow has great healing power, and sometimes when a patient is brought from a distance, a rude stone shed is built under the tree, and there he is laid till the cure is completed by the water of the Holy Stone. On leaving he ties a votive offering to the tree, which is always covered with these memorials of gratitude.

In autumn the people go to bewail the dead at St. Patrick's Stone; and the mournful Irish chant may be often heard rising up in the still evening air with weird and solemn effect.

Lady Jane Francesca Agnes Wilde

Tober-na-Dara

Tober-na-Dara (the well of tears) was so called because it overflowed one time for a mile round, from the tears of the Irish wives and mothers who came there to weep for their fallen kindred, who had been slain in a battle, fighting against Cromwell's troopers of the English army.

Lough Neagh

Wonderful tales are related about the formation of Lough Neagh; and the whole country round abounds with traditions. One of them affirms that the great Fionn Ma-Coul being in a rage one day, took up a handful of earth and flung it into the sea; and the handful was of such a size that where it fell it formed the Isle of Man, and the hollow caused by its removal became the basin of the present Lough Neagh.

Another legend is that a holy well once existed in the locality, blessed and sanctified by a saint with wonderful miraculous powers of healing; provided that every patient on leaving, after cure, carefully closed the wicket-gate that shut in the well. But once, however, a woman having forgotten this information, left the gate open, when instantly the indignant waters sprang from their bed and pursued the offender, who fled in terror before the advancing waves, until at last she sank down exhausted, when the waters closed over her, and she was no more seen. But along the track of her flight the waters remained, and formed the great lake now existing, which is exactly the length the woman traversed in her flight from the angry spirit of the lake.

Mysterious influences still haunt the locality all round Lough Neagh; for it is the most ancient dwelling-place of the fairies, and when they pass at night, from one island to another, soft music is heard floating by, and then the boatmen know that the fairies are out for a pleasure trip; and one man even averred that he saw them going by in the track of the moonbeam, a crowd of little men all dressed in green with red caps, and the ladies in silver gossamer. And he liked these pretty creatures, and always left a little *poteen* for them in the bottle when he was on the island. In return for which attention they gave him the best of good luck in fishing and in everything else; for never a gauger came next or nigh his place while the fairies protected him, and many a time they led the gauger into a bog, and otherwise discomfited him, when he and his men were after a still.

So the fisherman loved his little friends, and they took great care of him; for even in the troublous times of '98, when the wreckers were all over the country, they did him no harm; though indeed the same wreckers knew where to find a good glass of something when they came his way, and he always gave it to them with a heart and a half; for didn't they tell him they were going to free Ireland from the Sassenach tyranny.

Down deep, under the waters of Lough Neagh, can still be seen, by those who have the gift of fairy vision, the columns and walls of the beautiful palaces once inhabited by the fairy race when they were the gods of the earth; and this tradition of a buried town beneath the waves has been prevalent for centuries amongst the people.

Giraldus Cambrensis states, that in his time the tops of towers, "built after the fashion of the country," were distinctly visible in calm, clear weather, under the surface of the lake; and still the fairies haunt the ruins of their former splendour, and hold festivals beneath the waters when the full moon is shining; for the boatmen, coming home late at night, have often heard sweet music rising up from beneath the waves and the sound of laughter, and seen glimmering lights far down under the water, where the ancient fairy palaces are supposed to be.

The Doctor and the Fairy Princess

Late one night, so the story goes, a great doctor, who lived near Lough Neagh, was awoke by the sound of a carriage driving up to his door, followed by a loud ring. Hastily throwing on his clothes, the doctor ran down, when he saw a little sprite of a page standing at the carriage door, and a grand gentleman inside.

"Oh, doctor, make haste and come with me," exclaimed the gentleman. "Lose no time, for a great lady has been taken ill, and she will have no one to attend her but you. So come along with me at once in the carriage."

On this the doctor ran up again to finish his dressing, and to put up all that might be wanted, and was down again in a moment.

"Now quick," said the gentleman, "you are an excellent good fellow. Sit down here beside me, and do not be alarmed at anything you may see."

So on they drove like mad—and when they came to the ferry, the doctor thought they would wake up the ferryman and take the boat; but no, in they plunged, carriage and horses, and all, and were at the other side in no time without a drop of water touching them.

Now the doctor began to suspect the company he was in; but he held his peace, and they went on up Shane's Hill, till they stopped at a long, low, black house, which they entered, and passed along a narrow dark passage, groping their way, till, all at once, a bright light lit up the walls, and some attendants having opened a door, the doctor found himself in a gorgeous chamber all hung with silk and gold; and on a silken couch lay a beautiful lady, who exclaimed with the most friendly greeting—

"Oh, doctor, I am so glad to see you. How good of you to come."

"Many thanks, my lady," said the doctor, "I am at your ladyship's service."

And he stayed with her till a male child was born; but when he looked round there was no nurse, so he wrapped it in swaddling clothes and laid it by the mother.

"Now," said the lady, "mind what I tell you. They will try to put a spell on you to keep you here; but take my advice, eat no food and drink no wine, and you will be safe; and mind, also, that you express no surprise at anything you see; and take no more than five golden guineas, though you may be offered fifty or a hundred, as your fee."

"Thank you, madam," said the doctor, "I shall obey you in all things."

With this the gentleman came into the room, grand and noble as a prince, and then he took up the child, looked at it and laid it again on the bed.

Now there was a large fire in the room, and the gentleman took the fire shovel and drew all the burning coal to the front, leaving a great space at the back of the grate; then he took up the child again and laid it in the hollow at the back of the fire and drew all the coal over it till it was covered; but, mindful of the lady's advice, the doctor said never a word. Then the room suddenly changed to another still more beautiful, where a grand feast was laid out, of all sorts of meats and fair fruits and bright red wine in cups of sparkling crystal.

"Now, doctor," said the gentleman, "sit down with us and take what best pleases you."

"Sir," said the doctor, "I have made a vow neither to eat nor drink till I reach my home again. So please let me return without further delay."

"Certainly," said the gentleman, "but first let me pay you for your trouble," and he laid down a bag of gold on the table and poured out a quantity of bright pieces.

"I shall only take what is my right and no more," said the doctor, and he drew over five golden guineas, and placed them in his purse. "And now, may I have the carriage to convey me back, for it is growing late?"

On this the gentleman laughed. "You have been learning secrets from my lady," he said. "However, you have behaved right well, and you shall be brought back safely."

So the carriage came, and the doctor took his cane, and was carried back as the first time through the water—horses, carriage, and all—and so on till he reached his home all right just before daybreak. But when he opened his purse to take out the golden guineas, there he saw a splendid diamond ring along with them in the purse worth a king's ransom, and when he examined it he found the two letters of his own name carved inside. So he knew it was meant for him, a present from the fairy prince himself.

All this happened a hundred years ago, but the ring still remains in the doctor's family, handed down from father to son, and it is remarked, that whoever wears it as the owner for the time has good luck and honour and wealth all the days of his life.

"And by the light that shines, this story is true," added the narrator of the tale, using the strong form of asseveration by which the Irish-speaking peasants emphasize the truth of their words.

Lady Jane Francesca Agnes Wilde

A Holy Well

On the north side of Lough Neagh there is still a holy well of great power and sanctity. Three ancient white-thorn trees overshadow it, and about a mile distant is the fragmentary ruin of a wooden cross, erected in the olden time to mark the limit of the sacred ground.

It was the custom up to a recent date for the pilgrims to go round this well thirteen times barefoot on the 27th of June, drink of the water, wash in it, and then, holding themselves freed from all past sin, return to the old worldly life, and begin again after the usual fashion the old routine of business or pleasure, or reckless folly, conscious that they could come once more the following year and clear off all the accumulated stains of an ill life by a lavation in the holy well.

A number of yellow crystals are found near, which the people say grow in the rocks in one night upon Midsummer Eve. And these crystals have power to avert all evil and bring luck and blessing to a house and family, and certain words are said while gathering them, known only to the adepts. The crystals are, however, very plentiful, and are found scattered for a space of two miles round the well, and in the crannies of the rocks. When burned in a crucible they become pure lime in one hour, and the powder ferments with spirits of vitriol; yet the waters of the well when analyzed present no appearance of lime.

At one time an effort was made to change the name of Lough Neagh to Lough Chichester, in honour of the Lord Deputy, Sir Arthur Chichester, but the Irish would not accept the new baptism, and the old name still remains unchanged.

A Sacred Island

At Toome Island there is the ruin of an ancient church, where the dead walk on November Eve. It is a solemn and sacred place, and nothing is allowed to be taken from it; neither stone nor branch of the shadowing trees, for fear of angering the spirits. One day three men who were on the island cut down some branches of an elder-tree that grew there to repair a private

313

still, and carried them off in their boat; but when just close to the shore a violent gust of wind upset the boat, and the men were drowned. The wood, however, floated back to the island, and a cross was made of it which was erected on the beach, to commemorate the fate of the doomed men.

It is recorded, also, that a certain stone having been taken away by some masons from the ancient ruin, to build into the wall of the parish church, which they were erecting in the place, the water in the town well suddenly began to diminish, and at last dried up, to the great consternation and terror of the inhabitants, who were at their wits' end to know the cause; when luckily an old woman of the place dreamed a dream about the abduction of the stone, which gave the solution of the mystery.

At once the people took the matter into their own hands, and they went in a body and cast down the wall till they came on the stone, which was then placed in a boat, and carried back with solemn ceremonial to the island, where it was replaced in its original site, and, immediately after, the water flowed back again into the well, and the supply became even more copious than ever.

The Lake of Revenge

Near the great mountain of Croagh-Patrick there is a lake called *Clonvencagh*, or the Lake of Revenge, to which evil-disposed persons used to resort in order to imprecate maledictions on their enemies. It was the custom also to erect monuments round the well by placing on end a long flagstone, and heaping round it a pyramid of sand in order to keep it fixed firmly in its place. Over these pillar-stones certain mystic rites were then performed by the pilgrims, and prayers were said which took the form of the most terrible imprecations. It was therefore with awe and terror that one man said of another, "He has been cursed by the stone."

Scenes at a Holy Well

Scenes of holy faith, of tender love, and human pity are, however, happily more frequent amongst the devotees at the holy wells of Ireland than the fierce mutterings of malediction. At these sacred places may be seen the mother praying for her child, the girl for her lover, the wife for her husband; going the rounds on their bare knees, with the crucifix in their clasped hands and their eyes raised to heaven in silent prayer, with a divine faith that this prayer will be answered; and who can say but that the fervour of the supplication has often brought down the blessing of healing for the sick, or comfort for the sorrowing? The picturesque grouping round the holy well, the background of purple mountains, the antique stone cross at which the pilgrims kneel, the costumes and often the beautiful faces of the praying women, with their long dark hair and purple Irish eyes, form a scene of wonderful poetic and dramatic interest, which has been immortalized by Sir Frederick Burton in his great national picture, *The Blind Girl at the Holy Well*—a work that at once made the young painter famous, and laid the foundation of the subsequent career of this distinguished and perfect artist.

Lough Foyle

Lough Foyle means the borrowed lake, for in old times there were two weird sisters dwelling beyond the Shannon, who were skilled in necromancy. And the elder sister said to the younger—

"Give me the loan of your silver lake, for I have none; and I promise to restore it to you next Monday."

So the younger, being good-natured, rolled up the lake in a sheet and despatched it over hills and dales to her sister. But when the time came for return, the elder sister, being deceitful and cunning, made answer to the messenger sent for it—

"Truly, I said Monday, but I meant the Day of Judgment. So I shall keep the lake till then."

And the lake therefore remains in her country to this day, while the great hollow whence it was taken can still be seen in Connaught, bare and barren, waiting for the waters that never will return.

The Hen's Castle

At the head of Lough Corrib, deep in the water about a gunshot from the land, stands the ancient castle of *Caisleen-na-Cearca*, said to have been built in one night by a cock and a hen, but in reality it was founded by the ill-fated Roderick O'Connor, the last king of Ireland. Strange lights are sometimes seen flitting through it, and on some particular midnight a crowd of boats gather round it, filled with men dressed in green with red sashes. And they row about till the cock crows, when they suddenly vanish and the cries of children are heard in the air. Then the people know that there has been a death somewhere in the region, and that the Sidhe have been stealing the young mortal children, and leaving some ill-favoured brat in the cradle in place of the true child.

The old castle has many historic memories; the celebrated *Graina Uaile*, the great chieftainess of the West, made it her abode for some time, and carried thither the young heir of Howth, whom she had abducted from Howth Castle, when on one of her piratical expeditions. Afterwards, during the Wars of Elizabeth, a distinguished lady of the sept of the O'Flaherties, Bevinda O'Flahertie, shut herself up there with her only daughter and heiress, and a following of twenty resolute men. But further to ensure her safety, she wrote to the Queen, requesting permission to arm the guard; Queen Elizabeth in return sent an autograph letter granting the request, but addressed to "her good friend, Captain Bevan O'Flahertie," evidently thinking that the custodian of such a castle must certainly be a man.

In the solemn solitude of this picturesque and stately *Caisleen-na-Cearca*, the great lake fortress of Lough Corrib, with its rampart of purple mountains and its water pathway fifty miles long, the young heiress grew up tall and beautiful, the pride of the west. And in due time she married Blake of Menlo Castle. And from this historic pair is descended the present baronet and owner of the property, Sir John Blake of Menlo.

Cromwell ruthlessly dismantled the castle, and it has remained a ruin ever since; but the massive walls, and the beautiful twelfth century ornamentation of doors and windows still attest the ancient grandeur of the edifice, before

316

"the curse of Cromwell" fell upon it, and upon the country and on the people of Ireland.

Sliabh-Mish, County Kerry

Every one knows that Sliabh-Mish, County Kerry, is haunted. The figure of a man, accompanied by a huge black dog, is frequently seen standing on a high crag, but as the traveller approaches, the forms disappear, although they rise up again before him on another crag, and so continue appearing and disappearing as he journeys on. Many travellers have seen them, but no one has ever yet been able to meet the man and the dog face to face on the mountain side, for they seem to melt away in the mist, and are seen no more on reaching the spot. It happened, once upon a time, that a man journeying alone over the mountain path, took out his snuff-box to solace himself with a pinch, and was putting it up again in his waistcoat pocket, when he heard a voice near him saying, "Not yet! not yet! I am near you, wait."

He looked-round, but not a soul was to be seen. However, he thought it right to be friendly, so he shook some snuff from the box in the palm of his hand and held it out in the air. But his hair stood on end, and he trembled with fright, when he felt invisible fingers on his hand picking up the snuff, and when he drew it back the snuff had disappeared.

"God and the saints between us and harm!" exclaimed the poor man, ready to drop down from terror.

"Amen," responded the clear voice of some invisible speaker close beside him.

Then the man quickly made the sign of the cross over the hand touched by the spirit, and so went on his way unharmed.

The Skelligs of Kerry

The Skellig Rocks are situated about eleven miles from the mainland, and are considered of great sanctity. In the Middle Ages, during the penitential weeks of Lent, the monks used to leave the adjacent convent and retire to the Skelligs Rocks for silence, prayer, and abstinence. Several ancient stone-roofed cells are still in existence at the top of the rock, showing where they dwelt. These cells are of the most ancient cyclopean order of building known in Ireland, and are far older than the church near them, which does not date earlier than the seventh century.

Certainly no place more awful in its loneliness and desolation could be imagined than the summit of the bleak rock, reached only by a narrow way, almost inaccessible, even to those accustomed to climb precipitous paths, but which makes the ordinary traveller giddy with fear and dread.

As marriages were not allowed in Lent, it became a custom for the young people of both sexes to make a pilgrimage to the Skellig Rocks during the last Lenten week. A procession was formed of the young girls and bachelors, and tar-barrels were lighted to guide them on the dangerous paths. The idea was to spend the week in prayer, penance, and lamentation; the girls praying for good husbands, the bachelors repenting of their sins. But the proceedings gradually degenerated into such a mad carnival of dancing, drinking, and fun, that the priests denounced the pilgrimage, and forbade the annual migration to the Skelligs. Still the practice was continued until the police had

orders to clear the rocks. Thus ended the ancient custom of "going to the Skelligs:" for the mayor having pronounced judgment over the usage as "subversive of all morality and decorum," it was entirely discontinued; and the wild fun and frolic of the Skelligs is now but a tradition preserved in the memory of the oldest inhabitant.

Popular Notions Concerning the Sidhe Race

From the earliest ages the world has believed in the existence of a race midway between the angel and man, gifted with

318

power to exercise a strange mysterious influence over human destiny. The Persians called this mystic race Peris; the Egyptians and the Greeks named them demons, not as evil, but as mysterious allies of man, invisible though ever present; capable of kind acts but implacable if offended.

The Irish called them the Sidhe, or spirit-race, or the *Feadh-Ree*, a modification of the word Peri. Their country is the *Tir-na-oge*, the land of perpetual youth, where they live a life of joy and beauty, never knowing disease or death, which is not to come on them till the judgment day, when they are fated to pass into annihilation, to perish utterly and be seen no more. They can assume any form and they make horses out of bits of straw, on which they ride over the country, and to Scotland and back. They have no religion, but a great dread of the *Scapular* (Latin words from the Gospels written by a priest and hung round the neck). Their power is great over unbaptized children, and such generally grow up evil and have the evil eye, and bring ill luck, unless the name of God is instantly invoked when they look at any one fixedly and in silence.

All over Ireland the fairies have the reputation of being very beautiful, with long yellow hair sweeping the ground, and lithe light forms. They love milk and honey, and sip the nectar from the cups of the flowers, which is their fairy wine.

Underneath the lakes, and deep down in the heart of the hills, they have their fairy palaces of pearl and gold, where they live in splendour and luxury, with music and song and dancing and laughter and all joyous things as befits the gods of the earth. If our eyes were touched by a fairy salve we could see them dancing on the hill in the moonlight. They are served on vessels of gold, and each fairy chief, to mark his rank, wears a circlet of gold round his head.

The Sidhe race were once angels in heaven, but were cast out as a punishment for their pride. Some fell to earth, others were cast into the sea, while many were seized by demons and carried down to hell, whence they issue as evil spirits, to tempt men to destruction under various disguises; chiefly, however, as beautiful young maidens, endowed with the power of song and gifted with the most enchanting wiles. Under the influence of these beautiful sirens a man will commit any and every crime. Then when his soul is utterly black they carry him down to hell, where he remains for ever tortured by the demons to whom he sold himself.

The fairies are very numerous, more numerous than the human race. In their palaces underneath the hills and in the lakes and the sea they hide away much treasure. All the treasure of wrecked ships is theirs; and all the gold that men have hidden and buried in the earth when danger was on them, and then died and left no sign of the place to their descendants. And all the gold of the mine and the jewels of the rocks belong to them; and in the Sifra, or fairy-house, the walls are silver and the pavement is gold, and the banquet-hall is lit by the glitter of the diamonds that stud the rocks.

If you walk nine times round a fairy rath at the full of the moon, you will find the entrance to the Sifra; but if you enter, beware of eating the fairy food or drinking the fairy wine. The Sidhe will, indeed, wile and draw many a young man into the fairy dance, for the fairy women are beautiful, so beautiful that a man's eyes grow dazzled who looks on them, with their long hair floating like the ripe golden corn and their robes of silver gossamer; they have perfect forms, and their dancing is beyond all expression graceful; but if a man is tempted to kiss a *Sigh-oge*, or young fairy spirit, in the dance, he is lost for ever—the madness of love will fall on him, and he will never again be able to return to earth or to leave the enchanted fairy palace. He is dead to his kindred and race for ever more.

On Fridays the fairies have special power over all things, and chiefly on that day they select and carry off the young mortal girls as brides for the fairy chiefs. But after seven years, when the girls grow old and ugly, they send them back to their kindred, giving them, however, as compensation, a knowledge of herbs and philtres and secret spells, by which they can kill or cure, and have power over men both for good and evil.

It is in this way the wise women and fairy doctors have acquired their knowledge of the mysteries and the magic of herbs. But the fairies do not always keep the mortal women in a seven years' bondage. They sometimes only take away young girls for a dance in the moonlight, and then leave them back in their own home lulled in a sweet sleep. But the vision of the night was so beautiful that the young girls long to dream again and be made happy with the soft enchantments of the music and dance.

The fairies are passionately fond of music; it is therefore dangerous for a young girl to sing when she is all alone by the lake, for the spirits will draw her down to them to sing to them in the fairy palace under the waves, and her people will see her no more. Yet sometimes when the moonlight is on the water, and the waves break against the crystal columns of the fairy palace far down in the depths, they can hear her voice, and they know that she is singing to the fairies in the spirit land beneath the waters of the lake.

There was a girl in one of the villages that could see things no one else saw, and hear music no one else heard, for the fairies loved her and used to carry her away by night in a dream to dance with the fairy chiefs and princes. But, above all, she was loved by Finvarra the king, and used to dance with him all night till sunrise though her form seemed to be lying asleep on the bed.

One day she told some of her young companions that she was going that night to a great fairy dance on the rath, and if they chose she would bring them and put a salve on their eyes so that they would see wonders.

The young girls went with her, and on coming to the rath she said—

"Now put your foot on my foot and look over my left shoulder, and you will see the king and queen and all the beautiful lords and ladies with gold bands round their heads dancing on the grass. But take care when you see them to make no sign of the cross, nor speak the name of God, or they will vanish away, and perhaps even your life would be in danger."

On hearing this the girls ran away in fear and terror without ever using the spell or seeing the fairies. But the other remained, and told her friends next day that she had danced all night to the fairy music, and had heard the sweetest singing, so that she longed to go back and live for ever with the spirits on the hill.

And her wish was granted, for she died soon after, and on the night of her death soft music was heard floating round the house, though no one was visible. And it was said also that beautiful flowers grew on her grave, though no hand planted them there, and shadowy forms used to gather in the moonlight and sing a low chant over the place where she was laid.

The fairies can assume all forms when they have special ends in view, such as to carry off a handsome girl to Fairyland. For this purpose they sometimes appear at the village festivities as tall, dark, noble-looking gentlemen, and they wile away the young girls as partners in the dance by their grand air and the grace of their dancing. And ever after the young girl who has danced with them moves and dances with a special fairy grace, though sometimes she pines away and seems to die, but every one knows that her soul has been carried off to the *Tir-na-oge*, where she will be made the bride of the fairy king and live in luxury and splendour evermore.

Yet, though the fairies are fond of pleasure, they are temperate in their mode of living, and are besides honest in their dealings and faithful to their promises. If they borrow wine from the gentry they always repay it in blessings, and never indulge much in eating or drinking. But they have no objection to offer to mortals the subtle red wine at the fairy banquets, which lulls the soul to sleep and makes the reason powerless. The young men that they beguile into their fairy palaces become their bond-slaves, and are set to hard tasks. One man said he had marched with Finvarra's men all the way from Mayo to Cork, but there they had to leave him as they were going to Spain and could not take him across the sea on their white horses.

They also much desire the aid of a powerful mortal hand to assist them in their fairy wars, for they have often disputes and battles amongst themselves for the possession of some coveted rath or dancing ground.

Once a fairy prince came to a great chieftain of Connaught, one of the Kirwans, and begged for aid against a hostile fairy tribe that had invaded his territories. The required aid being given, the fairies and their mortal auxiliaries plunged into the lake and fought the enemy and conquered; after which the Connaught men returned to shore laden with rich presents of silver and gold and crystal wine-cups as the expression of gratitude from the fairy prince.

Lady Jane Francesca Agnes Wilde

It is said that Kirwan of Castle Hackett, the great Connaught chief, also received a beautiful fairy bride on that occasion, and it is certain that all the female descendants of the family are noted for their beauty, their grace in dancing, and their sweet voices in speaking. Lady Cloncurry, mother of the present Lord Cloncurry, was of this race, and in her youth was the acknowledged leading beauty of the Irish Court and celebrated for the rare fascination of her manner and voice.

The Hurling Match

The fairies, with their true artistic love of all the gentle graces of life, greatly dislike coarse and violent gestures, and all athletic sports, such as hurling and wrestling; and they often try to put an end to them by some evil turn.

One day a great cloud of dust came along the road during a hurling match and stopped the game. On this the people grew alarmed, for they said the fairies are out hunting and will do us harm by blinding us; and thousands of the Sidhe swept by, raising a terrific dust, though no mortal eye could see them.

Then one man, a good player and musician, ran for his fiddle and began to play some vigorous dance tunes, "for now," said he, "the fairies will begin to dance and forget us, and they will be off in no time to hold a revel on the rath to the music of their own fairy pipes."

And so it was, for at once the whirlwind of dust swept on to the hill of the fairy rath, and the hurling ground was left clear for the game to go on again in safety.

It must be acknowledged that the fairies are a little selfish, or they would not have interfered with the great national sport of hurling, which is the favourite amusement of the country, and used to be held as a high festival, and arranged with all the ceremonial of a tournament; at least before the bad times destroyed all the fun and frolic of the peasant life.

The prettiest girl of the village was chosen as the hurling girl—the *Colleen-a-bhailia*. Dressed in white, and accompanied by her maidens, she proceeded to the hurling ground, the piper and fiddlers going before her playing gay dance tunes.

There she was met by the procession of the young men surrounding the chief hurler—always a stalwart youth of over six feet. And the youth and the maiden joined hands and began the dance—all the people cheering.

This was called the opening of the hurling. And for the next match another pair would be selected, each village girl anxiously hoping to be the *Colleen-a-bhailia* chosen to lead the ceremonial dance for the second or following games. Naturally the hurling tournament ended with a festive supper, much love-making, and many subsequent marriages between the pretty colleens and stalwart young hurlers, despite all the envy and jealousy of the fairies, who maliciously tried to mar the pleasures of the festival.

The Ride with the Fairies

The fairies take great delight in horsemanship, and are splendid riders. Many fine young men are enticed to ride with them, when they dash along with the fairies like the wind, Finvarra himself leading, on his great black horse with the red nostrils, that look like flames of fire. And ever after the young men are the most fearless riders in the country, so the people know at once that they have hunted with the fairies. And after the hunt some favourite of the party is taken to a magnificent supper in the fairy palace, and when he has drunk of the bright red wine they lull him to sleep with soft music. But never again can he find the fairy palace, and he looks in vain for the handsome horseman on his fine black steed, with all the gay young huntsmen in their green velvet dresses, who rushed over the field with him, like a flash of the storm wind. They have passed away for ever from his vision, like a dream of the night.

Once on a time a gentleman, also one of the Kirwans of Galway, was riding by the fairy hill—where all the fairies of the West hold their councils and meetings, under the rule of Finvarra the king—when a strange horseman, mounted on a fiery black steed, suddenly appeared. But as the stranger bid him the time of day with distinguished grace, Mr. Kirwan returned his greeting courteously, and they rode on together side by side, discoursing pleasantly—for the stranger seemed to know every one and everything, though Mr. Kirwan could not remember ever having seen him before.

"Now," said the black horseman, "I know that you are to be at the races to-morrow, so just let me give you a hint: if you wish to be certain of winning, allow me to send you my man to ride your horse. He never failed in a race yet, and he shall be with you early, before the start."

With that, at a turn of the road, the stranger disappeared; for he was no other than Finvarra himself, who had a friendly liking for the tribe of the Kirwans, because all the men were generous who came of the blood, and all the women handsome.

Next morning, as Mr. Kirwan was setting out for the race, his groom told him that a young jockey was waiting to see him. He was the strangest looking little imp, Mr. Kirwan thought, he had ever set eyes on, but he felt compelled to give him all the rights and power that was necessary for the race, and the young imp was off in a moment, like a flash of lightning.

Mr. Kirwan knew no more—he seemed like one in a dream—till the silver cup was handed to him as winner of the race, and congratulations poured down on him, and every one asked eagerly where he got the wonderful jockey who seemed to make the horse fly like the spirit of the wind itself. But the jockey by this time had disappeared. However, the stranger on the black horse was there, and he constrained Mr. Kirwan to come with him to dinner; and they rode on pleasantly, as before, till they reached a grand, beautiful house, with a crowd of gorgeous servants waiting on the steps to receive the lord and master and his guest.

One of them led Mr. Kirwan to his room to dress for dinner, and there he found a costly suit of violet velvet ready, in which the valet arrayed him. Then he entered the dining-hall. It was all lit up splendidly, and there were garlands of flowers twining round crystal columns, and golden cups set with jewels for the wine, and golden dishes.

The host seemed an accomplished man of the world, and did the honours with perfect grace. Conversation flowed freely, while soft music was heard at intervals from invisible players, and Mr. Kirwan could not resist the charm and beauty of the scene, nor the bright red wine that his host poured out for him into the jewelled cups.

Then, when the banquet was over, a great crowd of ladies and gentlemen came in and danced to sweet low music, and they circled round the guest and tried to draw him into the dance. But when he looked at them it seemed to him that they were all the dead he had once known; for his own brother was there, that had been drowned in the lake a year before; and a man who had been killed by a fall when hunting; and others whose faces he knew well. And they were all pale as death, but their eyes burned like coals of fire.

And as he looked and wondered, a lovely lady came over to him, wearing a necklace of pearls. And she clasped his wrist with her little hand, and tried to draw him into the circle.

"Dance with me," she whispered, "dance with me again. Look at me, for you once loved me."

And when he looked at her he knew that she was dead, and the clasp of her hand was like a ring of fire round his wrist; and he drew back in terror, for he saw that she was a beautiful girl he had loved in his youth, and to whom he had given a necklace of pearls, but who died before he could make her his bride.

Then his heart sank with fear and dread, and he said to his host—

"Take me from this place. I know the dancers; they are dead. Why have you brought them up from their graves?"

But the host only laughed and said, "You must take more wine to keep up your courage." And he poured him out a goblet of wine redder than rubies.

And when he drank it, all the pageant and the music and the crowd faded away from before his eyes, and he fell into a profound sleep, and knew no more till he found himself at home, laid on his bed. And the servant told him that a strange horseman had accompanied him to the door late in the night, who had charged them to lay the master gently in his bed and by no means to awake him till noon next day, for he was weary after the race; and he bade them take the hunter to the stables and tend him carefully, for the animal was covered with foam, and all trembling.

At noon Mr. Kirwan awoke, and rose up as well as ever: but of all the fairy revels nothing remained to him but the mark round his wrist of the clasp of a woman's hand, that seemed burned into his flesh.

So he knew the night's adventure was no mere dream of the fancy, and the mark of the dead hand remained with him to his last hour, and the form of the young girl with her necklace of pearls often came before him in a vision of the night; but he never again visited the fairy palace, and never saw the dark horseman any more. As to the silver cup, he flung it into the lake, for he thought it had come to him by devil's magic and would bring no good luck to him or to his race. So it sank beneath the waves, and the silver cup was seen no more.

The Fairy Spy

Sometimes the fairies appear like old men and women, and thus gain admission to houses that they may watch and spy, and bewitch the butter, and abduct the children, and carry off the young girls for fairy brides.

There was a man in the west who was bedridden for seven years, and could do no work and had to be lifted by others when he moved. Yet the amount of food he consumed was enormous, and as every one pitied him, people were constantly bringing him all sorts of good things; and he ate up everything but grew no stronger.

Now on Sundays when the family went to mass, they locked him up, but left him plenty of food, for there was no one in the house to help him. One Sunday, however, they left chapel earlier than usual, and as they were going by the shore they saw a great crowd of strangers hurling, and in the midst of them, hurling and running and leaping, was the sick man, as well and jolly as ever a man could be. They called out to him, on which he turned round to face them, but that instant he disappeared.

So the family hastened home, unlocked the door, and went straight up to the room, where they found the man in bed as usual, thin and weak and unable to move; but he had eaten up all the food and was now crying out for more. On this the family grew very angry and cried, "You have been deceiving us. You are in league with the witch-folk; but we'll soon see what you really are, for if you don't get up out of that bed at once, we'll make down a fire and lay you on it, and make you walk."

Then he cried and roared: but they seized him to drag him to the fire. So when he saw they were in earnest he jumped up and rushed to the door, and before they could touch him he had disappeared, and was seen no more.

Now, indeed, they knew that he was in league with the devil, and they burned his bed and everything belonging to him, and poured holy water on the room. And when all was burned, nothing remained but a black stone with strange signs on it. And by this, no doubt, he performed his enchantments. And the people were afraid of it and gave it to the priest, who has it to this day, so there can be no doubt as to the truth of the story.

And the priest knows the hidden meaning of the strange signs which give power to the stone; but will reveal the secret to no one, lest the people might try to work devil's magic with it, and unlawful spells by the power of the stone and the power of the signs.

The Dark Horseman

One day a fine, handsome young fellow, called Jemmy Nowlan, set off to walk to the fair at Slane, whither some cattle of his had been sent off for sale that same morning early. And he was dressed in his best clothes, spruce and neat; and not one in all the county round could equal Jemmy Nowlan for height, strength, or good looks. So he went along quite gay and merry in himself, till he came to a lonely bit of the road where never a soul was to be seen; but just then the sky became black-dark, as if thunder were in the air, and suddenly he heard the tramp of a horse behind him. On turning round he saw a very dark, elegant looking gentleman, mounted on a black horse, riding swiftly towards him.

"Jemmy Nowlan," said the dark horseman, "I have been looking for you all along the road. Get up now, quickly, behind me, and I'll carry you in no time to the great fair of Slane; for, indeed, I am going there myself, and it would be very pleasant to have your company."

"Thank your honour kindly," said Jemmy; "but it's not for the likes of me to ride with your lordship; so I would rather walk, if it's pleasing to your honour; but thanks all the same."

Truth to tell, Jemmy in his own mind had a fear of the strange gentleman and his black horse, and distrusted them both, for had he not heard the people tell strange stories of how young men had been carried off by the fairies, and held prisoners by their enchantments down deep in the heart of the hill under the earth, where never a mortal could see them again or know their fate; and they were only allowed to come up and see their kindred on the nights the dead walked, and then they walked with them as they rose from the graves? So again he began to make his excuses, and meanwhile kept looking round for some path by which he could escape if possible.

"Come now," said the dark horseman, "this is all nonsense, Jemmy Nowlan; you really must come with me."

And with that he stooped down and touched him lightly on the shoulder with his whip, and in an instant Jemmy found himself seated on the horse, and galloping away like the wind with the dark horseman; and they never stopped nor stayed till they came to a great castle in a wood, where a whole set of servants in green and gold were waiting on the steps to receive them. And they were the smallest people Jemmy had ever seen in his life; but he made no remark, for they were very civil, and crowded round to know what they could do for him.

"Take him to a room and let him dress," said the gentleman, who appeared to own the castle. And in the room Jemmy found a beautiful suit of velvet, and a cap and feather. And when the little servants had dressed him they led him to the large hall that was all lit up and hung with garlands of flowers; and music and dancing were going on, and many lovely ladies were present, but not one in the hall was handsomer than Jemmy Nowlan in his velvet suit and cap and feather.

"Will you dance with me, Jemmy Nowlan?" said one lovely lady.

"No, Jemmy: you must dance with me," said another.

And they all fought for him, so he danced with them all, one after the other, the whole night through, till he was dead tired and longed to lie down and sleep.

"Take Jemmy Nowlan to his room, and put him to bed," said the gentleman to a red-haired man; "but first he must tell me a story."

"I have no story, your honour," said Jemmy, "for I am not book-learned; but I am very tired, let me lie down and sleep."

"Sleep, indeed," said the gentleman; "not if I can help it. Here, Davy"—and he called the red-haired man—"take Jemmy Nowlan and put him out; he can tell no story. I will have no one here who can't tell me a story. Put him out, he is not worth his supper."

So the red-haired man thrust Jemmy out at the castle gate, and he was just settling himself to sleep on a bench outside, when three men came by bearing a coffin.

"Oho, Jemmy Nowlan," they said, "you are welcome. We just wanted a fourth man to carry the coffin."

And they made him get under it with them, and away they marched over hedge and ditch, and field and bog, through briars and thorns, till they reached the old churchyard in the valley, and then they stopped.

"Who will dig a grave?" said one.

"Let us draw lots," said another.

And the lot fell on Jemmy. So they gave him a spade, and he worked and worked till the grave was dug broad and deep.

"This is not the right place at all for a grave," said the leader of the party when the grave was finished. "I'll have no one buried in this spot, for the bones of my father rest here."

So they had to take up the coffin again, and carry it on over field and bog till they reached another churchward, where Jemmy was obliged to dig a second grave; and when it was finished, the leader cried out—

"Who shall we place in the coffin?"

And another voice answered—

"We need draw no lots; lay Jemmy Nowlan in the coffin!"

And the men seized hold of him and tried to cast him to the ground. But

Jemmy was strong and powerful, and fought them all. Still they would not let go their hold, though he dealt them such blows as would have killed any other men. And at last he felt faint, for he had no weapon to fight with, and his strength was going.

Then he saw that the leader carried a hazel switch in his hand, and he knew that a hazel switch brought luck; so he made a sudden spring and seized it, and whirled it three times round his head, and struck right and left at his assailants, when a strange and wondrous thing happened; for the three men who were ready to kill him, fell down at once to the ground, and remained there still as the dead. And the coffin stood white in the moonlight by itself, and no hand touched it, and no voice spoke.

But Jemmy never waited to look or think, for the fear of the men was on him, lest they should rise up again; so he fled away, still holding the hazel twig in his hand, and ran on over field and bog, through briars and thorns, till he found himself again at the castle gate. Then all the grand servants came out, and the little men, and they said—

"You are welcome, Jemmy Nowlan. Come in; his lordship is waiting for you."

And they brought him to a room where the lord was lying on a velvet couch, and he said—

"Now, young man, tell me a story, for no one in my castle is allowed to eat, drink, or sleep till they have related something wonderful that has happened to them."

"Then, my lord," said Jemmy, "I can tell you the most wonderful of stories; and very proud I am to be able to amuse your lordship."

So he told him the story of the three men and the coffin, and the lord was so pleased that he ordered the servants to bring the youth a fine supper, and the best of wine, and Jemmy ate like a prince from gold dishes, and drank from crystal cups of the wine, and had the best of everything; but after the supper he felt rather queer and dazed-like, and fell down on the ground asleep like one dead.

After that he knew nothing till he awoke next morning, and found himself lying under a haystack in his own field, and all his beautiful clothes were gone—the velvet suit and cap and feather that he had looked so handsome in at the dance, when all the fine ladies fell in love with him. Nothing was left to him of all the night's adventure save the hazel twig, which he still held firmly in his hand.

And a very sad and down-hearted man was Jemmy Nowlan that day, especially when the herd came to tell him that none of the cattle were sold at the fair, for the men were waiting for the master, and wondering why he did not come to look after his money, while all the other farmers were selling their stock at the finest prices.

And Jemmy Nowlan has never yet made out why the fairies played him such a malicious and ill turn as to prevent him selling his cattle. But if ever again he meets that dark stranger on the black horse, he is determined to try the strength of his shillelagh on his head, were he ever such a grand man among the fairies. For at least he might have left him the velvet suit; and it was a shabby thing to take it away just when he couldn't help himself, and had fallen down from fair weakness and exhaustion after all the dancing, and the wine he drank at supper, when the lovely ladies poured it out for him with their little hands covered with jewels.

It was truly a bad and shabby trick, as Jemmy said to himself that May morning, when he stood up from under the hay-rick; and just shows us never to trust the fairies, for with all their sweet words and pleasant ways and bright red wine, they are full of malice and envy and deceit, and are always ready to ruin a poor fellow and then laugh at him, just for fun, and for the spite and jealousy they have against the human race.

Sheela-na-Skean

There is an old ruin of a farmhouse in the County Cork, near Fermoy, that has an evil reputation, and no one would build it up or inhabit it.

Years and years ago a rich farmer lived there, who was reputed to have hoards of gold hid away in his sleeping-room. Some said he never slept without the sack of gold being laid under his pillow. However, one night he was found cruelly murdered, and all the gold in the house was missing except a few pieces stained with blood, that had evidently been dropped by the murderers in their flight.

The old man at the time was living quite alone. His wife was dead, and his only son was away in a distant part of the country. But on news of the murder the son returned, and a close investigation was made. Suspicion finally fell on the housekeeper and a lover she used to bring to the house. They were arrested in consequence and brought to trial. The housekeeper, *Sheela-na-Skean*, or Sheela of the Knife, as she was called afterwards, was a dark, fierce, powerful woman, noted for her violent and vindictive temper. The lover was a weak, cowardly fellow, who at the last turned evidence to save his life. He had taken no part, he said, in the actual murder, though he had helped Sheela to remove and bury the gold. According to his story, Sheela entered the old man's room at night, and taking a sharp short sword that always hung at the head of his bed, she stabbed him fiercely over and over till not a breath of life was left. Then, calling her lover, they ransacked the room, and found quantities of golden guineas, which they put in a bag and carried out to the field, where they buried it in a safe spot, known only to themselves; but this place neither Sheela nor the lover would reveal unless they received a pardon.

The murder, however, was too atrocious for pardon, and Sheela was hung amid the howlings and execrations of the people. But she remained fierce and defiant to the last, still refusing obstinately to reveal the place where the money was buried.

The lover, meanwhile, had died in prison from fright, for after sentence was pronounced, he fell down in a fit, from which he never recovered. So the secret of the gold died with them.

After this the son came to live in the place; and the tradition of the hidden gold was still kept alive in the family, but all efforts to find it proved useless.

Now a strange thing happened. The farmer dreamed for three nights in succession that if he went at midnight to an old ruined castle in the neighbourhood, he would hear words that might tell him the secret of the gold; but he must go alone. So after the third dream the farmer resolved to do as he was ordered, and he went forth at midnight to the place indicated. His two sons, grown-up young men, anxiously awaited his return. And about an hour after midnight the father came home pale as a ghost, haggard and trembling. They helped him to his bed, and after a little he was able to tell them his adventures. He said, on reaching the old ruin he leaned up straight against the wall, and waited for the promised words in silence. Then a breath seemed to pass over his face, and he heard a low voice whispering in his ear—

"If you want to find the bag of gold, take out the third stone."

"But here," said the farmer mournfully, "the voice stopped before the place was named where the gold lay; for at that instant a terrific screech was heard, and the ghost of Sheela appeared gigantic and terrible; her hands dripping with blood, and her eyes flaming fire; and she rushed to attack me, brandishing a short, sharp sword round her head, the very same, perhaps, with which she had committed the murder. At sight of this awful apparition I fled homeward, Sheela still pursuing me with leaps and yells till I reached the boundary of the castle grounds, when she sank into the earth and disappeared. But," continued the farmer, "I am certain, from the voice, that the bag of gold lies hid under the third stone in—"

He could say no more, for at that instant the door of the bedroom was violently flung open, as if by a strong storm wind, the candle was blown out, and the unfortunate man was lifted from his bed by invisible hands, and dashed upon the floor with a terrible crash. In the darkness the young men could hear the groans, but they saw no one.

When the candle was relit they went over to help their father, but found he was already dead, with a black mark round his throat as if from strangulation by a powerful hand. So the secret of the gold remained still undiscovered.

After the funeral was over, and all affairs settled, the brothers agreed that they would still search for the gold in the old ruins of the castle, undeterred by the apparition of the terrible Sheela. So on a certain midnight they set forth with spades and big sticks for defence, and proceeded to examine every third stone in the huge walls, to the height of a man from the ground, seeking some secret mark or sign by which, perhaps, the true stone might be discovered. But as they worked, a thin blue light suddenly appeared at some distance in the inner court of the castle, and by it stood the ghost of their father, pointing with his outstretched hand to a certain stone in the wall. Now, they thought, that must certainly be the spot where the gold is hid; and they rushed on; but before they could reach the place, the terrible form of Sheela appeared, more awful than words could describe, clothed in white, and with a circle of flame round her head. And she seized the ghost with her gory hands, and dragged him away with horrible yells and imprecations. And far off in the darkness they could hear the fight going on, and the yells of Sheela as she pursued the ghost.

"Now," said the young men, "let us work while they are fighting;" and they worked away at the third stone from the end, where the blue light had rested—a large flat stone, but easily lifted; and when they had rolled it away from the place, there underneath lay a huge bag of bright golden guineas. And as they raised it up from the earth, a terrific unearthly din was heard in the distance, and a shrill scream rang on the air. Then a rush of the wind came by them and the blue light vanished, but they heeded nothing, only lifted the bag from the clay, and carried it away with them through the darkness and storm. And the yells seemed to pursue them till they reached the boundary of the castle grounds, then all was still; and they traversed the rest of the way in peace, and reached home safely.

From that time the ghost of *Sheela-na-Skean* ceased to haunt the castle, but lamenting and cries used sometimes to be heard at night in and around the old farmhouse; so the brothers pulled it down and left it a ruin, and built a handsome residence with some of their treasure; for now they had plenty of gold, and they lived happily and prospered ever after, with all their family and possessions. And on the spot where the gold was found they erected a cross, in memory of their father, to whom they owed all their wealth, and through whom this prosperity had come; for by him the evil spirit of *Sheela-na-Skean* was conquered at last, and the gold restored to the family of the murdered farmer.

Captain Webb, the Robber Chief

About a hundred years ago a most notorious robber, called Captain Webb, used to make the County Mayo his headquarters; and dreadful tales are still current amongst the people of his deeds of violence and cruelty.

Many beautiful young girls he carried off by force or fraud; and when he grew tired of them it was his practice to strip the unhappy victims naked, and plunge them down a deep hole near Lough Corrib, which is still known throughout the county as "Captain Webb's Hole."

One day, however, fate worked out a revenge on the audacious highwayman by the hands of a woman.

He had committed a daring robbery on the highroad—plundered a carriage, shot the horses, and carried off a noble and lovely girl, who was returning home with her mother from an entertainment, which had been given by a great lord in the vicinity. Consequently, as the robber knew, the ladies were dressed magnificently, and wore the most costly jewels. After stripping the mother of all her ornaments, he left her half dead upon the highway; but wrapping a cloak round the young lady, Captain Webb flung her on the horse before him and galloped off to one of the many hiding-places he had through the country.

For some time he gave up all his other favourites for the sake of the beautiful girl, and carried her about with him on all his wild expeditions, so great was the madness of his love for her.

But at length he grew tired even of her beauty, and resolved to get rid of her, in the same way as he had got rid of the others, by a cruel and sudden death.

So one day, when she was out riding beside him, as he always forced her to do, he brought her to the fatal hole where so many of his victims had perished, intending to cast her down headlong as he had done to so many others; but first he told her to dismount and to take off all her rich garments of silk and gold and her jewels, for she would need them no longer.

"For pity, then," she said, "do not look on me while I undress, for it is not seemly or right to look on a woman undressing; but turn your back and I shall unclasp my robe and fling it off."

So the captain turned his back as she desired him, for he could not refuse her last request; but still he kept close to the edge of the hole ready to throw her in; when suddenly she sprang upon him, and placing both hands on his shoulders, pushed him over the edge down into the fathomless gulf, from which no mortal ever rose alive, and in this manner the country was freed for evermore from the terrible robber fiend, by the courage of a brave and beautiful girl.

The Mayo Robber and Feenish the Mare

Another desperate character that made an evil reputation in the same county was Captain Macnamara. Though a man of family and good means and of splendid appearance, he led a life of the wildest excess, and stopped at no crime so as he could gratify the passion or the caprice of the moment, or find money to spend on his pleasures, with the reckless, senseless, foolish extravagance of an evil, dissolute nature; for he had early squandered away all his own patrimony, and now only lived by fraud, lying, and insolent contempt of the rights and claims of others.

Just at the time when his finances were at the lowest, he was summoned to attend his trial at the county assizes for some malpractices concerning land and stock belonging to a wealthy widow lady, who had a fine place in the neighbourhood, though she seldom lived there, being constantly abroad, in Paris or Rome, with her only son, a young lad, the heir of the property. It happened, however, that she returned home just in time for the trial, which interested her, as it concerned an audacious appropriation of some of her best land from which the stock had been drawn off and sold by Macnamara. Highly indignant at the insult offered to her, the wealthy widow appeared in court resolved on vengeance; and was received by all the officials with the utmost distinction and deference. The defendant was put through a most torturing examination, in which all his evil practices were laid bare with ruthless severity. But the widow heeded nothing of the record of wicked deeds; she only saw before her a splendid stalwart man in the prime of life, with a magnificent presence, flashing eyes, and raven hair. At once she was subjugated, as if by magic, by the handsome prisoner in the dock, and calling over her counsel, she gave orders that the suit should be stopped and no damages claimed. After this, as was natural, a warm intimacy sprang up between plaintiff and defendant, which ended in a short time by the marriage of the rich widow and the spendthrift captain; the widow's only son and heir to the estate being brought home from school to live with them, for, as the captain observed, it was necessary that the boy should be early instructed in the management of the property.

One evening, however, Macnamara set a rope across a lonely part of the road where he knew the lad must pass when riding home. In consequence the horse stumbled, and threw the rider; and at night when the servants and people went out with torches to look for the young heir, he was found lying quite dead by the roadside.

The whole property now devolved to the widow, who gave up the management entirely to Macnamara; and he lost no time in making good use of the large sums of money that came under his control, by constantly plunging into renewed courses of dissolute extravagance. How the home life went on no one knew, for little was seen of the wife while the husband carried on his orgies; but after a year had passed by, the country heard with surprise of the death of the rich widow, as she was still called—suddenly, it was said, by a fit, a stroke. She was found lying dead in her bed one morning, and her husband was in the greatest grief—this was the orthodox narrative. But strange whispers at the same time went through the neighbourhood, that round the neck of the poor dear lady was found a black mark, and many had grave suspicions of foul play, though they feared to take any measures against the captain, so great was the terror he inspired.

Meantime, he consoled himself with another wife, a young girl who had been a favourite of his long before his first wife's death. And they led a reckless life together till all the widow's money was gambled away or spent in dissolute frolics. Then he joined a wild band of sharpers and desperadoes who fought and cheated every one at the fairs and races, and were the terror of the whole country. But, especially they warred upon the Big Joyces of Connemara, who thereupon swore to be revenged.

Now the captain had a famous mare called *Feenish*, who could fly like the wind and live for days without food. And he taught her all sorts of strange tricks—to stand on her hind legs, to go in at a window and to walk upstairs; and the way the robber chief got the secret of power over men and animals was in this wise.

There was an old raven lived near him up in a big tree, and one day Macnamara stole the eggs, took them home, boiled them and then set them back again in the nest, to see what the old bird would do. Now he saw the wisdom of the raven, for she flew off at once to a neighbouring mountain, and having found a certain stone of magic virtue carried it back in her beak to the nest. With this stone she rubbed the eggs all over, till the life came back into them; and in due time the young ravens were flying about as strong and joyous as the rest.

Macnamara having observed this process, watched his opportunity, and one day when the raven was absent, he stole the magic stone from the nest. His first trial of the power was to rub himself all over, as he had seen the raven do with the eggs; and with a very remarkable result, for he at once became possessed of marvellous gifts. He could foresee events, and force people to do his will: he knew when danger was near, and what path to take to avoid his enemies when they were on his track. Then he rubbed Feenish, the mare, all over, and instantly she became as wise as a Christian, and knew every word that was said to her.

So Macnamara, armed with all these new powers, went on with his wild wicked life, and robbed and plundered worse than ever; and the blood of many a man, besides, was on his hands.

At last the Joyce faction resolved to make an end of the audacious robber, and all the Big Joyces of Connemara gathered in force and pursued him from place to place and over bog and mountain through half the country. At one time Macnamara plunged into a bog; where Feenish lost her four shoes; then he made her swim the river at Cong after a hard day's ride through mountain passes; but when the poor mare got to the other side she fell down dead, to the great grief of the robber chief, who had her buried on an island in Lough Corrib that still bears her name—Innis-Feenish. However, when he had laid his faithful friend in the clay, all energy forsook him, and all his good luck departed—his riches melted away, his children squandered his property, and his two sons met a violent death; finally, broken in spirit, beggared, and alone in the world, the last of his race, he found himself with nothing left of his ill-gotten gains except an old grey pony. On this animal he rode to Cork, where he took his passage in an emigrant ship to America, and sailed away from the old country, laden with the curses of all who had ever known him; and from that hour he was heard of no more. So ended the wicked career of the spendthrift and gambler and the suspected murderer of many victims.

Sketches of the Irish Past

The Bardic Race

The magi, the Sephoe, the gymnosophists, and the Irish adepts, held much the same creed and the same dogmas with regard to the conduct of life necessary to heighten the spiritual power. They all abstained from animal food at such times as the rush of inspiration was on them and the madness of prophetic rage; and at all times they favoured solitude, living apart in the House of Learning or Bardic College, where they admitted no obtrusive intimacies with lower intellects to disturb their lofty and exalted moods of thought. The means, also, by which they obtained mastery over diseases and the minds of men, with the strange and subtle use they made of herbs, were all kept secret amongst themselves; for they held that the prying eyes of shallow unbelievers should never be suffered to intrude upon the sacred mysteries. And it is certain that the bards possessed strange and mystic powers of wisdom beyond and above all other men. It was therefore very dangerous to offend a poet. If any one refused him a request he would take the lobe of the person's ear and grind it between his fingers, and the man would die. Yet the bards were capable of much human emotion, and were the sweet singers of sympathy when sorrow touched a household.

The following elegy from the Irish, written about two hundred years ago by the Ard-Filé, or chief poet of the tribe, has many natural, pathetic touches, and when chanted in Irish to the harp had power to melt the hearts of all the hearers to tears.

AN ELEGY.

O Boyne, once famed for battles, sports, and conflicts,
And great heroes of the race of Conn,
Art thou grey after all thy blooms?
O aged old woman of grey-green pools,
O wretched Boyne of many tears.
Where is the glory of thy sires?
The glory of Art with the swift arrow;
Of Meiltan, with the swift-darting spears
Of the lordly race of the O'Neil?
To thee belonged red victory,
When the Fenian wrath was kindled,
And the heroes in thousands rode to war,
And the bridles clanked on the steeds.
O river of kings and the sons of kings,
Of the swift bark and the silver fish,
I lay my blessing on thee with my tears,
For thou art the watcher by a grave—
My treasures lie in the earth at thy side—
O Boyne of many tears.
My sons lie there in their strength,
My little daughter in her beauty—
Rory, and Brian, and Rose—
These have I given against my will,
My blood, my heart, my bone and kin,
My love and my life, to the grave.
The blessing of men was on them,

341

The blessings of thousands that loved them,
From Kells of the Crosses to Drogheda—
Eight thousand blessings to Dowth of the Trees.
Peace be on the earth where they lie!
By the royal stream of the kings,
In the land of the great O'Neil.

The Bardic song amongst all nations was the first expression of the human soul, with all its strong, passionate emotions and heroic impulses. It is remarkable that, although several invasions of Ireland are on record, yet but one language seems to have existed there from the earliest times down to the coming of the Anglo-Normans in the twelfth century. The Bards held it as their peculiar duty to raise this language to the highest perfection, and the laws of Celtic poetry, especially, were most elaborate and the structure of the verse exceedingly difficult. Ten years of study were allowed the students at the Druids' College to gain perfection in the art, and also to practise the memory; for at the royal festivals the Ard-Filé was expected to recite fully and perfectly whatever heroic tale might be called for by the king at the banquet. On great occasions also, when the meeting was held in the open air, the chiefs sat round in a circle on mounds of turf, to the accompaniment of the harp, the chorus joining in the while the bards, standing in the centre, recited the heroic narrative lyrical portions at intervals, and a circle of harpists at the outermost ring of the assemblage introduced occasional symphonies of pure instrumental music to give the bards time for rest between the parts of the recitation.

There were three chief measures in music in use amongst the poets—"the Sorrowful," or the chant for the dead; "the Delightful," reserved for dances and festivities; and "the Reposing," devoted entirely to love sonnets and the plaintive softness of lyrical expression. But the *Ross-Catha*, or battle-hymn, was the great war-song to which the warriors marched to battle, and which inspired them with the heroic madness that braved death for victory.

Everything connected with the bards is interesting. They were so gifted, so learned, and so beautiful. For even genius was not considered enough, without beauty, to warrant a young man being enrolled in the ranks of the poets. A noble, stately presence was indispensable, and the poet was required not only to be gifted, but to be handsome. Then he was promoted through all the grades until he reached the last and highest, called "The Wisdom of the Gods," but the knowledge then acquired by the initiated was kept sacred from the crowd, and the adept swore by the sun, the stars, and the hosts of heaven never to reveal the mysteries acquired by his initiation, to the profane.

The high-born maidens amongst the noble families were also trained by the Druids in poetry and music, and in the exercise of the chase, such as archery and throwing the lance, to give their bodies health, vigour and beauty, while those endowed with peculiar intellect were admitted into the bardic orders, and became the priestess, prophetess, or poetess of the tribe; who inspired men by her eloquence and had power by her incantations over the deep mysteries of life. Such was Eodain, the chief poetess of Erin, the guide and inspirer of Eugene, the king of the South, the prophetess of her nation, who saved him and his kingdom from ruin by her wisdom, and redeemed him by her counsels from his dissolute and evil life.

The Ancient Race

But thousands of years ago, long before kings, bards, and Druids, with all their learning and comparative civilization, flourished in Ireland, and before the traditions of a beautiful fairy race were brought from the far East by a people accustomed to the sight of beauty, grace and splendour, an ancient race existed in the world—a mysterious, primitive wave of human life that spread over all Europe, perhaps over all the earth, and even surged upon the shores of our own Western island; possibly a pre-Adamic race, inferior in all points, physical as well as mental, to the Adamic race that succeeded them.

They have left no name or history, yet evidences of their nature, habits, intellect, and modes of life can be scientifically deduced from the abundant strange and curious antiquarian remains to be seen in the Museum of the Royal Irish Academy, of which Sir William Wilde in his illustrated catalogue has given such a perfect and comprehensive description. Records of a period so remote that the use of metals even was unknown; yet these ancient records reveal the story of the rude half-developed, early humanity of the world in as clear a symbol to the expert and the archæologist, as if written in alphabetical letters on monoliths, like those of Babylon.

Without, therefore, being forced into shadowy theory or nebular hypothesis, we may readily construct the whole life of the primitive man, his mode of being and doing, of dressing and of eating, of living, dying and sepulture, simply from the rude implements fashioned by his hand that cover the walls of the Academy, and are the letters in which an eternal page of human history is written.

But, this first pre-Adamic rudimental humanity was not wholly extirpated by the subsequent Adamic race. Representatives of them still remained throughout the world, and are yet existing, though these half-souled specimens of an early, inferior humanity, are gradually dying out and disappearing before the advance of the higher Adamic race, the destined lords and rulers of earth.

In Ireland the inferior primitive tribes became the bond-slaves for the higher humanity—the Tuatha-de-Dananns and Milesians that succeeded them; and specimens of this slave people can still be seen in remote districts in Ireland along the coast-line of the West, and in the secluded mountain passes. They are held in much contempt by the descendants of the nobler race, and are stigmatized even now as "the slave people," and the bondsmen of their forefathers.

It seems, then, an incontrovertible truth that the early inhabitants of Ireland, as of all Europe—in fact, the whole pre-Adamite humanity of the world—lived and died throughout how many ages we know not in a state little higher than the animal creation, without the knowledge of even the simplest elements of civilization, which all the Adamic races possess, from their higher organization and intellect, and which they seem to have had from the date of their earliest appearance on earth.

The clothing of the primitive man was of the skins of animals fastened with thongs, or tunics made of rushes, such as were found some years ago in Spain, on the skeleton forms of pre-historic date buried in a cave of the Sierra Nevada. Their only weapons and tools were of stone, manufactured by another stone. Their ornaments were of shells and fish-bones; and their dwellings such only as instinct has suggested to all animals.

There are abundant evidences in our National Museum to prove the existence of this primary stratum of barbarism underlying all the culture of modern Europe; and we might almost hesitate to link so low a type of humanity with our own if we did not recognize in it also the characteristic instinct of man, entirely wanting in the animals—an irrepressible tendency towards progression and improvement, and, above all, to ornamentation, which is a distinctive human quality.

The Antiquities of Ireland

We commence the study of this early race with the first rude stone implement with which a savage man killed an animal scarcely more savage. Then, simple designs of ornamentation are discernible—the first twilight dawning of soul through matter. The rude stone implement becomes decorated, more symmetrical in form, more adapted to its uses. There is evidence of a growing sense of beauty, and heightened reasoning powers. After the introduction of metals, we trace the original stone forms reproduced first in simple unalloyed copper, afterwards in that perfect and beautiful bronze of a ruddy yellow, like gold, which no modern bronze has ever equalled. There is no violent disruption of ideas, as if the new incoming race had entirely vanquished and crushed the earlier and elder; but on the contrary, a gradual and continuous development of the original ideas of this elder race itself, always co-working with whatever new influences may have come to it from without.

Many writers have held the belief that the first colonists of Ireland were a highly-civilized people, clothed with Tyrian silk, fine linen of Egypt, and adorned with costly ornaments of gold. But stern facts refute this theory. The same primitive race who used only stone weapons were unacquainted with the art of weaving, and knew of no other garment than the untanned skin of the animal they killed for food. Theorists might still, however, argue, doubt, and disbelieve, if one of the ancient race had not himself risen, as it were, from the grave, after a sleep of thousands of years, to give his testimony concerning his people. In 1821 this primitive Irishman, clad completely in skins laced with thongs, was found in a peat bog, ten feet below the surface. The teeth, long dark hair and beard, were perfect. Portions of this dress have been preserved in the Museum of the Royal Irish Academy. The material used in sewing was fine gut, and the regularity and closeness of the stitching are most remarkable. Specimens of the antique skin mocassins and skin caps have been also found at various times in the peat bogs, and secured for the Museum, so that we have the dress of the ancient Irishman complete.

Long after this period of barbarism, but still at a time so distant that it is anterior to all historic record, we find that the Irish had attained some knowledge of metals and the art of weaving. The Museum contains numerous highly-finished illustrations of the beautifully-formed, slender, leaf-shaped swords and daggers of bronze, which began gradually to supersede the use of the primitive celt. Many of these swords are of the pure Grecian type, formed apparently on the model of the leaf of the aloe or the agave. One sword found on an ancient battle-field is curved like a Turkish yataghan; and in "The Book of Rights" "curved swords of battle" are frequently referred to. But the specimens of the broad scythe-shaped sword, "which is especially and peculiarly Irish," are the most numerous, as many as forty-one of these heavy, thick, round-pointed battle-axe swords being in the Museum.

The same progress of artistic development is observable in the ancient swords as was noticed in the primitive celt—as the art advanced, the manufacturer began to exercise his artistic faculties in fanciful and costly decoration. The blade was adorned with either cast or engraved ornamentation, and the hilt inlaid or studded with gold. Thus, Brian Boroimhe is described as carrying a gold-hilted sword in his right hand at the battle of Clontarf.

It is very remarkable that, throughout the whole series, from the rudest to the most highly finished, a peculiar idea is traceable in the ornamentation, by which they can at once be recognized as Irish; and this idea seems to have travelled from Irish Paganism to Irish Christianism. The ornamentation on the sepulchral stones of New Grange is repeated on the stone celts; it is carried on into the age of Bronze; it decorated the swords and spears of the kings, as well as their costly diadems and ornaments of gold, and still continued to be traced, with a kind of loving fidelity to the ancient symbols, upon the manuscripts illuminated by priestly hands, so late as the tenth and eleventh centuries.

For the illustration of the costume of the early Irish, after it passed from primitive helpless barbarism to comparative civilization, by the aid of the knowledge of metals and the art of weaving, fortunately we are not left to mere theories; for, by a singular chance, the representative of the advanced period, like him of the barbaric age, arises also from the grave of the Past to bear witness for himself.

In 1824, a male body, completely clad in woollen antique garments, was found in a bog near Sligo, six feet below the surface; and so perfect was the body when first discovered, that a magistrate was called upon to hold an inquest on it. The garments also were in such complete preservation, that a photograph was made of a person clad in this antique suit, with the exception of the shoes, which were too small for an adult of our day, and a drawing from this photograph is one of the best and most beautifully executed illustrations of the Museum catalogue. The costume of this ancient Irish gentleman is exceedingly picturesque, consisting of trews of a plaid pattern, made wide above, like Turkish trousers, but fitting close to the leg and ankle; over them was a tunic of soft cloth, most elaborately gored and gussetted, showing high perfection in the tailoring art. The skirt of the tunic, which extends to the knee, is set on full, and measures eight feet in circumference at the bottom. The sleeves are tight, and open to the elbow, like an Albanian jacket; and over all was thrown the immemorial Irish mantle, so invariably worn, so indispensable a portion of Irish costume that it passed into a proverb among our neighbours, the Welsh, "like an Irishman for the cloak."

This graceful garment, as found upon the hero of the bog, and now visible in our Museum, is composed of brown, soft cloth, made straight on the upper edge, which is nine feet long, but cut nearly into the segment of a circle on the lower. The form resembles closely that worn by the Calabrian peasant at this day. These cloaks were often of great value; kings were paid tribute of them. They were made of various colours, each colour being a symbol to denote the rank of the wearer. The number of colours also in a dress had a significant value, and was regulated by law. Thus, one colour only was allowed to slaves; two for soldiers; three for goodly heroes, or young lords; six for the learned men; five for a poetess; and seven was the regal number for kings and queens.

In the "Book of Rights," the earliest accessible authority on the subject of costume prior to the Norman Invasion, we read of cloaks of various colours presented in tribute to the kings—cloaks of purple, red cloaks, green, white, black; in fact, cloaks of all colours. Some are mentioned as bordered with gold. The tunic is also described frequently, "with golden borders—with gold ornaments—with golden hems." Another form of cloak was fashioned with a hood like the Arab bornous, and was bordered with a deep fringe of goat's hairs.

Irish costume seems, in fact, to have been half-Oriental, half-Northern, like the compound race that peopled the island. The trews were the same as the Germanic *braccœ*; while the tunic was Albanian, and the mantle Eastern; as well as the high, conical head-dress, which is identical in form with the Persian cap of the present day. On this subject Sir William Wilde remarks—

"Every day's observation and research bring to light new affinities with early Irish costume. In the great French work, 'Herculaneum et Pompeii,' there is a battle scene, copied from a mosaic at Pompeii, in which the arms and dress of the combatants are almost identical with those of ancient Ireland. The vanquished wear tight-fitting trousers, close tunics, several of which are plaided, and cloaks with the hood coming over the head precisely like the Irish cochall. The chief figures wear torques round the neck, and bracelets on the wrists, and the hood is retained in its place by a narrow frontlet, apparently of gold. The colours of the garments are also peculiarly Irish. In some, the cloak is yellow; the mantle, dark red; and the tunic, purple bordered with white; the latter spangled with triple stars of gold, precisely after the fashion figured in the 'Book of Kells.' The chariot in which the principal figure stands resembles some figured on our ancient crosses, and the charioteer wears a pointed cap, green tunic, and tartan vest. All the vanquished wear beards, and their hoods envelop their chins."

The study of ancient costume has especial interest for the historian, as the culture, civilization, and commercial relations of a people can be readily deduced from it; and in the numerous and curious illustrations of the catalogue, taken from ancient records, illuminated manuscripts, and the ancient crosses and sepulchral monuments of the country, everything has been brought together that could throw light on this obscure subject. One most remarkable illustration is a full-length portrait of Dermot M'Morrough, king of Leinster, taken from an illuminated copy of Giraldus Cambrensis in the possession of Sir Thomas Philips, which portrait was very probably drawn from the life.

From all that is known on the subject, it would appear that linen and cloth of every degree of fineness, according to the rank of the wearer, were the principal materials used in ancient Irish dress. No remains of silk garments have been discovered; nor do the historical records, as far as we are aware, make any mention of silk being employed in personal wear. It is remarkable also, that while a traditional belief exists that linen has been known from time immemorial to Ireland, yet the Academy does not possess a single specimen of ancient linen. The linen shirts worn at the time of the Norman Invasion are said to have been of immense size, and dyed a saffron colour. But there is undeniable proof, that the tartan, or cloth of divers colours, which we are accustomed to associate only with Scotland, was worn universally in Ireland in ancient times. Portions of tartans are preserved in the Museum, and probably each grade of rank and clan possessed a characteristic plaid as well as a special dress. A love of variegated and glowing colours, and a tendency to gorgeous decoration, seem to have been always instinctive to the Irish nature.

The female dress of Ireland at a period subsequent to the barbaric age is also illustrated not from conjecture, but from actual observation; for in 1843 a complete female antique dress was discovered many feet below the surface in a bog (these museums of Nature, where she stores up and preserves her specimens of antique life with a care and perfection that no mortal curator can ever hope to equal), and is now to be seen in the Academy's museum.

It consists of a boddice with a long waist, open in front, and attached to a full plaited skirt; which, like the Albanian fustanell, consists of several narrow gored breadths, gathered into small plaits at top, and spreading into a broad quilling at the bottom; each plait being stitched on the inside to preserve the form.

The bottom of the skirt measures twenty-two and a half feet in circumference, and there are ninety-two plaits, most elaborately arranged, so that the joining of each of the narrow breadths should fall within a plait. The material is of a brown woollen cloth.

No pictorial representations exist of female costume earlier than the fourteenth or fifteenth centuries but from the sculptured effigies on tombs, we find it consisted of either a flowing robe and veil, or of the plaited skirt and tight boddice already described, while the head-dress varied according to the fashion of the day.

The subject of personal decoration is perfectly illustrated in the Museum; the Academy possessing one of the largest collections in Europe, beginning at the first rude effort at adornment of the barbaric age, up to the rich golden ornaments of a later, though still pre-historic period.

It is not pleasant to national pride, after feeding on the gorgeous fables of our earliest annalists, to contemplate the primitive Irishman fastening his mantle of untanned deerskin with a fish-bone or a thorn, as we know the Germans did in the time of Tacitus; yet, unhappily, antiquarian research will not allow us to doubt the fact of the simple savageness of the first colonists. But when the intellect of the rude man stirred within him, he began to carve the bones of the animals he killed into articles of ornament and use. Thus the slender bones of fowls were fashioned into cloak pins, especially the leg bone, where the natural enlargement at one end suggested the form, and afforded surface for artistic display. From this first rude essay of the child-man can be traced the continuous development of his ideas in decorative art, from the carving of bones to the casting of metal, up to the most elaborate working in enamel, gold, and precious stones. Our Museum is rich in these objects, containing more than five hundred specimens. Pins, fibulæ, [10] and brooches having been discovered in Ireland in immense quantities and variety, some of which are unsurpassed for beauty of design and workmanship.

"In these articles," Sir William remarks, "the process of development is displayed in a most remarkable manner; for, from the simple unadorned pin or spike of copper, bronze or brass (the metallic representation of the thorn), to the most elaborately wrought ring-brooch of precious metal, the patterns of which are now used by our modern jewellers—every stage of art, both in form and handicraft, is clearly defined, not one single link is wanting. In the first stage all the artist's powers were lavished on the decoration of the pin itself, or in the development of the head, which was enlarged and decorated into every possible shape and conceivable pattern. When it was almost impossible to improve the head, a ring or loop was added, passed through a hole in the neck. In the next stage, the ring was doubled, or many rings added. Finally, the ring was enlarged, flattened out, decorated, enamelled, covered with filigree, and jewelled, until, in those magnificent specimens of silver and gold found in Ireland of late years, it reached a degree of perfection which modern art can with difficulty imitate."

The forms of many of the Irish brooches, pins, and fibulæ, are identical with numbers found in Scandinavia, but the peculiar ornamentation—a curiously involved spiral or serpent coil, which can be traced back through all ages of Irish art to the most remote antiquity—is met nowhere else; neither in Etruscan nor Teutonic art, though some assert its origin can be traced to Assyria and Egypt. However, this *Opus Hibernicum*, as it was termed by the learned Kemble, is one of the tests by which an antiquary can distinguish national from imported work. It is also remarkable that the ornaments of like form found so copiously in Scandinavia are all of bronze, while the Irish are of gold, a metal which, there is every reason to believe, existed in Ireland abundantly in former times, and is still found in small quantities. That it was used for ornament, even coeval with the stone celt, is also probable, as the rudest savage can make the ductile metal assume any form by simply flattening it between two stones.

Many centuries before the Christian era, according to the annals, gold was smelted in Wicklow, to the east of the Liffey. Goblets and brooches were covered with it, and the artificer's name was Ucadan; but no further mention of native gold occurs throughout our ancient histories. However, two thousand years after, the story of the old annalist was singularly confirmed; for, in the year 1796, in the same part of Wicklow, perhaps on the very site of the furnace of Ucadan, upwards of £10,000 worth of native gold was obtained in about two months, and small quantities have been gathered there from time to time ever since.

The subject of the gold antiquities is one full of interest, and even of mystery. The quantity of antique manufactured gold ornaments dug up in Ireland, even in recent times, has been estimated as exceeding half a million of money. As much more may be lying beneath our feet, for, every year, as new cuttings are made for railroads, or bogs are drained, deposits of gold ornaments come to light. Two or three years ago a deposit of massive gold bracelets, in value nearly £5,000, as bright and beautiful as if just finished, was dug up in Carlow; and, still more recently, several antique golden frontlets were found by a labourer while working in a field, who, utterly unconscious of their value, threw them to his children, and the author of the Catalogue actually discovered, one day, the son of the man cutting them up into nose-rings for his pigs. They were happily rescued, and are now in the Academy. The form is beautiful and classic; it is a half-moon diadem, resembling accurately some seen in Etruscan sculpture.

What inestimable treasures may have been thus lost! not merely from ignorance, but also from cupidity; for numbers of gold articles have disappeared in the smelting-pot of the jewellers, who bought them from the country people at perhaps a fractional part of their value. The very small annual sum allowed to the Academy by Government is another cause why the work of destruction still goes on. Valuable gold ornaments are frequently offered there for sale—too valuable, unhappily, for the Academy to purchase, and with an indignant regret that is almost like a sense of shame, the members are obliged to leave them to their fate. Of course legislation could remedy all this, as it has done in Denmark, where the State has secured the possession of all antiquities found in the country for the National Museum, without any wrong being done to the finder, who is paid the full value of all he brings. But in Denmark there is a strong national pride in the subject, and the peasant, who is early taught by the local authorities the value of such things, would as soon think of destroying an antiquity as of burning his Bible.

It is still a question among the learned whether this enormous amount of manufactured gold, far exceeding all yet discovered in England and Scandinavia, was altogether native, or to some extent imported. An analysis of some of the gold has been made, to test the identity of its constituents with the gold of Wicklow, and in the instance selected the gold was found similar. This fact and the ornamentation are proofs to uphold the native theory: while opponents state that they came in the way of commerce from the Carthaginians who traded here. Ornaments identical with the Irish in form—the twisted torques, the bracelets, the diadems, and frontlets, having been found in the interior of Africa, and along the Gold Coast; in India, Barbary, Spain, and the islands of the Mediterranean.

Several ancient Irish musical instruments, the chief of which were the harp and trumpet, and numerous fragments of harps have been found also in the oldest crannoges, proving how ancient was the knowledge and the practice of music in Ireland—a fact confirmed by the Welsh Annals, which state that the Irish surpassed all nations in their proficiency on the harp.

The Museum possesses sixteen antique bronze trumpets, one of which—the finest specimen yet found in Europe—measures about eight feet in length, and the joining is curiously riveted with metal studs, a fact proving its antiquity, as it must have been formed in an age unacquainted with the art of soldering. With regard to coins, Sir William Wilde utterly denies that bronze ring-money was ever used in Ireland, as stated by Sir William Betham, who borrowed his idea from Vallancy: for all the articles hitherto described as ring-money, are now proved undeniably to belong to chain-dress or armour. The ancient medium of barter seems to have been so many head of cattle, or so many ounces of gold. A native coinage was utterly unknown. The amount of bronze discovered in Ireland is enormous, and proves the long duration of a period when it was in general use, before iron was known. Specimens of every object necessary to a people's life have been found fabricated of it—weapons, tools, armour, swords, and spears; culinary vessels, caldrons, spoons, and other minor requisites; hair-pins for the flowing locks of the women; brooches for the graceful mantles of the chiefs, but not of the dark, dingy, modern compound that bears the name. Irish antique bronze was a metal of bright, glowing, golden beauty, and the effect of an army marching with spears of this metal in the flashing sunlight, we can imagine to have been truly magnificent.

The people of this remote age must have attained considerable skill in the manufacturing arts—must have had laws, religion, and social culture—yet how little would have been known of them if these mute witnesses of a past humanity had not been interpreted by science. Archæology and philology are the only solvents of the past; and no theory can henceforth be tolerated that will not stand the test of being assayed by them. The philologist traces the origin and affinities of our people in the roots of the Irish language; while their habits, modes of life, their position in the scale of civilization throughout the long duration of the unwritten age, can only be read in the letters of stone, bronze, and gold upon the walls of our Academy.

Irish manuscripts, though the oldest in North-western Europe, date back scarcely further than the fifth or sixth century. Beyond that period we enter a region of darkness, through which no literature or letters radiate their light;

yet, unassisted by either, the archæologist can reconstruct the primitive world and the primitive man with greater truth and certainty than if he possessed both; for the facts of a museum are changeless and enduring, and can suffer no mutation from prejudice or ignorance, yet we must remember that it is science alone that gives value to these facts. Without its aid a museum would be only an aggregate of curious lumber. The archæologist must combine, in a synthetic and comprehensive view—must arrange in their proper sequence—must elucidate by a world-wide learning, these sibyline fragments of the past; or this writing on the wall, though it express the most irrefragable truths of history, will remain an undeciphered hieroglyphic, as useless and unprofitable to the student as the alphabet of an unknown language, which he is unable to form into intelligible words. All this Sir William Wilde accomplished for the Museum of the Academy, and in his clear and well-arranged volumes we can read the stone pages of our history by the light of all the learning and antiquarian research of the past and present age gathered to one focus.

The conclusion to be drawn from the facts laid before us is, that in an age of remote antiquity (M. Boucher de Perthes, the well-known French author and antiquarian, has written a book to prove that it was prior to the Deluge) the entire face of the earth was covered by a nomad people, speaking the one language, and living after the same rude fashion, with no other weapons than sharpened stone. This race passed away, and no research has ever yet discovered their name, their language, their religion, or the era of their existence. Not an inscription, not a word, not a letter graven on any stone have they left to allay the torturing curiosity of the inquirer. Yet traces of them have been found from Mexico to Japan; from the steppes of Tartary to the Pampas; round the shores of every European sea, and along the coasts of the two oceans. Wherever man's foot has trodden within historic times, they trod before all history. Even in this outlying isle of ours vestiges of this people are strewn so thickly that the very soil seems made of their remains. Then another race swept across Europe—a comparatively cultured race, bearing with them the chief element of civilization—a knowledge of metals. They spread over both sides of the Danube; left their footprints in Italy and on the shores of the Baltic; overran Switzerland, France, and Belgium, giving names to the rivers they passed, the mountains they crossed, and the towns they founded, which names cling to them even to this day. From Belgium they spread to Britain, and from thence, or by the seacoast of Spain, they reached Ireland, where they founded the existing Irish race, and brought with them the knowledge of metals, the art of music and poetry, and the still existing Irish language. Historians name these people the Celts. On the Continent they were gradually crushed down beneath the Roman and Gothic races, and in Britain also by successive conquests. But Ireland suffered no conquest. Here the old Celtic race lived and flourished, and here alone their language, which everywhere else melted into a compound with the Gothic and Latin, maintained its distinct existence. The English language is the gradually formed product and result of the successive conquests of England. But no invading people ever gained sufficient strength in Ireland to influence the original language. It exists still amongst us, living and spoken the same as when thousands of years ago the Celtic people first crossed the Danube and gave it the name it now bears. For this reason all the archæologists of Europe turn their eyes to our sacred isle, as to the one great museum of the Celtic race. Thus, Professor Keller, of Zurich, anxiously studies the formation of Irish crannoges, to compare them with the Swiss; and the learned Pictet, of Geneva, demands the long-deferred completion of the Irish Dictionary, with an ardour that puts to shame our own apathy, as without it comparative philology wants its chief corner-stone. The great facts of our Museum, illustrated, described, and laid before the learned of Europe in a comprehensive form, will go far to correct the crude, imperfect notions of Continental writers concerning Irish antiquities. For instance, Professor Lindenschmidt, of Mayence, asserted in one of his earlier published works, that all the ancient bronze articles found on this side of the Alps were imported from Etruria, as a people so barbarous as the Irish could never have produced them. The fact being, that the largest, most varied, most highly decorated collection of bronze celts existing is to be found in our Museum, along with numerous specimens of the moulds in which they were cast, discovered on the very spot where the ancient workman had lit his furnace. This universal interest and demand for information are enough to stimulate our learned men to exertion, seeing that they are, in a measure, answerable to Europe for the proper preservation of our antiquities, the very rudest of which can tell some tale of the past, as the mere furrows along the streets of the dead Pompeii show that life once passed there.

Early Irish Art

Early Irish art illustrates in a very remarkable manner those distinctive qualities of Irish nature, which we know from the legendary traditions have characterized our people from the earliest times. The earnest religious faith, the love of gorgeous colouring, the tendency to express ideas by symbol, and the vivid imagination that delights in the strange and unusual, often fantastic and grotesque, in place of the absolute and real, combined with the patient and minute elaboration of details, so truly Oriental in its spirit, specially mark Irish ornamentation. All these reverential, artistic, fanciful, and subtle evidences of the peculiar Celtic spirit find a full and significant expression in the wonderful splendours of early Irish art, as seen chiefly in the ancient illuminated manuscripts.

The reputation of Irish artists for excellence in these costly productions became so extended throughout Christian Europe in the early ages, that at the request of many nations Ireland sent forth numbers of her most cultured artists as teachers and scribes to the great foreign schools and colleges; and numerous examples of skilled Irish work are still existing in Continental Libraries, where they are held as amongst the most sacred of the national treasures. For a full and comprehensive illustration of this subject it would be impossible to over-estimate the artistic and historic value of Mr. Westwood's magnificent book on Anglo-Saxon and Irish Manuscripts. The volume contains *facsimiles* from all the principal illuminated Celtic manuscripts of Europe, executed with the most scrupulous care, chiefly by Mr. Westwood himself, the majority of them with the aid of a magnifying glass, so minute and delicate are the lines of ornamentation to be represented. In fact, for accuracy of information and richness of illustration, the volume surpasses anything yet published on Celtic art in the United Kingdom, and may claim equality with the grand, but enormously expensive work of Count Bastard, on early French Manuscripts. Mr. Westwood, in a learned preliminary dissertation, gives his views on the origin and development of Hiberno-Saxon art during the first thousand years of the Christian era, and finds in the ornamentation, as observed by Kemble and others, a distinct *Opus Hibernicum* and an *Opus Anglicum*, but the Irish the more perfect of the two, and wholly different from Continental art of the same era.

The earliest manuscripts of Greece and Rome show nothing like this distinctive Celtic art; nor the Italian mosaics, nor the wall paintings of Herculaneum or Pompeii—beautiful as are the representations of the human figure found there; nor does Byzantine art afford any similar types. From whence, then, did the Irish, the acknowledged founders of Celtic art in Europe, derive their ideas of ornamentation? This is one of the historical mysteries which, like the origin of the Round Towers, still awaits solution. One must travel a long way, even to the far East, before finding in the decorations of the ancient Hindoo temples anything approaching to the typical idea that runs through all Irish ornamentation. It is, however, an incontrovertible fact, and one proved to demonstration by Mr. Westwood's learning, labour, and researches, that a time when the pictorial art was almost extinct in Italy and Greece, and indeed scarcely existed in other parts of Europe—namely, from the fifth to the end of the eighth century—a style of art had been originated, cultivated, and brought into a most marvellous state of perfection in Ireland absolutely distinct from that of any other part of the civilized world; and which being carried abroad by Irish and Saxon missionaries was adopted and imitated in the schools of Charlemagne, and in all the other great schools and monasteries founded by them upon the Continent.

In the middle of the ninth century the influence of the artists of Germany reacted on the productions of England, and in consequence of the more frequent communications of learned men with Rome, classical models began to be adopted, floral decorations were introduced, and figures in the Byzantine style. With these the Irish ornamentation was combined, principally in the framework of the design. Then it gradually disappeared from England, where it was replaced by Franco-Saxon and Teutonic art; so that after the tenth century Mr. Westwood has not found any Anglo-Saxon manuscript executed in the Lindisfarne or Irish style. But it remained for several centuries longer in use in Ireland, though the ornamental details exhibit little of the extreme delicacy of the earlier productions. With reference to these, Mr. Digby Wyatt observes that, in delicacy of handling and minute but faultless execution, the whole range of palæography offers nothing comparable to the early Irish manuscripts, especially "The Book of Kells," the most marvellous of them all. One cannot wonder, therefore, that Giraldus Cambrensis, when over in Ireland in the reign of Henry II., on being shown an illuminated Irish manuscript, exclaimed, "This is more like the work of angels than of men!"

The peculiarities which characterize true Celtic art, whether in stone, metal work, or manuscript illumination, consist in the excessive and minute elaborations of intricate ornamental details, such as the spirals, the interlaced ribands, and the entwined serpents and other animal forms, so familiar to the students of our national art treasures in the museum of the Royal Irish Academy. These forms are invariably found in all Irish decoration. The initial letters and ornamentations of the ancient manuscripts are reproduced in the gigantic stone crosses and the more delicate metal work of the shrines and reliquaries; and from this identity of ornamentation the age can be determined of all art monuments or remains, and objects readily classified as cotemporaneous. The Irish adhered with wonderful fidelity to their peculiar art ideas for at least eight hundred years; and while the Saxons coquetted with Frankish art, and finally gave themselves up wholly to Norman influence, the Irish continued their exclusive devotion to the ancient and national Celtic type. Intensely national, indeed, were those early artists; they gave ideas to the world, but received none in exchange. In their pictures Goliath appears as an Irish warrior, and David bears an Irish harp in his hands while our Lord Himself, in one of the Irish sculptures, is represented wearing the Irish dress. When the nation fell under Norman sway in the twelfth century, Norman ideas naturally became triumphant; but everything that is most beautiful and interesting in antique Irish art belongs to the pre-Norman period—the gold ornaments, the gorgeous manuscripts, such as the Gospels of Durrow and of Kells; the grandest of the sculptured crosses, Cormac's Chapel, that architectural gem of Western Europe; the richly decorated shrines, such as that of St. Monchan, "the most important ancient shrine now in existence in these islands," Mr. Westwood states; and specially interesting to us Irish, from the recorded fact that it was covered with pure gold by Roderick O'Connor, the last king of Ireland, and was, as the Annals state, the most beautiful piece of art ever made in Erin. All these evidences of high cultivation and artistic skill were in existence long before the Norman adventurers set foot on our shores. Irish art, however, died out with Irish Nationality; and in two centuries or so, after the Norman Conquest, it ceased to exist, and was replaced by the pseudo-Roman or Irish Romanesque style. Irish art can be easily traced throughout the Continent by the peculiar ornamentation which characterized it; and wherever, amongst the early manuscripts in foreign libraries, one is found surpassing all the rest in the singular beauty and firmness of the writing, and the exquisite delicacy of the minute and elaborate illuminations, there at once an Irish hand is recognized as worker, or an Irish intellect as teacher. The same symbols and ideas run through all of them—there are the same strange, elongated, contorted, intertwined figures; the same rich mosaics of interlaced lines—so minute, so delicate, so rich in brilliant colours, that the border of the page seems powdered with crushed jewels. There is something almost melancholy in this devotion to a species of art in which there was nothing to stimulate the feelings or to warm the heart. No representation of nature's glories in tree or flower, or the splendour of human beauty; the artist's aim being rather, it would seem, to kill the human in him, by forcing his genius to work only on the cold abstractions of spirals and curves, and endless geometrical involutions, and the infinite monotony of those interlaced lines, still coiling on, for ever and ever, through the centuries, like the windings of the serpent of evil, which they were meant to symbolize, through the successive generations of our fated humanity. Truly, these artists offered up the sacrifice of love. Their lives and the labour of their lives were given humbly, silently, reverently to God, and the glory of God's Word. They had no other aim in life, and when the work was done, a work so beautiful that even now the world cannot equal it, there was no vainglorious boast of himself came from the lips of the artist worker, but the manuscript ends with some simple devotional words, his name, and the desire to be remembered as the writer, like the *orate pro me* on the ancient tombstones; this was all he asked or hoped for in return for the years of youth and life he had incarnated in the illuminated pages of the Gospels. For in those early ages art had no existence save in union with religion. Humanity brought together all its most precious ointments to pour upon the feet of Jesus. In Ireland especially—the Island of Saints—whatever genius could devise or the hand of the artist could execute was lavished upon some work that would recall the presence of God to the people, stimulate His worship, or make known His word; upon the Psalters, the Gospels, the crosses, the costly shrines, the jewelled cases for a saint's relics, the golden covers for the holy books. But nothing of that period has come down to us that shows a luxury in domestic life. The Word of God was shrined in gold, made rich with gems and enamels, but the people lived their old simple life in their old rude huts; and even the kings gave their wealth, not to erect palaces, but to build churches, to endow abbeys, to help the cause of God, and speed the holy men who were His ministers, in their crusade against evil, ignorance and darkness.

It is no idle boast to say that the Irish were the teachers of Europe from the seventh to the tenth century in art and religion. Mr. Westwood has visited all the great libraries of England and the Continent and found abundant evidence that Irish art, or Hiberno-Saxon art, was diffused over Europe during that period. The Greek and Latin manuscripts are not illuminated, but are adorned with intercalated pictures; Irish art differs from them in many respects—amongst others, in having the figures and rich ornamentations printed on the leaves and borders of the book itself. He has given *facsimiles* from Irish manuscripts now existing in the libraries of Oxford, Cambridge, Durham, Lichfield, Salisbury, Lambeth, the British Museum, and other places; and, passing to the Continent, has laid under contribution the great libraries of Paris, Rouen, Boulogne, St. Gall, Milan, Rome, Munich, Darmstadt, Stockholm, Copenhagen, and even St. Petersburg, and thus proved the excellence to which Irish artists, or Saxon artists educated in Irish schools, attained more than a thousand years ago. Nor is it strange that Ireland should have been the teacher, considering its early Christianity, which had made some progress amongst the people even in St. Jerome's time; a little later amongst the Britons; but at the end of the sixth century Augustine and his monks found the stolid Anglo-Saxons still in the bonds of their ancient paganism and Wodenism. The Celtic race received the Christian faith gladly as early as the fourth century, but it was a difficult matter to bring light to the Saxon soul. It has at all times proved itself rather opaque in nature. The Saxon tribes of Germany did not renounce their idols till forced to it by the strong coercive power and keen sword of Charlemagne, in the latter half of the eighth century.

With Christianity came to Ireland the knowledge of letters; at least no older inscription has been found than that on the pillar stone of Lugnadon, St. Patrick's nephew, which may still be seen beside the ruin of St. Patrick's oratory in one of the beautiful islands of Lough Corrib; [11] and the oldest manuscript existing in Ireland is the Book of Armagh, a copy of St. Jerome's Latin version of the Gospels written in the old Roman letters, and very valuable for the beauty of the writing and the various drawings it contains. Learning was at once consecrated to the service of God in those early days, and to multiply copies of the Gospels was the praiseworthy and devout task of the first great teachers and missionaries. The Book of Durrow and the Book of Kells, both of the early part of the sixth century, are believed to be the work of St. Columba himself. The latter, the Book of Kells, has filled all critics with wonder and admiration. It is more decorated than any existing copy of the Gospels, and is pronounced by learned authorities to be "the most beautiful manuscript in existence of so early a date, and the most magnificent specimen of penmanship and illumination in the Western World." They are both written in the Latin uncial character, common to Europe at the time; and here it may be noticed, in passing, that the so-called Irish alphabet is simply the Latin alphabet modified by the first missionaries to suit the Irish sounds, as Ulphila, the apostle of the Goths, invented an alphabet of mingled Greek and Latin characters, in order to enable him to make his translation of the Gospels into Gothic; and as the Greek missionaries invented the Russian alphabet, which is a modified form of the Greek, for a like purpose. That the Irish should retain the old form of the Latin letters, while most of the other nations of Europe have discarded it, is to be regretted, as nothing would facilitate the study of Irish so much at the present day, when one has so little leisure to spell out with much painful endeavour the barbarous symbols of a bygone age, as the adoption of the modern English alphabet. The first Irish book that was ever printed appeared in 1571, and is now in the Bodleian Library. It is a catechism of Irish grammar, and the Irish alphabet has suffered no modification or improvement since. It was about the end of the sixth century that the fame of Irish learning and the skill of Irish artists began to extend to England, and from thence to the Continent; and Irish scribes were employed to make copies of the Gospels and teach the splendid art of illumination in the English monasteries. From that period till the end of the ninth century the Irish were a power in Europe from their learning and piety—eminent in Greek as well as Latin, and the great teachers of scholastic theology to the Christian world. The Gospels of Lindisfarne, executed by monks of Iona in the seventh century, and now "the glory of the British Museum," form a most important element in the early history of Celtic art, as this book seems to have been the principal model for succeeding artists.

In the splendid folio copy of the Gospels at Copenhagen of the tenth century, supposed to have been brought to Denmark by King Canute, the figure of St. Matthew seated, while another saint draws back a curtain, is copied from the Gospels of Lindisfarne, while the border is in the tenth century style. The Gospels of St. Chad, now in Lichfield Library, are in the Irish style of the eighth century, and are very noticeable as having marginal notes in Latin, Anglo-Saxon, and ancient British, the latter being the oldest specimen of the ancient British language now in existence. The illuminations also are copied from the Lindisfarne book. St. Chad, it is known, was educated in Ireland, in the school of St. Finian. There are Irish Gospels at Durham of the eighth century. The Gospels of Mac-Regal are at Oxford, and the Gospels of Mac-Duran, the smallest and most beautiful known, are in the Archbishop's palace at Lambeth. As Saxon art progressed and became influenced by Roman models, the Irish scribes were chiefly employed wherever elegance, harmony of colour, and extreme delicacy of touch were particularly requisite, as in the borders and initial letters. Thus, the Psalter of St. Augustine, said to be from Rome, and which resembles in style the manuscript Virgil of the fifth century, in the Vatican, is framed in pure Celtic art. On the Continent, also, the borders of the great manuscripts were generally confined to Irish hands. A Latin copy of the Gospels at Treves, evidently produced by one of the establishments founded by the Irish upon the Rhine, is remarkable for a combination of Celtic, Teutonic, and Franco-Byzantine art. The borders are Irish while the figures are Byzantine. These illuminated borders have the glitter and radiance of a setting of jewels, and are thus admirably suited to fulfil the true object of all ornamentation, which Mr. Ruskin defines as being "beautiful in its place, and perfect in its adaptation to the purpose for which it was employed."

In the sixth century St. Gall, born in Ireland, accompanied St. Columbanus to the Continent, and founded the monastery in Switzerland that bears his name. Here many interesting manuscripts and fragments are still preserved, remarkable for the old Irish marginal notes to the Latin text. Those are considered by philologists of such importance that thirteen quarto plates and *facsimiles* from them are given by Dr. Ferdinand Keller in the Zurich Society's Transactions. An interesting relic of an Irish saint is also preserved in the Cathedral of Wurtzburg—a copy of the Gospels of St. Kilian, martyred in 689, and which was found stained with his blood on opening his tomb about fifty years after.

Thus, the Irish can be tracked, as it were, across Europe by their illuminated footsteps. They were emphatically the witnesses of God, the light-bearers through the dark ages, and above all, the faithful guardians and preservers of God's sacred Word. A hundred years before Alfred came to Ireland to be educated, and went back to civilize his native country by the knowledge he had acquired there, the Christian schools of Germany, under the direction of Irishmen, had been founded by Charlemagne. Through France, along the Rhine, through Switzerland, Italy, and Spain, the Irish missionaries taught and worked, founding schools and monasteries, and illuminating by their learning the darkest pages of European history. One of the great treasures of the Imperial Library of Paris is a beautiful Irish copy of the Latin Gospels. The College of St. Isidore, at Rome, possesses many Irish manuscripts—one of them is a Psalter, folio size, written throughout in letters a quarter of an inch long, and which is considered to be the finest of the later works of the Irish school. The celebrated Golden Gospels of Stockholm are of Hiberno-Saxon art of the ninth century. This book has a singular history. It was stolen from England, and disappeared for ages, but finally was discovered at Mantua in the seventeenth century, and purchased for the Royal Library at Stockholm. St. Petersburg also possesses a highly illuminated copy of the Gospels, which was taken from France at the time of the great Revolution, and found its way to the far North. It is a perfect and beautiful specimen of the Irish style of the eight century, and the initial letters can only be compared to those of the Book of Kells. All these Irish manuscript Gospels are, without exception, copies of St. Jerome's Latin version. No Irish translation of the Gospels has ever been found. Learning was evidently considered a sacred thing, indispensable for the priesthood, but not necessary for the masses; yet it seems strange that while the learned and pious Irish saints and missionaries were devoting their lives to multiplying copies of the Gospels for other nations, and disseminating them over Europe, they never thought of giving the people of their own land the Word of God to read in their own native tongue. The leading Teutonic races, on the contrary, with their free spirit, were not satisfied with accepting the doctrines of the faith, simply as an act of obedience to their teachers. They demanded the right of private judgment, the exercise of individual reason, and the Gospels were translated into Gothic as early as the fourth century by Bishop Ulphila for the use of the Gothic nation.

This remarkable book, called the "Codex Argenteus," is now in the Royal Library of Upsala, having, after many dangers and vicissitudes, at last found its way to the people who hold themselves the true descendants of the Goths, and whose king still bears the proud title of "King of the Swedes, Goths, and Vandals;" and an edition of it, with annotations, has been published by the learned Professor Andreas Uppstrom, of Upsala.

Towards the close of the tenth century the Frankish style of ornamentation, a blending of the classical and the Byzantine, had almost entirely superseded the beautiful and delicate Celtic art both in England and on the Continent, and about the fifteenth century it disappeared even from our own Ireland, the country of its origin. The gorgeous missals and illuminated Gospels, instinct with life, genius, holy reverence, and patient love, were destined to be replaced soon after by the dull mechanism of print; while Protestantism used all its new-found strength to destroy that innate tendency of our nature which seeks to manifest religious fervour, faith, and zeal by costly offerings and sacrifices. The golden-bordered holy books, the sculptured crosses, the jewelled shrines were crushed under the heel of Cromwell's troopers; the majestic and beautiful abbeys were desecrated and cast down to ruin, while beside them rose the mean and ugly structures of the Reformed faith, as if the annihilation of all beauty were then considered to be the most acceptable homage which man could offer to the God who created all beauty, and fitted the human soul to enjoy and manifest the spiritual, mystic, and eternal loveliness of form, and colour, and symmetry.

Since that mournful period when the conquering iconoclasts cast down the temples and crushed the spirit of our people, there has been no revival of art in Ireland. It is not wonderful, therefore, that we cling with so much of fond, though sad, admiration to the beautiful memorials of the past, and welcome with warm appreciation the efforts of able, learned and distinguished men to illustrate and preserve them, as in this splendid and costly book which Mr. Westwood has contributed to Celtic art.

Our Ancient Capital

The history of Dublin, so admirably narrated by Mr. Gilbert in his learned and instructive volumes, [12] begins the modern period of Irish history when Ireland became indissolubly united with the British Empire—the greatest empire of the world—and legendary lore, like all the ancient usages and superstitions, began to fade and perish before advancing civilization, as the luxurious undergrowth of a primeval forest before advancing culture.

A sketch of the rise of the capital of Ireland, with all the changes produced in Irish life by the new modes of thought and action introduced by Norman influence, forms therefore a fitting close to the legendary and early-historic period, so full of poetry and charm for the imagination, with its splendour of kings and bards, its shadowy romance and mist-woven dreams, and its ideal fairy world of beauty and grace, of music and song; when the people lived the free, joyous life of the childhood of humanity under their native princes, and the terrible struggle of a crushed and oppressed nation against a foreign master had not yet begun; the struggle that has lasted for seven centuries, and still goes on with exhaustless force and fervour.

The history of cities is the history of nations—the most perfect index of the social altitude, mental development, physical perfection, and political freedom, which at any given period a people may have attained. Every stone within a city is a hieroglyphic of the century that saw it raised. By it we trace human progression through all its phases; from the first rude fisher's hut, the altar of the primitive priest, the mound of the first nomad warrior, the stone fortalice or simple fane of the early Christian race, up to the stately and beautiful temples and palaces which evidence the luxury and refinement of a people in its proudest excess, or human genius in its climax of manifestation.

Thus Babylon, Thebes, Rome, Jerusalem, are words that express nations. The ever-during interest of the world circles round them, for their ruins are true and eternal pages of human history. Every fallen column is a fragment of a past ritual, or a symbol of a dynasty. The very dust is vital with great memories, and a philosopher, like the comparative anatomist, might construct the entire life of a people—its religion, literature, and laws—from these fragments of extinct generations—these fossil paleographs of man.

Statue and column, mausoleum and shrine, are trophies of a nation's triumphs or its tragedies. The young children, as they gaze on them, learn the story of the native heroes, poets, saints, and martyrs, leaders and lawgivers, who have flung their own glory as a regal mantle over their country. Spirits of the past, from the phantom-land, dwell in the midst of them. We feel their presence, and hear their words of inspiration or warning, alike in the grandeur or decadence of an ancient city.

Modern capitals represent also, not only the history of the past, but the living concentrated will of the entire nation. Thus is it with London, Berlin, and Vienna, while Paris, the *cité verbe*, as Victor Hugo calls her, represents not only the tendencies of France, but of Europe.

Dublin, however, differs from all other capitals, past or present, in this wise—that by its history we trace, not the progress of the native race, but the triumphs of its enemies; and that the concentrated will of Dublin has always been in antagonism to the feelings of a large portion of the nation.

The truth is, that though our chief city of Ireland has an historical existence older than Christianity, yet this fair *Ath-Cliath* has no pretension to be called our ancient mother. From first to last, from a thousand years ago till now, Dublin has held the position of a foreign fortress within the kingdom; and its history has no other emblazonment beyond that of unceasing hostility or indifference to the native race.

"The inhabitants are mere English, though of Irish birth," wrote Hooker, three hundred years ago. "The citizens," says Holingshed, "have from time to time so galled the Irish, that even to this day the Irish fear a ragged and jagged black standard that the citizens have, though almost worn to the stumps." Up to Henry the Seventh's reign, an Englishman of Dublin was not punished for killing an Irishman, nor were Irishmen admitted to any office within the city that concerned the government either of the souls or bodies of the citizens. The Viceroys, the Archbishops, the Judges, the Mayors, the Corporations, were all and always English, down to the very guild of tailors, of whom it stands on record that they would allow no Irishman to be of their fraternity. As the American colonists treated the red man, as the Spaniards of Cortez treated the Mexicans, as the English colony of India treated the ancient Indian princes, tribes, and people, so the English race of Dublin treated the Irish nation. They were a people to be crushed, ruined, persecuted, tormented, extirpated; and the Irish race, it must be confessed, retorted the hatred with as bitter an animosity. The rising of 1641 was like all Irish attempts—a wild, helpless, disorganized effort at revenge; and seven years later we read that Owen Roe O'Neil burned the country about Dublin, so that from one steeple there two hundred fires could be seen at once.

This being the position of a country and its capital, it is evident that no effort for national independence could gain nourishment in Dublin. Our metropolis is associated with no glorious moment of a nation's career, while in all the dark tragedies of our gloomy history its name and influence predominate. Dublin is connected with Irish patriotism only by the scaffold and the gallows. Statue and column do indeed rise there, but not to honour the sons of the soil. The public idols are foreign potentates and foreign heroes. Macaulay says eloquently on this subject, "The Irish people are doomed to see in every place the monuments of their subjugation; before the senate-house, the statue of their conqueror—within, the walls tapestried with the defeats of their fathers."

No public statue of an illustrious Irishman until recently ever graced the Irish capital. No monument exists to which the gaze of the young Irish children can be directed, while their fathers tell them, "This was to the glory of your countrymen." Even the lustre Dublin borrowed from her great Norman colonists has passed away. Her nobility are remembered only as we note the desecration of their palaces; the most beautiful of all our metropolitan buildings but reminds us that there the last remnant of political independence was sold; the stately Custom-house, that Dublin has no trade; the regal pile of Dublin Castle, that it was reared by foreign hands to "curb and awe the city."

It is in truth a gloomy task to awaken the memories of Dublin, even of this century. There, in that obscure house of Thomas Street, visions rise of a ghastly night-scene, where the young, passionate-hearted Geraldine was struggling vainly in death-agony with his betrayers and captors. Pass on through the same street, and close by St. Catherine's Church you can trace the spot where the gallows was erected for Robert Emmet. Before that sombre prison pile two young brothers, handsome, educated, and well-born, and many a fair young form after them, expiated by death their fatal aspirations for Irish freedom. Look at that magnificent portal, leading now to the tables of the money-changers; through it, not a century ago, men, entrusted with the nation's rights, entered to sell them, and came forth, not branded traitors, but decorated, enriched, and rewarded with titles, pensions, and honours.

Yet the anomalous relation between our country and its capital springs naturally from the antecedents of both. Dublin was neither built by the Irish nor peopled by the Irish; it is a Scandinavian settlement in the midst of a southern nation. Long even before the Norman invasion two races existed in Ireland, as different as the lines of migration by which each had reached it; and though ages have rolled away since Scythian and Southern first met in this distant land, yet the elemental distinctions have never been lost: the races have never blended into one homogeneous nationality. Other nations, like the English, have blended with their conquerors, and progression and a higher civilization have been the result. Roman, Saxon, Dane, and Norman, each left their impress on the primitive Briton; and from Roman courage, Saxon thrift, and Norman pride has been evolved the strong, wise, proud island-nation that rules the world—the Ocean-Rome. A similar blending of opposite elements, but in different proportions, has produced Scotch national character—grave, wise, learned, provident, industrious, and unconquerably independent. But the Irish race remains distinct from all others, as Jew or Zincali. It has no elective affinities, enters into no new combinations, forms no new results, attracts to itself no Scythian qualities of stern self-reliance and the indomitable pride of independence, but still retains all the old virtues and vices of their semi-oriental nature, which make the history of Ireland so sad a record of mere passionate impulses ending mostly in failure and despair. The English, slow in speech and repellent in manner, are yet able not only to rule themselves well and ably, but to rule the world; while the Irish, so fascinating, eloquent, brave, and gifted, have never yet achieved a distinctive place in the political system of Europe. We had even the advantage of an earlier education; we taught England her letters, Christianized her people, sheltered her saints, educated her princes; we give her the best generals, the best statesmen, the best armies; yet, withal, we have never yet found the strength to govern our own kingdom. Ethnologists will tell you this comes of race. It may be so. Let us then sail up the stream of time to Ararat, and try to find our ancestry amongst the children of the eight primal gods, as the ancients termed them, who there stepped forth from their ocean prison to people the newly baptized world.

A very clever German advises all reviewers to begin from the Deluge, so that by no possibility can a single fact, direct or collateral, escape notice connected with the matter in hand. When treating of Ireland this rule becomes a necessity. Our nation dates from the dispersion, and our faults and failings, our features and our speech, have an authentic hereditary descent of four thousand years. Other primitive nations have been lost by migration, annihilated by war, swallowed up in empires, overwhelmed by barbarians: thus it was that the old kingdoms of Europe changed masters, and that the old nations and tongues passed away. Here only, in this island prison of the Atlantic, can the old race of primitive Europe be still found existing as a nation, speaking the same tongue as the early tribes that first wandered westward, when Europe itself was an unpeopled wilderness.

We learn from sacred record that the first migrations of the human family, with "one language and one speech," were *from* the East; and every successive wave of population has still flowed from the rising towards the setting sun. The progression of intellect and science is ever westward. The march of humanity is opposed to the path of the planet. Life moves contrary to matter. A metaphor, it may be, of our spirit exile—this travelling "daily further from the East;" yet, when at the farthest limit, we are but approaching the glory of the East again.

Gradually, along the waters of the Mediterranean, the beautiful islands on its bosom serving as resting-places for the wanderers, or bridges for the tribes to pass over, the primal families of the Japhetian race reached in succession the three great Peninsulas of the Great Sea, in each leaving the germ of a mighty nation. Still onward, led by the providence of God, they passed the portals of the Atlantic, coasted the shores of the vine-clad France, and so reached at length the "Isles of the Setting Sun," upon the very verge of Western Europe.

But many centuries may have elapsed during the slow progression of these maritime colonies, who have left their names indelibly stamped on the earth's surface, from Ionia to the Tartessus of Spain; and Miriam may have chanted the death-song of Pharaoh, and Moses led forth the people of God, before the descendants of the first navigators landed amidst the verdant solitudes of Ireland.

The earliest tribes that reached our island, though removed so far from the centre of light and wisdom, must still have been familiar with all science necessary to preserve existence, and to organize a new country into a human habitation. They cleared the forests, worked the mines, built chambers for the dead, after the manner of their kindred left in Tyre and Greece, wrought arms, defensive and offensive, such as the heroes of Marathon used against the long-haired Persians; they raised altars and pillar-stones, still standing amongst us, mysterious and eternal symbols of a simple primitive creed; they had bards, priests, and lawgivers, the old tongue of Shinar, the dress of Nineveh, and the ancient faith whose ritual was prayer and sacrifice.

The kindred races who remained stationary, built cities and temples, still a world's wonder, and arts flourished amongst them impossible to the nomads of the plains, or the wanderers by the ocean islands; but the destiny of dispersion was still on the race, and from these central points of civilization, tribes and families constantly went forth to achieve new conquests over the yet untamed earth.

Whatever wisdom the early island colonizers had brought with them, would have died out for want of nourishment, had not these new tribes, from countries where civilization had become developed and permanent, constantly given fresh impulses to progress. With stronger and more powerful arts and arms, they, in succession, gained dominion over their weaker predecessors, and by commerce, laws, arts, and learning, they organized families into nations, enlightening while they subjugated.

The conquest of Canaan gave the second great impetus to the human tides ever flowing westward. Irish tradition has even, in a confused manner, preserved the names of two amongst the leaders of the Sidonian fugitives who landed in Ireland. Partholan, with his wife Elga, and Gadelius, with his wife Scota.

"This Gadelius," say the legends, "was a noble gentleman, right wise, valiant, and well spoken, who, after Pharaoh was drowned, sailed for Spain, and from thence to Ireland, with a colony of Greeks and Egyptians, and his wife Scota, a daughter of Pharaoh's; and he taught letters to the Irish, and warlike feats after the Greek and Egyptian manner."

These later tribes brought with them the Syrian arts and civilization, such as dyeing and weaving, working in gold, silver, and brass, besides the written characters, the same that Cadmus afterwards gave to Greece, and which remained in use amongst the Irish, it is said, until modified by Saint Patrick into their present form, to assimilate them to the Latin.

Continued intercourse with their Syrian kindred soon filled Ireland with the refinement of a luxurious civilization. From various sources, we learn that in those ancient times, the native dress was costly and picturesque, and the habits and modes of living of the chiefs and kings splendid and Oriental. The high-born and the wealthy wore tunics of fine linen of immense width, girdled with gold and with flowing sleeves after the Eastern fashion. The fringed cloak, or *cuchula*, with a hood, after the Arab mode, was clasped on the shoulders with a golden brooch. Golden circlets, of beautiful and classic form, confined their long, flowing hair, and, crowned with their diadems, the chiefs sat at the banquet, or went forth to war. Sandals upon the feet, and bracelets and signet rings, of rich and curious workmanship, completed the costume. The ladies wore the silken robes and flowing veils of Persia, or rolls of linen wound round the head like the Egyptian Isis, the hair curiously plaited down the back and fastened with gold or silver bodkins, while the neck and arms were profusely covered with jewels. [13]

For successive centuries, this race, half Tyrian and half Greek, held undisputed possession of Ireland, maintaining, it is said, constant intercourse with the parent state, and, when Tyre fell, commercial relations were continued with Carthage. Communication between such distant lands was nothing to Phœnician enterprise. Phœnicians in the service of an Egyptian king had sailed round Africa and doubled the Cape of Good Hope two thousand years before the Portuguese. The same people built the navy of King Solomon a thousand years before Christ; and led the fleet to India for the gold necessary for the Temple. They cast the brazen vessels for the altar, employing for the purpose the tin which their merchants must have brought from the British Isles. Thus, to use the words of Humboldt, there can be no doubt that three thousand years ago "the Tyrian flag waved from Britain to the Indian Ocean."

A king of the race, long before Romulus founded Rome, erected a college at Tara, where the Druids taught the wisdom of Egypt, the mysteries of Samothrace, and the religion of Tyre. Then it was that Ireland was known as *Innis-Alga*—the Holy Island—held sacred by the Tyrian mariners as the "Temple of the Setting Sun:" the last limit of Europe, from whence they could watch his descent into the mysterious western ocean.

But onward still came the waves of human life, unceasing, unresting. Driven forth from Carthage, Spain, and Gaul, the ancient race fled to the limits of the coast, then surged back, fought and refought the battle, conquering and yielding by turns, till at length the Syrian and the Latin elements blended into a new compound, which laid the foundation of modern Europe. But some tribes, disdaining such a union, fled from Spain to Ireland, and thus a new race, but of the old kindred, was flung on our shores by destiny.

The leaders, brave, warlike, and of royal blood, speedily assumed kingly sway, and all the subsequent monarchs of Ireland, the O'Briens, the O'Connors, the O'Neils, the O'Donnels, and other noble races, claim descent from them; and very proud, even to this day, are the families amongst the Irish who can trace back their pedigree to these princely Spaniards.

We have spoken hitherto but of the maritime colonists—that portion of the primal race who launched their ships on the Mediterranean to found colonies and kingdoms along its shores; then passing out through the ocean straits, the human tides surged upon the western limits of Europe, till the last wave found a rest on the green sward of ancient Erin. The habits of these first colonists were agricultural, commercial, and unwarlike; and ancient historians have left us a record of their temperament; volatile and fickle; passionate in joy and grief, with quick vivid natures prone to sudden excesses; religious and superstitious; a small, dark-eyed race, lithe of limb and light of heart; the eternal children of humanity.

For illustrations we need not here refer to the Royal Irish Academy, for as they looked and lived three thousand years ago, they may be seen to this day in the mountains of Connemara and Kerry.

While this race travelled westward to the ocean by the great southern sea, other families of the Japhetian tribes were pressing westward also, but by the great northern plains. From Western India, by the Caspian and the Caucasus, past the shores of the Euxine, and still westward along the great rivers of Central Europe, up to the rude coasts of the Baltic, could be tracked "the westward marches of the unknown crowded nations," carrying with them fragments of the early Japhetian wisdom, and memories of the ancient primal tongue brought from the far East; but, as they removed further from the great lines of human intercourse, and were subjected to the influence of rigorous climates and nomadic habits, gradually becoming a rude, fierce people of warriors and hunters, predatory and cruel, living by the chase, warring with the wild wolves for their prey, and with each other for the best pasture-grounds. Driven by the severity of the seasons to perpetual migration, they built no cities and raised no monuments, save the sepulchral mound, which can be traced from Tartary to the German Ocean.

Without the civilizing aids of commerce or literature, their language degenerated into barbarous dialects; their clothing was the skin of wild beasts; their religion, confused relics of ancient creeds, contributed by the wandering colonies of Egypt, Media, Greece, and Tyre, which occasionally blended with the Scythian hordes, wherein Isis, Mercury, and Hercules, the symbols of wisdom, eloquence, and courage, were the objects worshipped, though deteriorated by savage and sanguinary rites, whose sacrifices were human victims, and whose best votary was he who had slain most men.

From long wandering through the gloomy regions where the sun is darkened by perpetual clouds, they called themselves the "Children of the Night," and looked on her as the primal mother of all things.

Their pastimes symbolized the fierce daring of their lives. At their banquets they quaffed mead from the skulls of the slain, and chanted war-songs to the music of their clashing bucklers, while their dances were amid the points of their unsheathed swords.

From the influence of climate, and from constant intermarriage amongst themselves, certain physical and mental types became permanently fixed, and the gigantic frame, the fair hair and "stern blue eyes" [14] of the Scythian tribes, along with their bold, free, warlike, independent spirit, are still the marked characteristic of their descendants. For amidst these rude races of lion-hearted men, who cleared the forests of Central Europe for future empires, there were great and noble virtues born of their peculiar mode of life: a love of freedom, a lofty sense of individual dignity, bold defiance of tyranny, a fortitude and courage that rose to heroism—the spirit that brooks no fetter either on the mind or frame. We see that such men were destined for world-rulers. To them Europe is indebted for her free political systems; the chivalry that ennobled warfare and elevated women, and the religious reformation that freed Christianity from superstition. Every charter of human freedom dates from the Scythian forests.

The great northern concourse of fierce, wild tribes, comprehended originally under the name of Scythians, or Wanderers, having spread themselves over the north to the very kingdom of the Frost-Giants, amidst frozen seas and drifting glaciers, turned southward, tempted by softer climes and richer lands, and under the names of Goth, Vandal, Frank, and Norman, devastating tribes of the Scythian warriors poured their rude masses upon the early and refined civilization of the Mediterranean nations, conquering wherever they appeared and holding bravely whatever they conquered.

The Roman empire trembled and vanished before the terrible might of the long-haired Goths. They sacked Rome and threatened Constantinople: Africa, Italy, Spain, France, and Germany yielded to the barbaric power. Before the fifth century the Scythians had conquered the world, and every kingdom in Europe is ruled by them to this hour.

How strangely contrasted the destinies of the two great Japhetian races! What vicissitudes of fortune! The refined, lettered, oriental light-bringers to Europe—the founders of all kingdoms, the first teachers of all knowledge, the race that peopled Tyre, Carthage, Greece, Italy, Spain, and Gaul, degraded, humbled, and almost annihilated; the last poor remnant of them crushed up in the remote fastnesses of the hills along the coast-line of Europe; step by step driven backwards to the Atlantic, as the red man of America had been driven to the Pacific, till, over the whole earth they can be found nowhere as a nation, save only in Ireland, while the rude, fierce Scandinavian hordes have risen up to be the mightiest of the earth. Greece subdued Asia, and Rome subdued Greece, but Scythia conquered Rome! The children of night and of the dark forests rule the kingdoms that rule the world.

They have given language and laws to modern empires, and at the present day are at the head of all that is most powerful, most thoughtful, most enterprising, and most learned throughout the entire globe.

The story of how the Scythian first came to the British Islands, has been preserved in the Welsh annals, which date back three thousand years. The legend runs that their ancestors, the nation of the Cimbri, wandered long over Europe, forgetting God's name, and the early wisdom. At length they crossed "the hazy sea" (the German Ocean) from the country of the pools (Belgium) and came to Britain, the sea-girt land, called by them Cambria, [15] or, first mother; and they were the first who trod the soil of Britain. There their poets and bards recovered the lost name of God, the sacred I.A.O., and the primal letters their forefathers had known, called the ten signs. And ever since they have possessed religion and literature, though the bards kept the signs secret for many ages, so that all learning might be limited to themselves.

The paramount monarch of the Cimbri nation reigned at London, and a state of poetry and peace long continued, till the Dragon-Aliens appeared on their coasts. The ancient Cimbri retreated into Wales, where they have ever since remained. The Picts seized on Caledonia, and the Saxons on England, until, in their turn, they were conquered by the Danes.

Ireland at that period was the most learned and powerful island of the West. Through all changes of European dynasties she retained her independence. From the Milesian to the Norman, no conqueror had trod her soil. [16]

Meanwhile England, who never yet successfully resisted an invading enemy, passed under many a foreign yoke. For five hundred years the Romans held her as a province to supply their legions with recruits, and the abject submission of the natives called forth the bitter sarcasm, that "the good of his country was the only cause in which a Briton had forgot to die."

The acquisition of Ireland was eagerly coveted by the imperial race, but though Agricola boasted he would conquer it with a single legion, and even went so far towards the completion of his design as to line all the opposite coasts of Wales with his troops, yet no Roman soldier ever set foot on Irish soil.

Rome had enough of work on hand just then, for Alaric the Goth is at her gates, and Attila, the scourge of God, is ravaging her fairest provinces. The imperial mother of Colonies can no longer hold her own or aid her children; England is abandoned to her fate, and the Irish from the west, the Scythian from the north, the Saxon from the east, assault, and desolate, and despoil her.

The Scythian Picts pour down on her cities, "killing, burning, and destroying." The Irish land in swarms from their *corrahs*, and "with fiery outrage and cruelty, carry, harry, and make havoc of all." Thus bandied between two insolent enemies, the English sent ambassadors to Rome "with their garments rent, and sand upon their heads," bearing that most mournful appeal of an humbled people—"to Ætius, thrice Consul: the groans of the Britons. The barbarians drive us to the sea, the sea drives us back to the barbarians; thus, between two kinds of death, we are either slaughtered or drowned."

But no help comes, for Rome herself is devastated by Hun and Vandal, and the empire is falling like a shattered world.

Thus England passed helplessly under the Saxon yoke, and so rested some hundred years; Ireland the while remaining as free from Saxon thrall as she had been from Roman rule.

Through all these centuries the current of human life still flowed westward from the unknown mysterious regions of Central Asia.

It was about the close of the eighth century, when the Scythian Charlemagne was crowned Emperor of Rome in the city of the Cæsars, that the fierce children of Thor and Odin, after having swept across Northern Europe to the limit of the land, flung their fortunes to the stormy seas, and began to earn that terrible yet romantic renown with which history and saga have invested the deeds of the Scandinavian sea kings. The raven on their black banner was the dreaded symbol of havoc and devastation all along the sea coasts and islands of the Atlantic. In England, Saxon rule fell helplessly before the power of the new invaders, as wave after wave of the ruthless sea-ravagers dashed upon the sluggish masses of the heptarchy.

After two hundred years of protracted agony and strife, Saxon sway was annihilated for ever, and Canute the Dane reigned in England.

Meanwhile, the well-appointed fleets of Norsemen and Danes were prowling about the cost of Ireland, trying to obtain a footing on her yet unconquered soil.

When these pagan pirates first appeared on our shores, Ireland had enjoyed a Christian civilization of four centuries. The light of the true faith had been there long before it shone upon rude Saxon England. The Irish of that early era excelled in music, poetry, and many arts. They had a literature, colleges for the learned, an organized and independent hierarchy, churches and abbeys, whose ruins still attest the sense of the beautiful, as well as the piety which must have existed in the founders. Their manuscripts, dating from this period, are older than those of any other nation of Northern Europe; their music was distinguished by its pathetic beauty, and the ballads of their bards emulated in force of expression those of ancient Homer. At the time that the Scots were totally ignorant of letters, and that the princes of the heptarchy had to resort to Irish colleges for instruction in the liberal sciences, Ireland held the proud title of the "Island of Saints and Scholars;" and learned men went forth from her shores to evangelize Europe.

One Irish priest founded an abbey at Iona; another was the friend and counsellor of Charlemagne; a third, of equal celebrity, founded monasteries both in France and England. The Irish of eleven centuries ago were the apostles of Europe!

The Norsemen, or "white strangers," as the Irish called them who swept like a hurricane over this early civilization, were fierce pagans, who respected neither God nor man. Not till three centuries after their arrival in Ireland were they converted to the Christian faith. They pillaged towns, burned churches, destroyed manuscripts of the past which no future can restore, plundered abbeys of all that learning, sanctity and civilization had accumulated of the sacred, the costly, and the beautiful, and gave the Irish nothing in return but lessons of their own barbarous ferocity. Then it was we hear how Irish mothers gave their infants food on the point of their father's sword, and at the baptism left the right arms of their babes unchristened that they might strike the more relentlessly. The Syrian and the Scythian, the children of the one Japhetian race, met at last in this *ultima thule* of Europe, after a three thousand years' divergence; and even then, though they met with fierce animosity and inextinguishable hatred, yet lingerings of a far-off ancient identity in the language, the traditions, and the superstitions of each, could still be traced in these children of the one mighty father.

Great consternation must have been in Ireland when the report spread that a fleet of sixty strange sail was in the Boyne, and that another of equal number was sailing up the Liffey. The foreigners leaped from their ships to conquest. Daring brought success; they sacked, burned, pillaged, murdered; put a captive king to death in his own gyves at their ships; drove the Irish before them from the ocean to the Shannon; till, with roused spirit and gathered force, the confederate kings of Ireland in return drove back the white foreigners from the Shannon to the ocean. But they had gained a footing, and inroads, with plunder and devastation, never ceased from that time till the whole eastern sea-border of Ireland was their own. There they established themselves for four centuries, holding their first conquests, but never gaining more, until they were finally expelled by the Normans.

To these red-haired pirates and marauders Dublin owes its existence as a city. The *Ath-Cliath* of the Irish, though of ancient fame, was but an aggregate of huts by the side of the Liffey, which was crossed by a bridge of hurdles. The kings of Ireland never made it a royal residence, even after Tara was cursed by St. Rodan. Their palaces were in the interior of the island; but no doubt exists that *Ath-Cliath*, the Eblana of Ptolemy, was a well-known port, the resort of merchantmen from the most ancient times. There were received the Spanish wines, the Syrian silks, the Indian gold, destined for the princes and nobles; and from thence the costly merchandize was transported to the interior.

But Dublin, with its fine plain watered by the Liffey, its noble bay, guarded by the sentinel hills, at once attracted the special notice of the bold Vikings. Their chiefs fixed their residence there, and assumed the title of Kings of Dublin, or Kings of the Dark Water, as the word may be translated. They erected a fortress on the very spot where the Norman Castle now rules the city, and, after their conversion, a cathedral, still standing amongst us, venerable with the memories of eight hundred years.

Their descendants are with us to this day, and many families might trace back their lineage to the Danish leaders, whose names have been preserved in Irish history. Amongst sundry of "these great and valiant captains" are named Swanchean, Griffin, Albert Roe, Torbert Duff, Goslyn, Walter English, Awley, King of Denmark, from whom descend the Macaulays, made more illustrious by the modern historian of their race than by the ancient pirate king. There are also named Randal O'Himer, Algot, Ottarduff Earl, Fyn Crossagh, Torkill, Fox Wasbagg, Trevan, Baron Robert, and others; names interesting, no doubt, to those who can claim them for their ancestry.

The Norsemen having walled and fortified Dublin, though including but a mile within its circumference—whereas now the city includes ten—proceeded to fortify Dunleary, now Kingstown, in order to secure free passage to their ships. Then, from their stronghold of Dublin, they made incessant inroads upon the broad rich plains of the interior. They spread all along Meath, which received its name from them, of "Fingall" (the land of the white stranger); they devastated as far north as Armagh, as far west as the Shannon; Wexford, Waterford, and Limerick became half Danish cities. Everywhere their course was marked by barbaric spoliation. At one time it is noticed that they carried off a "great prey of women"—thus the Romans woo'd their Sabine brides; indeed the accounts in the Irish annals of the shrines they burned, the royal graves they plundered, the treasures they pillaged, the ferocities they perpetrated, are as interminable as they are revolting.

When beaten back by the Irish princes they crouched within their walled city of Dublin, till an opportunity offered for some fresh exercise of murderous cunning, some act of audacious rapine. Thus the contest was carried on for four centuries between the colonists and the nation; mutual hatred ever increasing; the Irish kings of Leinster still claiming the rights of feudal lords over the Danes; the Danes resisting every effort made to dislodge them, though they were not unfrequently forced to pay tribute.

Sometimes the Irish kings hired them as mercenaries to assist in the civil wars which raged perennially amongst them. Sometimes there were intermarriages between the warring foes—the daughter of Brian Boro' wedded Sitric, King of the Danes of Dublin. Occasionally the Irish kings got possession of Dublin, and ravaged and pillaged in return. Once the Danes were driven forth completely from the city, and forced to take refuge upon "Ireland's Eye," the lone sea rock, since made memorable by a tragic history. Malachy, King of Meath, besieged Dublin for three days and three nights, burned the fortress, and carried off the Danish regalia; hence the allusion in Moore's song to "The Collar of Gold which he won from the proud invader." But the most terrible defeat the Danes ever sustained was at Clontarf, when ten thousand men in coats of mail were opposed to King Brian; but "the ten thousand in armour were cut in pieces, and three thousand warriors slain besides." Even the Irish children fought against the invader. The grandchild of King Brian, a youth of fifteen, was found dead with his hand fast bound in the hair of a Dane's head, whom the child had dragged to the sea. [17]

Still the Danish colony was not uprooted, though after this defeat they grew more humble, kept within their city of Dublin, and paid tribute to the kings of Leinster, and to the paramount monarch of Ireland.

Up to this period, therefore, we see that the Irish race had no relationship whatever with their capital city; they never saw the inside of their metropolis unless they were carried there as prisoners, or that they entered with fire and sword; and, stranger still, during the many centuries of the existence of Dublin as a city, up to the present time, the Irish race have never ruled there, or held possession of the fortress of their capital.

But the time of judgment upon the Danes was approaching, though it did not come by Irish hands. As the Saxons in England fell before the Danes, so the Danes had fallen before the Normans. The Normans, a Scythian race likewise, but more beautiful, more brave, more chivalrous, courtly, and polished, than any race that had preceded them, came triumphant from Italy and France to achieve the conquest of England, which yielded almost without a struggle. One great battle, and then no more. William the Norman, or rather the Scythian Frenchman, ascends the throne of Alfred. Dane and Saxon fall helplessly beneath his feet, and his tyrannies, his robberies, his confiscations, are submitted to by the subjugated nation without an effort at resistance.

His handful of Norman nobles seized upon the lands, the wealth, the honours, the estates of the kingdom, and retain them to this hour. And justly; so noble a race as the Norman knights were made for masters. The Saxons sank at once to the level of serfs, of traders and menials, from which they have never risen, leaving England divided into a Norman aristocracy who have all the land, and a Saxon people who have all the toil; crushed by the final conquerors, they sank to be the sediment of the kingdom.

The Irish had a different destiny; for five hundred years they fought the battle for independence with the Normans, nor did their chiefs sink to be the pariahs of the kingdom, as the Saxons of England, but retain their princely pretensions to this day. The O'Connors, the O'Briens, O'Neils, Kavanaghs, O'Donnels, yield to no family in Europe in pride of blood and ancestral honours; while, by intermarriage with the Norman lords, a race was founded of Norman Irish—perhaps the finest specimens of aristocracy that Europe produced—the Geraldines at their head, loving Ireland, and of whom Ireland may be proud.

A hundred years passed by after the Norman conquest of England. Three kings of the Norman race had reigned and died, and still the conquest of Ireland was unattempted; no Norman knight had set foot on Irish soil.

The story of their coming begins with just such a domestic drama as Homer had turned into an epic two thousand years before. A fair and faithless woman, a king's daughter, fled from her husband to the arms of a lover. All Ireland is outraged at the act. The kings assemble in conclave and denounce vengeance upon the crowned seducer, Dermot, King of Leinster.

He leagues with the Danes of Dublin, the abhorred of his countrymen, but the only allies he can find in his great need. A battle is fought in which Dermot is defeated, his castle of Ferns is burned, his kingdom is taken from him, and he himself is solemnly deposed by the confederate kings, and banished beyond the seas. Roderick, King of all Ireland, is the inexorable and supreme judge. He restores the guilty wife to her husband; but the husband disdains to receive her, and she retires to a convent, where she expiates her crime and the ruin of her country by forty years of penance. The only records of her afterwards are of her good deeds. She built a nunnery at Clonmacnoise; she gave a chalice of gold to the altar of Mary, and cloth for nine altars of the Church; and then Dervorgil, the Helen of our Iliad, is heard of no more.

Dermot, her lover, went to England, seeking aid to recover his kingdom of Leinster. In a year he returns with a band of Welsh mercenaries, and marches to Dublin; but is again defeated by the confederate kings, and obliged to pay a hundred ounces of gold to O'Rourke of Breffny, "for the wrong he had done him respecting his wife," and to give up as hostage to King Roderick his only son. But while parleying with the Irish kings, Dermot was secretly soliciting English aid, and not unsuccessfully.

Memorable was the year 1170, when the renowned Strongbow, Gilbert de Clare, Earl of Pembroke, and his Norman knights, landed at Wexford to aid the banished king; and when Dermot welcomed his illustrious allies, little he thought that by his hand

"The emerald gem of the Western world,

Was set in the crown of a stranger."

The compact with the foreigners was sealed with his son's blood. No sooner did King Roderick hear of the Norman landing, than he ordered the royal Kavanagh, the hostage of King Dermot, to be put to death; and henceforth a doom seemed to be on the male heirs of the line of Dermot, as fatal as that which rested upon the house of Atrides.

Dermot had an only daughter remaining. He offered her in marriage to the Earl of Pembroke, with the whole kingdom of Leinster for her dowry, so as he would help him to his revenge. After a great battle against the Danes, in which the Normans were victorious, the marriage was celebrated at Waterford.

"Sad Eva gazed
All round that bridal field of blood, amazed;
Spoused to new fortunes." [18]

No record remains to us of the beauty of the bride, or in what language the Norman knight wooed her to his arms; this only we know, that Eva, Queen of Leinster in her own right, and Countess of Pembroke by marriage, can number amongst her descendants the present Queen of England. Of the bridegroom, Cambrensis tells us that he was "ruddy, freckle-faced, grey-eyed, his face feminine, his voice small, his neck little, yet of a high stature, ready with good words and gentle speeches."

The same authority describes Dermot from personal observation—"A tall man of stature, of a large and great body, a valiant and bold warrior, and by reason of his continued hallooing his voice was hoarse. He rather chose to be feared than loved. Rough and generous, hateful unto strangers, he would be against all men and all men against him."

From Waterford to Dublin was a progress of victory to Dermot and his allies, for they marched only through the Danish settlements of which Dermot was feudal lord. At Dublin King Roderick opposed them with an army. Three days the battle raged; then the Danes of Dublin, fearing Dermot's wrath, opened their gates, and offered him gold and silver in abundance if he would spare their lives; but, heedless of treaties, the Norman knights rushed in, slew the Danes in their own fortress, drove the rest to the sea; and thus ended the Danish dynasty of four centuries. Never more did they own a foot of ground throughout the length or breadth of the land. An Irish army, aided by Norman skill, had effected their complete extinction. The Kingdom of Leinster was regained for Dermot, and he and his allies placed a garrison in Dublin. This was the last triumph of the ancient race. The kingdom was lost even at the moment it seemed regained. That handful of Scythian warriors, scarcely visible amid Dermot's great Irish army, are destined to place the yoke upon the neck of ancient Ireland.

The brave Roderick gathered together another army, and, with sixty thousand men, laid siege to Dublin, O'Rourke of Breffny aiding him. They were repulsed. O'Rourke was taken prisoner, and hanged with his head downwards, then beheaded and the head stuck on one of the centre gates of the castle, "a spectacle of intense pity to the Irish;" and Roderick retired into Connaught to recruit more forces.

There is something heroic and self-devoted in the efforts which, for eighteen years, were made by Roderick against the Norman power. Brave, learned, just, and enlightened beyond his age, he alone of all the Irish princes saw the direful tendency of the Norman inroad. All the records of his reign prove that he was a wise and powerful monarch. He had a fleet on the Shannon, the like of which had never been seen before. He built a royal residence in Connaught, the ruins of which are still existing to attest its former magnificence, so far beyond all structures of the period, that it was known in Ireland as the beautiful house. He founded a chair of literature at Armagh, and left an endowment in perpetuity, to maintain it for the instruction of the youth of Ireland and Scotland. A great warrior, and a fervent patriot, his first effort, when he obtained the crown, was to humble the Danish power. Dublin was forced to pay him tribute, and he was inaugurated there with a grandeur and luxury unknown before. When Dermot outraged morality, he deposed and banished him. When Dermot further sinned, and traitorously brought over the foreigner, Roderick, with stern justice, avenged the father's treason by the son's life. His own son, the heir of his kingdom, leagued with the Normans, and was found fighting in their ranks. Roderick, like a second Brutus, unpitying, yet heroically just, when the youth was brought a prisoner before him, himself ordered his eyes to be put out. His second son also turned traitor, and covenanted with the Normans to deprive his father of the kingdom. Then Roderick, surrounded by foreign foes and domestic treachery, quitted Connaught, and went through the provinces of Ireland, seeking to stir up a spirit as heroic as his own in the hearts of his countrymen. Soon after his unworthy son was killed in some broil, and Roderick resumed the kingly functions; but while all the other Irish princes took the oath of fealty to King Henry, he kept aloof beyond the Shannon, equally disdaining treachery or submission. His last son, the only one worthy of him, being defeated in a battle by the Normans, slew himself in despair.

The male line of his house was now extinct; the independence of his country was threatened; Norman power was growing strong in the land, and his continued efforts for eighteen years to arouse the Irish princes to a sense of their danger was unavailing. Wearied, disgusted, heartbroken, it may be, he voluntarily laid down the sceptre and the crown, and retired to the monastery of Cong, where he became a monk, and thus, in penance and seclusion, passed ten years—the weary ending of a fated life.

He died there, twenty-eight years after the Norman invasion, "after exemplary penance, victorious over the world and the devil;" and the chroniclers record his title upon his grave where he is laid—

"Roderick O'Connor,
King of all Ireland, both of the Irish and English."

Seven centuries have passed since then, yet even now, which of us could enter the beautiful ruins of that ancient abbey, wander through the arched aisles tapestried by ivy, or tread the lonely silent chapel, once vocal with prayer and praise, without sad thoughts of sympathy for the fate of the last monarch of Ireland, and perchance grave thoughts likewise over the destiny of a people who, on that grave of native monarchy, independence, and nationality, have as yet written no RESURGAM.

Exactly ten months after the Normans took possession of Dublin, King Dermot, "by whom a trembling sod was made of all Ireland, died of an insufferable and unknown disease—for he became putrid while living—without a will, without penance, without the body of Christ, without unction, as his evil deeds deserved."

Immediately the Earl of Pembroke assumed the title of King of Leinster in right of his wife Eva. Whereupon Henry of England grew alarmed at the independence of his nobility, and hastened over to assert his claims as lord paramount. To his remonstrances Strongbow answered, "What I won was with the sword; what was given me I give you." An agreement was then made by which Strongbow retained Dublin, while Henry appointed what nobles he chose over the other provinces of Leinster.

When the first Norman monarch landed amongst us, the memorable 18th day of October, 1172, no resistance was offered by any party; no battle was fought. The Irish chiefs were so elated at the Danish overthrow, that they even volunteered oaths of fealty to the foreign prince who had been in some sort their deliverer. Calmly, as in a state pageant, Henry proceeded from Wexford to Dublin; his route lay only through the conquered Danish possessions, now the property of the Countess Eva; there was no fear therefore of opposition. On reaching the city, "he caused a royal palace to be built, very curiously contrived of smooth wattels, after the manner of the country, and there, with the kings and princes of Ireland, did keep Christmas with great solemnity," on the very spot where now stands St. Andrew's Church.

King Henry remained six months in Ireland, the longest period which a foreign monarch has ever passed amongst us, and during that time he never thought of fighting a battle with the Irish. As yet, the whole result of Norman victories was the downfall of the Danes, in which object the Irish had gladly assisted. Strongbow and Eva reigned peacefully in our capital. Henry placed governors over the other Danish cities, and in order that Dublin, from which the Danes had been expelled, might be repeopled, he made a present of our fair city to the good people of Bristol.

Accordingly a colony from that town, famed for deficiency in personal attractions, came over and settled here; but thirty years after, the Irish, whose instincts of beauty were no doubt offended by the rising generation of Bristolians, poured down from the Wicklow hills upon the ill-favoured colony, and made a quick ending of them by a general massacre.

In a fit of penitence, also, for the murdered À Becket, Henry founded the Abbey of Thomas Court, from which Thomas Street derives its name, and then the excommunicated king quitted Ireland, leaving it unchanged, save that Henry the Norman held the possessions of Torkil the Dane, and Dublin, from a Danish, had become a Norman city. Five hundred years more had to elapse before English jurisdiction extended beyond the ancient Danish pale, and a Cromwell or a William of Nassau was needed for the final conquest of Ireland, as well as for the redemption of England.

Nothing can be more absurd than to talk of a Saxon conquest of Ireland. The Saxons, an ignorant, rude, inferior race, could not even maintain their ascendency in England. They fell before the superior power, intelligence, and ability of the Norman, and the provinces of Ireland that fell to the first Norman nobles were in reality not gained by battles, but by the intermarriage of Norman lords with the daughters of Irish kings. Hence it was that in right of their wives the Norman nobles early set up claims independent of the English crown, and the hereditary rights, being transmitted through each generation, were perpetually tempting the Norman aristocracy into rebellion. English supremacy was as uneasily borne by the De Lacys, the Geraldines, the Butlers, and others of the Norman stock, as by the O'Connors, the Kavanaghs, the O'Neils, or the O'Briens. The great Richard de Burgho married Odierna, grand-daughter of Cathal Crovdearg, king of Connaught. Hence the De Burghos assumed the title of Lords of Connaught.

King Roderick, as we have said, left no male issue. His kingdom descended to his daughter, who married the Norman knight, Hugo de Lacy. Immediately De Lacy set up a claim as independent prince in right of his wife, assumed legal state, took the title of King of Meath, and appeared in public with a golden crown upon his head, and so early as twenty-five years after the invasion, John de Courcy and the son of this De Lacy marched *against* the English of Leinster and Munster. Many a romance could be woven of the destiny and vicissitudes of this great race, half Irish, half Norman; independent princes by the one side, and English subjects by the other.

The great Earl of Pembroke lived but a few years after his capture of Dublin. The Irish legends say that St. Bridget killed him. However, he and Eva had no male heir, and only one daughter, named Isabel, after the Earl's mother, who was also aunt to the reigning king of Scotland.

This young girl was sole heiress of Leinster and of her father's Welsh estates. Richard Cœur de Lion took her to his court at London, and she became his ward. In due time she married William Marshall, called the great

Earl, hereditary Earl Marshal of England, and Earl of Pembroke and Leinster, in right of his wife. High in office and favour with the king, we read that he carried the sword of state before Richard at his coronation, and as a monument of his piety, he left Tintern Abbey, in the County Wexford, erected by him on his wife's property.

Isabel and Earl William had five sons and five daughters. The five sons, William, Walter, Gilbert, Anselm, and Richard (Isabel called no son of hers after the royal traitor Dermot, her grandfather) inherited the title in succession, and all died childless. We have said there was a doom upon Dermot's male posterity.

The inheritance was then divided between the five daughters, each of whom received a province for a dower. Carlow, Kilkenny, the Queen's County, Wexford, and Kildare were the five portions. Maud, the eldest, married the Earl of Norfolk, who became Earl Marshal of England in right of his wife.

Isabel, the second, married the Earl of Gloucester, and her granddaughter, Isabel also, was mother to the great Robert Bruce, who was therefore great-great-great-grandson of Eva and Strongbow. Eva, the third daughter, married the Lord de Breos, and from a daughter of hers, named Eva likewise, descended Edward the Fourth, King of England, through whose granddaughter Margaret Queen of Scotland, daughter of Henry the Seventh, the present reigning family of England claim their right to the throne. Through two lines, therefore, our Most Gracious Majesty can trace back her pedigree to Eva the Irish princess.

Joan, whose portions were Wexford, married Lord Valentia, half-brother to King Henry the Third, and the male line failing, the inheritance was divided between two daughters, from one of whom the Talbots, Earls of Shrewsbury, inherit their Wexford estates.

From Sybil, the youngest, who married the Earl of Ferrars and Derby, descended the Earls of Winchester, the Lords Mortimer, and other noble races. She had seven daughters, who all married Norman lords, so that scarcely a family could be named of the high and ancient English nobility, whose wealth has not been increased by the estates of Eva, the daughter of King Dermot; and thus it came to pass that Leinster fell by marriage and inheritance, not by conquest, into the possession of the great Norman families, who, of course, acknowledged the King of England as their sovereign; and the English monarchs assumed thenceforth the title of Lords of Ireland—a claim which they afterwards enforced over the whole country.

The destiny of the descendants of De Lacy and King Roderick's daughter was equally remarkable. They had two sons, Hugh and Walter, who, before they were twenty-one, threw off English allegiance, and set up as independent princes. To avoid the wrath of King John they fled to France, and took refuge in an abbey, where, disguised as menials, the two young noblemen found employment in garden-digging, preparing mud and bricks, and similar work. By some chance the abbot suspected the disguise, and finally detected the princes in the supposed peasants. He used his knowledge of their secret to obtain their pardon from King John, and Hugh De Lacy was created Earl of Ulster. He left an only daughter, his sole heir. She married a De Burgho, who, in right of his wife, became Earl of Ulster, and from them descended Ellen, wife of Robert Bruce, King of Scotland. It is singular that the mother of Robert Bruce should have been descended from Eva, and his wife from King Roderick's daughter. The granddaughter of Robert Bruce, the Princess Margery, married the Lord High Steward of Scotland, and through her the Stuarts claimed the crown. From thence it is easy to trace how the royal blood of the three kingdoms meet in the reigning family of England. Another descendant of the Earls of Ulster (an only daughter likewise) married Lionel, Duke of Clarence, son of Edward the Third, who, in the right of his wife, became Earl of Ulster and Lord of Connaught, and these titles finally merged in the English crown in the person of Edward the Fourth. From all these genealogies one fact may be clearly deduced, that the present representative of the royal Irish races of Eva and Roderick, and the lineal heiress of their rights, is Her Majesty Queen Victoria.

The proud and handsome race of Norman Irish, that claimed descent from these intermarriages, were the nobles, of whom it was said, "They were more

Irish than the Irish themselves." The disposition to become independent of England was constantly manifested in them. They publicly asserted their rights, renounced the English dress and language, and adopted Irish names. Thus Sir Ulick Burke, ancestor of Lord Clanricarde, became MacWilliam Oughter (or upper), and Sir Edmond Albanagh, progenitor of the Earl of Mayo, became MacWilliam Eighter (or lower). Richard, son of the Earl of Norfolk, and grandson of Eva, set up a claim to be independent King of Leinster, and was slain by the English. We have seen that Walter and Hugh De Lacy, grandsons of Roderick, were in open rebellion against King John. A hundred years later, two of the same race, named Walter and Hugh likewise, were proclaimed traitors for aiding the army of Robert Bruce, who claimed the crown of Ireland for his brother Edward, and the two De Lacys were found dead by the side of Edward Bruce at the great battle of Dundalk, where the Scotch forces were overthrown.

Once, even the Geraldines and the Fitzmaurices took prisoner the Justiciary of Dublin, as the Lord-Lieutenant of that day was named. Meanwhile the Irish princes of the West retained their independence; sometimes at feud, sometimes in amity with the English of the Eastern coast. We read that "the English of Dublin invited Hugh, King of Connaught, to a conference, and began to deal treacherously with him; but William Mareschall, his friend, coming in with his forces, rescued him, in despite of the English, from the middle of the Court, and escorted him to Connaught." Both races were equally averse to the domination of the English crown. The Geraldines and Butlers, the De Burghos and De Lacys, were as intractable as the O'Connors of Connaught, or the O'Neils of Tyrone; even more so. The Great O'Neil submitted to Elizabeth; but two hundred years later the Geraldines had still to add the name of another martyr for liberty to the roll of their illustrious ancestors.

Frequently the Normans fought amongst themselves as fiercely as if opposed to the Irish. The Earl of Ulster, a De Burgho, the same who is recorded to have given the first entertainment at Dublin Castle, took his kinsman, Walter Burke, prisoner, and had him starved to death in his own castle; a tragedy which might have been made as memorable as that of Ugolino in the *Torre del Fame*, had there been a Dante in Ireland to record it. For this act the kinsmen of Walter Burke murdered the Earl of Ulster on the Lord's Day, as he was kneeling at his prayers, and cleft his head in two with a sword.

It was unfortunate for Ireland that her Irish princes were so unconquerable, and that her Norman lords should have caught the infection of resistance to the crown. Eight hundred years ago the Saxons of England peaceably settled down with the Normans to form one nation, with interests and objects identical.

The Norman conquerors, better fitted, perhaps, for rulers than any other existing in Europe, established at once a strong, vigorous government in England. The Kings, as individuals, may have been weak or tyrannous, but there was a unity of purpose, a sense of justice, and a vigour of will existing in the ruling class that brought the ruled speedily under the order and discipline of laws. Not a century and a half had elapsed from the Conquest before Magna Charta and representation by Parliament secured the liberty of the people against the caprices of kings; and the Norman temperament which united in a singular degree the instincts of loyalty with the love of freedom, became the hereditary national characteristic of Englishmen. But Ireland never, at any time, comprehended the word nationality. From of old it was broken up into fragments, ruled by chiefs whose principal aim was mutual destruction. There was no unity, therefore no strength.

If, at the time of the Norman invasion, a king of the race had settled here as in England, the Irish would gradually have become a nation under one ruler, in place of being an aggregate of warring tribes; but for want of this chief corner-stone the Norman nobles themselves became but isolated chiefs—new petty kings added to the old—each for himself, none for the country. It was contrary to all natural laws that the proud Irish princes, with the traditions of their race going back two thousand years, should at once serve with love and loyalty a foreign king whose face they never saw and from whom they derived no benefits. And thus it was that five hundred years elapsed, from Henry Plantagenet to William of Nassau, before Ireland was finally adjusted in her subordinate position to the English crown.

Meanwhile the Danish Dublin was fast rising into importance as the Norman city, the capital of the English pale. Within that circle the English laws, language, manners and religion were implicitly adopted; without, there was a fierce, warlike, powerful people, the ancient lords of the soil, but with them the citizens of Dublin had no affinity; and the object of the English rulers was to keep the two races as distinct as possible. Amongst other enactments tending to obliterate any feeling of kindred which might exist, the inhabitants of the pale were ordered to adopt English surnames, derived from everything which by the second commandment we are forbidden to worship. Hence arose the tribes of fishes—cod, haddock, plaice, salmon, gurnet, gudgeon, &c.; and of birds—crow, sparrow, swan, pigeon; and of trades, as carpenter, smith, baker, mason; and of colours—the blacks, whites, browns, and greens, which in Dublin so copiously replace the grand old historic names of the provinces. Determined also on annihilating the picturesque, at least in the individual, lest the outward symbol might be taken for an inward affinity, the long flowing hair and graceful mantle, after the Irish fashion, were forbidden to be worn within the pale.

Neither was the Irish language tolerated within the English jurisdiction, for which Holingshed gives good reason, after this fashion—"And here," he says, "some snappish carpers will snuffingly snib me for debasing the Irish language, but my short discourse tendeth only to this drift, that it is not expedient that the Irish tongue should be so universally gagled in the English pale; for where the country is subdued, there the inhabitants should be ruled by the same laws that the conqueror is governed, wear the same fashion of attire with which the victor is vested, and speak the same language which the victor parleth; and if any of these lack, doubtless the conquest limpeth." The English tongue, however, seems to have been held in utter contempt and scorn by the Irish allies of the pale. After the submission of the Great O'Neil, the last who held the title of king in Ireland, which he exchanged for that of Earl of Tyrone, as a mark and seal of his allegiance to Queen Elizabeth, "One demanded merrilie," says Holingshed, "why O'Neil would not frame himself to speak English? 'What,' quoth the other in a rage, 'thinkest thou it standeth with O'Neil his honour to writhe his mouth in clattering English.'"

As regarded religion, the English commanded the most implicit obedience to the Pope, under as strict and severe penalties as, five hundred years later, they enacted against those who acknowledged his authority. One provision of the ancient oath imposed upon the subjugated Irish was—"You acknowledge yourself to be of the Mother Church of Rome, now professed by all Christians." But, that the Irish of that era little heeded papal or priestly ordinances may be inferred from the fact that, during the wars of Edward Bruce, the English complained that their Irish auxiliaries were more exhausting than the Scots, as they ate meat all the time of Lent; and it is recorded, that in 1133, when the Leinster Irish rose against the English, "they set fire to everything, even the churches, and burned the church of Dunleary, with eighty persons in it, and even when the priest in his sacred vestments, and carrying the Host in his hands, tried to get out, they drove him back with their spears and burned him. For this they were excommunicated by a Papal Bull, and the country was put under an interdict. But they despised these things, and again wasted the county of Wexford." [19]

The energetic and organizing spirit of the Normans was, however, evidenced by better deeds than those we have named. Courts of law were established in Dublin, a mayor and corporation instituted, and Parliaments were convened after the English fashion. Within fifty years after the Norman settlement, the lordly pile of Dublin Castle rose upon the site of the old Danish fortress, built, indeed, to overawe the Irish, as William the Conqueror built the Tower of London to overawe the English; yet, by Norman hands, the first regal residence was given to our metropolis. St. Patrick's Cathedral was next elected by the colonists, and gradually our fair city rose into beauty and importance through Norman wealth and Norman skill. From henceforth, the whole interest of Irish history centres in the chief city of the pale, and the history of Dublin becomes the history of English rule in Ireland. For centuries its position was that of a besieged city in the midst of a hostile country; for centuries it resisted the whole force of the native race; and finally triumphantly crushed, annihilated, and revenged every effort made for Irish independence.

In truth, Dublin is a right royal city, and never fails in reverential respect towards her English mother.

Many great names are associated with the attempt to write a history of Dublin. The work in all ages was laborious; there were no printed books to consult, and the records of Ireland, as Hooker complains three hundred years ago, "were verie slenderlie and disorderlie kept." Whitelaw's work, though it employed two editors ten hours a day for ten years, yet goes no farther than a description of the public buildings; but the object of Mr. Gilbert's history is distinct from all that precedes it. It is from the decaying streets and houses that he disentombs great memories, great fragments of past life. It is not a mere record of Ionic pillars, Corinthian capitals, or Doric pediments he gives us. Whitelaw has supplied whole catalogues of these; but records of the human life, that has throbbed through the ancient dwellings of our city century after century; of the vicissitudes of families, to be read in their ruined mansions; of the vast political events which in some room, in some house, on some particular night, branded the stigmata deeper on the country; or the tragedies of great hopes crushed, young blood shed, victims hopelessly sacrificed, which have made some street, some house, some chamber, for ever sacred.

The labours of such an undertaking are manifest; yet none can appreciate them fully who has not known what it is to spend days, weeks, months buried in decaying parchments, endless pipe-rolls, worm-eaten records, dusty deeds and leases, excavating some fact, or searching for some link necessary for the completion of a tale, or the elucidation of a truth.

Mr. Gilbert tells us that twelve hundred statutes and enactments of the Anglo-Irish Parliament still remain unpublished. From these and such-like decayed and decaying manuscripts, ancient records which have become almost hieroglyphics to the present age, he has gathered the life-history of an ancient city; he has made the stones to speak, and evoked the shadows of the past to fill up the outline of a great historical picture.

Fifty, even twenty years hence, the production of such a work would be impossible; the ancient records will probably have perished; the ancient houses, round which the curious may yet gather, will have fallen to the ground; and the ancient race, who cherished in their hearts the legends of the past with the fidelity of priests, and the fervour of bards, will have almost passed away.

Dublin is fortunate, therefore, in finding a historian endowed with the ability, the energetic literary industry, the untiring spirit of research, and the vast amount of antiquarian knowledge necessary for the production of so valuable a work, before records perish, mansions fall, or races vanish.

In a history illustrated by human lives and deeds, and localized in the weird old streets, once the proudest, now the meanest of our city, many a family will find an ancestral shadow starting suddenly to light, trailing long memories with it of departed fashion, grandeur, and magnificence.

Few amongst us who tread the Dublin of the present in all its beauty, think of the Dublin of the past in all its contrasted insignificance. True, the eternal features are the same; the landscape setting of the city is coeval with creation. Tyrian, Dane, and Norman have looked as we look, and with hearts as responsive to Nature's loveliness, upon the emerald plains, the winding rivers, the hills draperied in violet and gold, the mountain gorges, thunder-riven, half veiled by the foam of the waterfall, and the eternal ocean encircling all; scenes where God said a city should arise, and the mountain and the ocean are still, as of old, the magnificent heritage of beauty conferred on our metropolis.

But the early races, whether from southern sea or northern plain, did little to aid the beauty of nature with the products of human intellect. Dublin, under the Danish rule, consisted only of a fortress, a church, and one rude street. Under the rule of the Normans, those great civilizers of the western world, those grand energetic organizers, temple and tower builders, it rose gradually into a beautiful capital, the chief city of Ireland, the second city of the empire. At first the rudimental metropolis gathered round the castle, as nebulæ round a central sun, and from this point it radiated westward and southward; the O'Briens on the south, the O'Connors on the west, the O'Neils on the north, perpetually hovering on the borders, but never able to regain the city, never able to dislodge the brave Norman garrison who had planted their banners on the castle walls. In that castle, during the seven hundred years of its existence, no Irishman of the old race has ever held rule for a single hour.

And what a history it has of tragedies and splendours; crowned and discrowned monarchs flit across the scene, and tragic destinies, likewise, may be recorded of many a viceroy! Piers Gravestone, Lord-Lieutenant of King Edward, murdered; Roger Mortimer—"The Gentle Mortimer"—hanged at Tyburn; the Lord Deputy of King Richard II. murdered by the O'Briens; whereupon the King came over to avenge his death, just a year before he himself was so ruthlessly murdered at Pomfret Castle. Two viceroys died of the plague; how many more were plagued to death, history leaves unrecorded; one was beheaded at Drogheda; three were beheaded on Tower Hill. Amongst the names of illustrious Dublin rulers may be found those of Prince John, the boy Deputy of thirteen; Prince Lionel, son of Edward III., who claimed Clare in right of his wife, and assumed the title of Clarence from having conquered it from the O'Briens.

The great Oliver Cromwell was the Lord-Lieutenant of the Parliament, and he in turn appointed his son Henry to succeed him. Dire are the memories connected with Cromwell's reign here, both to his own party and to Ireland. Ireton died of the plague after the siege of Limerick; General Jones died of the plague after the surrender of Dungarvon; a thousand of Cromwell's men died of the plague before Waterford. The climate, in its effect upon English constitutions, seems to be the great Nemesis of Ireland's wrongs.

Strange scenes, dark, secret, and cruel, have been enacted in that gloomy pile. No one has told the full story yet. It will be a Ratcliffe romance of dungeons and treacheries, of swift death or slow murder. God and St. Mary were invoked in vain for the luckless Irish prince or chieftain that was caught in that Norman stronghold; but that was in the old time—long, long ago.

Now the castle courts are crowded only with loyal and courtly crowds, gathered to pay homage to the illustrious successor of a hundred viceroys.

The strangest scene, perhaps, in the annals of vice-royalty, was when Lord Thomas Fitzgerald (Silken Thomas), son of the Earl of Kildare, and Lord-Lieutenant in his father's absence, took up arms for Irish independence. He rode through the city with seven score horsemen, in shirts of mail and silken fringes on their head-pieces (hence the name Silken Thomas), to St. Mary's Abbey, and there entering the council chamber, he flung down the sword of state upon the table, and bade defiance to the king and his ministers; then hastening to raise an army, he laid siege to Dublin Castle, but with no success. Silken Thomas and his five uncles were sent to London, and there executed; and sixteen Fitzgeralds were hanged and quartered at Dublin. By a singular fatality, no plot laid against Dublin Castle ever succeeded; though to obtain possession of this foreign fortress was the paramount wish of all Irish rebel leaders. This was the object with Lord Maguire and his Catholics, with Lord Edward Fitzgerald and his republicans, with Emmet and his enthusiasts, with Smith O'Brien and his nationalists—yet they all failed. Once only, during seven centuries, the green flag waved over Dublin Castle, with the motto—"NOW OR NEVER! NOW AND FOR EVER!" It was when Tyrconnel held it for King James.

In the ancient stormy times of Norman rule, the nobility naturally gathered round the Castle. Skinner's Row was the "May Fair" of mediæval Dublin. Hoey's Court, Castle Street, Cook Street, Fishamble Street, Bridge Street, Werburgh Street, High Street, Golden Lane, Back Lane, &c., were the fashionable localities inhabited by lords and bishops, chancellors and judges; and Thomas Street was the grand prado where viceregal pomp and Norman pride were oftenest exhibited. A hundred years ago the Lord-Lieutenant was entertained at a ball by Lord Mountjoy in Back Lane. Skinner's Row was distinguished by the residence of the great race of the Geraldines, called "Carbrie House," which from them passed to the Dukes of Ormond, and after many vicissitudes, the palace from which Silken Thomas went forth to give his young life for Irish independence, fell into decay, "and on its site now stand the houses known as 6, 7, and 8 Christ Church Place, in the lower stories of which still exist some of the old oak beams of the Carbrie House."

In Skinner's Row also, two hundred years ago, dwelt Sir Robert Dixon, Mayor of Dublin, who was knighted at his own house there by the Lord-Lieutenant, the afterwards unfortunate Strafford. The house has fallen to ruins, but the vast property conferred on him by Charles I. for his good services, has descended to the family of Sir Kildare Burrowes, of Kildare. In those brilliant days of Skinner's Row, it was but seventeen feet wide, and the pathways but one foot broad. All its glories have vanished now; even the name no longer exists; yet the remains of residences once inhabited by the magnificent Geraldines and Butlers can still be traced.

Every stone throughout this ancient quarter of Dublin has a history. In Cook Street Lord Maguire was arrested at midnight, under circumstances very similar to the capture of Lord Edward Fitzgerald; and "to commemorate this capture in the parish it was the annual custom, down to the year 1829, to toll the bells of St. Andrew's Church at twelve o'clock on the night of the 22nd of October."

In Bridge Street great lords and peers of the realm resided. The Marquis of Antrim, the Duke of Marlborough's father; Westenra, the Dutch merchant who founded the family afterwards ennobled, and others. It was the Merrion Square of the day. In Bridge Street the rebellion of '98 was organized at the house of Oliver Bond; and one night Major Swan, led by Reynolds the informer, seized twelve gentlemen there, all of whom were summarily hanged as rebels. Castle Street was the focus of the rebellion of 1641; Sir Phelim O'Neill and Lord Maguire had their residences there, and concocted together how to seize the Castle, destroy all the lords and council, and re-establish Popery in Ireland. But a more useful man than either lived there also—Sir James Ware, whose indefatigable ardour in the cause of Irish literature caused him to collect, with great trouble and expense, a vast number of Irish manuscripts, which, after passing through many vicissitudes, are now deposited in the British Museum. The French family of Latouche came to Castle Street about one hundred years ago, and one of them, in 1778, upheld the shattered credit of the Government by a loan of £20,000 to the Lord-Lieutenant. Fishamble Street has historical and classic memories, and traditions of Handel consecrate this now obscure locality.

Handel spent a year in Dublin. His "Messiah" was composed there, and first performed for the benefit of Mercer's Hospital. How content he was with his reception is expressed in a letter to a friend. "I cannot," he says, "sufficiently express the kind treatment I receive here, but the politeness of this generous nation cannot be unknown to you."

Dublin Quays are likewise illustrated by great names. On Usher's Quay may still be seen the once magnificent Moira House, the princely residence of Lord Moira, afterwards Marquis of Hastings, Governor-General of India. A hundred years ago it was the Holland House of Dublin, sparkling with all the wit, splendour, rank, and influence of the metropolis. The decorations were unsurpassed in the kingdom for beauty and grandeur. The very windows were inlaid with mother-o'-pearl.

After the Union, the family in disgust quitted Ireland; Moira house was left tenantless for some years, and then finally was sold for the use of the pauper poor of Dublin. The decorations were removed, the beautiful gardens turned into offices, the upper story of the edifice was taken off, and the entire building pauperized as much as possible to suit its inmates and its title—"The Mendicity."

In the good old times the Lord Mayor treated the Lord-Lieutenant to a new play every Christmas, when the Corporation acted Mysteries upon the stage in Hoggin Green, where the College now stands. The Mysteries were on various subjects. In one, the tailors had orders to find Pilate and his wife clothed accordingly; the butchers were to supply the tormentors; the mariners and vintners represented Noah. At that period the Lord-Lieutenants held their court at Kilmainham, or Thomas Court, for Dublin Castle was not made a viceregal residence until the reign of Elizabeth. The parliaments, too, were ambulatory. Sometimes they met in the great aisle of Christ Church, that venerable edifice whose echoes have been destined to give back such conflicting sounds. What changes in its ritual and its worshippers! What scenes have passed before its high altar since first erected by the Danish bishop, whose body, in pallium and mitre, lay exposed to view but a few years since, after a sleep of eight hundred years. Irish kings and Norman conquerors have trod the aisles. There Roderick was inaugurated, the last king of Ireland; there Strongbow sleeps, first of the Norman conquerors, and, until the middle of the last century, all payments were made at his tomb, as if in him alone, living or dead, the citizens had their strength; there Lambert Simnel was crowned with a crown taken from the head of the Virgin Mary; there Cromwell worshipped before he went forth to devastate; there the last Stuart knelt in prayer before he threw the last stake at the Boyne for an empire; and there William of Nassau knelt in gratitude for the victory, with the crown upon his head, forgotten by James in his ignominious flight.

And how many rituals have risen up to heaven from that ancient altar, each *anathema maranatha* to the other—the solemn chants of the early church; the gorgeous ritual of the mass; in Elizabeth's time, the simple liturgy of the English Church in the English tongue; this, too, was prohibited in its turn, and for ten years the Puritans wailed and howled against kings and liturgies in the ancient edifice; there the funeral oration for the death of Cromwell was pronounced, entitled, "*Threni Hibernici,* or Ireland sympathizing with England for the loss of their Josiah (Oliver Cromwell)." Once again rose the incense of the mass while King James was amongst us; but William quenched the lights on the altar, and established once more the English Liturgy in its simplicity and beauty. But so little, during all these changes, had the Irish to do with the cathedral of their capital, that by an Act passed in 1380 no Irishman was permitted to hold in it any situation or office; and so strictly was the law enforced, that Sir John Stevenson was the first Irishman admitted, as even vicar-choral.

Many are the themes of interest to be found in Mr. Gilbert's "History of Dublin," concerning those ancient times when Sackville Street was a marsh, Merrion Square an exhausted quarry, the undulations so beautiful in its present verdant state being but the accident of excavation; when St. Stephen's Green, with its ten fine Irish acres, was a compound of meadow, quagmire, and ditch; when Mountjoy Square was a howling wilderness, and North Georges Street and Summer Hill were far away in the country, and when the Danes, rudely expelled by Norman swords from the south of the Liffey, were stealing over the river to found a settlement on the north side.

Our fathers have told us of Dublin in later times, before the Union, when a hundred lords and two hundred commoners enriched and enlivened our city with their wealth and magnificence. Dublin was then at the summit of its glory; but when the colonists sold their parliament to England, and the Lords and Commons vanished, and their mansions became hospitals and poorhouses, and all wealth, power, influence, and magnificence were transferred to the loved mother country, then the "City of the Dark Water" sank into very pitiable insignificance. The proud Norman spirit of independence was broken at last, and there was no great principle to replace it. Having no large sympathies with the Irish nation, no idea of country, nationality, or any other grand word by which is expressed the resolve of self-reliant men to be self-governed, the colonists became petty, paltry, and selfish in aim; imitative in manners and feelings; apathetic, even antagonistic to all national advance; bound to England by helpless fear and servile hope; content so as they could rest under her great shadow, secure from the mysterious horrors of Popery, preserved in the blessing of a church establishment, and allowed to worship even the shadow of transcendent Majesty. Then Dublin ambition was satisfied and happy; for there is no word so instinctively abhorrent, so invincibly opposed to all the prejudices of Dublin society, as patriotism.

From this cursory glance over the antecedents of our metropolis, the cause of her anti-Irishism is plainly deducible from the fact, that at no epoch was Dublin an Irish city. The inhabitants are a blended race, descended of Danes, Normans, Saxon settlers, and mongrel Irish. The country of their affections is England. They have known no other mother. With the proud old princes and chiefs of the ancient Irish race they have no more affinity than (to use Mr. Macaulay's illustration) the English of Calcutta with the nation of Hindustan, and from this colonial position a certain Dublin idiosyncrasy of character has resulted, which makes the capital distinct in feeling from the rest of Ireland.

Meanwhile the destiny of the ancient race is working out, not in happiness or prosperity, but in stern, severe discipline. Unchanged and unchangeable they remain, so far as change is effected by impulses arising from within. "Two thousand years," says Moore, "have passed over the hovel of the Irish peasant in vain." Such as they were when the first light of history rested on them, they are now; indolent and dreamy, patient and resigned as fatalists, fanatical as Bonzees, implacable as Arabs, cunning as Greeks, courteous as Spaniards, superstitious as savages, loving as children, clinging to the old home and the old sod and the old families with a tenderness that is always beautiful, sometimes heroic; loving to be ruled, with veneration in excess; ready to die like martyrs for a creed, a party, or the idol of the hour, but incapable of extending their sympathies beyond the family or the clan; content with the lowest place in Europe; stationary amid progression; isolated from the European family; without power or influence; lazily resting in the past while the nations are wrestling in the present for the future. Children of the ocean, yet without commerce; idle by thousands, yet without manufactures; gifted with quick intellect and passionate hearts, yet literature and art die out amongst them for want of aid or sympathy; without definite aims, without energy or the earnestness which is the vital life of heroic deeds; dark and blind through prejudice and ignorance, they can neither resist nobly nor endure wisely; chafing in bondage, yet their epileptic fits of liberty are marked only by wild excesses, and end only in sullen despair.

Yet it was not in the providence of God that the fine elements of humanity in such a people should still continue to waste and stagnate during centuries of inaction, while noble countries and fruitful lands, lying silent since creation, were waiting the destined toilers and workers, who, by the sweat of the brow, shall change them to living empires.

Two terrible calamities fell upon Ireland—famine and pestilence; and by these two dread ministers of God's great purposes, the Irish race were uprooted and driven forth to fulfil their appointed destiny. A million of our people emigrated; a million of our people died under these judgments of God. Seventeen millions worth of property passed from time-honoured names into the hands of strangers. The echoes of the old tongue—call it Pelasgian, Phœnician, Celtic, Irish, what you will, still the oldest in Europe, is dying out at last along the stony plains of Mayo and the wild sea-cliffs of the storm-rent western shore. Scarcely a million and a half are left of people too old to emigrate, amidst roofless cabins and ruined villages, who speak that language now. Exile, confiscation, or death, was the final fate written on the page of history for the much-enduring children of Ireland. One day they may reassert themselves in the new world, or in other lands. Australia, with its skies of beauty and its pavement of gold, may be given to them as America to the Saxon, but how low must a nation have fallen at home when even famine and plague come to be welcomed as the levers of progression and social elevation. Some wise purpose of God's providence lies, no doubt, at the reverse side, but we have not yet turned the leaf.

The ancient race who, thousands of years ago, left the cradle of the sun to track him to the ocean, are now flung on the coast of another hemisphere to begin once more their destined westward march; and like the Israelites of old, they, too, might tell in that new country: "A Syrian ready to perish was our father!"

They fled across the Atlantic like a drift of autumn leaves—"pestilence-stricken multitudes"—and the sea was furrowed by the dead as the plague-ships passed along.

One would say a doom had been laid upon our people—the wandering Io of humanity—a destiny of weeping and unrest.

Of old the kings at Tara sat throned with their faces to the west: was it a symbol or a prophecy of the future of their nation? when from every hill in Ireland could be seen—

"The remnant of our people
Sweeping westward, wild and woful,
Like the cloud-rack of a tempest,
Like the withered leaves of autumn."

Lady Jane Francesca Agnes Wilde

From the Atlantic to the Pacific, where the Rocky Mountains bar like a portal the land of gold—through the islands of the Southern Ocean to the great desolate world of Australia, seeking as it were the lost home of their fathers, and doomed to make the circuit of the earth—still onward flows the tide of human life—that inexhaustible race which has cleared the forests of Canada, built the cities and made all the railroads of the States, given thousands to the red plains of the Crimea, overran California and peopled Australia—the race whose destiny has made them the instruments of all civilization, though they have never reaped its benefits.

Yet we cannot believe that the Irish race is doomed for ever to work and suffer without the glory of success; for the Celtic element is necessary to humanity as a great factor in human progress. It is the subtle, spiritual fire that warms and permeates the ruder clay of other races, giving them new, vivid, and magnetic impulses to growth and expansion.

The children of the early wanderers from the Isles of the Sea will still continue to fulfil their mission as world-workers and world-movers. Across the breadth of earth they will found new nations, each a greater and a stronger Ireland, where they will have the certainty of power, station, and reward denied them at home. But neither change nor progress nor the severing ocean will destroy the electric chain that binds them lovingly to their ancient mother in that true sympathy with country and kinship that ever burns in the Irish heart.

The new Ireland across the seas, whether in America or in Australia, will still cherish with sacred devotion the beautiful legends, the pathetic songs, the poetry and history and the heroic traditions of the old, well-loved country as eternal verses of the Bible of humanity, with all the light and music of the fanciful fairy period, such as I have tried to gather into a focus in these volumes, along with the holy memories of those martyrs of our race whose names are for ever associated with the words Liberty and Nationhood, but whose tragic fate has illustrated so many mournful pages in the history of the Irish past.

On the Ancient Races of Ireland [20]

That there was a time—after "the Spirit of God moved on the face of the waters, and separated the dry land from the sea"—when the present British Isles formed a continuous and integral portion of the European Continent is the received opinion of the scientific. With that continuity of surface (whether before or after the glacial period matters not in the present inquiry) there was, we know, a uniform dispersion of vegetable and animal life over this portion of the globe; and so long as this country enjoyed the temperature and climate it now possesses, it must have been an emerald land—humid, green, and fertile, affording pasturage and provender for the largest herbivoræ—the mammoth, elephant, and musk ox, the reindeer, the wild boar, and perhaps even the woolly rhinoceros. The primitive races of horned cattle, possibly the red deer, and undoubtedly the largest and noblest of cervine creatures, the gigantic Irish deer, or *Cervus megaceros*, besides the wild pig, and smaller mammals, as well as birds and fishes innumerable, must then have existed here.

How long that condition of the land known now as Ireland existed, what geological revolutions occurred, or what time elapsed during its continuance, is but matter of speculation; but a "repeal of the union" took place, and Great Britain and Ireland became as they now are, and as they are likely to remain, geographically separated, although united in interest as well as government. In all probability the great pine forests, with some of the yews, the oaks, and the birch, had at this time been submerged beneath the lowest strata of our bogs.

It was after this epoch, I believe, that man first set foot upon the shores of Erin—a country well wooded, abundantly stocked with animals, and abounding in all nature's blessings suited to the well-being of the human race; with fowls in its woods and on its shores; fish in its seas, lakes and rivers; deer and other game in its forest glades, oxen on its pastures, fuel in its bogs; and a climate, although moist and variable, on the whole mild and temperate.

Let us now go back for a moment and take a glance at the map of the world. The sacred writings tell us, and the investigations of historians, antiquarians, and philologists confirm the statement, that the cradle of mankind was somewhere between the Caspian Sea and the great River Euphrates. Without entering too minutely into the subject, I may state briefly that the human family separated in process of time into three great divisions—the African, the Asiatic, and the Indo-European. With the latter only we have to deal. As population increased, it threw off its outshoots; and emigration, the great safeguard of society, and the ordained means of peopling as well as cultivating and civilizing the earth, began to impel the races and tribes still farther and farther from the birthplace of humanity. But in those days the process was somewhat slower and more gradual than that which now sends an Irish family across 3,500 miles of ocean in a week.

With but the rudest means of transit, hordes of the primitive races passed up the banks of the great rivers, the Euphrates, the Nile, the Volga, the Danube, and the Rhone; while other tribes, in all likelihood more advanced and cultivated, wandered along the coasts, peopling as they went the northern shores of the Mediterranean and the Black Sea.

That an early and uncultivated people passed up the Danube in their immigration, and settled for centuries on its banks, when Europe was a tangled wilderness, inhabited by the auroch and the gigantic deer, there can be no manner of doubt; for they have left memorials of their existence in the unerring and enduring remains of their sepulchres, their tools, and weapons, from the Black Sea to Switzerland and Savoy. In Switzerland this primitive people rested for a considerable period, perhaps for many centuries, forming for themselves those peculiar piled lacustrine habitations on the shores of its picturesque inland waters, known as "Pfaulbauten"—the analogues, and in all probability the types, of the crannoges recently discovered in Ireland and Scotland, to which countries the scattered fragments of that race finally carried this special form of domestic architecture. The lowest strata of implements were deposited beneath the sites of these pfaulbauten; and in some of the more ancient ones the only remains are those of stone, flint, and pottery—the former resembling in a remarkable manner the stone tools and weapons of the primitive Irish.

What the language of this early Helvetian people was, we have no means of ascertaining; but that their exodus was one of haste and compulsion, and probably the result of invasion by a superior and more cultivated race, is almost certain. Driven from their mountain homes, they passed down the banks of the Rhine and the Elbe, and helped to people North-western Europe, forming with those who arrived coastwise the great nation of the Gauls and Belgæ. It is not unlikely that this littoral wave of population carried with them the metallurgic arts; for we find in their tombs and barrows on the coasts of Spain, France, and Brittany, bronze celts identical in shape with some of those discovered in our own country.

Still passing westwards towards the setting sun, some members of this early people stood at length face to face with the white cliffs of Kent. Impelled by curiosity and the thirst for knowledge, man's undeviating enterprise soon sent these hardy people across the narrow strait that divides Britain from the continent of Europe, centuries before the ships of Tarshish voyaged from Tyre and Sidon to trade with Britain for the tin of Cornwall, to alloy, harden, and beautify into bronze the copper with which Solomon decorated the temple of Jerusalem.

To the restless Celt the breadth of this new possession was but a slight impediment to his western progress, and once more he looked upon the blue waters of the salt sea, and beyond them, to the green hills of Erin. A plank—a single-piece canoe—formed out of an oak-tree by fire and a sharp stone, or a wicker curragh covered with hides, would soon waft him from Portpatrick to Donaghadee, or even from Anglesea to Howth.

Here, then, the story of our race begins, and the immediate object of this inquiry commences. That man, as he first stood on this island, was in a rude, uncultivated state, without a knowledge of letters or manufactures—skilled in those arts only by which, as a nomad hunter and fisher, he supported life and ministered to his simple wants—there can be no manner of doubt. Clad in the skins of animals he slew, which were sewn together with their sinews or intestines—his weapons and tools formed of flint, stone, bone, wood or horn—his personal decoration, shells, amber, attractive pebbles collected on the beach, or the teeth of animals strung together in a rude necklace, or bound round the wrists and arms; and his religion, if any, Pagan, Sun-worship, or Druidism, man first stood, in all probability, on the north-eastern shores of Erin. It may be unpalatable to our national vanity to learn that the early colonists of Ireland did not come here clad in purple and gold direct from Phœnicia, in brazen-prowed triremes, with the mariner's compass and the quadrant; or stood for the first time upon the shores of Hibernia armed *cap-à-pied* in glittering armour, as Minerva sprang from the front of Jove; but it is, nevertheless, indisputably true, that the first people were such as I have described them.

No date can be assigned to the period of the first inhabitation, but as evidence of the primitive condition of the race it is sufficient to state that human bodies clad in deer-skin have been discovered in our bogs; that flint weapons in abundance have been found all over Ireland, but especially in the North, where that peculiar lithological condition chiefly exists; and that stone tools have been dug up in thousands all over the country, but more particularly from the beds of our rivers, marking the sites of contested fords, which were the scenes of sanguinary conflicts, as on the Shannon and the Bann; and that all these are referrible to a period when the Irish had no knowledge of metals, and could neither spin nor weave.

To Northern archæologists belongs the credit of that theory which divides the ages of man according to the material evidences of the arts of bygone times, as into those of stone, of copper, gold, and bronze, and of iron and silver. While I have no doubt that, generally speaking, such was the usual progress of development in those particulars, I deny that this division can, as a rule, be applied to Ireland, where undoubtedly each period overlapped the succeeding, so as to mix the one class of implement with another, even as I myself have seen on the great cultivated plain of Tyre harrow-pins formed of flints and sharp stones stuck into the under surface of a broad board; and on that battle field—

"Where Persia's victim hordes

First bowed beneath the brunt of Hella's sword,"

I have picked up flint and obsidian arrow-heads, although we know that the Athenians, whose remains still lie beneath the tumulus of Marathon, gave way before the long-handled metallic spears of Asia; and the stone missile, in one of its most formidable shapes, is not yet abandoned in this country.

I hold it as susceptible of demonstration, that man in similar stages of his career all over the world acts alike, so far as is compatible with climate, his wants, and the materials that offer to his hand, even from the banks of the Niger or Zambesi to the islands of the South Sea, or the regions inhabited by the Laps and Esquimaux. Thus, whenever man acquires or discovers a new art, he first applies it to continue the fashion of its predecessor, until accident, necessity, or ingenuity induces him to modify the reproduction. The first arrow-head and spear is almost the same all over the world, and is the type of that in metal; and the stone celt or hatchet formed, as I have proved elsewhere, the model for the copper or bronze implement for a like use in both ancient Etruria and ancient Ireland.

Discussions may arise as to whether our knowledge of metals was a separate, independent discovery of our own, or was acquired by intercourse with other nations more advanced than ourselves. In answer thereto I can only say that we have no evidence or authority for the latter supposition; and that, as we possessed abundant materials on the one hand, and had sufficient native ingenuity on the other, it is most likely that our discovery of metals—at least of gold, copper, and tin—was independent of extrinsic influence. So far removed from the centres of civilization, unconquered by the Roman legion, uninfluenced by Saxon or Frankish art, and with undoubted evidences of development and styles of art peculiar to ourselves, both in form and decoration, it is but fair, until some stronger arguments have been brought against it, to believe that we were the discoverers and smelters of our minerals, and the fabricators of our metallic weapons, tools, and ornaments. That some Grecian influence pervaded the early Irish metallurgic art, as exhibited by some of our leaf-shaped sword blades, is true; but it is an exceptional instance, and the form is common to almost all countries in which bronze sword blades have been found.

With regard to the dwellings of the early race we are not left to mere conjecture, for not long ago a log hut was discovered fourteen feet below the surface of a bog in the county of Donegal. This very antique dwelling was twelve feet square, and nine high; and consisted of an upper and lower chamber, which were probably mere sleeping apartments. The oaken logs of which it was constructed are believed to have been hewn with stone hatchets, some of which were found on the premises, thus identifying it with the pre-metallic period of our history. Man soon becomes gregarious, and passes from the hunter and the fisher to the shepherd, and thence to the agriculturist. The land is cleared of wood; the wild animals either die out, or are rendered subservient to his will. The domestication of animals in most instances precedes, and always accompanies, the pastoral state of existence; and to that condition the patriarchal stage ensues, and afterwards that of the monarchical. To such phases of development, from the age of escape from the rudest barbarism, to the most cultivated condition in government, polite literature, art and science, Ireland was, I believe, no exception. Of the shepherd state we still possess the most abundant proofs, in the numerous earthen raths, lisses, and forts scattered all over the country, and from which so many of our townlands and other localities take their names; but especially marking the sites of the primitive inhabitation on our goodly pastures, although now mere grassy, annular elevations, varying in area from a few perches to several acres, and in many instances alone preserved by the hallowed traditions or popular superstitions of the people.

Such of those landmarks of the past as still remain, out of thousands that have been obliterated, show us that in those parts of Ireland, at least, where they exist, there was once a dense population, even during the shepherd stage of its inhabitation. And if in the progress of events, uncontrolled by human agency, and brought about by influences that we have so recently mourned over and still deplore, but could not prevent, we are now again becoming a pastoral people, we are only returning to that state of existence for which this country is peculiarly adapted, and was, I believe, originally intended—that of being the greatest grass and green-crop soil and climate in the world.

The pastoral was undoubtedly the normal, one of the oldest, and beyond all question, the longest continued state in Ireland; and, although changed by internal dissensions, invasion, confiscation, and foreign rule, is still remembered by the people among whom its influence, slumbering, but not dead, now and then crops out in questions of "tenant right." Years ago I showed, from the animal remains found in our forts, bogs, and crannoges, that centuries upon centuries before short-horned improved breeds of cattle and sheep commanded at our agricultural shows the admiration of Europe, we had here breeds of oxen which are not now surpassed by the best races of Holland and Great Britain; and which are unequalled in the present day even by those on the fertile plains of Meath, Limerick, or Roscommon, or throughout the golden vale of Tipperary. We were then a cattle-rearing, flesh-eating people; our wealth was our cattle; our wars were for our cattle; the ransom of our chieftains was in cattle; our taxes were paid in cattle; the price paid for our most valuable manuscripts was so many cows. Even in comparatively modern times our battle cloaks were made of leather; our traffic and barter were the Pecuaniæ of our country; and the "Tain-bo-Cuailne," the most famous metrical romance of Europe, after the "Niebelungenlied," is but the recital of a cattle raid from Connaught into Louth during the reign of Mave, Queen of Connaught—a personage transmitted to us by Shakspeare, as the Queen Mab of the "Midsummer Night's Dream." And, although the Anglo-Norman invasion is usually attributed to the love of an old, one-eyed, hoarse-voiced King of Leinster, sixty years of age, for Dervorgil (attractive, we must presume, though but little his junior in years), and who became the Helen of the Irish Iliad, when "the valley lay smiling before her," she was but an insignificant item in the stock abduction from the plains of Breffny along the boggy slopes of Shemore.

The Boromean, or cattle tribute, which the King of Tara demanded from the Leinstermen, was perhaps the cause of the greatest intestinal feud which ever convulsed so small a space of European ground for so great a length of time. This triennial cattle tax, besides 5,000 ounces of silver, 5,000 cloaks, and 5,000 brazen vessels, consisted of 15,000 head of cattle of different descriptions, the value of which, at the present price of stock, would amount to about £130,000. The cattle tribute also paid to the Prince or petty King of Cashel upwards of a thousand years ago was 6,500 cows, 4,500 oxen, 4,500 swine, and 1,200 sheep; in all, 16,700, or, at the present value of stock, between £80,000 and £100,000. In addition to which we read of horses and valuables of various descriptions.

Brian O'Kennedy, who drove the Norsemen from the shores of Clontarf, derived his cognomen of Borrome from his reimposition of this cattle tax. And in the *Leabhar-na-Garth*, or ancient Book of Rights and Privileges of the Kings of Erin, the cattle statistics, as they are there set forth, show that the Irish were solely a pastoral people; and the whole text and tenor of the Irish annals and histories, and the notices of the wars of the Desmonds and of O'Neil, confirm this view.

The great raths of Ireland, where the people enclosed their cattle by night, have been erroneously termed "Danish forts," but when the shannaghees are pressed for further information as to the date of their erection they say, "They were made by them ould Danes that came over with Julius Cæsar." If, however, inquiry be made of the old illiterate Irish-speaking population, they will tell you that they were made by "the good people," and are inhabited by the fairies. Hence the veneration that has in a great measure tended to their preservation; and I have no doubt that the ancient indigenous and venerated thorns that still decorate their slopes or summits are the veritable descendants of the quickset hedges that helped to form the breastworks, or staked defences, on their summits.

These forts are almost invariably to be found in the fattest pastures; so that if any of my friends were in the present day to ask me where they could best invest in land, I would fearlessly answer, "Wherever you find most ancient raths remaining;" and I know that many of our cattle prizes have been carried off by sheep and oxen fed upon the grass lands cleared and fertilized by the early Celts more than a thousand years ago, and a sod of which has not been turned for centuries. They were not originally the gentle slopes that now diversify the surface, but consisted in steep ramparts or earthworks, with an external ditch, on which a stout paling was erected against man or beast, a form of structure still seen in the kraal of the New Zealander. The Irish rath-maker was an artificer of skill, and held in high esteem, and occupied a dignified position at the great feasts of Tara—second only to the ollamh and the physician. That the soil of which they were constructed had been not only originally rich, but had been subjected to man's industry, is proved by the fact that it is now frequently turned out upon the neighbouring sward as one of the best of manures. Within these raths, some of which had double, and even treble entrenchments, were erected the dwellings of the people and their chiefs, the latter of whom were often interred within the mounds, or beneath the cromlechs that still exist in their interior, as, for example, in the "Giant's Ring," near Belfast. In some instances they also contained in their sides and centres stone caves, that were probably used as store-houses, granaries, or places of security.

The earliest historic race of Ireland was a pastoral people called Firbolgs, said to be of Greek or Eastern origin; probably a branch of that great Celtic race which, having passed through Europe and round its shores, found a resting-place at last in Ireland. Of the Fomorians, Nemedians, and other minor invaders, we need not speak, as they have left nothing by which to track their footsteps. The old annalists bring them direct from the Ark, and in a straight line from Japhet. The coming of Pharaoh's daughter from Egypt with her ships may be also considered apocryphal. But the Firbolgs begin our authentic history. They had laws and social institutions, and established a monarchical government at the far-famed Hill of Tara, about which our early centres of civilization sprung, and where we have now most of those great pasturelands—those plains of Meath that can beat the world for their fattening qualities, and which supply neighbouring countries with their most admired meats.

I cannot say that the Firbolg was a cultivated man, but I think he was a shepherd and an agriculturist. I doubt if he knew anything, certainly not much, of metallurgy; but it does not follow that he was a mere savage, no more than the Maories of New Zealand were when we first came in contact with them.

The Firbolgs were a small, straight-haired, swarthy race, who have left a portion of their descendants with us to this very day. A genealogist (their own countryman resident in Galway about two hundred years ago) described them as dark-haired, talkative, guileful, strolling, unsteady, "disturbers of every Council and Assembly," and "promoters of discord." I believe they, together with the next two races about to be described, formed the bulk of our so-called Celtic population—combative, nomadic on opportunity, enduring, litigious, but feudal and faithful to their chiefs; hard-working for a spurt (as in their annual English emigration); not thrifty, but, when their immediate wants are supplied, lazy, especially during the winter.

To these physical and mental characters described by MacFirbis let me add those of the unusual combination of blue or blue-grey eyes and dark eyelashes with a swarthy complexion. This peculiarity I have only remarked elsewhere in Greece; the mouth and upper gum is not good, but the nose is usually straight. In many of this and the next following race there was a peculiarity that has not been alluded to by writers—the larynx, or, as it used to be called, the *pomum Adami*, was remarkably prominent, and became more apparent from the uncovered state of the neck. The sediment of this early people still exists in Ireland, along with the fair-complexioned Dananns, and forms the bulk of the farm-labourers, called in popular phraseology *Spalpeens*, that yearly emigrate to England. In Connaught they now chiefly occupy a circle which includes the junction of the counties of Mayo, Galway, Roscommon, and Sligo. They, with their fair-faced brothers (at present the most numerous), are also to be found in Kerry and Donegal; and they nearly all speak Irish.

By statistics procured from our Great Midland Western Railway alone I learn that on an average 30,000 of these people, chiefly the descendants of the dark Firbolgs and the fair Dananns, emigrate annually to England for harvest work, to the great advantage of the English farmer and the Irish landlord. The acreage of arable land for these people runs from two to six acres.

Connecting this race with the remains of the past, I am of opinion that they were the first rath or earthen-mound and enclosure makers; that they mostly buried their dead without cremation, and, in cases of distinguished personages, beneath the cromlech or the tumulus. Their heads were oval or long in the anteroposterior diameter, and rather flattened at the sides: examples of these I have given and descanted upon when I first published my Ethnological Researches, which have been fully confirmed by the late Andreas Retzius. It is, however, unnecessary, even if space or advisability permitted, for me to allude to such matters, as that great work the "Crania Britannica" has lithographed typical specimens of this long-headed race.

The next immigration we hear of in the "Annals" is that of the *Tuatha-de-Dananns*, a large, fair-complexioned, and very remarkable race; warlike, energetic, progressive, skilled in metal work, musical, poetical, acquainted with the healing art, skilled in Druidism, and believed to be adepts in necromancy and magic, no doubt the result of the popular idea respecting their superior knowledge, especially in smelting and in the fabrication of tools, weapons, and ornaments. From these two races sprang the Fairy Mythology of Ireland.

It is strange that, considering the amount of annals and legends transmitted to us, we have so little knowledge of Druidism or Paganism in ancient Ireland. However, it may be accounted for in this wise: That those who took down the legends from the mouths of the bards and annalists, or those who subsequently transcribed them, were Christian missionaries whose object was to obliterate every vestige of the ancient forms of faith.

The Dananns spoke the same language as their predecessors, the Firbolgs. They met and fought for the sovereignty. The "man of metal" conquered and drove a great part of the others into the islands on the coast, where it is said the Firbolg race took their last stand. Eventually, however, under the influence of a power hostile to them both, these two people coalesced, and have to a large extent done so up to the present day. They are the true old Irish peasant and small farming class.

The Firbolg was a bagman, so called, according to Irish authorities, because he had to carry up clay in earthen bags to those terraces in Greece now vine-clad. As regards the other race there is more difficulty in the name. Tuath or Tuatha means a tribe or tribe-district in Irish. Danann certainly sounds very Grecian; and if we consider their remains, we find the long, bronze, leaf-shaped sword, so abundant in Ireland, identical with weapons of the same class found in Attica and other parts of Greece.

Then, on the other hand, their physiognomy, their fair or reddish hair, their size, and other circumstances, incline one to believe that they came down from Scandinavian regions after they had passed up as far as they thought advisable into North-western Europe. If the word Dane was known at the time of their arrival here, it would account for the designation of many of our Irish monuments as applied by Molyneux and others. Undoubtedly the Danann tribes presented Scandinavian features, but did not bring anything but Grecian art. After the "Stone period," so called, of which Denmark and the south of Sweden offer such rich remains, I look upon the great bulk of the metal work of the North, especially in the swords in the Copenhagen and Stockholm Museums, as Asiatic; while Ireland possesses not only the largest native collection of metal weapon-tools, usually denominated "celts," of any country in the world, but the second largest amount of swords and battle-axes. And moreover these, and all our other metal articles, show a well-defined rise and development from the simplest and rudest form in size and use to that of the most elaborately constructed and the most beautifully adorned.

I believe that these Tuatha-de-Dananns, no matter from whence they came, were, in addition to their other acquirements, great masons, although not acquainted with the value of cementing materials. I think they were the builders of the great stone Cahirs, Duns, Cashels, and Caves in Ireland; while their predecessors constructed the earthen works, the raths, circles, and forts that diversify the fields of Erin. The Dananns anticipated Shakespeare's grave-digger, for they certainly made the most lasting sepulchral monuments that exist in Ireland, such, for example, as New Grange, Douth, Knowth, and Slieve-na-Calleagh and other great cemeteries. Within the interior and around these tombs were carved, on unhewn stones, certain archaic markings, spires, volutes, convolutes, lozenge-shaped devices, straight, zigzag, and curved lines, and incised indentations, and a variety of other insignia, which, although not expressing language, were symbolical, and had an occult meaning known only to the initiated. These markings, as well as those upon the urns, were copied in the decorations of the gold and bronze work of a somewhat subsequent period. The Dananns conquered the inferior tribes in two celebrated pitched battles, those of the Northern and Southern Moytura. On these fields we still find the caves, the stone circles, the monoliths, and dolmans or cromlechs that marked particular events, and the immense cairns that were raised in honour of the fallen chieftains.

Although many of the warriors of the Firbolgs fled to their island fastnesses on the coasts of Galway and Donegal, no doubt a large portion of them remained in the inland parts of the country, and in that very locality to which I have adverted, which is almost midway between the sites of the two battles, in a line stretching between Mayo and Sligo, where in time the two races appear to have coalesced by that natural law which brings the dark and the fair together.

Moreover it has been recorded that the conquering race sent their small dark opponents into Connaught, while they themselves took possession of the rich lands further east, and not only established themselves at Tara but spread into the south. It is remarkable that in time large numbers of the Dananns themselves were banished to the West, and likewise that the last forcible deportation of the native Irish race (so late as the seventeenth century) was when the people of this province got the choice of going "to Connaught or Hell," in the former of which, possibly, they joined some of the original stock. The natural beauty of the lakes and mountains of Connaught remains as it was thousands of years ago; but no doubt if some of the legislators of the period to which I have already referred could now behold its fat pasture-plains, they might prefer them to the flax lands of Ulster.

These Dananns had a globular form of head, of which I have already

Lady Jane Francesca Agnes Wilde

published examples. For the most part I believe they burned their dead or sacrificed to their manes, and placed an urn with its incinerated contents—human or animal—in the grave, where the hero was either stretched at length or crouched in an attitude similar to that adopted by the ancient Peruvians, as I have elsewhere explained. These Irish urns, which are the earliest relics of our ceramic art that have come down to the present time, are very graceful in form, and some of them most beautifully decorated, as may be seen in our various museums.

Specimens of this Danann race still exist, but have gradually mixed with their forerunners to the present day. Here is what old MacFirbis wrote of them two hundred years ago: "Every one who is fair-haired, vengeful, large, and every plunderer, professors of musical and entertaining performances, who are adepts of Druidical and magical arts, they are the descendants of the Tuatha-de-Dananns." They were not only fair but sandy in many instances, and consequently extensively freckled.

It is affirmed that the Dananns ruled in Ireland for a long time, until another inroad was made into the island by the Milesians—said to be brave, chivalrous, skilled in war, good navigators, proud, boastful, and much superior in outward adornment as well as mental culture, but probably not better armed than their opponents. They deposed the three last Danann kings and their wives, and rose to be, it is said, the dominant race—assuming the sovereignty, becoming the aristocracy and landed proprietors of the country, and giving origin to those chieftains that afterwards rose to the title of petty kings, and from whom some of the best families in the land with anything like Irish names claim descent, and particularly those with the prefix of the "O" or the "Mac." When this race arrived in Ireland I cannot tell, but it was some time prior to the Christian era. It is said they came from the coast of Spain, where they had long remained after their Eastern emigration.

Upon the site of what is believed to be the ancient Brigantium, now the entrance to the united harbours of Corunna and Ferrol, stands the great lighthouse known to all ships passing through the Bay of Biscay. Within this modern structure still exists the celebrated "Pharos of Hercules," which I investigated and described many years ago. That tower, it was said in metaphorical language, commanded a view of Ireland, and as such became the theme of Irish poems and legends. Certain it is that sailing north or north-westward from it the ships of the sons of Milesius and their followers could have reached Ireland without much coasting. If the story of Breogan's Tower is true, then it must have been erected in the time of lime-and-mortar building, and that is during the Roman occupation of Iberia and Gaul. How many thousands, rank and file, of these Spanish Milesians came here in their six or eight galleys and tried the fortunes of war from "the summit of the ninth wave from the shore" and conquered the entire Danann, Firbolg, and Fomorian population, I am unable to give the slightest inkling of, no more than I can of the so-called Phœnician intercourse with this country. Perhaps without going into the fanciful descriptions of the "Battle of Ventry Harbour," or the southern conquest of Ireland by the Iberian Milesians, we may find some more trustworthy illustrations of Spanish dwellings in the architecture of the town of Galway, and some picturesque representatives in the lithe upright figures and raven-haired, but blue-eyed maidens of the City of the Tribes. Here is what old MacFirbis, who, I suppose, claimed descent from the sons of Milesius, wrote about them: "Every one who is white of skin, brown of hair, bold, honourable, daring, prosperous, bountiful in the bestowal of property, and who is not afraid of battle or combat, they are the descendants of the sons of Milesius in Erin."

This high panegyric is only equalled by the prose and verse compositions of the ancient bards and rhymers and the modern historians, who have recorded the deeds of the great warriors, Ith, Heber, and Heremon, whose descendants boast to have been the rulers of the land. Even Moore, although he wrote such beautiful lyrics concerning this race in his early days, yet when he came to study history, he felt the same difficulty I do now. I do not dispute their origin or supremacy; but I fail to distinguish their early customs, their remains, or race from those of the Firbolgs or Dananns whom they conquered, and who left undoubted monuments peculiar to their time.

Now all these people—the piratical navigator along our coasts, the mid-

Lady Jane Francesca Agnes Wilde

Europe primitive shepherd and cultivator, the Northern warrior, and the Iberian ruler—were, according to my view, all derived from the one Celtic stock. They spoke the same language, and their descendants do so still. When they acquired a knowledge of letters they transmitted their history through the Irish language. No doubt they fused; but somehow a quick fusion of races has not been the general characteristic of the people of this country. Unlike the Anglo-Norman in later times, the Milesian was a long way from home; the rough sea of the Bay of Biscay rolled between him and his previous habitat; and if he became an absentee he was not likely to find much of his possessions on his return. It is to be regretted that while we have here such a quantity of poetical and traditional material respecting the Milesian invasion of Ireland, the Spanish annals or traditions have given us but very little information on that subject.

It would be most desirable if the Government or some Irish authority would send a properly instructed commissioner to investigate the Spanish annals, and see whether there is anything relating to the Spanish migrations to Ireland remaining in that country.

Besides the sparse introduction of Latin by Christian missionaries in the fifth century, some occasional Saxon words springing from peaceful settlers along our coasts and in commercial emporiums, and whatever Danish had crept into our tongue around those centres where the Scandinavians chiefly located themselves, and which were principally proper names of persons and places that became fixed in our vernacular, we find but one language among the Irish people until the arrival of the Anglo-Normans at the end of the twelfth century.

The linguistic or philological evidence on this subject is clearly decisive. The residue of the early races already described spoke one language, called Gaelic; so did the Scotch, the Welsh, and probably, in early times, the Britons and the Bretons. It was not only the popular conversational tongue used in the ordinary intercourse of life, but it was also employed in genealogies, annals, and other records in a special character, not quite peculiar to this country, but then common in Europe. Much has been said

423

about the necessity for a glossary of our ancient MSS., such as those at Saint Gall, in Trinity College, in the Royal Irish Academy, and in Belgian and English libraries; but there are very few ancient languages that do not require to be glossed in the present day, even as the words of Chaucer do.

The Government are now, under the auspices of our Master of the Rolls, and the special direction and supervision of Mr. J. T. Gilbert, giving coloured photographs of some of our ancient writings, and have promised that some of our remaining manuscripts will be translated. I see no occasion now for waiting for more elaborated philological dictionaries or glossaries while there are still some few Irish scholars in this country capable of giving a free but tolerably literal translation of these records that do not require any great acumen in rendering them into English. Is history to wait upon the final decision of philologists respecting a word or two in a manuscript, and to decide as to whether it may be of Sanscrit or any other origin?

No doubt some of my hearers may ask, What about the Oghams (or Ohams)? do they not show a very early knowledge of an alphabet? As yet this is a moot question. A rude pillar-stone, having upon it a tolerably straight edge, was in early times notched along its angle which served as a stem-line by nicks formed on it, and straight or oblique lines, singly or in clusters, proceeding from the stem. The decipherers of these inscriptions have, one and all, agreed upon the fact that these lines represented letters, syllables, or words, and that the language is either Irish or Latin. Therefore the persons who made them must have been aware of alphabetic writing and grammar. These carved monoliths are chiefly found in Kerry and Cork. Upon some of them Christian emblems are figured. The incising of the stone has evidently been performed by some rude instrument, either a flint or metallic pick; and it is remarkable that these pillars present scarcely any amount of dressing.

In Connaught, in my youth, the exception in remote districts was where the person spoke *both* English and Irish. In 1851, when we first took a census of the Irish-speaking population, after the country had lost three-quarters of a million of people, chiefly of the Irish race, we had then (to speak in round numbers) one and a half millions of Irish-speaking population. In 1861 they had fallen off by nearly half a million; and upon the taking of the last census in 1871 the entire Irish-speaking population was only 817,865. The percentages, according to the total population in our different provinces, were these: in Leinster 1.2, in Munster 27.7, in Ulster 4.6, and in Connaught 39.0; for the total of Ireland 15.1. Kilkenny and Louth are the counties of Leinster where the language is most spoken. In Munster they are Kerry, Clare, and Waterford; in Ulster, Donegal, where 28 per cent. of the population speak Irish; but in Connaught, to which I have already alluded as containing the remnant of the early Irish races, we have no less than 56 per cent. of Irish-speaking population in the counties of Mayo and Galway respectively. Of my own knowledge I can attest that a great many of these people cannot speak English. We thus see that of the population of Ireland, which in the present day might be computed at about five and a half millions, there were, at the time of taking the census in April, 1871, only 817,865; and I think I may prophesy that that is the very largest number that in future we will ever have to record. On the causes of this decadence it is not my province to descant. These Celts have been the great pioneers of civilization, and are now a power in the world. Are they not now numerically the dominant race in America? and have they not largely peopled Australia and New Zealand?

We have now arrived at a period when you might naturally expect the native annalist to make some allusion to conquest or colonization by the then mistress of the world. Without offering any reason for it, I have here only to remark that neither as warriors nor colonizers did the Romans ever set foot in Ireland; and hence the paucity of any admixture of Roman art amongst us.

To fill up a hiatus which might here occur in our migrations, I will mention a remarkable circumstance. A Christian youth of Romano-Saxon parentage, and probably of patrician origin, was carried off in a raid of Irish marauders, and employed as a swineherd in this very Ulster, the country of the Dalaradians, and lived here for several years, learning our customs and speaking our language. He escaped, however, to Munster, and thence to his native land of Britain or Normandy, from whence he returned in A.D. 432

with friends, allies, and missionaries, and passing in his galley into the mouth of the Boyne, walked up the banks of that famed stream, raised the paschal fire at Slane, and speedily introduced Christianity throughout Ireland.

In thus briefly alluding to the labours of St. Patrick, I wish to be understood to say that about the time of his mission there was much Saxon intercourse with this country, and the great missionary had not only many friends but several relatives residing here, and some of them on the very banks of the Boyne; and I believe that a considerable amount of civilization and some knowledge of Christianity had been introduced long previously; so that, although old King Laoghaire or Loury and his Druids did not bow the knee to the Most High God, nor accept the teaching of the beautiful hymn that Patrick and his attendants chanted as they passed up the grassy slopes of Tara, still there were many hundred people in Ireland ready to receive the glad tidings of the gospel of salvation.

Having finished with the Milesians, we now come to the Danes (so-called), the Scandinavians or Norsemen—the pagan Sea-Kings who made inroads on our coasts, despoiled our churches and monasteries, but at the same time, it must be confessed, helped to establish the commercial prosperity of some of our cities and towns from 795 to the time of the battle of Clontarf, A.D. 1014, when the belligerent portion of the Scandinavians were finally expelled the country. During the time I have specified, Dublin, Limerick, and Waterford belonged to these Northern people. They not only coasted round the island and never lost an opportunity of pillage and plunder, but they passed through the interior and carried their arms into the very centre of the land. The Danes left us very little ornamental work beyond what they lavished upon their swords and helmets; but, on the other hand, it should be borne in mind that there are no Irish antiquities, either social, warlike, or ecclesiastical, in the Scandinavian Museums.

Concerning their ethnological characters, I must again refer to the "Crania Britannica." In the records they were designated strangers, foreigners, pagans, gentiles, and also white and black foreigners, so that there were undoubtedly two races—the dark, and the fair or red, like as in the case of the Firbolgs or

Dananns. They were also styled "Azure Danes," probably on account of the shining hue of their armour.

I believe the fair section of that people to have been of Norwegian origin, while the dark race came from Jutland and the coast of Sweden; and both by the Orkneys, the coasts of Scotland, and the Isle of Man. Their skulls were large and well formed; they had a thorough knowledge of metal work, and especially iron; and, as I have shown elsewhere, their swords and spears were of great size and power, the former wielded as a slashing weapon, while those of their early opponents were of bronze, weak, and intended for stabbing. In nowhere else in Europe (that I am aware of) have these rounded, pointed, or bevelled heavy iron swords been found except in Ireland and Norway.

Large quantities of Danish remains have been discovered in deep sinkings made in Dublin; and several weapons, tools, and ornaments, believed to be of Scandinavian origin, have been found within a few inches of the surface on one of the battle-fields on the south side of the Liffey, within the last few years. Upon most of these I have already reported and given illustrations. I may mention one circumstance connected with this race. I never examined a battle-field of the Danes, nor a collection of Danish weapons or implements, that I did not find the well-adjusted scales and weights which the Viking had in his pocket for valuing the precious metals he procured either by conquest or otherwise.

Although considered hostile, these Scandinavian Vikings must have fraternized with the Irish. We know that they intermarried; for, among many other instances that might be adduced, I may mention that during the battle of Clontarf, when Sitric, the Danish king of Dublin, looked on the fight from the walls of the city, he was accompanied by his wife, the daughter of the aged king known as "Brian the Brave."

When, however, the Irish chieftains were not fighting with one another, they were often engaged in petty wars with the Scandinavians, who, in turn, were attacked by their own countrymen, the "Black Gentiles," especially on the plain of Fingall, stretching from Dublin to the Boyne, and which the white race chiefly occupied. It must not be supposed that the battle of

Clontarf ended the Danish occupation of Ireland; they still held the cities of Dublin, Limerick, and Waterford at least, and largely promoted the commercial prosperity in these localities—a prosperity which has not quite yet departed. I should like to present you with some remains of the Scandinavian language in Ireland, but the materials are very scanty.

We are now coming to a later period. The Romans had occupied Britain, the Saxons followed; the Danes had partial possession for a time; the Heptarchy prevailed until Harold, the last of the Saxon kings, fell at Hastings, and England bowed beneath that mixture of Norman, Gaulish, Scandinavian, and general Celtic blood that William brought with him from the shores of France. The Saxon dynasty was at an end, but the Britons of the day accepted their fate; and not only the soldiers, but the Norman barons fused with the people of that kingdom, and largely contributed to make it what it now is. This fusion of races, this assimilation of sentiments, this interchange of thought, this kindly culture, the higher elevating the lower, among whom they permanently reside, must always tend to great and good ends in raising a people to a nobler intellectual state.

The Anglo-Normans came here in 1172, a very mixed race, but their leaders were chiefly of French or Norman extraction. Why they came, or what they did, it is not for me to expatiate upon. I wish, however, to correct an assertion commonly made, to the effect that the Norman barons of Henry II. *then* conquered Ireland. They occupied some towns, formed a "Pale," levied taxes, sent in soldiery, distributed lands, and introduced a new language; but the "King's writ did not run;" the subjugation of Ireland did not extend over the country at large, and it remained till 1846 and the five or six following years to complete the conquest of the Irish race, by the loss of a tuberous esculent and the Governmental alteration in the value of a grain of corn. Then there went to the workhouse or exile upwards of two millions of the Irish race, besides those who died of pestilence. Having carefully investigated and reported upon this last great European famine, I have come to the conclusion just stated, without taking into consideration its political, religious, or national aspects.

Lady Jane Francesca Agnes Wilde

It appears to me that one of our great difficulties in Ireland has been the want of fusion—not only of races, but of opinions and sentiments, in what may be called a "give and take" system. As regards the intermixture, I think there cannot be a better one than the Saxon with the Celt. The Anglo-Normans, however, partially fused with the native Irish; for Strongbow married Eva the daughter of King Dermot; and from this marriage it has been clearly shown that Her Most Gracious Majesty the present Queen of Ireland and Great Britain is lineally descended. Several of the noble warriors who came over about that period have established great and widespread names in Ireland, among whom I may mention the Geraldines in Leinster, the De Burgos in Connaught, and the Butlers in Munster; and they and their descendants became, according to the old Latin adage, "more Irish than the Irish themselves."

Look what the intermixture of races has done for us in Ireland; the Firbolg brought us agriculture; the Danann the chemistry and mechanics of metal work; the Milesians beauty and governing power; the Danes commerce and navigation; the Anglo-Normans chivalry and organized government; and, in later times, the French emigrants taught us an improved art of weaving.

It would be more political than ethnological were I to enter upon the discussion of that subsequent period which would conduct us to the days of Cromwell or the Boyne, or, perhaps, to later periods, involving questions not pertinent to the present subject.

But I must here say a word or two respecting Irish art. In architecture, in decorative tone-work, from archaic markings that gave a tone and character to all subsequent art, in our beauteous crosses, in our early metal work, in gold and bronze, carried on from the pagan to the Christian period, and in our gorgeously illuminated MS. books, we have got a style of art that is specially and peculiarly Irish, and that has no exact parallel elsewhere, and was only slightly modified by Norman or Frankish design.

Time passed, and events accumulated; political affairs intermingle, but the anthropologist should try and keep clear of them. At the end of the reign of Elizabeth a considerable immigration of English took place into the South of

429

Ireland. Subsequently the historic episode of the "Flight of the Earls," O'Neil and O'Donnell, brought matters to a climax; and the early part of the reign of the first James is memorable for the "Plantation of Ulster," when a number of Celtic Scots with some Saxons returned to their brethren across the water; and about the same time the London companies occupied large portions of this fertile province, and the early Irish race were transplanted by the Protector to the West, as I have already stated. It must not be imagined that this was the first immigration. The Picts passed through Ireland, and no doubt left a remnant behind them. And in consequence of contiguity, the Scottish people must early have settled upon our northern coasts. When the adventurous Edward Bruce made that marvellous inroad into Ireland at the end of the fourteenth century and advanced into the bowels of the land, he carried with him a Gaelic population cognate with our own people, and in all probability left a residue in Ulster, thus leavening the original Firbolgs, Tuatha-de-Danann, and Milesians, with the exception of the county of Donegal, which still holds a large Celtic population speaking the old Irish tongue, and retaining the special characters of that people as I have already described them. This Scotic race, as it now exists in Ulster, and of which we have specimens before us, I would sum up with three characteristics. That they were courageous is proved by their shutting the gates and defending the walls of Derry; that they were independent and lovers of justice has been shown by their establishment of tenant right; and that they were industrious and energetic is manifest by the manufacturers of Belfast. Do not, I entreat my brethren of Ulster, allow these manufactures to be jeopardized, either by masters or men, by any disagreements, which must lead to the decay of the fairest and wealthiest province and one of the most beautiful cities in this our native land.

Footnotes

[1]The terms Dryad and Druid may be compared as containing the same root and reference.

[2]Now called Moytura.

[3]There is a strange idea current in Europe at the present time that one of the most remarkable potentates now living has this fatal gift and power of the Evil Eye.

[4]In Ancient Egypt the ivy was sacred to Osiris, and a safeguard against evil.

[5]The correct names for these islands are Innis-Erk (the Island of St. Erk), and Innis-bo-finn (the Island of the White Cow).

[6]The fairies have a right to whatever is spilt or falls upon the ground.

[7]Leprehaun, or *Leith Brogan*, means the "Artisan of the Brogae."

[8]The ancient serpent-idol was called in Irish, "The Great Worm." St. Patrick destroyed it, and had it thrown into the sea. There are no serpents now to be found in Ireland, not even grass snakes or scorpions.

[9]Extract from a letter by the Marchioness of Waterford, on the Currahmore Crystal.

[10]This word "fibulæ" is a heathenish and imported term, quite foreign to the Irish tongue. There is no other word known in the Irish language to designate a brooch, be it of bone or be it of gold, than *Dealg*, which signifies a thorn.

[11]See Sir William Wilde's work, "Lough Corrib: its Shores and Islands," where a drawing of this inscription is given.

[12]"The History of Dublin." 3 vols. By J. T. Gilbert, M.R.I.A. Dublin.

[13]These relics of a civilization three thousand years old, may still be gazed upon by modern eyes in the splendid and unrivalled antiquarian collection of the Royal Irish Academy. The golden circlets, the fibulas, torques, bracelets, rings, &c., worn by the ancient race, are not only costly in value, but often so singularly beautiful in the working out of minute artistic details, that modern art is not merely unable to equal them, but unable even to comprehend how the ancient workers in metals could accomplish works of such delicate, almost microscopic minuteness of finish.

[14]The expression of Tacitus.

[15]This is the Latinized form of the original word.

[16]The Danes were never more than a colony in Ireland.

[17]Hogan, the great historical sculptor of Ireland, has illustrated this era of

Irish history by a fine group, heroic and poetical in idea, as well as beautiful in execution, like every work that proceeded from the gifted mind of this distinguished artist.

[18]The Irish Celt to the Irish Norman, from "Poems," by Aubrey de Vere.

[19]Grace's Annals. Rev. R. Butler's translation.

[20]Extracts from the Address to the Anthropological Section of the British Association. Belfast, 1874. By Sir WILLIAM WILDE, M.D., M.R.I.A., Chevalier of the Swedish Order of the North Star.